Teach
Yourself®

Essential Spanish Verbs

María Rosario Hollis

Revised by Keith Chambers

Series editor
Paul Coggle

For UK order enquiries: please contact
Bookpoint Ltd, 130 Milton Park, Abingdon, Oxon OX14 4SB.
Telephone: +44 (0) 1235 827720. *Fax:* +44 (0) 1235 400454.
Lines are open 09.00–17.00, Monday to Saturday, with a 24-hour
message answering service. Details about our titles and how to
order are available at www.teachyourself.com

For USA order enquiries: please contact McGraw-Hill Customer
Services, PO Box 545, Blacklick, OH 43004-0545, USA.
Telephone: 1-800-722-4726. *Fax:* 1-614-755-5645.

For Canada order enquiries: please contact McGraw-Hill
Ryerson Ltd, 300 Water St, Whitby, Ontario L1N 9B6, Canada.
Telephone: 905 430 5000. Fax: 905 430 5020.

Long renowned as the authoritative source for self-guided
learning – with more than 50 million copies sold worldwide –
the *Teach Yourself* series includes over 500 titles in the fields of
languages, crafts, hobbies, business, computing and education.

British Library Cataloguing in Publication Data: a catalogue record
for this title is available from the British Library.

Library of Congress Catalog Card Number: on file.

First published in UK 1994 as Teach Yourself Spanish Verbs
by Hodder Education, part of Hachette UK, 338 Euston Road,
London NW1 3BH.

First published in US 1994 by The McGraw-Hill Companies, Inc.

This edition published 2010.

The *Teach Yourself* name is a registered trade mark of
Hodder Headline.

Typeset by MPS Limited, a Macmillan Company.

Printed in Great Britain for Hodder Education, an Hachette UK
Company, 338 Euston Road, London NW1 3BH.

The publisher has used its best endeavours to ensure that the URLs
for external websites referred to in this book are correct and active
at the time of going to press. However, the publisher and the
author have no responsibility for the websites and can make no
guarantee that a site will remain live or that the content will remain
relevant, decent or appropriate.

Hachette UK's policy is to use papers that are natural, renewable
and recyclable products and made from wood grown in sustainable
forests. The logging and manufacturing processes are expected to
conform to the environmental regulations of the country of origin.

Impression number	10 9 8 7 6 5 4 3 2
Year	2014 2013 2012 2011

Contents

Personal introduction by Keith Chambers

Verbs are an essential feature of language and this book is designed to take the mystery out of this aspect of learning Spanish. Whether you are a complete beginner or a relatively advanced learner, you can consult this book when you need to check the form of a certain verb. You may also browse through the different sections to see the use of different tenses, see the patterns of regular verbs, iron out difficulties with irregular verbs or gain new insights to the Spanish verb system. Whatever your approach and level, whether you read from cover to cover, or just dip in when you need some help, you should find **Essential Spanish Verbs** a useful support to your language learning.

The book starts with short overviews of what a verb is, how verbs function and how Spanish and English verbs compare and contrast. This is followed by more detailed sections on tenses, parts of the verb and illustrations of usage. Finally, comprehensive lists of regular and irregular verbs provide a valuable reference tool.

This revised edition has useful new features, including insight boxes which provide helpful tips on specific verbs and, on our website at www.teachyourself.com, you will find an audio feature and a questionnaire for self-examination **¡Buena suerte!**

Only got a minute?

What is a verb?

The verb is the basic building block of any sentence – indeed, a sentence cannot exist without a verb.

When we think of a verb, we normally think of an action: we <u>learn</u> Spanish, the dog <u>barks</u>, they <u>write</u> a letter. This action may not just be physical or tangible; it can also be aspirational or emotional: they <u>want</u> happiness; we <u>need</u> the money; you <u>love</u> each other, I <u>long</u> for peace.

The verb can also help to describe the status of someone or something: you <u>seem</u> unhappy, she <u>is</u> pretty, I <u>am</u> a teacher, you <u>are</u> <u>sleeping</u>.

The verb can also indicate a change or a transition from one thing to another: she <u>became</u> rich, the room <u>darkened</u>, the film <u>begins</u> at eight.

If a verb takes a direct object, it is said to be *transitive*: they <u>read</u> the book; we <u>cooked</u> the meal, she <u>spent</u> the money.

If the verb makes sense without having a direct object, it is called *intransitive*: they <u>work</u> hard, we <u>slept</u>, how cheerfully they <u>sing</u>.

One thing is for sure, if you take out the verb in any of the above examples, the expression loses its essential meaning.

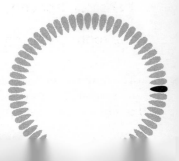

5 Only got five minutes?

How the Spanish verb works – basic principles

Most verbs in English are relatively straightforward – the form of the verb hardly changes from one context to the other. Take *put*, for example.

We <u>put</u> the radio on every morning but yesterday I <u>put</u> the television on instead. Tomorrow I shall <u>put</u> it on again while you <u>put</u> the breakfast on the table. Please <u>put</u> on the news. If they <u>put</u> music on instead, I wouldn't <u>put</u> up with it! My friend, however, <u>puts</u> on the sports programme and this <u>puts</u> him in a good mood for the rest of the day.

English tends to clarify who is doing the action and when it occurs by using additional markers, such as *I*, *we*, *they*, *yesterday*, *tomorrow*, *please*, etc.

If you changed the above paragraph into Spanish, the verb itself would need several different forms, with each form denoting information about who is doing the putting and when. In Spanish, the ending of the verb is very important. Get it wrong and the whole meaning of the sentence can change.

If you look in a dictionary for the Spanish equivalent of *put*, you will probably find **poner**. This form is called the <u>infinitive</u>, since it is not linked to any particular person or time. In English we often indicate the infinitive by adding *to*; so **poner** = *to put*.

The infinitive in Spanish always ends in **-ar** (the majority), **-er** (the second most numerous group) or **-ir**, e.g. **habl<u>ar</u>** = *to speak*; **com<u>er</u>** = *to eat*; **viv<u>ir</u>** = *to live*.

But Spanish has to change the verb ending in most cases.
This depends on the following.

The person or persons

These are conventionally numbered first, second and third. *I* = the
first person you normally think of in a crisis!, *you* = the second
person, and *he/she* = the third person. In the plural, these are
we (first), *you* (second) and *they* (third).

These *personal pronouns* as they are known are essential in English,
but are usually omitted in Spanish, since the ending of each verb
indicates who is performing the action:

Creo que es difícil.   *I think that it is difficult.*
¿En qué piensas?   *What are you thinking about?*

Personal pronouns can be added for emphasis or clarity, so here
they are anyway! Note that in most forms Spanish can distinguish
between masculine and feminine persons.

Singular masculine/feminine			Plural masculine/feminine	
1st person	yo	*I*	nosotros/ nosotras	*we*
2nd person	tú	*you (familiar)*	vosotros/ vosotras	*you (familiar)*
3rd person	él, ella	*he, she*	ellos/ellas	*they*
	usted	*you (polite)*	ustedes	*you (polite)*

In modern Spanish the second person is used in a familiar context –
talking to family, friends, children, close colleagues, etc.

A slight complication is that Spanish has polite forms for *you* as
well (**usted** and **ustedes**), but these are considered as being <u>third</u>

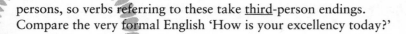

persons, so verbs referring to these take <u>third</u>-person endings. Compare the very formal English 'How is your excellency today?'

Familiar:

¿Cómo estás, amigo?	*How are you, my friend?*
¿Cómo estáis, amigos?	*How are you, my friends?*

Polite:

¿Cómo está usted, señor?	*How are you, sir?*
¿Cómo están ustedes, señores?	*How are you, gentlemen?*

It is not essential to include the **usted/ustedes** but this is often done for extra politeness with strangers.

American Spanish rarely uses the second-person plural **vosotros/vosotras** form. Instead **ustedes** (but always with *third*-person plural verb endings) takes on the familiar role as well. This is also found in some areas of Spain.

Insight

Usted and **ustedes** are sometimes abbreviated to **Vd** and **Vds** (**Ud** and **Uds** in American Spanish).

The Tense

In the context of verbs, tense means 'time'. Something happening or being done now is referred to as the present tense'.

Bebo vino. *I drink wine.*

Actions that took place in the past require a verb ending indicating past tense.

Ayer bebí café.   *Yesterday I drank coffee.*

Just as English can distinguish subtleties such *as I worked/I used to work/I was working*, etc., Spanish has a variety of past tenses to reflect shades of meaning.

Similarly, something yet to come or to happen is the future tense. Simple, isn't it?

Mañana beberé té.   *Tomorrow I shall drink tea.*

There are some other aspects, such as mood, commands, conditions, but these will be examined later.

To get started, always check the following: PERSON, NUMBER, TENSE.

Who is performing the action? Is it one person, or more than one person?

If the subject is 'you', are you speaking informally or politely?

When is the action occurring? Is it now, in the past, or in the future?

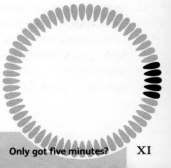

10 Only got ten minutes?

Points of Contrast – The Yin and Yang of Spanish Verbs

Spanish verbs fall into three main groups, whose infinitives end in **-ar**, **-er** or **-ir**. Fortunately, the endings for each group are usually predictable and follow regular patterns for each tense. Indeed, verbs in **-er** and **-ir** copy each other and share the same endings in the majority of tenses, so perhaps we can look on the bright side and say there are only really two and a half main groups!

As Spanish spelling follows a word's pronunciation, minor changes are sometimes necessary to comply with conventions of spelling. These changes are for the most part obvious or readily understood. Similarly, use of the accent mark is generally governed by clearly defined rules to mark where the stress deviates from normal rules.

With some types of verb, known as root-changing or radically-changing verbs, the position of the stressed syllable brings about a change to a vowel but again the overall principle can be relatively easily noted and applied with a little practice. The main changes are **e** squashes to **ie**, and **o** squashes to **ue** under stress in the affected verbs of all main groups, as in **contar**, *to count*: **cuento, contamos**; **perder**, *to lose*: **pierdo, perdemos**; **dormir**: **duermo, dormimos**. A small handful of **-ir** verbs can have additional changes of **e** to **i**, and **o** to **u**, even when not under stress: (**divertir**, *to amuse*: **divierto, divertimos. divirtió, divirtiendo**; **morir**, *to die*: **muero, morimos, murió, muriendo**).

A cluster of verbs has more marked changes in the stem of the simple past (preterite) tense, similar to English verbs such as *give/gave; do/did; say/said*, but in most cases there is a fairly discernible pattern. As in English, many of the verbs affected are those most commonly used. These include **hacer, decir, poner, poder, saber, tener, venir, caber**, verbs ending in **-ucir** – all of which have an additional trick up their sleeve by not stressing their endings or using an accent in the preterite, in contrast to the normal pattern. The **-ar** verb **dar**, *to give*, has a change of heart and behaves like an **-ir** verb in the preterite, and becomes **di, diste, dio, dimos, disteis, dieron**!

Ser, *to be*, and **ir**, *to go*, are a law unto themselves: they share the same forms throughout the preterite, with the unrelated **fui, fuiste, fue, fuimos, fuisteis, fueron**.

As in most languages, there are some verbs that seem to deviate wilfully from the norm – **ser**, *to be*, like its English equivalent with *am, is, are, was, will be, has been*, pursues its own path in many tenses. To add to the fun, Spanish has a choice of two verbs meaning *to be*: **ser** and **estar**. Both of these have some irregularities. **Ir**, *to go*, borrows its forms from three basic stems: **voy** (present), **iré** (future), **fui** (past).

The English-speaking learner can nevertheless take heart and know that in many ways Spanish verbs echo English usage with regard to how tenses are formed. Spanish verbs, for example, have equivalent forms to *speaking, spoken, spoke, going to speak, shall have spoken*, etc., and compared with some other languages, the choice of appropriate tense is not difficult to make. Compound tenses are formed with **haber**, *to have*, as in English but not also with *to be*, as happens in French, Italian or German! Of course there are some important points to watch, but that is part of the joy and challenge of learning another language.

Spanish uses a range of so-called 'modal' verbs, such as **poder, deber, querer**, with a following infinitive in the same way as English *can (go), must (work), want (to sleep)*. On the other hand, some English verbs have to be replaced by another expression in Spanish: *I like something*, for example, is turned on its head and becomes *something is pleasing to me* – **me gusta**.

Spanish and English both distinguish between active and passive voice – *The dog chewed the bone/The bone was chewed by the dog* – and form the passive in similar ways, using the verb *to be*, **ser: el perro mordió el hueso/El hueso fue mordido por el perro**, though Spanish tends to avoid the passive and prefers where possible to use other constructions, including the reflexive. There are some instances where Spanish has concepts that are less familiar. Reflexive verbs, for example, distinguish between an action done to another person or object and to oneself: **lavar**, *to wash* (a car, the baby, etc.) but **lavarse**, *to get washed*. This pattern extends across a whole range of personal activities: **levantarse**, *to get up*; **acostarse**, *to go to bed*; **vestirse**, *to get dressed*; **ducharse**, *to have a shower*, and several more. Sometimes reflexive verbs merely intensify an action: **ir**, *to go*; **irse**, *to go away*; **dormir**, *to sleep*; **dormirse**, *to go to sleep*.

Some usages which might sound old-fashioned or very bookish in English are still the rule in Spanish. The subjunctive mood is virtually obsolete in modern English or is confined to a handful of cases, such as *if I were rich* or *be that as it may*. But the subjunctive still has an essential role in everyday Spanish: **si fuera rico; sea lo que sea**. Whereas English says quite happily *I wanted you to know*, Spanish has to adopt the more cumbersome *I wanted that you knew*, with a past subjunctive: **Quería que lo supieras!** Indeed most (but not all) of the normal 'indicative' tenses have a corresponding subjunctive partner.

Commands need some extra care in Spanish. Not only do you have to remember the various forms of *you* and distinguish between singular and plural, familiar and formal, in the case of familiar commands you also have to differentiate between a positive (do it!) and a negative (don't!) order. From **hablar**, *to speak*, for example, you have **habla/no hables/hablad/no habléis/(no) hable/(no) hablen**. You also have to remember to put any object or reflexive pronoun after a positive command – and normally add an accent! – but in front of a negative command, as in **levántese/no se levante**.

The following section examines these topics in greater detail.

Introduction

HOW TO USE THIS BOOK

Read the introductory overviews if you are a little uncertain about basic concepts then read the section on verbs and how they work.

Look up the verb you want to use in the verb list at the back of the book. You will need what is known as the *infinitive*, the equivalent to the *to* ... form in English (e.g. **venir** *to come*).

The verbs have been given a number between 1 and 200. If the number is in **bold print**, the verb is one of the 200 presented in the verb tables; if it is not among the 200, the reference number (in ordinary print) will direct you to a verb that behaves in the same way as the verb you want to use.

Turn to the verb(s) referred to for details of your verb. If you are not sure which verb form to use in a given context, turn to the relevant section of 'How Spanish verbs work'.

The examples listed with the 200 verbs show basic uses of the verb, followed by some idioms and other useful connected expressions, as well as words sharing the same origin.

Credits

Front cover: © Oxford Illustrators

Back cover and pack: © Jakub Semeniuk/iStockphoto.com, © Royalty-Free/Corbis, © agencyby/iStockphoto.com, © Andy Cook/iStockphoto.com, © Christopher Ewing/iStockphoto.com, © zebicho – Fotolia.com, © Geoffrey Holman/iStockphoto.com, © Photodisc/Getty Images, © James C. Pruitt/iStockphoto.com, © Mohamed Saber – Fotolia.com

How Spanish verbs work

1 *HOW DOES THE VERB SHOW TENSE?*

Most languages use changes in the verb form to indicate an aspect of time, which may be present, past or future. It is, of course, perfectly possible to convey a sense of time without applying the concept of tense to the verb. Although the following examples are ungrammatical, most people would be able to understand

Yesterday I work all day.
Today I work hard.
Tomorrow I work for only one hour.

since the sense of time is indicated by the words *yesterday*, *today* and *tomorrow* rather than by changes to the verb. But to be correct you will make changes to the verb form (making use of tense) to convey the sense of time:

He works hard as a rule. = Present tense
I worked for eight hours non-stop. = Past tense

2 *FORMING DIFFERENT TENSES*

In many languages, this involves adding various endings to what is called the *stem* of the verb. In the examples above, the stem is *work*. You add *-s* to make the third person singular present form of the verb; *-ed* is added to make the past tense, whatever the person. In Spanish, the same principle applies. To form the stem, you remove the **-ar**, **-er** or **-ir** from the infinitive; for example, the stem of **hablar** is **habl-**. You then add the appropriate endings. For example:

Hablé con tu madre.   *I spoke to your mother.*
Hablaban en voz alta.   *They were talking loudly.*

Tenses formed in this way are called simple tenses. They include the present, preterite, imperfect, future and conditional tenses.

3 OTHER FEATURES OF THE VERB IN CONTEXT

a Auxiliary verbs

A verb used to support the main verb, for example, *I **am** working*, *you **are** working*, is called an *auxiliary* verb. *Working* tells us what activity is going on; *am/are* tell us that it is continuous.

The most important auxiliary verbs in English are *to be*, *to have* and *to do*. You use *do*, for example, to ask questions and to negate statements:

***Do** you work on Saturdays?*
*Yes, but I **do** not work on Sundays.*

Spanish does not use **hacer** (*to make, do*) as an auxiliary for asking questions or for negating statements, but does use **estar** (*to be*) to form continuous tenses, as in **Están preparando la comida** (*They are preparing the meal*) and **haber** (*to have*) to form a range of tenses.

b Simple and compound tenses

We know that tenses formed by adding endings to the verb stem are called *simple* tenses, for example:

Trabajé aquí el verano pasado.   *I worked here last summer.*

Compound tenses are formed with the auxiliary verb **haber** (*to have*) and include the perfect, pluperfect, conditional perfect, past anterior.

In the sentence **He trabajado aquí todos los veranos** (*I have worked here every summer*), the auxiliary verb *to have* has been introduced to form what is usually known as the perfect tense. Other examples of compound tenses are:

El tren ha llegado tarde.   *The train has arrived late.*
Habrá habido muchas   *There will have been many more*
  oportunidades más.   *opportunities.*

| Habían entrado por la ventana. | They had come in through the window. |

c Participles and gerunds

In the above examples of compound tenses, the auxiliary verbs *to have* or *to be* are used with a form of the main verb known as a *participle*. The *past participle* is used to form the perfect tense in both Spanish and English:

he estudiado	I have studied
he comido	I have eaten
he salido	I have gone out

In English, a form of the verb ending in *-ing*, called the *present participle*, is used to form the continuous tenses:

*I am **working, eating** and **sleeping***
*I was **working, eating** and **sleeping***

Spanish forms continuous tenses using the endings **-ando** for **-ar** verbs, **-iendo** for **-er** and **-ir** verbs. This is usually called the gerund (**gerundio**) and is used with **estar**, or sometimes **ir**.

From **correr**

| Estoy corriendo | I am running |
| Estaba corriendo | I was running |

The gerund is also used in constructions such as these:

| Salió de la oficina, dando un portazo. | He went out of the office, slamming the door. |
| Le vi trabajando (from **trabajar**). | I saw him working. |

And with **continuar/seguir**, *to continue*

| Siguieron andando (from **andar**). | They went on walking. |

4 REGULAR AND IRREGULAR VERBS

Most languages have verbs which do not behave according to a set pattern and which are referred to as irregular verbs.

In English, the verb *to work* is regular because it conforms to a set pattern. The verb *to be*, however, does not.

Fortunately, many Spanish verbs are regular, forming their tenses according to a set pattern. There are three groups of verb which are identified by their type of conjugation and endings. Here is a model verb of each type:

- ▶ -**ar** *hablar*
- ▶ -**er** *comer*
- ▶ -**ir** *vivir*

These endings are given in full at the beginning of the verb tables.

Irregular verbs (ones which do not behave like those in the three groups listed above) have to be learned individually. Many of the verbs in the Verb Tables in this book have some irregularity. But many of the so-called irregular verbs are more or less regular in their behaviour. Spanish has a number of verbs where the irregularity is a change in the vowel of the stem of the verb, whenever the stem – rather than the ending – carries the stress (cer<u>r</u>ar, c<u>ie</u>rra; ped<u>ir</u>, p<u>id</u>e; cost<u>ar</u>, c<u>ue</u>sta; etc.). These are known as 'root-changing' or 'radical-changing' verbs.

Here are some common examples of each of the four types of vowel change:

e → ie	e → i	o → ue	u → ue
cerrar *to close*	pedir *to ask*	costar *to cost*	*jugar *to play*
entender *to understand*	corregir *to correct*	probar *to try*	
divertir *to amuse*	reír *to laugh*	dormir *to sleep*	
preferir *to prefer*		morir *to die*	

*jugar is the only verb in this category.

Sometimes the irregularity is merely a change in spelling to maintain consistency of pronunciation: **buscar → bus<u>qué</u>**, **pagar → pa<u>gué</u>**. These verbs present an abnormality that recurs constantly and creates a pattern that can be quite easily learnt.

Insight
Remember that in Spanish spelling follows the pronunciation. Say the infinitive out loud and the sound of the **c, z** or **g** will remain constant throughout the various verb forms. So **buscar** (hard *c*), **busqué; empezar** (*th* sound), **empecé; llegar** (hard *g*), **llegué.** Other examples will be found in the verb tables.

Other verbs are totally irregular. They simply present no logical explanations for their forms. Three common verbs are:

ir	*to go*
decir	*to say*
ser	*to be*

Soy Juan.	*I am Juan.*
Somos amigos.	*We are friends.*
Eran enemigos.	*They used to be enemies.*
Fueron estudiantes durante cinco años.	*They were students for five years.*

5 FORMATION AND USE OF TENSES

a The present

To form the present tense, simply take off the **-ar**, **-er** or **-ir** part of the infinitive to find the stem; then add the endings:

-ar verbs	-er verbs	-ir verbs
habl**o**	com**o**	viv**o**
habl**as**	com**es**	viv**es**
habl**a**	com**e**	viv**e**
habl**amos**	com**emos**	viv**imos**
habl**áis**	com**éis**	viv**ís**
habl**an**	com**en**	viv**en**

The present tense (**presente**) is used:

▶ to indicate an action that occurs at a present time.

Veo un pájaro. *I see a bird.*

▶ to refer to regular activities or ongoing states.

Toco el piano todas las tardes. *I play the piano every evening.*

▶ in certain circumstances, to refer to the immediate future.

Mañana voy a Londres. *I go/am going to London tomorrow.*

There is also a present continuous tense which is formed with the verb **estar** + gerund.

Estoy hablando. *I am (at this moment) speaking.*

b The imperfect

-ar verbs	-er verbs	-ir verbs
habl**aba**	com**ía**	viv**ía**
habl**abas**	com**ías**	viv**ías**
habl**aba**	com**ía**	viv**ía**
habl**ábamos**	com**íamos**	viv**íamos**
habl**abais**	com**íais**	viv**íais**
habl**aban**	com**ían**	viv**ían**

The imperfect (**pretérito imperfecto**) is used:

▶ to refer to an ongoing state, or a repeated or continuous action in the past:

Comía a las dos. *I used to eat at 2 pm.*
Vivíamos en Madrid entonces. *We lived/were living in Madrid then.*

▶ to refer to an action which was in progress when something else happened. In this case, the verb referring to the new action is in the preterite tense:

Hablaban de ti cuando llegué. *They were talking about you when I arrived.*

The verbs **ser** (*to be*), **estar** (*to be*), **tener** (*to have*) and the impersonal form of **haber** (*to have*) (**había** *there was*), are those most frequently used when describing the past:

El hotel estaba enfrente de la iglesia. *The hotel was opposite the church.*
Había muy pocos turistas. *There were very few tourists.*

c The preterite and the perfect

The preterite tense (**pretérito indefinido**), or 'simple past' is
an important tense in Spanish. It is used to refer to completed
actions which are now considered as over and consigned to
the past.

-ar verbs	-er verbs	-ir verbs
habl**é**	com**í**	viv**í**
habl**aste**	com**iste**	viv**iste**
habl**ó**	com**ió**	viv**ió**
habl**amos**	com**imos**	viv**imos**
habl**asteis**	com**isteis**	viv**isteis**
habl**aron**	com**ieron**	viv**ieron**

Note that in this tense, the verbs are stressed on the end, and
accents are required on the first and third persons singular.

A few verbs comprise a group called the **'pretérito grave'**. These
do not stress the endings – which are the same for all verbs in

this group – and do not take accents. The stem of the verb also changes. The group includes:

estar to be	tener to have	venir to come
estuve	tuve	vine
estuviste	tuviste	viniste
estuvo	tuvo	vino
estuvimos	tuvimos	vinimos
estuvisteis	tuvisteis	vinisteis
estuvieron	tuvieron	vinieron

The perfect (**pretérito perfecto**) is a compound tense formed by the relevant form of the present tense of the auxiliary verb **haber** with the past participle of the main verb.

-ar verbs	-er verbs	-ir verbs
he hablado	**he** comido	**he** vivido
has hablado	**has** comido	**has** vivido
ha hablado	**ha** comido	**ha** vivido
hemos hablado	**hemos** comido	**hemos** vivido
habéis hablado	**habéis** comido	**habéis** vivido
han hablado	**han** comido	**han** vivido

Past participles are normally formed by adding **-ado** to the stem of **-ar** verbs and **-ido** to the stem of **-er** and **-ir** verbs. About a dozen verbs have irregular past participles, including

decir to say	**dicho**
hacer to do, make	**hecho**

Insight

Remember the Spanish equivalent of 'no sooner said than done' – **dicho y hecho**. Two irregular past participles!

ver *to see*	**visto**
romper *to break*	**roto**
poner *to put*	**puesto**
escribir *to write*	**escrito**
freír *to fry*	**frito**
morir *to die*	**muerto**
abrir *to open*	**abierto**

The perfect tense is used to refer to actions carried out in the recent past, but associated in some way with the present.

Él no ha comido todavía.	*He has not eaten yet.*
No he estado nunca en Francia.	*I have never been to France.*
Llego tarde porque esta mañana he venido en autobús.	*I'm late because I came by bus this morning.*

Insight

A good general rule is that if the English past tense is formed with *have/has*, use the perfect. Otherwise, use the preterite. Compare the following.

Hemos dicho que no.	*We have said no.*
Dijimos que no.	*We said no.*

Note, however, that where an action that started in the past is continuing into the present, Spanish uses the present tense and not the perfect.

Espero el autobús desde hace dos horas.	*I have been waiting for the bus for two hours (and am still waiting!).*

d The pluperfect
The pluperfect (**pretérito pluscuamperfecto**) is a compound tense and is formed by the relevant form of the imperfect tense of the auxiliary verb **haber** with the past participle of the main verb.

-ar verbs	-er verbs	-ir verbs
había hablado	**había** comido	**había** vivido
habías hablado	**habías** comido	**habías** vivido
había hablado	**había** comido	**había** vivido
habíamos hablado	**habíamos** comido	**habíamos** vivido
habíais hablado	**habíais** comido	**habíais** vivido
habían hablado	**habían** comido	**habían** vivido

It is used in English to express an action in the past that was completed before another one was started.

Cuando llegó ya te habías ido. *When he arrived you had already left.*

e The past anterior

The past anterior (**pretérito anterior**) is a compound tense formed by the relevant form of the preterite tense of the auxiliary verb **haber** with the past participle of the main verb. Its use nowadays is mostly literary and is frequently replaced by the preterite alone, or the pluperfect.

-ar verbs	-er verbs	-ir verbs
hube hablado	**hube** comido	**hube** vivido
hubiste hablado	**hubiste** comido	**hubiste** vivido
hubo hablado	**hubo** comido	**hubo** vivido
hubimos hablado	**hubimos** comido	**hubimos** vivido
hubisteis hablado	**hubisteis** comido	**hubisteis** vivido
hubieron hablado	**hubieron** comido	**hubieron** vivido

The past anterior indicates a past action that had occurred before another past action:

Apenas hubo cenado se acostó. *As soon as he had had his supper he went to bed.*

f The future
The future tense (**futuro imperfecto**) is formed by adding the appropriate endings to the full verb infinitive.

-ar verbs	*-er verbs*	*-ir verbs*
hablar**é**	comer**é**	vivir**é**
hablar**ás**	comer**ás**	vivir**ás**
hablar**á**	comer**á**	vivir**á**
hablar**emos**	comer**emos**	vivir**emos**
hablar**éis**	comer**éis**	vivir**éis**
hablar**án**	comer**án**	vivir**án**

Insight
For ease of pronunciation, some verbs drop **e** or **i** from the infinitive, or insert **d**, before adding the endings.

Examples are **querré** (**querer**), **habré** (**haber**), **saldré** (**salir**), **tendré** (**tener**), **vendré** (**venir**).

The future tense has three main uses:

▶ to express an action or state which will occur in the future.

Estaré hasta que cierren.   *I shall stay until closing time.*

▶ to express probability.

Tendrás hambre.   *You will (no doubt) be hungry.*

▶ in the second person it can be used as an imperative or as an obligatory order.

Irás a casa.   *You'll go home.*

g The future perfect
The future perfect tense (**futuro perfecto**) is a compound tense formed by the relevant form of the future tense of the auxiliary verb **haber**, and the past participle of the main verb.

-ar verbs	-er verbs	-ir verbs
habré hablado	**habré** comido	**habré** vivido
habrás hablado	**habrás** comido	**habrás** vivido
habrá hablado	**habrá** comido	**habrá** vivido
habremos hablado	**habremos** comido	**habremos** vivido
habréis hablado	**habréis** comido	**habréis** vivido
habrán hablado	**habrán** comido	**habrán** vivido

The future perfect indicates a future action that will have been completed by a certain time in the future:

Cuando llegues ya habré acabado. *I will have finished by the time you arrive.*

Note that the verb in the **cuando** clause is in the subjunctive (see below). The future perfect can also indicate probability, surprise or even hesitation:

Habrá salido ya. *He must have left already.*

6 INDICATIVE, SUBJUNCTIVE, IMPERATIVE ... : MOOD

The term *mood* is used to group verb phrases into three broad categories according to the general kind of meaning they convey.

a The indicative mood
This is used for making statements or asking questions of a factual kind.

We are not going today.
Does he work here?
Crime does not pay.

All the tenses you have just been looking at are in the indicative mood.

b The conditional
This indicative tense is often closely linked with the subjunctive and is used to express conditions or possibilities.

I would accept her offer, if ...

In Spanish, the present conditional (**potencial simple**) is formed by adding the appropriate endings to the infinitive.

-ar verbs	-er verbs	-ir verbs
hablar**ía**	comer**ía**	vivir**ía**
hablar**ías**	comer**ías**	vivir**ías**
hablar**ía**	comer**ía**	vivir**ía**
hablar**íamos**	comer**íamos**	vivir**íamos**
hablar**íais**	comer**íais**	vivir**íais**
hablar**ían**	comer**ían**	vivir**ían**

The present conditional indicates a future or present action as advice, a suggestion, aspiration, politeness, possible or impossible wishes:

Deberías estudiar más.   *You should study more.*
Podríamos ir mañana.   *We could go tomorrow.*

If the verb in the main clause is in the past, and the verb in the subordinate clause refers to the future, you must use the conditional.

Me dijiste que vendrías.   *You told me that you would come.*

Insight
Those verbs that modify the infinitive with the future make similar changes in the conditional. So, **querría, habría, saldría, tendría, vendría**, etc.

The conditional perfect (**potencial compuesto**) is formed with the conditional of **haber** and the past participle.

-ar verbs	-er verbs	-ir verbs
habría hablado	**habría** comido	**habría** vivido
habrías hablado	**habrías** comido	**habrías** vivido
habría hablado	**habría** comido	**habría** vivido
habríamos hablado	**habríamos** comido	**habríamos** vivido
habríais hablado	**habríais** comido	**habríais** vivido
habrían hablado	**habrían** comido	**habrían** vivido

The conditional perfect is used to express what might have happened or what might have been done.

Me habría gustado cenar con ellos.	*I would have liked to have dined with them.*

c The subjunctive mood
This is used for expressing wishes, conditions and non-factual matters.

It is my wish that John be allowed to come.
If I were you …

The use of the subjunctive in English is rare nowadays, but it is still frequently used in Spanish. There is an equivalent subjunctive form for most tenses, many of which are given in the box below.

The present subjunctive is often introduced by verbs of hoping and doubting, together with **que** (*that*):

Espero que te guste.	*I hope (that) you like it.*
Dudo que ellos vengan.	*I doubt (whether) they will come.*

The subjunctive is also used in negative expressions indicating doubt or uncertainty.

No creo que sea necesario.	*I don't think it is necessary.*

but

Creo que es necesario.	*I think it is necessary.*

-ar verbs	-er verbs	-ir verbs
Present		
habl**e**	com**a**	viv**a**
habl**es**	com**as**	viv**as**
habl**e**	com**a**	viv**a**
habl**emos**	com**amos**	viv**amos**
habl**éis**	com**áis**	viv**áis**
habl**en**	com**an**	viv**an**
Imperfect		
habl-**ara/ase**	com-**iera/iese**	viv-**iera/iese**
habl-**aras/ases**	com-**ieras/ieses**	viv-**ieras/ieses**
habl-**ara/ase**	com-**iera/iese**	viv-**iera/iese**
habl-**áramos/ásemos**	com-**iéramos/iésemos**	viv-**iéramos/iésemos**
habl-**arais/aseis**	com-**ierais/ieseis**	viv-**ierais/ieseis**
habl-**aran/asen**	com-**ieran/iesen**	viv-**ieran/iesen**
Perfect		
haya hablado	haya comido	haya vivido
hayas hablado	hayas comido	hayas vivido
haya hablado	haya comido	haya vivido
hayamos hablado	hayamos comido	hayamos vivido
hayáis hablado	hayáis comido	hayáis vivido
hayan hablado	hayan comido	hayan vivido
Pluperfect		
hub-iera/iese hablado	hub-iera/iese comido	hub-iera/iese vivido
hub-ieras/ieses hablado	hub-ieras/ieses comido	hub-ieras/ieses vivido
hub-iera/iese hablado	hub-iera/iese comido	hub-iera/iese vivido
hub-iéramos/iésemos hablado	hub-iéramos/iésemos comido	hub-iéramos/iésemos vivido
hub-ierais/ieseis hablado	hub-ierais/ieseis comido	hub-ierais/ieseis vivido
hub-ieran/iesen hablado	hub-ieran/iesen comido	hub-ieran/iesen vivido

The imperfect and pluperfect subjunctive have two forms which are used interchangeably. The imperfect is frequently dependent on a clause which contains a verb in the conditional.

Nos gustaría que vinieses.   *We would like you to come.*

It is used after **si** (*if*) to introduce an idea which is unlikely to occur.

Si hubiese algún problema te   *If there were any problem*
  llamaría.   *I would call you.*

Certain verbs indicating advice, suggestion or command require the subjunctive:

Te sugiero que no salgas.   *I suggest you don't go out.*

The subjunctive is used after **cuando** (*when*), **en cuanto** (*as soon as*), **después (de) que** (*after*), etc., when referring to an event in the future.

En cuanto vuelvas.   *As soon as you get back.*

Insight

The subjunctive is always used with **antes (de) que** (*before*).

Váyase antes (de) que venga la policia. *Go away before the police come.*

Lo hizo antes de que le pudieran impedir. *He did it before they could stop him.*

d The imperative mood
This is used to give directives or commands.

Give me a hand.
Help Sharon with her homework.

Because we have only one version of the second person (you) in English, we have only one form of the second person imperative. However, as Spanish has polite and informal forms of the second person, the imperative is more complex. It is further complicated by the fact that the negative version is quite different from the affirmative version. This means that there are *eight* versions for giving someone a command in Spanish (familiar singular, polite singular, familiar plural, polite plural – and all these again in the negative!).

There are actually only two forms of the imperative, those relating to the second person (**tú** or **vosotros/vosotras**) and only with positive commands. The rest, including the negative forms, are expressed by using the appropriate form of the subjunctive:

habla *do speak*   **no hables** *do not speak*
hablad *speak, all of you*   **no habléis** *do not speak*
¡Que lo hagan ellos mismos!   *Let them do it themselves!*

7 THE ACTIVE AND PASSIVE VOICE

Most actions can be viewed in one of two ways:

The dog bit the postman.
The postman was bitten by the dog.

In the first example the dog is clearly the initiator of the action and the postman receives or suffers the action. This type of sentence is referred to as the *active voice*.

In the second example, the postman occupies first position in the sentence even though he is the object of the action. The subject, the dog, has been relegated to third position (after the verb) and could even be omitted. This type of sentence is referred to as the *passive voice*. The object has become the subject of the sentence.

In Spanish the passive voice is formed by the appropriate tense of the verb **ser** and the past participle of the verb concerned.

La canción ha sido cantada.	*The song has been sung.*
Peter ha sido besado.	*Peter has been kissed.*
El agua ha sido bebida.	*The water has been drunk.*

Note that the past participle must agree in number and gender with the subject of the verb.

Don Juan es amado.	*Don Juan is loved.*
Carmen es amada.	*Carmen is loved.*

A model of a verb in the passive is given on the next page.

Note, however, that wherever possible Spanish speakers prefer to use a reflexive verb rather than the passive (see Section 9).

8 TRANSITIVE AND INTRANSITIVE VERBS

To a large extent the verb you choose determines what other elements are used with it. With the verb *to happen*, for instance, you say what occurred but you do not have to provide any further information.

The accident happened.

With a verb like *to give*, on the other hand, you state *who* or *what* did the giving and also have to state *who* or *what* was given:

Steve gave a compact disc.

It is admittedly just possible to say *Steve gave* in the sense that he made a donation, but this is a very special use of *give*. With this verb it would also be very common to state the recipient of the giving:

Steve gave a compact disc to Kate.

ser amado *to be loved*

INDICATIVE

Present	Imperfect	Perfect
soy amado/a	era amado/a	he sido amando/a
eres amado/a	eras amado/a	has sido amado/a
es amado/a	era amado/a	ha sido amado/a
somos amados/as	éramos amados/as	hemos sido amados/as
sois amados/as	erais amados/as	habéis sido amados/as
son amados/as	eran amados/as	han sido amados/as

Future	Pluperfect	Preterite
seré amado/a	había sido amado/a	fui amado/a
será amado/a	habías sido amado/a	fuiste amado/a
será amado/a	había sido amado/a	fue amado/a
seremos amados/as	habíamos sido amados/as	fuimos amados/as
seréis amados/as	habíais sido amados/as	fuisteis amados/as
serán amados/as	habían sido amados/as	fueron amados/as

Future perfect	Past anterior
habré sido amado/a	hube sido amado/a
habrás sido amado/a	hubiste sido amado/a
habrá sido amado/a	hubo sido amado/a
habremos sido amados/as	hubimos sido amados/as
habréis sido amados/as	hubisteis sido amados/as
habrán sido amados/as	hubieron sido amados/as

CONDITIONAL / SUBJUNCTIVE

Present (Conditional)	Present (Subjunctive)	Imperfect
sería amado/a	sea amado/a	fu-era/ese amado/a
serías amado/a	seas amado/a	fu-eras/eses amado/a
sería amado/a	sea amado/a	fu-era/ese amado/a
seríamos amandos/as	seamos amados/as	fu-éramos/ésemos amados/as
seríais amados/as	seáis amados/as	fu-erais/eseis amados/as
serían amados/as	sean amados/as	fu-eran/esen amados/as

Perfect	Perfect	Pluperfect
habría sido amado/a	haya sido amado/a	hub-iera/iese sido amado/a
habrías sido amado/a	hayas sido amado/a	hub-ieras/ieses sido amado/a
habría sido amado/a	haya sido amado/a	hub-iera/iese sido amado/a
habríamos sido amados/as	hayamos sido amados/as	hub-iéramos/iésemos sido amados/as
habríais sido amados/as	hayáis sido amados/as	hub-ierais/ieseis sido amados/as
habrían sido amados/as	hayan sido amados/as	hub-ieran/iesen sido amados/as

GERUND / PAST PARTICIPLE / IMPERATIVE

GERUND	PAST PARTICIPLE	IMPERATIVE
siendo amado/a	sido amado/a	sé amado, sé amada
		sed amados, sed amadas

or even better:

Steve gave Kate a compact disc.

In the above examples *a compact disc* is said to be the *direct object* of the verb *to give* because it is what is actually given. *To Kate* or *Kate* is said to be the *indirect object*, since this element indicates who the compact disc was given to.

Verbs which do not require a direct object are said to be *intransitive*.

to die	*The old man died.*
to wait	*I waited.*

Verbs which do require a direct object are said to be *transitive*:

to enjoy	*Noeline enjoys a swim.*
to need	*Gary needs some help.*

Because many verbs can be used either with or without a direct object, depending on the precise meaning of the verb, it is safer to talk of transitive and intransitive uses of verbs:

Intransitive	**Transitive**
He's sleeping.	*He's sleeping a deep sleep.*
I'm eating.	*I'm eating my dinner.*
She's writing.	*She's writing an essay.*

9 REFLEXIVE VERBS

The term *reflexive* is used when the initiator of an action (or *subject*) and the sufferer of the action (or *object*) are one and the same:

She washed herself.
We enjoyed ourselves.

Many more verbs are used reflexively in Spanish than in English, so it is important to understand the concept. For instance, Spanish says the equivalent of *The door opened itself* where English simply says *The door opened*.

La puerta se abrió.	*The door opened.*
Se cayó del caballo.	*She fell off her horse.*

Reflexive verbs can be recognized by the addition of **-se** after the infinitive: **lavarse** (*to wash oneself*), **caerse** (*to fall*), **irse** (*to go away*). They have the same endings as other verbs in their groups but are always preceded by a reflexive pronoun:

me	nos
te	os
se	se

lavarse	caerse	irse
me lavo	me caigo	me voy
te lavas	te caes	te vas
se lava	se cae	se va
nos lavamos	nos caemos	nos vamos
os laváis	os caéis	os vais
se lavan	se caen	se van

Spanish often uses a reflexive verb where English would use the passive.

Se me dijo que …	*I was told that …*
Se ha bebido el agua.	*The water has been drunk.*
Se mató al asesino.	*The murderer was killed.*
Se le vio en el mercado.	*He was seen in the market.*

When a verb is used reflexively there is often a change of meaning:

divertir *to amuse*	**divertirse** *to enjoy oneself*
dormir *to sleep*	**dormirse** *to go to sleep*
entender *to understand*	**entenderse** *to be understood, to agree*
ir *to go*	**irse** *to go away*
levantar *to raise, lift*	**levantarse** *to get up*

parecer *to seem*	**parecerse** *to look like each other*
poner *to put*	**ponerse** *to put on (clothes), to become*
volver *to turn, go back*	**volverse** *to turn round, to become*

Certain reflexive verbs, such as **hallarse** (*to find*), **quedarse** (*to remain*), **verse** (*to see*) are often used where English uses the passive:

Se halló engañada.	*She was deceived.*
Se quedaron atónitos.	*They were astonished.*
El ladrón se vio encarcelado.	*The thief was imprisoned.*

The reflexive pronoun **se** is also used in impersonal constructions where *one, we* or *you* might be used in English:

¿Se puede entrar?	*Can one come in?*
Si se estudia, se aprenderá.	*If you study, you will learn.*

10 MODAL VERBS

Verbs used to express concepts such as *being able to, knowing how to, wanting to, having to, must* and *should* are known as modal verbs and are followed in Spanish by the infinitive. Here are some examples:

No *podemos* **ir contigo a la playa.**	*We can't go with you to the beach.*
No *sé* **tocar la guitarra.**	*I can't play the guitar (= I don't know how to).*
Quiero **ver al gerente.**	*I want to see the manager.*
Ahora *tengo que* **volver a la casa.**	*I have to go home now.*
Debes **hacerlo en seguida.**	*You must do it at once.*
Deben de **llegar tarde.**	*They must have arrived late.*
No *debes* **comer tanto.**	*You shouldn't eat so much.*

....
Insight
 Deber de implies supposition – what someone imagines to the case – whereas **deber** suggests a degree of moral obligation.
....

11 *THE VERB* GUSTAR

To *say I like something* you use the verb **gustar**. This verb behaves quite differently from most other verbs as it uses mainly the third person forms, with the person or persons doing the liking as an indirect object of the verb. If what you like is *singular*, or if you like *doing* something, you use **gusta**, and in the present tense it looks like this:

Me gusta	*I like … or I like it*	**Nos gusta**	*We like (it)*
Te gusta	*You like (it)*	**Os gusta**	*You like (it)*
Le gusta	*He/she likes/you like (it)*	**Les gusta**	*They/you like (it)*

Here are some examples:

Me gusta el café pero no me gusta el té.	*I like coffee but I don't like tea.*
No le gusta escribir cartas.	*She doesn't like writing letters.*
¿No os gusta cocinar?	*Don't you (plural) like cooking?*
Les gusta ir al cine.	*They like going to the cinema.*

If what you like is plural you use **gustan**:

Me gustan las naranjas.	*I like oranges.*

Other tenses are used in the same way:

Me gustaría ver tu casa.	*I'd like to see your house.*
¿Te gustaba leer?	*Did you enjoy reading?*
Les ha gustado la película.	*They liked the film.*

It can be helpful to think of **gustar** as meaning *to be pleasing*.

Me gusta el café.	*Coffee is pleasing to me.*
¿Te gustaba leer?	*Was reading pleasing to you?*

There are a few other verbs which follow the same pattern as **gustar**. Common ones include:

encantar	**Me encanta el fútbol.**	*I love football.*
apetecer	**¿Te apetece beber algo?**	*Do you fancy something to drink?*
doler	**Me duele la cabeza.**	*My head hurts/I've got a headache.*

Verb tables

On the following pages you will find the various tenses of 200 Spanish verbs presented in full, with examples of how to use them.

Sometimes only the first person singular form is given. Tenses for these verbs are given in full in the 'Only, got five minutes? section and 'How Spanish verbs work'. You should also check back to this latter section if you are not sure when to use the different tenses.

Abbreviations used in this book

aux.	auxiliary	LA	Latin America
col.	colloquial	m.	masculine
fem.	feminine	(r.)	reflexive
imp.	impersonal	tr.	transitive
intr.	intransitive		

THE BIG THREE

MODEL VERB TABLES FOR THE THREE MAIN GROUPS OF REGULAR VERBS

-AR HABLAR *TO SPEAK*

INDICATIVE

Present	Imperfect	Perfect
-o	-aba	he -ado
-as	-abas	has -ado
-a	-aba	ha -ado
-amos	-ábamos	hemos -ado
-áis	-abais	habéis -ado
-an	-aban	han -ado
Future	**Pluperfect**	**Preterite**
-aré	había -ado	-é
-arás	habías -ado	-aste
-ará	había -ado	-ó
-aremos	habíamos -ado	-amos
-aréis	habíais -ado	-asteis
-arán	habían -ado	-aron
Future perfect	**Past anterior**	
habré -ado	hube -ado	

CONDITIONAL   SUBJUNCTIVE

Present	Present	Imperfect
-aría	-e	-ara/ase
-arías	-es	-aras/-ases
-aría	-e	-ara/-ase
-aríamos	-emos	-áramos/-ásemos
-aríais	-éis	-arais/-aseis
-arían	-en	-aran/-asen
Perfect	**Perfect**	**Pluperfect**
habría -ado	haya -ado	hub-iera/-iese -ado

GERUND   PAST PARTICIPLE   IMPERATIVE

GERUND	PAST PARTICIPLE	IMPERATIVE
-ando	-ado	-a, -ad
		-e (Vd), -en (Vds)

-ER COMER *TO EAT*

INDICATIVE

Present	Imperfect	Perfect
-o	-ía	he -ido
-es	-ías	has -ido
-e	-ía	ha -ido
-emos	-íamos	hemos -ido
-éis	-íais	habéis -ido
-en	-ían	han -ido

Future	Pluperfect	Preterite
-eré	había -ido	-í
-erás	habías -ido	-iste
-erá	había -ido	-ió
-eremos	habíamos -ido	-imos
-eréis	habíais -ido	-isteis
-erán	habían -ido	-ieron

Future perfect	Past anterior
habré -ido	hube -ido

CONDITIONAL · SUBJUNCTIVE

Present	Present	Imperfect
-ería	-a	-iera/-iese
-erías	-as	-ieras/-ieses
-ería	-a	-iera/iese
-eríamos	-amos	-iéramos/-iésemos
-eríais	-áis	-ierais/-ieseis
-erían	-an	-ieran/-iesen

Perfect	Perfect	Pluperfect
habría -ido	haya -ido	hub-iera/-iese -ido

GERUND · PAST PARTICIPLE · IMPERATIVE

GERUND	PAST PARTICIPLE	IMPERATIVE
-iendo	-ido	-e, -ed
		-a (Vd), -an (Vds)

-IR VIVIR *TO LIVE*

INDICATIVE

Present	Imperfect	Perfect
-o	-ía	he -ido
-es	-ías	has -ido
-e	-ía	ha -ido
-imos	-íamos	hemos -ido
-ís	-íais	habéis -ido
-en	-ían	han -ido

Future	Pluperfect	Preterite
-iré	había -ido	-í
-irás	habías -ido	-iste
-irá	había -ido	-ió
-iremos	habíamos -ido	-imos
-iréis	habíais -ido	-isteis
-irán	habían -ido	-ieron

Future perfect	Past anterior
habré -ido	hube -ido

CONDITIONAL · SUBJUNCTIVE

Present	Present	Imperfect
-iría	-a	-iera/iese
-irías	-as	-ieras/-ieses
-iría	-a	-iera/iese
-iríamos	-amos	-iéramos/-iésemos
-iríais	-áis	-ierais/-ieseis
-irían	-an	-ieran/-iesen

Perfect	Perfect	Pluperfect
habría -ido	haya -ido	hub-iera/-iese -ido

GERUND · PAST PARTICIPLE · IMPERATIVE

GERUND	PAST PARTICIPLE	IMPERATIVE
-iendo	-ido	-e, -id
		-a (Vd), -an (Vds)

1 acertar *to guess, be right* (tr./intr.)

INDICATIVE

Present	Imperfect	Perfect
acierto	acertaba	he acertado
aciertas	acertabas	has acertado
acierta	acertaba	ha acertado
acertamos	acertábamos	hemos acertado
acertáis	acertabais	habéis acertado
aciertan	acertaban	han acertado

Future	Pluperfect	Preterite
acertaré	había acertado	acerté
acertarás	habías acertado	acertaste
acertará	había acertado	acertó
acertaremos	habíamos acertado	acertamos
acertaréis	habíais acertado	acertasteis
acertarán	habían acertado	acertaron

Future perfect	Past anterior	
habré acertado	hube acertado	

CONDITIONAL / SUBJUNCTIVE

Present	Present	Imperfect
acertaría	acierte	acert-ara/ase
acertarías	aciertes	acert-aras/ases
acertaría	acierte	acert-ara/ase
acertaríamos	acertemos	acert-áramos/ásemos
acertaríais	acertéis	acert-arais/aseis
acertarían	acierten	acert-aran/asen

Perfect	Perfect	Pluperfect
habría acertado	haya acertado	hub-iera/iese acertado

GERUND	PAST PARTICIPLE	IMPERATIVE
acertando	acertado	acierta, acertad
		acierte (Vd), acierten (Vds)

Si acierta, ganará el premio. *If she guesses right, she'll win the prize.*
Acertó a la primera. *He guessed it/got it right first time.*
Lo has acertado. *You've got it right. You've hit the nail on the head.*
No sé si acertaremos. *I wonder if we'll get it right.*
No aciertas el modo de hacerlo. *You don't seem to have found the right way to do it.*

el acertijo *riddle*
acertadamente *correctly*
el acierto *good shot, success*

con acierto *successfully*
acertado/a *correct, right, sensible*
acertador(a) *good guesser*

2 acordar *to agree, correspond* (tr.)

INDICATIVE

Present	Imperfect	Perfect
acuerdo	acordaba	he acordado
acuerdas	acordabas	has acordado
acuerda	acordaba	ha acordado
acordamos	acordábamos	hemos acordado
accordáis	acordabais	habéis acordado
acuerdan	acordaban	han acordado

Future	Pluperfect	Preterite
acordaré	había acordado	acordé
acordarás	habías acordado	acordaste
acordará	había acordado	acordó
acordaremos	habíamos acordado	acordamos
acordaréis	habíais acordado	acordasteis
acordarán	habían acordado	acordaron

Future perfect	Past anterior
habré acordado	hube acordado

CONDITIONAL — SUBJUNCTIVE

Present	Present	Imperfect
acordaría	acuerde	acord-ara/ase
acordarías	acuerdes	acord-aras/ases
acordaría	acuerde	acord-ara/ase
acordaríamos	acordemos	acord-áramos/ásemos
acordaríais	acordéis	acord-arais/aseis
acordarían	acuerden	acord-aran/asen

Perfect	Perfect	Pluperfect
habría acordado	haya acordado	hub-iera/iese acordado

GERUND — PAST PARTICIPLE — IMPERATIVE

GERUND	PAST PARTICIPLE	IMPERATIVE
acordando	acordado	acuerda, acordad
		acuerde (Vd), acuerden (Vds)

Han acordado firmar el tratado. *They have agreed to sign the treaty.*
Los colores acuerdan. *The colours match.*
Se acordó hacerlo. *It was agreed to do it.*
Acordaron salir temprano. *They agreed to leave early.*
acordarse *to remember*
No me acuerdo. *I don't remember.*
Si mal no me acuerdo ... *If my memory serves me right ...*
¿Te acuerdas de Juan? *Do you remember Juan?*
No se acuerda ni del santo de su nombre. *He can't even remember his own name.*

elacuerdo *an agreement, accord*
estar de acuerdo *to agree*
acordado/a *agreed*

ponerse de acuerdo *to agree*
tomar un acuerdo *to pass a resolution*
llegar a un acuerdo *to reach an agreement*

3 acostarse *to go to bed, lie down* (r.)

INDICATIVE

Present	Imperfect	Perfect
me acuesto	me acostaba	me he acostado
te acuestas	te acostabas	te has acostado
se acuesta	se acostaba	se ha acostado
nos acostamos	nos acostábamos	nos hemos acostado
os acostáis	os acostabais	os habéis acostado
se acuestan	se acostaban	se han acostado

Future	Pluperfect	Preterite
me acostaré	me había acostado	me acosté
te acostarás	te habías acostado	te acostaste
se acostará	se había acostado	se acostó
nos acostaremos	nos habíamos acostado	nos acostamos
os acostaréis	os habíais acostado	os acostasteis
se acostarán	se habían acostado	se acostaron

Future perfect	Past anterior
me habré acostado	me hube acostado

CONDITIONAL / SUBJUNCTIVE

Present	Present	Imperfect
me acostaría	me acueste	me acost-ara/ase
te acostarías	te acuestes	te acost-aras/ases
se acostaría	se acueste	se acost-ara/ase
nos acostaríamos	nos acostemos	nos acost-áramos/ásemos
os acostaríais	os acostéis	os acost-arais/aseis
se acostarían	se acuesten	se acost-aran/asen

Perfect	Perfect	Pluperfect
me habría acostado	me haya acostado	me hub-iera/iese acostado

GERUND	PAST PARTICIPLE	IMPERATIVE
acostándose	acostado	acuéstate, acostaos
		acuéstese (Vd), acuéstense (Vds)

Leonor se acuesta a las 3. *Leonor goes to bed at 3.*
¿Te acuestas tarde? *Do you go to bed late?*
Se acuesta con cualquiera. *She goes to bed with anyone.*
Nos acostamos juntos desde hace tres años. *We have been living together for three years.*
Me acuesto por los palestinos. *I support the Palestinians.*
Nos acostamos contra la pared. *We leaned against the wall.*

la acostada *sleep, lie-down*
acostarse boca arriba *to lie down face up*
acostar al niño *to put the child to bed*
acostado/a *lying down, stretched out*
acostar el barco *to bring the ship alongside*

4 acrecentar *to increase* (tr.)

INDICATIVE

Present	Imperfect	Perfect
acreciento	acrecentaba	he acrecentado
acrecientas	acrecentabas	has acrecentado
acrecienta	acrecentaba	ha acrecentado
acrecentamos	acrecentábamos	hemos acrecentado
acrecentáis	acrecentabais	habéis acrecentado
acrecientan	acrecentaban	han acrecentado

Future	Pluperfect	Preterite
acrecentaré	había acrecentado	acrecenté
acrecentarás	habías acrecentado	acrecentaste
acrecentará	había acrecentado	acrecentó
acrecentaremos	habíamos acrecentado	acrecentamos
acrecentaréis	habíais acrecentado	acrecentasteis
acrecentarán	habían acrecentado	acrecentaron

Future perfect	Past anterior
habré acrecentado	hube acrecentado

CONDITIONAL SUBJUNCTIVE

Present	Present	Imperfect
acrecentaría	acreciente	acrecent-ara/ase
acrecentarías	acrecientes	acrecent-aras/ases
acrecentaría	acreciente	acrecent-ara/ase
acrecentaríamos	acrecentemos	acrecent-áramos/ásemos
acrecentaríais	acrecentéis	acrecent-arais/aseis
acrecentarían	acrecienten	acrecent-aran/asen

Perfect	Perfect	Pluperfect
habría acrecentado	haya acrecentado	hub-iera/iese acrecentado

GERUND	PAST PARTICIPLE	IMPERATIVE
acrecentando	acrecentado	acrecienta, acrecentad
		acreciente (Vd), acrecienten (Vds)

Ha acrecentado su número de acciones. *He has increased his number of shares.*
El calor acrecienta a lo largo del día. *The heat increases throughout the day.*
Puedes acrecentar la temperatura del horno. *You can increase the oven temperature.*
Acrecentaré mi colección de plantas. *I shall increase my plant collection.*
Acrecentó su fortuna. *She increased her fortune.*

el acrecentamiento *increase, growth*   **acrecentador(a)** *one that increases*
acrecentante *increasing, incremental*   **la acrecencia** *increase, growth*
acrecentarse *to increase, grow*

5 adiestrar to coach, train (tr.)

INDICATIVE

Present	Imperfect	Perfect
adiestro	adiestraba	he adiestrado
adiestras	adiestrabas	has adiestrado
adiestra	adiestraba	ha adiestrado
adiestramos	adiestrábamos	hemos adiestrado
adiestráis	adiestrabais	habéis adiestrado
adiestran	adiestraban	han adiestrado

Future	Pluperfect	Preterite
adiestraré	había adiestrado	adiestré
adiestrarás	habías adiestrado	adiestraste
adiestrará	había adiestrado	adiestró
adiestraremos	habíamos adiestrado	adiestramos
adiestraréis	habíais adiestrado	adiestrasteis
adiestrarán	habían adiestrado	adiestraron

Future perfect	Past anterior
habré adiestrado	hube adiestrado

CONDITIONAL / SUBJUNCTIVE

Present	Present	Imperfect
adiestraría	adiestre	adiestr-ara/ase
adiestrarías	adiestres	adiestr-aras/ases
adiestraría	adiestre	adiestr-ara/ase
adiestraríamos	adiestremos	adiestr-áramos/ásemos
adiestraríais	adiestréis	adiestr-arais/aseis
adiestrarían	adiestren	adiestr-aran/asen

Perfect	Perfect	Pluperfect
habría adiestrado	haya adiestrado	hub-iera/iese adiestrado

GERUND / PAST PARTICIPLE / IMPERATIVE

GERUND	PAST PARTICIPLE	IMPERATIVE
adiestrando	adiestrado	adiestra, adiestrad
		adiestre (Vd), adiestren (Vds)

Adiestra perros. *She trains dogs.*
Te adiestraré cuando tengamos tiempo. *I shall coach you when we have more time.*
Adiestraban a los niños en el manejo de las armas. *They used to train children in the use of arms.*
No tiene paciencia para adiestrarse. *He is not patient enough to train.*

el adiestramiento *training, drilling, practice*
el/la adiestrador(a) *trainer, coach, teacher*
adiestrado *trained, trainee*
la destreza *skill, dexterity, handiness*
el diestro *bullfighter, expert swordsman*
diestro/a *right, right hand; skilful, dexterous expert, clever*
la diestra *the right hand*

6 adquirir *to acquire* (tr.)

INDICATIVE

Present	Imperfect	Perfect
adquiero	adquiría	he adquirido
adquieres	adquirías	has adquirido
adquiere	adquiría	ha adquirido
adquirimos	adquiríamos	hemos adquirido
adquirís	adquiríais	habéis adquirido
adquieren	adquirían	han adquirido

Future	Pluperfect	Preterite
adquiriré	había adquirido	adquirí
adquirirás	habías adquirido	adquiriste
adquirirá	había adquirido	adquirió
adquiriremos	habíamos adquirido	adquirimos
adquiriréis	habíais adquirido	adquiristeis
adquirirán	habían adquirido	adquirieron

Future perfect	Past anterior
habré adquirido	hube adquirido

CONDITIONAL · SUBJUNCTIVE

Present	Present	Imperfect
adquiriría	adquiera	adquir-iera/iese
adquirirías	adquieras	adquir-ieras/ieses
adquiriría	adquiera	adquir-iera/iese
adquiriríamos	adquiramos	adquir-iéramos/iésemos
adquiriríais	adquiráis	adquir-ierais/ieseis
adquirirían	adquieran	adquir-ieren/iesen

Perfect	Perfect	Pluperfect
habría adquirido	haya adquirido	hub-iera/iese adquirido

GERUND	PAST PARTICIPLE	IMPERATIVE
adquiriendo	adquirido	adquiere, adquirid
		adquiera (Vd), adquieran (Vds)

Se adquiere aquí. *You can acquire it here.*
Lo adquirí en 1990. *I acquired it in 1990.*
Adquiriría uno si tuviera dinero. *I would get one if I had the money.*
¡Ojalá adquiramos uno! *I wish we could acquire one!*

los bienes adquiridos *acquired wealth*
el poder adquisitivo *purchasing power*
el adquiridor *acquirer, buyer*
adquirible *obtainable*

el adquiriente *acquirer*
la adquisición *acquisition*
adquisitivo *acquisitive (law); buying*

7 advertir *to warn, advise; to notice* (tr.)

INDICATIVE

Present	Imperfect	Perfect
advierto	advertía	he advertido
adviertes	advertías	has advertido
advierte	advertía	ha advertido
advertimos	advertíamos	hemos advertido
advertís	advertíais	habéis advertido
advierten	advertían	han advertido

Future	Pluperfect	Preterite
advertiré	había advertido	advertí
advertirás	habías advertido	advertiste
advertirá	había advertido	advirtió
advertiremos	habíamos advertido	advertimos
advertiréis	habíais advertido	advertisteis
advertirán	habían advertido	advirtieron

Future perfect	Past anterior
habré advertido	hube advertido

CONDITIONAL / SUBJUNCTIVE

Present	Present	Imperfect
advertiría	advierta	advirt-iera/iese
advertirías	adviertas	advirt-ieras/ieses
advertiría	advierta	advirt-iera/iese
advertiríamos	advirtamos	advirt-iéramos/iésemos
advertiríais	advirtáis	advirt-ierais/ieseis
advertirían	adviertan	advirt-ieran/iesen

Perfect	Perfect	Pluperfect
habría advertido	haya advertido	hub-iera/iese advertido

GERUND	PAST PARTICIPLE	IMPERATIVE
advirtiendo	advertido	advierte, advertid
		advierta (Vd), adviertan (Vds)

Te lo advierto, no lo hagas. *I warn you, don't do it.*
¿Has advertido que llevaba una caja? *Did you notice that he was carrying a box?*
Pedro les advirtó ayer. *Pedro warned them yesterday.*
Te advierto que no vale la pena. *I warn you, it's not worth it.*
Me lo advirtieron en Madrid. *I was notified in Madrid.*
Adviértele que se lleve el abrigo. *Advise him to take his coat.*

advertido/a *sharp, wide awake*
la advertencia *notice, warning*
el advertidor *detector*

el advertidor local *audio warning device*
el advertimiento *warning notice*
advertidamente *knowing, with forewarning*

8 alentar *to encourage; to breathe* (tr./intr.)

INDICATIVE

Present	Imperfect	Perfect
aliento	alentaba	he alentado
alientas	alentabas	has alentado
alienta	alentaba	ha alentado
alentamos	alentábamos	hemos alentado
alentáis	alentabais	habéis alentado
alientan	alentaban	han alentado

Future	Pluperfect	Preterite
alentaré	había alentado	alenté
alentarás	habías alentado	alentaste
alentará	había alentado	alentó
alentaremos	habíamos alentado	alentamos
alentaréis	habíais alentado	alentasteis
alentarán	habían alentado	alentaron

Future perfect	Past anterior
habré alentado	hube alentado

CONDITIONAL	SUBJUNCTIVE	
Present	**Present**	**Imperfect**
alentaría	aliente	alent-ara/ase
alentarías	alientes	alent-aras/ases
alentaría	aliente	alent-ara-ase
alentaríamos	alentemos	alent-áramos/ásemos
alentaríais	alentéis	alent-arais/aseis
alentarían	alienten	alent-aran/asen

Perfect	Perfect	Pluperfect
habría alentado	haya alentado	hub-iera/iese alentado

GERUND	PAST PARTICIPLE	IMPERATIVE
alentado	alentado	alienta, alentad
		aliente (Vd), alienten (Vds)

Juan siempre alienta a sus amigos. *Juan always encourages his friends.*
Me alentó a continuar. *She encouraged me to go on.*
Me alienta con su sonrisa. *She encourages me with her smile.*
Tuvimos que alentar hondo. *We had to take a deep breath.*
En sus almas alientan patriotismo. *They are very patriotic (lit. they breathe patriotism).*

el aliento *breath*
el alentador *encouraging, inspiring*
alentarse *to cheer up, take heart*

alentoso *brave, spirited*
alentado/a *tireless, comforting*
alentadamente *spiritedly, gallantly*

9 almorzar *to have lunch* (tr./intr.)

INDICATIVE

Present	Imperfect	Perfect
almuerzo	almorzaba	he almorzado
almuerzas	almorzabas	has almorzado
almuerza	almorzaba	ha almorzado
almorzamos	almorzábamos	hemos almorzado
almorzáis	almorzabais	habéis almorzado
almuerzan	almorzaban	han almorzado

Future	Pluperfect	Preterite
almorzaré	había almorzado	almorcé
almorzarás	habías almorzado	almorzaste
almorzará	había almorzado	almorzó
almorzaremos	habíamos almorzado	almorzamos
almorzaréis	habíais almorzado	almorzasteis
almorzarán	habían almorzado	almorzaron

Future perfect	Past anterior
habré almorzado	hube almorzado

CONDITIONAL | SUBJUNCTIVE

Present	Present	Imperfect
almorzaría	almuerce	almorz-ara/ase
almorazarías	almuerces	almorz-aras/ases
almorzaría	almuerce	almorz-ara/ase
almorzaríamos	almorcemos	almorz-áramos/ásemos
almorzarías	almorcéis	almorz-arais/aseis
almorzarían	almuercen	almorz-aran/asen

Perfect	Perfect	Pluperfect
habría almorzado	haya almorzado	hub-iera/iese almorzado

GERUND | PAST PARTICIPLE | IMPERATIVE

GERUND	PAST PARTICIPLE	IMPERATIVE
almorzando	almorzado	almuerza, almorzad
		almuerce (Vd), almuercen (Vds)

En México almorzamos a las 11. *In Mexico, we have brunch at 11.*
Almorzaremos tarde. *We'll have a late lunch.*
Almuerzo café con leche y un pastel. *I have white coffee and cake for elevenses.*
Vengo almorzado. *I have had lunch already.*

el almuerzo *lunch/brunch/elevenses/late breakfast*
tomar el almuerzo *to have lunch, etc.*

10 **amar** *to love, be fond of* (tr.)

INDICATIVE

Present	Imperfect	Perfect
amo	amaba	he amado
amas	amabas	has amado
ama	amaba	ha amado
amamos	amábamos	hemos amado
amáis	amabais	habéis amado
aman	amaban	han amado

Future	Pluperfect	Preterite
amaré	había amado	amé
amarás	habías amado	amaste
amará	había amado	amó
amaremos	habíamos amado	amamos
amaréis	habíais amado	amasteis
amarán	habían amado	amaron

Future perfect	Past anterior	
habré amado	hube amado	

CONDITIONAL SUBJUNCTIVE

Present	Present	Imperfect
amaría	ame	am-ara/ase
amarías	ames	am-aras/ases
amaría	ame	am-ara/ase
amaríamos	amemos	am-áramos/ásemos
amaríais	améis	am-arais/aseis
amarían	amen	am-aran/asen

Perfect	Perfect	Pluperfect
habría amado	haya amado	hub-iera/iese amado

GERUND PAST PARTICIPLE IMPERATIVE

GERUND	PAST PARTICIPLE	IMPERATIVE
amando	amado	ama, amad
		ame (Vd), amen (Vds)

Amo a los niños. *I love children.*
Romeo amaba a Julieta. *Romeo loved Juliet.*
Es bello amar. *To love is beautiful.*
Los soldados aman a la patria. *Soldiers love their homeland.*

el amor *love*
los amores *love affair*
el amante *lover*
el amoroso *loving, tender*

el amor propio *pride, self-respect*
hacer el amor *to make love*
amorosamente *lovingly*

11 andar *to walk, to go, to work (machinery, etc.)* (tr./intr.)

INDICATIVE

Present	Imperfect	Perfect
ando	andaba	he andado
andas	andabas	has andado
anda	andaba	ha andado
andamos	andábamos	hemos andado
andáis	andabais	habéis andado
andan	andaban	han andado

Future	Pluperfect	Preterite
andaré	había andado	anduve
andarás	habías andado	anduviste
andará	había andado	anduvo
andaremos	habíamos andado	anduvimos
andaréis	habíais andado	anduvisteis
andarán	habían andado	anduvieron

Future perfect	Past anterior
habré andado	hube andado

CONDITIONAL / SUBJUNCTIVE

Present	Present	Imperfect
andaría	ande	anduvi-era/ese
andarías	andes	anduvi-eras/eses
andaría	ande	anduvi-era/ese
andaríamos	andemos	anduvi-éramos/ésemos
andaríais	andéis	anduvi-erais/eseis
andarían	anden	anduvi-eran/esen

Perfect	Perfect	Pluperfect
habría andado	haya andado	hub-iera/iese andado

GERUND / PAST PARTICIPLE / IMPERATIVE

GERUND	PAST PARTICIPLE	IMPERATIVE
andando	andado	anda, andad
		ande (Vd), anden (Vds)

Vamos andando. *Let's walk.*
Anduvimos 10 km. *We walked 10 km.*
El coche anda bien. *The car goes well.*
Mi reloj no anda. *My watch isn't working.*
¿Cómo andan los negocios? *How's business going?*
Andamos mal de tiempo. *We're short of time.*
¿Cómo andas de pan? *How are you off for bread?*
Pedro anda por las nubes. *Peter has his head in the clouds.*
No te andes por las ramas. *Don't beat about the bush.*

andante *walking*	**andariego/a** *wandering, wanderer*
andar a gatas *to crawl*	**andador(a)** *wandering*
la andanza *happening, occurrence*	**andado/a** *trodden, frequented, common*
las andanzas *deeds, adventures*	**la andadura** *pace, progress*

12 apaciguar *to pacify, calm down* (tr.)

INDICATIVE

Present	Imperfect	Perfect
apaciguo	apaciguaba	he apaciguado
apaciguas	apaciguabas	has apaciguado
apacigua	apaciguaba	ha apaciguado
apaciguamos	apaciguábamos	hemos apaciguado
apaciguáis	apaciguabais	habéis apaciguado
apaciguan	apaciguaban	han apaciguado

Future	Pluperfect	Preterite
apaciguaré	había apaciguado	apacigüé
apaciguarás	habías apaciguado	apaciguaste
apaciguará	había apaciguado	apaciguó
apaciguaremos	habíamos apaciguado	apaciguamos
apaciguaréis	habíais apaciguado	apaciguasteis
apaciguarán	habían apaciguado	apaciguaron

Future perfect	Past anterior
habré apaciguado	hube apaciguado

CONDITIONAL · SUBJUNCTIVE

Present	Present	Imperfect
apaciguaría	apacigüe	apacigu-ara/ase
apaciguarías	apacigües	apacigu-aras/ases
apaciguaría	apacigüe	apacigu-ara/ase
apaciguaríamos	apacigüemos	apacigu-áramos/ásemos
apaciguaríais	apacigüéis	apacigu-arais/aseis
apaciguarían	apacigüen	apacigu-aran/asen

Perfect	Perfect	Pluperfect
habría apaciguado	haya apaciguado	hub-iera/iese apaciguado

GERUND · PAST PARTICIPLE · IMPERATIVE

GERUND	PAST PARTICIPLE	IMPERATIVE
apaciguando	apaciguado	apacigua, apaciguad
		apacigüe (Vd), apacigüen (Vds)

Apacigua a los niños. *He calms the children down.*
Sabe apaciguar. *He knows how to calm people down.*
Apaciguó a los rebeldes. *He pacified the rebels.*
Se apacigua con música. *Music calms him down.*

apaciguarse *to quieten, calm down*
apacible *mild, placid*
el apaciguamiento *pacifying, appeasement*

apaciguado *pacified*
apaciguador(a) *soothing, calming*
la apacibilidad *gentleness, calmness*

13 apostar *to bet; to post* (tr./intr.)

INDICATIVE

Present	Imperfect	Perfect
apuesto	apostaba	he apostado
apuestas	apostabas	has apostado
apuesta	apostaba	ha apostado
apostamos	apostábamos	hemos apostado
apostáis	apostabais	habéis apostado
apuestan	apostaban	han apostado

Future	Pluperfect	Preterite
apostaré	había apostado	aposté
apostarás	habías apostado	apostaste
apostará	había apostado	apostó
apostaremos	habíamos apostado	apostamos
apostaréis	habíais apostado	apostasteis
apostarán	habían apostado	apostaron

Future perfect	Past anterior
habré apostado	hube apostado

CONDITIONAL | SUBJUNCTIVE

Present	Present	Imperfect
apostaría	apueste	apost-ara/ase
apostarías	apuestes	apost-aras/ases
apostaría	apueste	apost-ara/ase
apostaríamos	apostemos	apost-áramos/ásemos
apostaríais	apostéis	apost-arais/aseis
apostarían	apuesten	apost-aran/asen

Perfect	Perfect	Pluperfect
habría apostado	haya apostado	hub-iera/iese apostado

GERUND | PAST PARTICIPLE | IMPERATIVE

GERUND	PAST PARTICIPLE	IMPERATIVE
apostando	apostado	apuesta, apostad
		apueste (Vd), apuesten (Vds)

¿Qué te apuestas? *What do you bet?*
¡Apuesto a que sí! *I bet it is!*
Te apuesto a que no viene. *I bet you he doesn't come.*
Les han apostado en Escocia. *They have been posted to Scotland.*
Apostaremos los caballos en el prado. *We'll station the horses on the field.*
Se las apuesta con cualquiera a beber. *He competes with anybody for drinking.*

la apuesta *a bet*
apuesto/a *neat, elegant, handsome*
apostador(a) *punter, bookie*

el apostadero *station post, naval station*
aposta, apostadamente *on purpose*

14 apretar *to grip, press together* (tr./intr.)

INDICATIVE

Present	Imperfect	Perfect
aprieto	apretaba	he apretado
aprietas	apretabas	has apretado
aprieta	apretaba	ha apretado
apretamos	apretábamos	hemos apretado
apretáis	apretabais	habéis apretado
aprietan	apretaban	han apretado

Future	Pluperfect	Preterite
apretaré	había apretado	apreté
apretarás	habías apretado	apretaste
apretará	había apretado	apretó
apretaremos	habíamos apretado	apretamos
apretaréis	habíais apretado	apretasteis
apretarán	habían apretado	apretaron

Future perfect	Past anterior
habré apretado	hube apretado

CONDITIONAL | SUBJUNCTIVE

Present	Present	Imperfect
apretaría	apriete	apret-ara/ase
apretarías	aprietes	apret-aras/ases
apretaría	apriete	apret-ara/ase
apretaríamos	apretemos	apret-áramos/ásemos
apretaríais	apretéis	apret-arais/aseis
apretarían	aprieten	apret-aran/asen

Perfect	Perfect	Pluperfect
habría apretado	haya apretado	hub-iera/iese apretado

GERUND | PAST PARTICIPLE | IMPERATIVE

apretando	apretado	aprieta, apretad
		apriete (Vd), aprieten (Vds)

Peter me aprieta entre sus brazos. *Peter hugs me in his arms.*
¿Te aprietan los zapatos? *Are your shoes tight?*
Le apretó contra la pared. *He pinned him against the wall.*
Tuve que apretar la maleta. *I had to press hard to shut the case.*
Estamos apretados de dinero. *We are tight for money.*
Tenemos que apretarnos el cinturón. *We have to tighten our belts.*
El calor aprieta. *The heat is oppressive.*
¡Aprieta a correr! *Start running/Run faster/harder!*

apretadamente *tightly, densely*
la apretadera *strap, rope, pressure*
apretado/a *tight, difficult, cramped*

aprieto *jam, trouble, distress*
el apretón *squeeze, grip; jam, crush*

15 aprobar *to approve, pass* (tr./intr.)

INDICATIVE

Present	Imperfect	Perfect
apruebo	aprobaba	he aprobado
apruebas	aprobabas	has aprobado
aprueba	aprobaba	ha aprobado
aprobamos	aprobábamos	hemos aprobado
aprobáis	aprobabais	habéis aprobado
aprueban	aprobaban	han aprobado

Future	Pluperfect	Preterite
aprobaré	había aprobado	aprobé
aprobarás	habías aprobado	aprobaste
aprobará	había aprobado	aprobó
aprobaremos	habíamos aprobado	aprobamos
aprobaréis	habíais aprobado	aprobasteis
aprobarán	habían aprobado	aprobaron

Future perfect	Past anterior	
habré aprobado	hube aprobado	

CONDITIONAL / SUBJUNCTIVE

Present	Present	Imperfect
aprobaría	apruebe	aprob-ara/ase
aprobarías	apruebes	aprob-aras/ases
aprobaría	apruebe	aprob-ara/ase
aprobaríamos	aprobemos	aprob-áramos/ásemos
aprobaríais	aprobéis	aprob-arais/aseis
aprobarían	aprueben	aprob-aran/asen

Perfect	Perfect	Pluperfect
habría aprobado	haya aprobado	hub-iera/iese aprobado

GERUND	PAST PARTICIPLE	IMPERATIVE
aprobando	aprobado	aprueba, aprobad
		apruebe (Vd), aprueben (Vds)

Se ha aprobado la propuesta. *The motion has been passed.*
Aprobé en español. *I passed in Spanish.*
Me ha aprobado el presupuesto. *He has passed my budget.*
Seguro que se aprobará mi proyecto. *I am sure my project will be approved.*
El ministro va a aprobar una resolución. *The minister is going to adopt a resolution.*
Quieren aprobar un contrato. *They want to ratify a contract.*

aprobado *passed, approved*
aprobatoria *approving*
la aprobación del Parlamento
  parliamentary approval

aprobar un documento *to certify a document*
la aprobación *approval, consent*
aprobado oficialmente por las autoridades
  officially approved by the authorities

16 argüir *to argue, reason* (tr./intr.)

INDICATIVE

Present	Imperfect	Perfect
arguyo	argüía	he argüido
arguyes	argüías	has argüido
arguye	argüía	ha argüido
argüimos	argüíamos	hemos argüido
argüís	argüíais	habéis argüido
arguyen	argüían	han argüido

Future	Pluperfect	Preterite
argüiré	había argüido	argüí
argüirás	habías argüido	argüiste
argüirá	había argüido	arguyó
argüiremos	habíamos argüido	argüimos
argüiréis	habíais argüido	argüisteis
argüirán	habían argüido	arguyeron

Future perfect	Past anterior
habré argüido	hube argüido

CONDITIONAL / SUBJUNCTIVE

Present	Present	Imperfect
argüiría	arguya	argu-yera/yese
argüirías	arguyas	argu-yeras/yeses
argüiría	arguya	argu-yera/yese
argüiríamos	arguyamos	argu-yéramos/yésemos
argüiríais	arguyáis	argu-yerais/yeseis
argüirían	arguyan	argu-yeran/yesen

Perfect	Perfect	Pluperfect
habría argüido	haya argüido	hub-iera/iese argüido

GERUND / PAST PARTICIPLE / IMPERATIVE

GERUND	PAST PARTICIPLE	IMPERATIVE
arguyendo	argüido	arguye, argüid
		arguya (Vd), arguyan (Vds)

No podemos argüir con él. *We can't reason with him.*
Arguyó que teníamos obligaciones con mi familia. *He argued that we had obligations to my family.*
Juan argüiría con cualquiera. *Juan would argue with anybody.*
Si arguyese bien el caso... *If only he argued the case well...*

el argumento *argument, reasoning, outline; plot, story-line; (LA) quarrel*
la argumentación *argument, reasoning*

argumentista *script-writer, arguer*
argumentar *to argue, contend*

17 arrendar *to let, lease; hire out* (tr.)

INDICATIVE

Present	Imperfect	Perfect
arriendo	arrendaba	he arrendado
arriendas	arrendabas	has arrendado
arrienda	arrendaba	ha arrendado
arrendamos	arrendábamos	hemos arrendado
arrendáis	arrendabais	habéis arrendado
arriendan	arrendaban	han arrendado

Future	Pluperfect	Preterite
arrendaré	había arrendado	arrendé
arrendarás	habías arrendado	arrendaste
arrendará	había arrendado	arrendó
arrendaremos	habíamos arrendado	arrendamos
arrendaréis	habíais arrendado	arrendasteis
arrendarán	habían arrendado	arrendaron

Future perfect	Past anterior
habré arrendado	hube arrendado

CONDITIONAL · SUBJUNCTIVE

Present	Present	Imperfect
arrendaría	arriende	arrend-ara/ase
arrendarías	arriendes	arrend-aras/ases
arrendaría	arriende	arrend-ara/ase
arrendaríamos	arrendemos	arrend-áramos/ásemos
arrendaríais	arrendéis	arrend-arais/aseis
arrendarían	arrienden	arrend-aran/asen

Perfect	Perfect	Pluperfect
habría arrendado	haya arrendado	hub-iera/iese arrendado

GERUND · PAST PARTICIPLE · IMPERATIVE

GERUND	PAST PARTICIPLE	IMPERATIVE
arrendando	arrendado	arrienda, arrendad
		arriende (Vd), arrienden (Vds)

Arrendaré una habitación. *I shall let a room.*
Arrienda su casa y vive con su madre. *She rents out her house and lives with her mother.*
Yo que tú arrendaría el coche y usaría la moto. *If I were you, I would hire out the car and use the motorbike.*
Voy a arrendar la casa de nuevo. *I am going to re-lease the house.*

el arrendamiento *letting, leasing, hiring*
el arrendajo *jay (bird); mimic*
el/la arrendatario/a *tenant, leaseholder*
arrendable *leaseable, 'to let'*

el arrendador *landlord*
la arrendadora *landlady*
el arrendamiento financiero *lease*

18 asentar *to settle, set, make firm* (tr.)

INDICATIVE

Present	Imperfect	Perfect
asiento	asentaba	he asentado
asientas	asentabas	has asentado
asienta	asentaba	ha asentado
asentamos	asentábamos	hemos asentado
asentáis	asentabais	habéis asentado
asientan	asentaban	han asentado

Future	Pluperfect	Preterite
asentaré	había asentado	asenté
asentarás	habías asentado	asentaste
asentará	había asentado	asentó
asentaremos	habíamos asentado	asentamos
asentaréis	habíais asentado	asentasteis
asentarán	habían asentado	asentaron

Future perfect	Past anterior
habré asentado	hube asentado

CONDITIONAL   SUBJUNCTIVE

Present	Present	Imperfect
asentaría	asiente	asent-ara/ase
asentarías	asientes	asent-aras/ases
asentaría	asiente	asent-ara/ase
asentaríamos	asentemos	asent-áramos/ásemos
asentarías	asentéis	asent-arais/aseis
asentarían	asienten	asent-aran/asen

Perfect	Perfect	Pluperfect
habría asentado	haya asentado	hub-iera/iese asentado

GERUND   PAST PARTICIPLE   IMPERATIVE

GERUND	PAST PARTICIPLE	IMPERATIVE
asentando	asentado	asienta, asentad
		asiente (Vd), asienten (Vds)

La lluvia ha asentado el polvo. *The rain has settled the dust.*
Debes asentar los cimientos del edificio. *You must lay the foundations of the building.*
Vamos a asentar el campamento al lado del río. *We are going to set up camp by the river.*
Le asentó una bofetada. *He gave him a slap.*

el asiento *seat*
asentar en el libro *to enter into the books*
asentar ladrillos *to set bricks in cement*

asentar al haber de... *to credit someone with...*
asentar al deber *to debit*

19 asentir *to assent, agree* (intr.)

INDICATIVE

Present	Imperfect	Perfect
asiento	asentía	he asentido
asientes	asentías	has asentido
asiente	asentía	ha asentido
asentimos	asentíamos	hemos asentido
asentís	asentíais	habéis asentido
asienten	asentían	han asentido

Future	Pluperfect	Preterite
asentiré	había asentido	asentí
asentirás	habías asentido	asentiste
asentirá	había asentido	asintió
asentiremos	habíamos asentido	asentimos
asentiréis	habíais asentido	asentisteis
asentirán	habían asentido	asintieron

Future perfect	Past anterior
habré asentido	hube asentido

CONDITIONAL / SUBJUNCTIVE

Present	Present	Imperfect
asentiría	asienta	asint-iera/iese
asentirías	asientas	asint-ieras/ieses
asentiría	asienta	asint-iera/iese
asentiríamos	asintamos	asint-iéramos/iésemos
asentiríais	asintáis	asint-ierais/ieseis
asentirían	asientan	asint-ieran/iesen

Perfect	Perfect	Pluperfect
habría asentido	haya asentido	hub-iera/iese asentido

GERUND	PAST PARTICIPLE	IMPERATIVE
asintiendo	asentido	asiente, asentid
		asienta (Vd), asientan (Vds)

Todos asintieron a las palabras del presidente. *Everybody acquiesced to the words of the president.*
Lo asentiremos mañana. *We shall agree to it tomorrow.*
No asintió a dejarse retratar. *She did not agree to have her picture taken.*
Asiente con la cabeza. *Nod your head.*
Asentí a la verdad de su razonamiento. *I recognized the truth of his reasoning.*

el asentimiento *assent, consent* **el asentista** *contractor, supplier*
el asenso *consent*

20 asir *to grasp, seize* (tr./intr.)

INDICATIVE

Present	Imperfect	Perfect
asgo	asía	he asido
ases	asías	has asido
ase	asía	ha asido
asimos	asíamos	hemos asido
asís	asíais	habéis asido
asen	asían	han asido

Future	Pluperfect	Preterite
asiré	había asido	así
asirás	habías asido	asiste
asirá	había asido	asió
asiremos	habíamos asido	asimos
asiréis	habíais asido	asisteis
asirán	habían asido	asieron

Future perfect	Past anterior
habré asido	hube asido

CONDITIONAL / SUBJUNCTIVE

Present	Present	Imperfect
asiría	asga	as-iera/iese
asirías	asgas	as-ieras/ieses
asiría	asga	as-iera/iese
asiríamos	asgamos	as-iéramos/iésemos
asiríais	asgáis	as-ierais/ieseis
asirían	asgan	as-ieran/iesen

Perfect	Perfect	Pluperfect
habría asido	haya asido	hub-iera/iese asido

GERUND	PAST PARTICIPLE	IMPERATIVE
asiendo	asido	ase, asid
		asga (Vd), asgan (Vds)

Hay que asir la jarra por el asa. *You must grasp the jug by the handle.*
Asiré el momento. *I shall seize the moment.*
Manuel sabe asir las oportunidades. *Manuel knows how to grasp opportunities.*
Los bebés no pueden asir bien. *Babies cannot grasp things properly.*
Se asieron después del accidente. *They went for each other after the accident.*
Van a asirse de los pelos. *They will be at each other's throats.*

asir por el mango *to face a problem*
el asa *handle*
la asidera *saddle-strap*

asirse *to fight, grapple, go for each other*
ir asidos del brazo *to go arm in arm*
el asidero *handle, handhold, pretext*

21 atender *to attend, pay attention* (tr./intr.)

INDICATIVE

Present	Imperfect	Perfect
atiendo	atendía	he atendido
atiendes	atendías	has atendido
atiende	atendía	ha atendido
atendemos	atendíamos	hemos atendido
atendéis	atendíais	habéis atendido
atienden	atendían	han atendido

Future	Pluperfect	Preterite
atenderé	había atendido	atendí
atenderás	habías atendido	atendiste
atenderá	había atendido	atendió
atenderemos	habíamos atendido	atendimos
atenderéis	habíais atendido	atendisteis
atenderán	habían atendido	atendieron

Future perfect	Past anterior
habré atendido	hube atendido

CONDITIONAL · SUBJUNCTIVE

Present	Present	Imperfect
atendería	atienda	atend-iera/iese
atenderías	atiendas	atend-ieras/ieses
atendería	atienda	atend-iera/iese
atenderíamos	atendamos	atend-iéramos/iésemos
atenderíais	atendáis	atend-ierais/ieseis
atenderían	atiendan	atend-ieran/iesen

Perfect	Perfect	Pluperfect
habría atendido	haya atendido	hub-iera/iese atendido

GERUND	PAST PARTICIPLE	IMPERATIVE
atendiendo	atendido	atiende, atended
		atienda (Vd), atiendan (Vds)

Tengo compromisos que atender. *I have got obligations to meet.*
Atendieron el consejo. *They paid attention to the advice.*
Atendía a un cliente. *I was serving a customer.*
Atenderemos el giro. *We shall honour the draft.*
El médico atendió a un caso urgente. *The doctor had to see to an emergency.*
Atiende el teléfono. *She is minding the phone.*
¡Atención, cuidado con el perro! *Beware of the dog!*

la atención *attention, care*
en atención a esto... *regarding this...*
atento/a *attentive, observant, polite*
prestar atención *to pay attention*

22 atravesar to cross, go through (tr.)

INDICATIVE

Present	Imperfect	Perfect
atravieso	atrevesaba	he atravesado
atraviesas	atrevesabas	has atravesado
atraviesa	atrevesaba	ha atravesado
atravesamos	atrevesábamos	hemos atravesado
atravesáis	atravesabais	habéis atravesado
atraviesan	atravesaban	han atravesado

Future	Pluperfect	Preterite
atravesaré	había atravesado	atravesé
atravesarás	habías atravesado	atravesaste
atravesará	había atravesado	atravesó
atravesaremos	habíamos atravesado	atravesamos
atravesaréis	habíais atravesado	atravesasteis
atravesarán	habían atravesado	atravesaron

Future perfect	Past anterior
habré atravesado	hube atravesado

CONDITIONAL | SUBJUNCTIVE

Present	Present	Imperfect
atravesaría	atraviese	atraves-ara/ase
atravesarías	atravieses	atrave-aras/ases
atravesaría	atraviese	atrave-ara/ase
atravesaríamos	atravesemos	atrave-áramos/ásemos
atravesaríais	atraveséis	atrave-arais/aseis
atravesarían	atraviesen	atrave-aran/asen

Perfect	Perfect	Pluperfect
habría atravesado	haya atravesado	hub-iera/iese atravesado

GERUND | PAST PARTICIPLE | IMPERATIVE

GERUND	PAST PARTICIPLE	IMPERATIVE
atravesando	atravesado	atraviesa, atravesad
		atraviese (Vd), atraviesen (Vds)

Atravesamos el río de noche. *We crossed the river at night.*
La bala atravesó el metal. *The bullet pierced the metal.*
Atravieso un momento difícil. *I'm going through a difficult time.*
Le tengo atravesado. *I can't stand him.*
Siempre se atraviesa en mis negocios. *He's always interfering in my affairs.*
Me encanta atravesarme en una conversación. *I love to butt in on a conversation.*

atravesado/a *crossed, oblique; cross-eyed*
la travesía *crossing*
atravesarse *to come in between, interfere*

atravesando las olas *broadside to the waves*

23 beber *to drink* (tr./intr.)

INDICATIVE

Present	Imperfect	Perfect
bebo	bebía	he bebido
bebes	bebías	has bebido
bebe	bebía	ha bebido
bebemos	bebíamos	hemos bebido
bebéis	bebíais	habéis bebido
beben	bebían	han bebido

Future	Pluperfect	Preterite
beberé	había bebido	bebí
beberás	habías bebido	bebiste
beberá	había bebido	bebió
beberemos	habíamos bebido	bebimos
beberéis	habíais bebido	bebisteis
beberán	habían bebido	bebieron

Future perfect	Past anterior
habré bebido	hube bebido

CONDITIONAL SUBJUNCTIVE

Present	Present	Imperfect
bebería	beba	beb-iera/iese
beberías	bebas	beb-ieras/ieses
bebería	beba	beb-iera/iese
beberíamos	bebamos	beb-iéramos/iésemos
beberíais	bebáis	beb-ierais/ieseis
beberían	beban	beb-ieran/iesen

Perfect	Perfect	Pluperfect
habría bebido	haya bebido	hub-iera/iese bebido

GERUND PAST PARTICIPLE IMPERATIVE

bebiendo	bebido	bebe, bebed
		beba (Vd), beban (Vds)

Bebo café con leche por la mañana. *I drink white coffee in the morning.*
Es abstemio, nunca bebe alcohol. *He is a teetotaller.*
Se bebió tres coñacs después de comer. *After lunch he had three brandies.*
Bebamos a la salud del rey. *Let's drink to the king's health.*
Bebe un pote. *He's a heavy drinker.*
Bebe como una cuba. *He drinks like a fish.*

la bebida *drink*
el/la bebedor(a) *boozer, heavy drinker*
bebedizo, bebedero *drinkable*

bebido *tipsy, drunk*
darse a la bebida *to take to drink*
el bebedero *water trough; spout
  (of drinking vessels)*

24 buscar *to look for* (tr.)

INDICATIVE

Present	Imperfect	Perfect
busco	buscaba	he buscado
buscas	buscabas	has buscado
busca	buscaba	ha buscado
buscamos	buscábamos	hemos buscado
buscáis	buscabais	habéis buscado
buscan	buscaban	han buscado

Future	Pluperfect	Preterite
buscaré	había buscado	busqué
buscarás	habías buscado	buscaste
buscará	había buscado	buscó
buscaremos	habíamos buscado	buscamos
buscaréis	habíais buscado	buscasteis
buscarán	habían buscado	buscaron

Future perfect	Past anterior
habré buscado	hube buscado

CONDITIONAL | SUBJUNCTIVE

Present	Present	Imperfect
buscaría	busque	busc-ara/ase
buscarías	busques	busc-aras/ases
buscaría	busque	busc-ara/ase
buscaríamos	busquemos	busc-áramos/ásemos
buscaríais	busquéis	busc-arais/aseis
buscarían	busquen	busc-aran/asen

Perfect	Perfect	Pluperfect
habría buscado	haya buscado	hub-iera/iese buscado

GERUND | PAST PARTICIPLE | IMPERATIVE

GERUND	PAST PARTICIPLE	IMPERATIVE
buscando	buscado	busca, buscad
		busque (Vd), busquen (Vds)

Le busqué por todas partes. *I looked for him everywhere.*
Está buscando un trabajo. *He is looking for a job.*
Voy a buscarle a la estación. *I'm going to pick her up at the station.*
Se busca coche. *Car wanted.*
Miguel Ángel ha tenido que buscarse la vida. *Miguel Angel has had to fend for himself.*
Se lo buscó ella misma. *She brought it on herself.*
¡Te la estás buscando! *You're asking for it!*

la busca *search*
la búsqueda *search*
el/la buscador(a) *searcher*
el buscón *petty thief, rogue*

la buscona *whore*
el/la buscavidas *meddler, busybody*
el buscarruidos *troublemaker*

25 caber *to fit, have enough room* (intr.)

INDICATIVE

Present	Imperfect	Perfect
quepo	cabía	he cabido
cabes	cabías	has cabido
cabe	cabía	ha cabido
cabemos	cabíamos	hemos cabido
cabéis	cabíais	habéis cabido
caben	cabían	han cabido

Future	Pluperfect	Preterite
cabré	había cabido	cupe
cabrás	habías cabido	cupiste
cabrá	había cabido	cupo
cabremos	habíamos cabido	cupimos
cabréis	habíais cabido	cupisteis
cabrán	habían cabido	cupieron

Future perfect	Past anterior
habré cabido	hube cabido

CONDITIONAL   SUBJUNCTIVE

Present	Present	Imperfect
cabría	quepa	cup-iera/iese
cabrías	quepas	cup-ieras/ieses
cabría	quepa	cup-iera/iese
cabríamos	quepamos	cup-iéramos/iésemos
cabríais	quepáis	cup-ierais/ieseis
cabrían	quepan	cup-ieran/iesen

Perfect	Perfect	Pluperfect
habría cabido	haya cabido	hub-iera/iese cabido

GERUND   PAST PARTICIPLE   IMPERATIVE

GERUND	PAST PARTICIPLE	IMPERATIVE
cabiendo	cabido	cabe, cabed
		quepa (Vd), quepan (Vds)

No cabe por esa puerta. *It won't go through that door.*
¿Cabe el libro? *Is there room for the book?*
Caben más de tres en el ascensor. *There is room for more than three people in the lift.*
Caben tres litros en la botella. *The bottle holds three litres.*
Todo cabe en Carlos. *Carlos is capable of anything.*
¡No cabe más! *There's no more room./That's the lot!*
No cabía en sí de contenta. *She was bursting with joy.*

la cabida *space, room*	**no cabe duda** *there is no doubt*
la capacidad *capacity*	**no tiene cabida** *it is not acceptable*

26 caer to fall (intr.)

INDICATIVE

Present	Imperfect	Perfect
caigo	caía	he caído
caes	caías	has caído
cae	caía	ha caído
caemos	caíamos	hemos caído
caéis	caíais	habéis caído
caen	caían	han caído

Future	Pluperfect	Preterite
caeré	había caído	caí
caerás	habías caído	caíste
caerá	había caído	cayó
caeremos	habíamos caído	caímos
caeréis	habíais caído	caísteis
caerán	habían caído	cayeron

Future perfect	Past anterior
habré caído	hube caído

CONDITIONAL / SUBJUNCTIVE

Present	Present	Imperfect
caería	caiga	ca-yera/yese
caerías	caigas	ca-yeras/yeses
caería	caiga	ca-yera/yese
caeríamos	caigamos	ca-yéramos/yésemos
caeríais	caigáis	ca-yerais/yeseis
caerían	caigan	ca-yeran/yesen

Perfect	Perfect	Pluperfect
habría caído	haya caído	hub-iera/iese caído

GERUND	PAST PARTICIPLE	IMPERATIVE
cayendo	caído	cae, caed
		caiga (Vd), caigan (Vds)

El edificio se cayó al suelo. *The building fell to the ground.*
Se ha caído del caballo. *She has fallen off the horse.*
La noche está al caer. *Night is about to fall.*
Pam cayó en cama/enferma. *Pam fell ill.*
Dejó caer el cuchillo. *He dropped the knife.*
Antonio no me cae bien. *I don't like Antonio.*
Carlos se cae de miedo. *Carlos is terrified.*
La fiesta cae en martes. *The party is on a Tuesday.*

la caída *fall, tumble*
caedizo *unsteady, about to fall*
caído/a *fallen, wilting*

los caídos *the fallen*
estar caído de sueño *to be dead tired*

27 calentar *to warm, heat up* (tr.)

INDICATIVE

Present	Imperfect	Perfect
caliento	calentaba	he calentado
calientas	calentabas	has calentado
calienta	calentaba	ha calentado
calentamos	calentábamos	hemos calentado
calentáis	calentabais	habéis calentado
calientan	calentaban	han calentado

Future	Pluperfect	Preterite
calentaré	había calentado	calenté
calentarás	habías calentado	calentaste
calentará	había calentado	calentó
calentaremos	habíamos calentado	calentamos
calentaréis	habíais calentado	calentasteis
calentarán	habían calentado	calentaron

Future perfect	Past anterior
habré calentado	hube calentado

CONDITIONAL   SUBJUNCTIVE

Present	Present	Imperfect
calentaría	caliente	calent-ara/ase
calentarías	calientes	calent-aras/ases
calentaría	caliente	calent-ara/ase
calentaríamos	calentemos	calent-áramos/ásemos
calentaríais	calentéis	calent-arais/aseis
calentarían	calienten	calent-aran/asen

Perfect	Perfect	Pluperfect
habría calentado	haya calentado	hub-iera/iese calentado

GERUND   PAST PARTICIPLE   IMPERATIVE

GERUND	PAST PARTICIPLE	IMPERATIVE
calentando	calentado	calienta, calentad
		caliente (Vd), calienten (Vds)

Calienta la leche. *Warm up the milk.*
El sol calentará la piedra. *The sun will warm up the stone.*
Nos calentamos al fuego. *We warmed up by the fire.*
Me he calentado bastante. *I have warmed myself up enough.*
Lo calentó al rojo vivo. *He made it red hot.*
Les calentaron las orejas. *They told them off.*

el calentador *heater*
el calor *heat*
caliente *hot, warm; on heat, sexually aroused; (LA) angry*

hace calor *it is hot*
el calentamiento *heating, warming*
la calentura *fever, high temperature*

28 caminar *to walk* (tr./intr.)

INDICATIVE

Present	Imperfect	Perfect
camino	caminaba	he caminado
caminas	caminabas	has caminado
camina	caminaba	ha caminado
caminamos	caminábamos	hemos caminado
camináis	caminabais	habéis caminado
caminan	caminaban	han caminado

Future	Pluperfect	Preterite
caminaré	había caminado	caminé
caminarás	habías caminado	caminaste
caminará	había caminado	caminó
caminaremos	habíamos caminado	caminamos
caminaréis	habíais caminado	caminasteis
caminarán	habían caminado	caminaron

Future perfect	Past anterior
habré caminado	hube caminado

CONDITIONAL · SUBJUNCTIVE

Present	Present	Imperfect
caminaría	camine	camin-ara/ase
caminarías	camines	camin-aras/ases
caminaría	camine	camin-ara/ase
caminaríamos	caminemos	camin-áramos/ásemos
caminarías	caminéis	camin-arais/aseis
caminarían	caminen	camin-aran/asen

Perfect	Perfect	Pluperfect
habría caminado	haya caminado	hub-iera/iese caminado

GERUND · PAST PARTICIPLE · IMPERATIVE

GERUND	PAST PARTICIPLE	IMPERATIVE
caminando	caminado	camina, caminad
		camine (Vd), caminen (Vds)

Caminamos durante dos horas. *We walked for two hours.*
Caminé hasta la casa. *I walked to the house.*
Caminarán hasta el río. *They will walk to the river.*
¿Has caminado despacio? *Have you walked slowly?*
Don Francisco camina derecho. *Don Francisco behaves properly.*
Fredes camina con pena. *Fredes moves with difficulty.*

el camino *road, way*
la caminata *long walk, ramble*
el caminante *walker, traveller*

el caminero *road builder*
caminador(a) *fond of walking*
el caminejo *rough road, dirt track*

29 cantar *to sing, chant* (tr./intr.)

INDICATIVE

Present	Imperfect	Perfect
canto	cantaba	he cantado
cantas	cantabas	has cantado
canta	cantaba	ha cantado
cantamos	cantábamos	hemos cantado
cantáis	cantabais	habéis cantado
cantan	cantaban	han cantado

Future	Pluperfect	Preterite
cantaré	había cantado	canté
cantarás	habías cantado	cantaste
cantará	había cantado	cantó
cantaremos	habíamos cantado	cantamos
cantaréis	habíais cantado	cantasteis
cantarán	habían cantado	cantaron

Future perfect	Past anterior
habré cantado	hube cantado

CONDITIONAL | SUBJUNCTIVE

Present	Present	Imperfect
cantaría	cante	cant-ara/ase
cantarías	cantes	cant-aras/ases
cantaría	cante	cant-ara/ase
cantaríamos	cantemos	cant-áramos/ásemos
cantaríais	cantéis	cant-arais/aseis
cantarían	canten	cant-aran/asen

Perfect	Perfect	Pluperfect
habría cantado	haya cantado	hub-iera/iese cantado

GERUND	PAST PARTICIPLE	IMPERATIVE
cantando	cantado	canta, cantad
		cante (Vd), canten (Vds)

Me gusta cantar. *I like singing.*
Marta canta en la ópera de Madrid. *Marta sings in the Madrid Opera.*
Plácido Domingo cantará en Mérida. *Placido Domingo will sing in Merida.*
Sara y Elena cantan a dos voces. *Sara and Elena sing duets.*
Ana cantó de plano. *Ana made a full confession.*
Francisca cantará las claras. *Francisca will speak out frankly.*

la canción *song*
el cantar *song*
el cantar de gesta *epic poem*
el cántico *hymn, song*

el/la cantante *singer*
el cantarín, cantarina *tinkling, sing-song noise*
el cante flamenco, el cante jondo *Andalusian gypsy singing*

30 **castigar** *to punish* (tr.)

INDICATIVE

Present	Imperfect	Perfect
castigo	castigaba	he castigado
castigas	castigabas	has castigado
castiga	castigaba	ha castigado
castigamos	castigábamos	hemos castigado
castigáis	castigabais	habéis castigado
castigan	castigaban	han castigado

Future	Pluperfect	Preterite
castigaré	había castigado	castigué
castigarás	habías castigado	castigaste
castigará	había castigado	castigó
castigaremos	habíamos castigado	castigamos
castigaréis	habíais castigado	castigasteis
castigarán	habían castigado	castigaron

Future perfect	Past anterior
habré castigado	hube castigado

CONDITIONAL | SUBJUNCTIVE

Present	Present	Imperfect
castigaría	castigue	castig-ara/ase
castigarías	castigues	castig-aras/ases
castigaría	castigue	castig-ara/ase
castigaríamos	castiguemos	castig-áramos/ásemos
castigaríais	castiguéis	castig-arais/aseis
castigarían	castiguen	castig-aran/asen

Perfect	Perfect	Pluperfect
habría castigado	haya castigado	hub-iera/iese castigado

GERUND	PAST PARTICIPLE	IMPERATIVE
castigando	castigado	castiga, castigad
		castigue (Vd), castiguen (Vds)

No castigues al niño. *Don't punish the boy.*
Me castigaron por romper el vaso. *I was punished for breaking the glass.*
Si te portas mal te castigaré. *I shall punish you if you don't behave.*
Te vamos a castigar. *We are going to punish you.*
Pedro castiga mucho el caballo. *Pedro rides his horse hard.*

el castigo *punishment, penalty*
el castigo corporal *corporal punishment*
el/la castigador(a) *punisher, punishing*

la castigación *punishment*
castigado/a *punished*

31 cazar *to hunt, chase; to catch* (tr.)

INDICATIVE

Present	Imperfect	Perfect
cazo	cazaba	he cazado
cazas	cazabas	has cazado
caza	cazaba	ha cazado
cazamos	cazábamos	hemos cazado
cazáis	cazabais	habéis cazado
cazan	cazaban	han cazado

Future	Pluperfect	Preterite
cazaré	había cazado	cacé
cazarás	habías cazado	cazaste
cazará	había cazado	cazó
cazaremos	habíamos cazado	cazamos
cazaréis	habíais cazado	cazasteis
cazarán	habían cazado	cazaron

Future perfect	Past anterior	
habré cazado	hube cazado	

CONDITIONAL   SUBJUNCTIVE

Present	Present	Imperfect
cazaría	cace	caz-ara/ase
cazarías	caces	caz-aras/ases
cazaría	cace	caz-ara/ase
cazaríamos	cacemos	caz-áramos/ásemos
cazaríais	cacéis	caz-arais/aseis
cazarían	cacen	caz-aran/asen

Perfect	Perfect	Pluperfect
habría cazado	haya cazado	hub-iera/iese cazado

GERUND	PAST PARTICIPLE	IMPERATIVE
cazando	cazado	caza, cazad
		cace (Vd), cacen (Vds)

Estaba cazando un león en África. *He was hunting a lion in Africa.*
Cazarán jabalíes en setiembre. *They will hunt wild boar in September.*
No me gusta cazar. *I don't like hunting.*
Le cacé en el acto. *I caught him in the act.*
No le vas a cazar. *You will not catch him.*
Por fin le cacé en la fiesta. *I finally ran him to earth at the party.*
Miguel las caza al vuelo. *Miguel is pretty sharp.*
Fue cazado por el banco. *He was headhunted by the bank.*

la caza *hunting*
dar caza a *to give chase, go after*
ir a la caza *to go hunting/shooting*
el/la cazador(a) *hunter*

la cazadora *windcheater; leather jacket*
el cazagenios *talent spotter*

32 cegar *to blind; block* (tr./intr.)

Present	Imperfect	Perfect
ciego	cegaba	he cegado
ciegas	cegabas	has cegado
ciega	cegaba	ha cegado
cegamos	cegábamos	hemos cegado
cegáis	cegabais	habéis cegado
ciegan	cegaban	han cegado

Future	Pluperfect	Preterite
cegaré	había cegado	cegué
cegarás	habías cegado	cegaste
cegará	había cegado	cegó
cegaremos	habíamos cegado	cegamos
cegaréis	habíais cegado	cegasteis
cegarán	habían cegado	cegaron

Future perfect	Past anterior
habré cegado	hube cegado

CONDITIONAL	SUBJUNCTIVE	

Present	Present	Imperfect
cegaría	ciegue	ceg-ara/ase
cegarías	ciegues	ceg-aras/ases
cegaría	ciegue	ceg-ara/ase
cegaríamos	ceguemos	ceg-áramos/ásemos
cegarías	ceguéis	ceg-arais/aseis
cegarían	cieguen	ceg-aran/asen

Perfect	Perfect	Pluperfect
habría cegado	haya cegado	hub-iera/iese cegado

GERUND	PAST PARTICIPLE	IMPERATIVE
cegando	cegado	ciega, cegad
		ciegue (Vd), cieguen (Vds)

El sol me ciega. *The sun is blinding me.*
La explosión me cegó. *The explosion blinded me.*
El árbol le ciega la vista. *The tree blocks his view.*
Ha cegado el agujero. *He has blocked up the hole.*
Se cegaron de ira. *They were blinded with anger.*

cegato/a *short-sighted*
la ceguera *blindness*
la ceguera nocturna *night blindness*
la ceguedad *blindness*

ciego/a *blind*
quedar ciego *to go blind, be blinded*

33 cerrar *to close, shut, lock* (tr./intr.)

INDICATIVE

Present	Imperfect	Perfect
cierro	cerraba	he cerrado
cierras	cerrabas	has cerrado
cierra	cerraba	ha cerrado
cerramos	cerrábamos	hemos cerrado
cerráis	cerrabais	habéis cerrado
cierran	cerraban	han cerrado

Future	Pluperfect	Preterite
cerraré	había cerrado	cerré
cerrarás	habías cerrado	cerraste
cerrará	había cerrado	cerró
cerraremos	habíamos cerrado	cerramos
cerraréis	habías cerrado	cerrasteis
cerrarán	habían cerrado	cerraron

Future perfect	Past anterior
habré cerrado	hube cerrado

CONDITIONAL   SUBJUNCTIVE

Present	Present	Imperfect
cerraría	cierre	cerr-ara/ase
cerrarías	cierres	cerr-aras/ases
cerraría	cierre	cerr-ara/ase
cerraríamos	cerremos	cerr-áramos/ásemos
cerraríais	cerréis	cerr-arais/aseis
cerrarían	cierren	cerr-aran/asen

Perfect	Perfect	Pluperfect
habría cerrado	haya cerrado	hub-iera/iese cerrado

GERUND	PAST PARTICIPLE	IMPERATIVE
cerrando	cerrado	cierra, cerrad
		cierre (Vd), cierren (Vds)

Cierra la puerta. *Close the door.*
Cierro con llave. *I'm locking up.*
La puerta cierra mal. *The door doesn't shut properly.*
Cerramos a las seis. *We close at six.*
La fábrica ha cerrado. *The factory has closed down.*
Han cerrado la frontera. *They have closed the border.*
La carretera está cerrada por la nieve. *The road is blocked by the snow.*
Se ha cerrado en hacerlo. *He persists in doing it.*

el cierre *closing*
el cierre de radio y TV *close-down* (radio and TV)
la cerradura *lock; shutting*

la cerradura de seguridad *safety lock*
el/la cerrajero/a *locksmith*
la cerrajería *locksmith's craft, trade shop*

34 cocer *to boil, cook* (tr./intr.)

INDICATIVE

Present	Imperfect	Perfect
cuezo	cocía	he cocido
cueces	cocías	has cocido
cuece	cocía	ha cocido
cocemos	cocíamos	hemos cocido
cocéis	cocías	habéis cocido
cuecen	cocían	han cocido

Future	Pluperfect	Preterite
coceré	había cocido	cocí
cocerás	habías cocido	cociste
cocerá	había cocido	coció
coceremos	habíamos cocido	cocimos
coceréis	habías cocido	cocisteis
cocerán	habían cocido	cocieron

Future perfect	Past anterior
habré cocido	hube cocido

CONDITIONAL	SUBJUNCTIVE	
Present	**Present**	**Imperfect**
cocería	cueza	coc-iera/iese
cocerías	cuezas	coc-ieras/ieses
cocería	cueza	coc-iera/iese
coceríamos	cozamos	coc-iéramos/iésemos
coceríais	cozáis	coc-ierais/ieseis
cocerían	cuezan	coc-ieran/iesen

Perfect	Perfect	Pluperfect
habría cocido	haya cocido	hub-iera/iese cocido

GERUND	PAST PARTICIPLE	IMPERATIVE
cociendo	cocido	cuece, coced
		cueza (Vd), cuezan (Vds)

Tienes que cocer el agua. *You must boil the water.*
Lo cueces a fuego vivo. *You boil it vigorously.*
La leche está cociendo. *The milk is boiling.*
Coceré las patatas. *I shall boil the potatoes.*
Cocieron el pan al horno. *They baked the bread (in the oven).*
¿Está bien cocido? *It is well done?*
Me estoy cociendo viva. *I am boiling.*

cocer al horno *to bake*
el cocido *stew*
cocido/a *boiled*
la cocción *cooking, boiling time*
la cocina *kitchen, cookery; cooker, stove*

el/la cocinero/a *cook*
el cocinillas *meddler*
cocinar *to cook, do the cooking*

35 coger *to take, pick up, catch* (tr./intr.)

INDICATIVE

Present	Imperfect	Perfect
cojo	cogía	he cogido
coges	cogías	has cogido
coge	cogía	ha cogido
cogemos	cogíamos	hemos cogido
cogéis	cogíais	habéis cogido
cogen	cogían	han cogido

Future	Pluperfect	Preterite
cogeré	había cogido	cogí
cogerás	habías cogido	cogiste
cogerá	había cogido	cogió
cogeremos	habíamos cogido	cogimos
cogeréis	habíais cogido	cogisteis
cogerán	habían cogido	cogieron

Future perfect	Past anterior
habré cogido	hube cogido

CONDITIONAL | SUBJUNCTIVE

Present	Present	Imperfect
cogería	coja	cog-iera/iese
cogerías	cojas	cog-ieras/ieses
cogería	coja	cog-iera/iese
cogeríamos	cojamos	cog-iéramos/iésemos
cogeríais	cojáis	cog-ierais/ieseis
cogerían	cojan	cog-ieran/iesen

Perfect	Perfect	Pluperfect
habría cogido	haya cogido	hub-iera/iese cogido

GERUND	PAST PARTICIPLE	IMPERATIVE
cogiendo	cogido	coge, coged
		coja (Vd), cojan (Vds)

Coge la caja. *Pick up the box.*
Cogimos un taxi. *We took a taxi*
Hemos cogido los billetes. *We have collected the tickets.*
Vamos a coger el tren. *We are going to take the train.*
He cogido cariño al gato. *I've taken a liking to the cat.*
Cogí celos a Juan. *I became jealous of Juan.*
Se ha cogido los dedos en la puerta. *He's caught his fingers in the door.*
Me has cogido desprevenido. *You have caught me at a disadvantage.*

la cogestión *partnership in industry*
cogido *fold, pleat, tuck*
la cogida *catching; catch*

el cogedero *handle*
cogedero/a *ready for picking, ripe*
el cogedor *dustpan*

36 colar *to filter, strain* (tr./intr.)

INDICATIVE

Present	Imperfect	Perfect
cuelo	colaba	he colado
cuelas	colabas	has colado
cuela	colaba	ha colado
colamos	colábamos	hemos colado
coláis	colabais	habéis colado
cuelan	colaban	han colado

Future	Pluperfect	Preterite
colaré	había colado	colé
colarás	habías colado	colaste
colará	había colado	coló
colaremos	habíamos colado	colamos
colaréis	habíais colado	colasteis
colarán	habían colado	colaron

Future perfect	Past anterior
habré colado	hube colado

CONDITIONAL · SUBJUNCTIVE

Present	Present	Imperfect
colaría	cuele	col-ara/ase
colarías	cueles	col-aras/ases
colaría	cuele	col-ara/ase
colaríamos	colemos	col-áramos/ásemos
colaríais	coléis	col-arais/aseis
colarían	cuelen	col-aran/asen

Perfect	Perfect	Pluperfect
habría colado	haya colado	hub-iera/iese colado

GERUND	PAST PARTICIPLE	IMPERATIVE
colando	colado	cuela, colad
		cuele (Vd), cuelen (Vds)

Voy a colar las verduras. *I am going to strain the vegetables.*
Cuela el café. *Filter the coffee.*
Colaremos los zumos. *We shall filter the juices.*
¿Has colado todo el café? *Have you filtered all the coffee?*
Coló su mentira. *They believed his lie.*
¡No cuela! *I'm not swallowing that!*
Trataba de colar un billete falso. *He was trying to use a forged note.*
Me colé en el cine. *I managed to get into the cinema without paying.*

colar con lejía to bleach
el coladero, colador strainer, sieve
la coladura straining; blunder
la colada wash; washing

tender la colada to hang-out the washing
saldrá en la colada it will come out in the wash
colarse to slip in, slip past; jump the queue

37 colgar *to hang, hang up* (tr./intr.)

INDICATIVE

Present	Imperfect	Perfect
cuelgo	colgaba	he colgado
cuelgas	colgabas	has colgado
cuelga	colgaba	ha colgado
colgamos	colgábamos	hemos colgado
colgáis	colgabais	habéis colgado
cuelgan	colgaban	han colgado

Future	Pluperfect	Preterite
colgaré	había colgado	colgué
colgarás	habías colgado	colgaste
colgará	había colgado	colgó
colgaremos	habíamos colgado	colgamos
colgaréis	habíais colgado	colgasteis
colgarán	habían colgado	colgaron

Future perfect	Past anterior	
habré colgado	hube colgado	

CONDITIONAL | SUBJUNCTIVE

Present	Present	Imperfect
colgaría	cuelgue	colg-ara/ase
colgarías	cuelgues	colg-aras/ases
colgaría	cuelgue	colg-ara/ase
colgaríamos	colguemos	colg-áramos/ásemos
colgaríais	colguéis	colg-arais/aseis
colgarían	cuelguen	colg-aran/asen

Perfect	Perfect	Pluperfect
habría colgado	haya colgado	hub-iera/iese colgado

GERUND | PAST PARTICIPLE | IMPERATIVE

colgando	colgado	cuelga, colgad
		cuelgue (Vd), cuelguen (Vds)

Colgaremos el cuadro en la pared. *We'll hang the picture on the wall.*
¿Lo has colgado del clavo? *Have you hung it on the hook?*
Me colgó el teléfono. *He rang off./He hung up on me.*
Le colgaron la culpa a Juan. *They pinned the blame on Juan.*
¡Me quedé colgada! *I was left so disappointed!*
Hemos dejado colgado a Bob. *We let Bob down/failed him.*
¡Antes le veré colgado! *I'll see him hanged first!*

colgante *hanging, drooping*
el puente colgante *suspension bridge*
el colgadero *hanger, peg*
colgado/a *suspended, hanging down, uncertain*

el colgador *hanger*
la colgadura *drapery, tapestry*
el colgajo *appendage, rag, tatters*
colgadizo/a *hanging, loose*

38 comenzar *to start, begin* (tr./intr.)

INDICATIVE

Present	Imperfect	Perfect
comienzo	comenzaba	he comenzado
comienzas	comenzabas	has comenzado
comienza	comenzaba	ha comenzado
comenzamos	comenzábamos	hemos comenzado
comenzáis	comenzabais	habéis comenzado
comienzan	comenzaban	han comenzado

Future	Pluperfect	Preterite
comenzaré	había comenzado	comencé
comenzarás	habías comenzado	comenzaste
comenzará	había comenzado	comenzó
comenzaremos	habíamos comenzado	comenzamos
comenzaréis	habíais comenzado	comenzasteis
comenzarán	habían comenzado	comenzaron

Future perfect	Past anterior
habré comenzado	hube comenzado

CONDITIONAL / SUBJUNCTIVE

Present	Present	Imperfect
comenzaría	comience	comenz-ara/ase
comenzarías	comiences	comenz-aras/ases
comenzaría	comience	comenz-ara/ase
comenzaríamos	comencemos	comenz-áramos/ásemos
comenzaríais	comencéis	comenz-arais/aseis
comenzarían	comiencen	comenz-aran/asen

Perfect	Perfect	Pluperfect
habría comenzado	haya comenzado	hub-iera/iese comenzado

GERUND / PAST PARTICIPLE / IMPERATIVE

GERUND	PAST PARTICIPLE	IMPERATIVE
comenzando	comenzado	comienza, comenzad
		comience (Vd), comiencen (Vds)

Siempre comienza el primero. *He always starts first.*
Comenzó a las cuatro. *He started at four.*
Comenzaremos con Juan. *We shall start with Juan.*
¡Quiero comenzar por el postre! *I want to start with the dessert!*
Comienza a regir en mayo. *It becomes operative in May.*
El rey comenzará el acto. *The king will open the ceremony.*

el comenzamiento *start, beginning*
el comienzo *start, beginning*
al comienzo *at first, at the start*
en los comienzos de siglo *at the beginning of the century*

dar comienzo a (la carrera) *to start (the race)*
comienza y no acaba *it goes on for ever*

39 comer *to eat, have lunch* (tr./intr.)

INDICATIVE

Present	Imperfect	Perfect
como	comía	he comido
comes	comías	has comido
come	comía	ha comido
comemos	comíamos	hemos comido
coméis	comíais	habéis comido
comen	comían	han comido

Future	Pluperfect	Preterite
comeré	había comido	comí
comerás	habías comido	comiste
comerá	había comido	comió
comeremos	habíamos comido	comimos
comeréis	habíais comido	comisteis
comerán	habían comido	comieron

Future perfect	Past anterior
habré comido	hube comido

CONDITIONAL   SUBJUNCTIVE

Present	Present	Imperfect
comería	coma	com-iera/iese
comerías	comas	com-ieras/ieses
comería	coma	com-iera/iese
comeríamos	comamos	com-iéramos/iésemos
comeríais	comáis	com-ierais/ieseis
comerían	coman	com-ieran/iesen

Perfect	Perfect	Pluperfect
habría comido	haya comido	hub-iera/iese comido

GERUND   PAST PARTICIPLE   IMPERATIVE

GERUND	PAST PARTICIPLE	IMPERATIVE
comiendo	comido	come, comed
		coma (Vd), coman (Vds)

Comimos en un hotel. *We had lunch in a hotel.*
Comeré un bocadillo con Juan. *I shall have a sandwich with Juan.*
En España se come a las dos. *In Spain lunch is at 2 p.m.*
Da de comer al perro. *Feed the dog.*
Sin comerlo ni beberlo. *Without having anything to do with it.*
No comas a dos carrillos. *Don't gobble your food.*
Se come las palabras. *He mumbles.*

el comestible *food, foodstuff*
los comestibles *groceries, provisions*
comestible *eatable, edible*
la comida *food, meal*

la comidilla *hobby, favourite pastime*
el comedor *dining room*
comilón *big eater, glutton*

40 competir *to compete, contest* (intr.)

INDICATIVE

Present	Imperfect	Perfect
compito	competía	he competido
compites	competías	has competido
compite	competía	ha competido
competimos	competíamos	hemos competido
competís	competíais	habéis competido
compiten	competían	han competido

Future	Pluperfect	Preterite
competiré	había competido	competí
competirás	habías competido	competiste
competirá	había competido	compitió
competiremos	habíamos competido	competimos
competiréis	habías competido	competisteis
competirán	habían competido	compitieron

Future perfect	Past anterior
habré competido	hube competido

CONDITIONAL / SUBJUNCTIVE

Present	Present	Imperfect
competiría	compita	compit-iera/iese
competirías	compitas	compit-ieras/ieses
competiría	compita	compit-iera/iese
competiríamos	compitamos	compit-iéramos/iésemos
competiríais	compitáis	compit-ierais/ieseis
competirían	compitan	compit-ieran/iesen

Perfect	Perfect	Pluperfect
habría competido	haya competido	hub-iera/iese competido

GERUND / PAST PARTICIPLE / IMPERATIVE

GERUND	PAST PARTICIPLE	IMPERATIVE
compitiendo	competido	compite, competid
		compita (Vd), compitan (Vds)

Los atletas compiten en Sevilla. *The athletes compete in Seville.*
Tom compite con Jerry. *Tom competes against Jerry.*
Compito con Carmen por el primer puesto. *I compete with Carmen for first position.*
Competirán en los Juegos Olímpicos. *They will compete in the Olympic Games.*
Sony compite en ventas. *Sony outsells its competitors.*

la competición *competition*
el/la competidor(a) *competitor, rival, contestant*
la competitividad *competitiveness*
competitivo/a *competitive*

la competencia *competition, rivalry, competitiveness*
competencia desleal *unfair competition*

41 comprar *to buy, purchase* (tr.)

INDICATIVE

Present	Imperfect	Perfect
compro	compraba	he comprado
compras	comprabas	has comprado
compra	compraba	ha comprado
compramos	comprábamos	hemos comprado
compráis	comprabais	habéis comprado
compran	compraban	han comprado

Future	Pluperfect	Preterite
compraré	había comprado	compré
comprarás	habías comprado	compraste
comprará	había comprado	compró
compraremos	habíamos comprado	compramos
compraréis	habíais comprado	comprasteis
comprarán	habían comprado	compraron

Future perfect	Past anterior
habré comprado	hube comprado

CONDITIONAL SUBJUNCTIVE

Present	Present	Imperfect
compraría	compre	compr-ara/ase
comprarías	compres	compr-aras/ases
compraría	compre	compr-ara/ase
compraríamos	compremos	compr-áramos/ásemos
comprarías	compréis	compr-arais/aseis
comprarían	compren	compr-aran/asen

Perfect	Perfect	Pluperfect
habría comprado	haya comprado	hub-iera/iese comprado

GERUND	PAST PARTICIPLE	IMPERATIVE
comprando	comprado	compra, comprad
		compre (Vd), compren (Vds)

Me he comprado un coche. *I have bought a car.*
Compraremos pan mañana. *We shall buy bread tomorrow.*
Necesitamos comprar un piso. *We need to buy a flat.*
Compraron los regalos en Sevilla. *They bought the presents in Seville.*
Francisca compra al contado. *Francisca pays cash.*
No compres al fiado. *Don't buy on credit.*
Lo han comprado a plazos. *They have bought it on hire purchase.*

la compra *shopping, purchase, buying*
ir de compras *to go shopping*
el/la comprador(a) *buyer, purchaser*
la compraventa *buying and selling, dealing*

42 comprobar *to check, confirm* (tr.)

INDICATIVE

Present	Imperfect	Perfect
compruebo	comprobaba	he comprobado
compruebas	comprobabas	has comprobado
comprueba	comprobaba	ha comprobado
comprobamos	comprobábamos	hemos comprobado
comprobáis	comprobabais	habéis comprobado
comprueban	comprobaban	han comprobado

Future	Pluperfect	Preterite
comprobaré	había comprobado	comprobé
comprobarás	habías comprobado	comprobaste
comrobará	había comprobado	comprobó
comprobaremos	habíamos comprobado	comprobamos
comprobaréis	habíais comprobado	comprobasteis
comprobarán	habían comprobado	comprobaron

Future perfect	Past anterior
habré comprobado	hube comprobado

CONDITIONAL · SUBJUNCTIVE

Present	Present	Imperfect
comprobaría	compruebe	comprob-ara/ase
comprobarías	compruebes	comprob-aras/ases
comprobaría	compruebe	comprob-ara/ase
comprobaríamos	comprobemos	comprob-áramos/ásemos
comprobarías	comprobéis	comprob-arais/aseis
comprobarían	comprueben	comprob-aran/asen

Perfect	Perfect	Pluperfect
habría comprobado	haya comprabado	hub-iera/iese comprobado

GERUND	PAST PARTICIPLE	IMPERATIVE
comprobando	comprobado	comprueba, comprobad
		compruebe (Vd), comprueben(Vds)

Esto lo comprueba. *This verifies it.*
Tenemos que comprobar las facturas. *We have to check the invoices.*
Lo comprobaré con rayos X. *I shall X-ray to check it.*
Está comprobando la temperatura. *He is monitoring the temperature.*
Comprueban en obra. *They do spot checks.*

comprobable *provable, demonstrable*
la comprobación *checking, proof*
el comprobador *tester*
el comprobante *voucher, receipt*

el documento comprobante *supporting document*
comprobatorio/a *proving, confirming*

43 concebir *to conceive, imagine* (tr./intr.)

INDICATIVE

Present	Imperfect	Perfect
concibo	concebía	he concebido
concibes	concebías	has concebido
concibe	concebía	ha concebido
concebimos	concebíamos	hemos concebido
concebís	concebíais	habéis concebido
conciben	concebían	han concebido

Future	Pluperfect	Preterite
concebiré	había concebido	concebí
concebirás	habías concebido	concebiste
concebirá	había concebido	concibió
concebiremos	habíamos concebido	concebimos
concebiréis	habíais concebido	concebisteis
concebirán	habían concebido	concibieron

Future perfect	Past anterior
habré concebido	hube concebido

CONDITIONAL / SUBJUNCTIVE

Present	Present	Imperfect
concebiría	conciba	concib-iera/iese
concebirías	concibas	concib-ieras/ieses
concebiría	conciba	concib-iera/iese
concebiríamos	concibamos	concib-iéramos/iésemos
concebiríais	concibáis	concib-ierais/ieseis
concebirían	conciban	concib-ieran/iesen

Perfect	Perfect	Pluperfect
habría concebido	haya concebido	hub-iera/iese concebido

GERUND	PAST PARTICIPLE	IMPERATIVE
concibiendo	concebido	concibe, concebid
		conciba (Vd), conciban (Vds)

Ha concebido. *She is pregnant.*
Hemos concebido un plan. *We have made a plan.*
No concibo su plan. *I can't understand his plan.*
No lo puede concebir. *He can't imagine it.*
Concibo esperanzas. *I nourish hope.*
Concibió una antipatía por Simón. *He took a dislike to Simon.*
Me hizo concebir esperanzas. *It encouraged me.*

concebible *conceivable, thinkable*
inconcebible *unthinkable*
la concepción *conception; understanding*
los anticonceptivos *contraceptives*

el concepto *concept, idea, notion*
concebir un proyecto en líneas generales *to plan out a project*

44 concertar *to arrange, agree* (tr./intr.)

INDICATIVE

Present	Imperfect	Perfect
concierto	concertaba	he concertado
conciertas	concertabas	has concertado
concierta	concertaba	ha concertado
concertamos	concertábamos	hemos concertado
concertáis	concertabais	habéis concertado
conciertan	concertaban	han concertado

Future	Pluperfect	Preterite
concertaré	había concertado	concerté
concertarás	habías concertado	concertaste
concertará	había concertado	concertó
concertaremos	habíamos concertado	concertamos
concertaréis	habíais concertado	concertasteis
concertarán	habían concertado	concertaron

Future perfect	Past anterior
habré concertado	hube concertado

CONDITIONAL   SUBJUNCTIVE

Present	Present	Imperfect
concertaría	concierte	concert-ara/ase
concertarías	conciertes	concert-aras/ases
concertaría	concierte	concert-ara/ase
concertaríamos	concertemos	concert-áramos/ásemos
concertarías	concertéis	concert-arais/aseis
concertarían	concierten	concert-aran/asen

Perfect	Perfect	Pluperfect
habría concertado	haya concertado	hub-iera/iese concertado

GERUND	PAST PARTICIPLE	IMPERATIVE
concertando	concertado	concierta, concertad
		concierte (Vd), concierten (Vds)

Hemos concertado el precio. *We have agreed the price.*
Quiero concertar la venta. *I want to coordinate the sale.*
Vamos a concertarlo. *Let's come to terms about it.*
Lo concertamos para mañana. *We are arranging it for tomorrow.*
Tus noticias conciertan con las mías. *Your news coincides with mine.*
Están concertando un contrato. *They are drawing up a contract.*

concertado/a *orderly, concerted*
el matrimonio concertado *arranged marriage*
el/la concertista *player, performer*

concertarse *to harmonize*
el concierto *agreement; concert*
concertadamente *methodically*

45 conducir *to drive, conduct, lead* (tr./intr.)

INDICATIVE

Present	Imperfect	Perfect
conduzco	conducía	he conducido
conduces	conducías	has conducido
conduce	conducía	ha conducido
conducimos	conducíamos	hemos conducido
conducís	conducíais	habéis conducido
conducen	conducían	han conducido

Future	Pluperfect	Preterite
conduciré	había conducido	conduje
conducirás	habías conducido	condujiste
conducirá	había conducido	condujo
conduciremos	habíamos conducido	condujimos
conduciréis	habíais conducido	condujisteis
conducirán	habían conducido	condujeron

Future perfect	Past anterior
habré conducido	hube conducido

CONDITIONAL   SUBJUNCTIVE

Present	Present	Imperfect
conduciría	conduzca	conduj-era/ese
conducirías	conduzcas	conduj-eras/eses
conduciría	conduzca	conduj-era/ese
conduciríamos	conduzcamos	conduj-éramos/ésemos
conduciríais	conduzcáis	conduj-erais/eseis
conducirían	conduzcan	conduj-eran/esen

Perfect	Perfect	Pluperfect
habría conducido	haya conducido	hub-iera/iese conducido

GERUND	PAST PARTICIPLE	IMPERATIVE
conduciendo	conducido	conduce, conducid
		conduzca (Vd), conduzcan (Vds)

¿Sabes conducir? *Can you drive?*
Conduce muy deprisa. *She drives very fast.*
Nos condujeron por un túnel. *They led us along a tunnel.*
Estos cables conducen la electricidad. *These cables carry the electricity.*
No te conduce a nada. *It takes you nowhere.*
¿A qué conduce? *What's the point?*
La depresión le condujo a la bebida. *Depression drove him to drink.*

la conducción *leading, driving*
el/la conductor(a) *driver, conductor*
el conducto *pipe, tube, conduit*
la conducencia *transportation*

la conducta *conduct, behaviour, something transported*
conducente *conductive to, leading to*

46 confesar *to confess, admit* (tr.)

INDICATIVE

Present	Imperfect	Perfect
confieso	confesaba	he confesado
confiesas	confesabas	has confesado
confiesa	confesaba	ha confesado
confesamos	confesábamos	hemos confesado
confesáis	confesabais	habéis confesado
confiesan	confesaban	han confesado

Future	Pluperfect	Preterite
confesaré	había confesado	confesé
confesarás	habías confesado	confesaste
confesará	había confesado	confesó
confesaremos	habíamos confesado	confesamos
confesaréis	habíais confesado	confesasteis
confesarán	habían confesado	confesaron

Future perfect	Past anterior
habré confesado	hube confesado

CONDITIONAL / SUBJUNCTIVE

Present	Present	Imperfect
confesaría	confiese	confes-ara/ase
confesarías	confieses	confes-aras/ases
confesaría	confiese	confes-ara/ase
confesaríamos	confesemos	confes-áramos/ásemos
confesarías	confeséis	confes-arais/aseis
confesarían	confiesen	confes-aran/asen

Perfect	Perfect	Pluperfect
habría confesado	haya confesado	hub-iera/iese confesado

GERUND	PAST PARTICIPLE	IMPERATIVE
confesando	confesado	confiesa, confesad
		confiese (Vd), confiesen (Vds)

Me ha confesado su edad. *He has told me his age.*
Ha confesado el crimen. *He has admitted to the crime.*
Voy a confesar. *I'm going to confess my sins.*
Confesó antes de ir a la cárcel. *He confessed before going to jail.*

confesar sin reservas *to admit without reservation*
la confesión de culpabilidad *admission of guilt*
confesarse *to own up*
la confesión *confession, admission*

confesional *confessional*
el confesionario *confessional*
el confesante *penitent*
confeso *confessed, converted*
el confesor *confessor*

47 conocer *to know* (tr./intr.)

INDICATIVE

Present	Imperfect	Perfect
conozco	conocía	he conocido
conoces	conocías	has conocido
conoce	conocía	ha conocido
conocemos	conocíamos	hemos conocido
conocéis	conocíais	habéis conocido
conocen	conocían	han conocido

Future	Pluperfect	Preterite
conoceré	había conocido	conocí
conocerás	habías conocido	conociste
conocerá	había conocido	conoció
conoceremos	habíamos conocido	conocimos
conoceréis	habíais conocido	conocisteis
conocerán	habían conocido	conocieron

Future perfect	Past anterior
habré conocido	hube conocido

CONDITIONAL   SUBJUNCTIVE

Present	Present	Imperfect
conocería	conozca	conoc-iera/iese
conocerías	conozcas	conoc-ieras/ieses
conocería	conozca	conoc-iera/iese
conoceríamos	conozcamos	conoc-iéramos/iésemos
conoceríais	conozcáis	conoc-ierais/ieseis
conocerían	conozcan	conoc-ieran/iesen

Perfect	Perfect	Pluperfect
habría conocido	haya conocido	hub-iera/iese conocido

GERUND   PAST PARTICIPLE   IMPERATIVE

GERUND	PAST PARTICIPLE	IMPERATIVE
conociendo	conocido	conoce, conoced
		conozca (Vd), conozcan (Vds)

Conoce su oficio. *He knows his job.*
Le conozco desde hace mucho años. *I've known him for years.*
La conocimos en Burgos. *We met her in Burgos.*
¿Conoces Pamplona? *Do you know Pamplona?*
Te daré a conocer en la fiesta. *I'll introduce you at the party.*
¿De qué le conoces? *How do you know him?*
No me conoce de nada. *She doesn't know me.*

conocedor(a) *expert, knowledgeable*
conocido/a *well known, known*
el conocimiento *knowledge*
conocerse *to know, meet each other*
la conocencia *knowledge, confession*

conocible *knowable, recognizable*
conocidamente *clearly, distinctly*
se conoce que... *it is clear that.../ it is known that...*

48 conseguir *to get, achieve, manage to* (tr.)

INDICATIVE

Present	Imperfect	Perfect
consigo	conseguía	he conseguido
consigues	conseguías	has conseguido
consigue	conseguía	ha conseguido
conseguimos	conseguíamos	hemos conseguido
conseguís	conseguíais	habéis conseguido
consiguen	conseguían	han conseguido

Future	Pluperfect	Preterite
conseguiré	había conseguido	conseguí
conseguirás	habías conseguido	conseguiste
conseguirá	había conseguido	consiguió
conseguiremos	habíamos conseguido	conseguimos
conseguiréis	habíais conseguido	conseguisteis
conseguirán	habían conseguido	consiguieron

Future perfect	Past anterior
habré conseguido	hube conseguido

CONDITIONAL   SUBJUNCTIVE

Present	Present	Imperfect
conseguiría	consiga	consigu-iera/iese
conseguirías	consigas	consigu-ieras/ieses
conseguiría	consiga	consigu-iera/iese
conseguiríamos	consigamos	consigu-iéramos/iésemos
conseguiríais	consigáis	consigu-ierais/ieseis
conseguirían	consigan	consigu-ieran/iesen

Perfect	Perfect	Pluperfect
habría conseguido	haya conseguido	hub-iera/iese conseguido

GERUND   PAST PARTICIPLE   IMPERATIVE

GERUND	PAST PARTICIPLE	IMPERATIVE
consiguiendo	conseguido	consigue, conseguid consiga (Vd), consigan (Vds)

He conseguido hacerlo. *I have managed to do it.*
Consiguió un permiso especial. *He got a special permit.*
Esperamos conseguirlo. *We hope to achieve it.*
He conseguido el apoyo de la OTAN. *I have achieved the support of NATO.*
Tenemos que conseguir fondos. *We have to raise funds.*
Quiere conseguir un préstamo. *She wants to secure a loan.*

conseguido *successful*
el conseguimiento *achievement*
conseguible *obtainable*

49 consentir *to consent, allow* (tr./intr.)

INDICATIVE

Present	Imperfect	Perfect
consiento	consentía	he consentido
consientes	consentías	has consentido
consiente	consentía	ha consentido
consentimos	consentíamos	hemos consentido
consentís	consentíais	habéis consentido
consienten	consentían	han consentido

Future	Pluperfect	Preterite
consentiré	había consentido	consentí
consentirás	habías consentido	consentiste
consentiré	había consentido	consintió
consentiremos	habíamos consentido	consentimos
consentiréis	habíais consentido	consentisteis
consentirán	habían consentido	consintieron

Future perfect	Past anterior
habré consentido	hube consentido

CONDITIONAL   SUBJUNCTIVE

Present	Present	Imperfect
consentiría	consienta	consint-iera/iese
consentirías	consientas	consint-ieras/ieses
consentiría	consienta	consint-iera/iese
consentiríamos	consintamos	consint-iéramos/iésemos
consentiríais	consintáis	consint-ierais/ieseis
consentirían	consientan	consint-ieran/iesen

Perfect	Perfect	Pluperfect
habría consentido	haya consentido	hub-iera/iese consentido

GERUND   PAST PARTICIPLE   IMPERATIVE

consintiendo	consentido	consiente, consentid
		consienta (Vd), consientan (Vds)

No te consentirán hablar. *They won't let you speak.*
¡No se puede consentir eso! *We can't have that!*
No consiente más peso. *It won't take any more weight.*
Te consiento otro. *I'll allow you to have another one.*
Consiento en hacerlo. *I agree to do it.*

consentido/a *spoiled, pampered*
el marido consentido *complaisant husband*
consentidor(a) *indulgent, weak*

el consentimiento *consent*
el consenso *consensus*

50 contar *to count; to tell, narrate* (tr./intr.)

INDICATIVE

Present	Imperfect	Perfect
cuento	contaba	he contado
cuentas	contabas	has contado
cuenta	contaba	ha contado
contamos	contábamos	hemos contado
contáis	contabais	habéis contado
cuentan	contaban	han contado

Future	Pluperfect	Preterite
contaré	había contado	conté
contarás	habías contado	contaste
contará	habías contado	contó
contaremos	habíamos contado	contamos
contaréis	habíais contado	contasteis
contarán	habían contado	contaron

Future perfect	Past anterior
habré contado	hube contado

CONDITIONAL | SUBJUNCTIVE

Present	Present	Imperfect
contaría	cuente	cont-ara/ase
contarías	cuentes	cont-aras/ases
contaría	cuente	cont-ara/ase
contaríamos	contemos	cont-áramos/ásemos
contaríais	contéis	cont-arais/aseis
contarían	cuenten	cont-aran/asen

Perfect	Perfect	Pluperfect
habría contado	haya contado	hub-iera/iese contado

GERUND	PAST PARTICIPLE	IMPERATIVE
contando	contado	cuenta, contad
		cuente (Vd), cuenten (Vds)

Cuenta del 1 al 10. *Count from 1 to 10.*
Me solía contar cuentos de hadas. *She used to tell me fairy stories.*
Te contaré lo que pasó. *I'll tell you what happened.*
Es muy largo de contar. *It's a long story.*
Cuenta con que es más fuerte que tú. *Bear in mind that he's stronger than you.*
¡Cuenta conmigo! *Trust me!*
No contaban con eso. *They hadn't bargained for that.*
¡Cuéntaselo a tu abuela! *Tell it to the marines!*

el contador *counter, meter*
el cuento *story, tale*
el cuentista *storyteller; gossip*
el pago al contado *cash payment*
la cuenta *account, calculation, bill*

el cuentakilómetros *milometer, speedometer*
el cuentagotas *dropper*
el dinero contante (y sonante) *ready cash*

51 convertir *to convert, change* (tr.)

INDICATIVE

Present	Imperfect	Perfect
convierto	convertía	he convertido
conviertes	convertías	has convertido
convierte	convertía	ha convertido
convertimos	convertíamos	hemos convertido
convertís	convertíais	habéis convertido
convierten	convertían	han convertido

Future	Pluperfect	Preterite
convertiré	había convertido	convertí
convertirás	habías convertido	convertiste
convertirá	había convertido	convirtió
convertiremos	habíamos convertido	convertimos
convertiréis	habíais convertido	convertisteis
convertirán	habían convertido	convirtieron

Future perfect	Past anterior
habré convertido	hube convertido

CONDITIONAL · SUBJUNCTIVE

Present	Present	Imperfect
convertiría	convierta	convirt-iera/iese
convertirías	conviertas	convirt-ieras/ieses
convertiría	convierta	convirt-iera/iese
convertiríamos	convirtamos	convirt-iéramos/iésemos
convertirías	convirtáis	convirt-ierais/ieseis
convertirían	conviertan	convirt-ieran/iesen

Perfect	Perfect	Pluperfect
habría convertido	haya convertido	hub-iera/iese convertido

GERUND	PAST PARTICIPLE	IMPERATIVE
convirtiendo	convertido	convierte, convertid
		convierta (Vd), conviertan (Vds)

Quiero convertir libras en euros. *I want to change pounds into euros.*
Convertimos en divisas. *We change foreign currency.*
Conviértelo en efectivo. *Turn it into cash.*
Se ha convertido al catolicismo. *He has converted to Catholicism.*
Se convirtió en una rana. *He turned into a frog.*

el/la conversor(a) *converter*
convertible *convertible*
el convertidor *converter*
la conversión *conversion*

converso/a *coverted, convert*
la convertibilidad *convertibility*
convertirse en *to be transformed into*
convertirse a *to be converted to*

52 corregir *to correct, put right* (tr.)

INDICATIVE

Present	Imperfect	Perfect
corrijo	corregía	he corregido
corriges	corregías	has corregido
corrige	corregía	ha corregido
corregimos	corregíamos	hemos corregido
corregís	corregíais	habéis corregido
corrigen	corregían	han corregido

Future	Pluperfect	Preterite
corregiré	había corregido	corregí
corregirás	habías corregido	corregiste
corregirá	había corregido	corrigió
corregiremos	habíamos corregido	corregimos
corregiréis	habíais corregido	corregisteis
corregirán	habían corregido	corrigieron

Future perfect	Past anterior
habré corregido	hube corregido

CONDITIONAL / SUBJUNCTIVE

Present	Present	Imperfect
corregiría	corrija	corrig-iera/iese
corregirías	corrijas	corrig-ieras/ieses
corregiría	corrija	corrig-iera/iese
corregiríamos	corrijamos	corrig-iéramos/iésemos
corregiríais	corrijáis	corrig-ierais/ieseis
corregirían	corrijan	corrig-ieran/iesen

Perfect	Perfect	Pluperfect
habría corregido	haya corregido	hub-iera/iese corregido

GERUND	PAST PARTICIPLE	IMPERATIVE
corrigiendo	corregido	corrige, corregid
		corrija (Vd), corrijan (Vds)

Tengo que corregir exámenes. *I have to mark exams.*
Voy a corregir un defecto. *I'm going to remove a defect.*
Me corrigió delante de todos. *He corrected me in front of everybody.*
Te lo he corregido. *I have put it right for you.*

la corrección *correction, adjustment* **correccional** *reformatory*
correcto/a *right, correct; polite* **corregible** *rectifiable*
el/la corrector(a) *proofreader* **corregirse** *to reform oneself*

53 costar *to cost; to be difficult* (intr.)

INDICATIVE

Present	Imperfect	Perfect
cuesto	costaba	he costado
cuestas	costabas	has costado
cuesta	costaba	ha costado
costamos	costábamos	hemos costado
costáis	costabais	habéis costado
cuestan	costaban	han costado

Future	Pluperfect	Preterite
costaré	había costado	costé
costarás	habías costado	costaste
costará	había costado	costó
costaremos	habíamos costado	costamos
costaréis	habíais costado	costateis
costarán	habían costado	costaron

Future perfect	Past anterior
habré costado	hube costado

CONDITIONAL   SUBJUNCTIVE

Present	Present	Imperfect
costaría	cueste	cost-ara/ase
costarías	cuestes	cost-aras/ases
costaría	cueste	cost-ara/ase
costaríamos	costemos	cost-áramos/ásemos
costaríais	costéis	cost-arais/aseis
costarían	cuesten	cost-aran/asen

Perfect	Perfect	Pluperfect
habría costado	haya costado	hub-iera/iese costado

GERUND   PAST PARTICIPLE   IMPERATIVE

GERUND	PAST PARTICIPLE	IMPERATIVE
costando	costado	cuesta, costad
		cueste (Vd), cuesten (Vds)

¿Cuánto cuesta? *How much is it?*
Cuesta 1.000 €. *It costs 1000 euros.*
No cuestan muy caras. *They are not very expensive.*
Cuesta unos minutos hacerlo. *It takes a few minutes to do it.*
Cuesta un ojo de la cara. *It costs an arm and a leg.*
Me cuesta mucho hablar español. *I find it difficult to speak Spanish.*
Nos costó creerlo. *We found it difficult to believe.*

el coste *cost, price; expense*
el costo *cost*
costoso/a *expensive; costly*

costo efectivo *actual cost*
costo, seguro y flete *cost, insurance and freight*

54 **crecer** *to grow, increase* (intr.)

INDICATIVE

Present	Imperfect	Perfect
crezco	crecía	he crecido
creces	crecías	has crecido
crece	crecía	ha crecido
crecemos	crecíamos	hemos crecido
crecéis	crecíais	habéis crecido
crecen	crecían	han crecido

Future	Pluperfect	Preterite
creceré	había crecido	crecí
crecerás	habías crecido	creciste
crecerá	había crecido	creció
creceremos	habíamos crecido	crecimos
creceréis	habíais crecido	crecisteis
crcerán	habían crecido	crecieron

Future perfect	Past anterior
habré crecido	hube crecido

CONDITIONAL / SUBJUNCTIVE

Present	Present	Imperfect
crecería	crezca	crec-iera/iese
crecerías	crezcas	crec-ieras/ieses
crecería	crezca	crec-iera/iese
creceríamos	crezcamos	crec-iéramos/iésemos
creceríais	crezcáis	crec-ierais/ieseis
crecerían	crezcan	crec-ieran/iesen

Perfect	Perfect	Pluperfect
habría crecido	haya crecido	hub-iera/iese crecido

GERUND / PAST PARTICIPLE / IMPERATIVE

GERUND	PAST PARTICIPLE	IMPERATIVE
creciendo	crecido	crece, creced
		crezca (Vd), crezcan (Vds)

Algunas plantas crecen rápidamente. *Some plants grow very quickly.*
Se deja crecer el pelo y la barba. *He lets his hair and beard grow.*
El niño ha crecido mucho. *The boy has grown a lot.*
El árbol no hace más que crecer. *The tree does not stop growing.*
El río crece todos los inviernos. *The river swells every winter.*
Crece un punto. *Increase a stitch.*
Enrique ve crecer la hierba. *Enrique is very sharp.*

la luna creciente *crescent moon*
el crecimiento *growing, growth,*
  increase, rise
las creces *increase, excess*
devolver con creces *to repay with interest*

crecedero/a *growing*
la crecida *swelling of a river*
crecidamente *amply, abundantly,*
  in excess
crecido/a *grown, numerous*

55 dar *to give* (tr.)

INDICATIVE

Present	Imperfect	Perfect
doy	daba	he dado
das	dabas	has dado
da	daba	ha dado
damos	dábamos	hemos dado
dais	dabais	habéis dado
dan	daban	han dado

Future	Pluperfect	Preterite
daré	había dado	di
darás	habías dado	diste
dará	había dado	dio
daremos	habíamos dado	dimos
daréis	habíais dado	disteis
darán	habían dado	dieron

Future perfect	Past anterior	
habré dado	hube dado	

CONDITIONAL · SUBJUNCTIVE

Present	Present	Imperfect
daría	dé	di-era/ese
darías	des	di-eras/eses
daría	dé	di-era/ese
daríamos	demos	di-éramos/ésemos
daríais	deis	di-erais/eseis
darían	den	di-eran/esen

Perfect	Perfect	Pluperfect
habría dado	haya dado	hub-iera/iese dado

GERUND	PAST PARTICIPLE	IMPERATIVE
dando	dado	da, dad
		dé (Vd), den (Vds)

Dame el libro, por favor. *Give me the book, please.*
¿Le quieres dar el mensaje? *Can you give him the message?*
Me han dado un regalo. *I have been given a present.*
¡Ahí me las den todas! *That won't bother me!*
Han dado las cuatro. *It's four o'clock.*
¡Y dale que dale! *Here we go again!*
Da lo mismo. *It doesn't matter.*
No se me da mal. *I'm not doing too badly.*

el/la dador(a) *donor, giver, bearer*
el dador de sangre *blood donor*
los dares y tomares *give and take*

la dádiva *present, gift*
dar de comer *to feed*
dado que *provided that, given that*

56 deber to owe, must, ought to (tr.)

INDICATIVE

Present	Imperfect	Perfect
debo	debía	he debido
debes	debías	has debido
debe	debía	ha debido
debemos	debíamos	hemos debido
debéis	debíais	habéis debido
deben	debían	han debido

Future	Pluperfect	Preterite
deberé	había debido	debí
deberás	habías debido	debiste
deberá	había debido	debió
deberemos	habíamos debido	debimos
deberéis	habíais debido	debisteis
deberán	habían debido	debieron

Future perfect	Past anterior	
habré debido	hube debido	

CONDITIONAL / SUBJUNCTIVE

Present	Present	Imperfect
debería	deba	deb-iera/iese
deberías	debas	deb-ieras/ieses
debería	deba	deb-iera/iese
deberíamos	debamos	deb-iéramos/iésemos
deberíais	debáis	deb-ierais/ieseis
deberían	deban	deb-ieran/iesen

Perfect	Perfect	Pluperfect
habría debido	haya debido	hub-iera/iese debido

GERUND / PAST PARTICIPLE / IMPERATIVE

GERUND	PAST PARTICIPLE	IMPERATIVE
debiendo	debido	debe, debed
		deba (Vd), deban (Vds)

Me debes £5. *You owe me £5.*
Debo hacerlo. *I must do it.*
Deberían ir. *They ought to go.*
Debe ser así. *It must be like that.*
Has debido perderlo. *You must have lost it.*
Debe de ser argentino. *He must be Argentinian.*
¿A qué se debe esto? *What's that for?*

el deber *duty*	**debidamente** *properly*
los deberes *homework*	**el debe** *debit*
debido/a *due, proper, just*	**debido a** *due to*

57 decir *to say, tell* (tr.)

INDICATIVE

Present	Imperfect	Perfect
digo	decía	he dicho
dices	decías	has dicho
dice	decía	ha dicho
decimos	decíamos	hemos dicho
decís	decíais	habéis dicho
dicen	decían	han dicho

Future	Pluperfect	Preterite
diré	había dicho	dije
dirás	habías dicho	dijiste
dirá	había dicho	dijo
diremos	habíamos dicho	dijimos
diréis	habíais dicho	dijisteis
dirán	habían dicho	dijeron

Future perfect	Past anterior
habré dicho	hube dicho

CONDITIONAL · SUBJUNCTIVE

Present	Present	Imperfect
diría	diga	dij-era/ese
dirías	digas	dij-eras/eses
diría	diga	dij-era/ese
diríamos	digamos	dij-éramos/ésemos
diríais	digáis	dij-erais/eseis
dirían	digan	dij-eran/esen

Perfect	Perfect	Pluperfect
habría dicho	haya dicho	hub-iera/iese dicho

GERUND · PAST PARTICIPLE · IMPERATIVE

GERUND	PAST PARTICIPLE	IMPERATIVE
diciendo	dicho	di, decid
		diga (Vd), digan (Vds)

Dicen que hace calor. *They say it is hot.*
No dijo nada. *He said nothing.*
¿Cómo has dicho? *What did you say?*
Le dicen 'majo'. *They call him 'majo'.*
No lo digo por ti. *I don't mean you.*
como quien no dice nada *casually, as though it wasn't important*
digan lo que digan *whatever they may say*
¡Diga! ¡Dígame! *Hello! (on phone)*

el dicho *saying, proverb*
mejor dicho *rather*
dicho y hecho *no sooner said than done*

es un decir *it's just a saying*
decires *gossip*

58 defender *to defend* (tr.)

INDICATIVE

Present	Imperfect	Perfect
defiendo	defendía	he defendido
defiendes	defendías	has defendido
defiende	defendía	ha defendido
defendemos	defendíamos	hemos defendido
defendéis	defendíais	habéis defendido
defienden	defendían	han defendido

Future	Pluperfect	Preterite
defenderé	había defendido	defendí
defenderás	habías defendido	defendiste
defenderá	había defendido	defendió
defenderemos	habíamos defendido	defendimos
defenderéis	habíais defendido	defendisteis
defenderán	habían defendido	defendieron

Future perfect	Past anterior
habré defendido	hube defendido

CONDITIONAL   SUBJUNCTIVE

Present	Present	Imperfect
defendería	defienda	defend-iera/iese
defenderías	defiendas	defend-ieras/ieses
defendería	defienda	defend-iera/iese
defenderíamos	defendamos	defend-iéramos/iésemos
defenderíais	defendáis	defend-ierais/ieseis
defenderían	defiendan	defend-ieran/iesen

Perfect	Perfect	Pluperfect
habría defendido	haya defendido	hub-iera/iese defendido

GERUND   PAST PARTICIPLE   IMPERATIVE

GERUND	PAST PARTICIPLE	IMPERATIVE
defendiendo	defendido	defiende, defended
		defienda (Vd), defiendan (Vds)

Se defienden de sus enemigos. *They defend themselves from their enemies.*
La gallina defiende a sus pollitos. *The hen defends her chicks.*
El muro nos defenderá del viento. *The wall will protect us from the wind.*
Sirve para defenderme contra el frío. *It's to protect me from the cold.*
Nos vamos defendiendo. *We are managing.*
Me defiendo en español. *I can get by in Spanish.*
Se defendieron bien. *They did well.*
¡Defiéndeme! *Help me!*

la defensa *defence*	**defensivo/a** *defensive*
en defensa propia *in self defence*	**el/la defensor(a)** *defender, protector*
la defensa pasiva *civil defence*	**estar a la defensiva** *to be on the defensive*
las defensas costeras *coastal defences*	

59 deferir *defer, delegate* (tr./intr.)

INDICATIVE

Present	Imperfect	Perfect
defiero	defería	he deferido
defieres	deferías	has deferido
defiere	defería	ha deferido
deferimos	deferíamos	hemos deferido
deferís	deferíais	habéis deferido
defieren	deferían	han deferido

Future	Pluperfect	Preterite
deferiré	había deferido	deferí
deferirás	habías deferido	deferiste
deferirá	había deferido	defirió
deferiremos	habíamos deferido	deferimos
deferiréis	habíais deferido	deferisteis
deferirán	habían deferido	defirieron

Future perfect	Past anterior
habré deferido	hube deferido

CONDITIONAL / SUBJUNCTIVE

Present	Present	Imperfect
deferiría	defiera	defir-iera/iese
deferirías	defieras	defir-ieras/ieses
deferiría	defiera	defir-iera/iese
deferiríamos	defiramos	defir-iéramos/iésemos
deferiríais	defiráis	defir-ierais/ieseis
deferirían	defieran	defir-ieran/iesen

Perfect	Perfect	Pluperfect
habría deferido	haya deferido	hub-iera/iese deferido

GERUND / PAST PARTICIPLE / IMPERATIVE

GERUND	PAST PARTICIPLE	IMPERATIVE
defiriendo	deferido	defiere, deferid
		defiera (Vd), defieran (Vds)

Quiero deferirle mi puesto. *I would like you to have my place.*
Te defiero mi responsabilidad. *I give you my responsibilities.*
No quiere deferir sus cargos. *He doesn't want to delegate his position.*
Estoy tan agradecida que les deferiré mis privilegios. *I am so grateful that I shall delegate my privileges to them.*

por deferencia *out of deference*
la deferencia *deference*
deferente *deferential*

deferido/a *referred*
el juramento deferido *oath*

60 delinquir *to break the law, offend* (intr.)

INDICATIVE

Present	Imperfect	Perfect
delinco	delinquía	he delinquido
delinques	delinquías	has delinquido
delinque	delinquía	ha delinquido
delinquimos	delinquíamos	hemos delinquido
delinquís	delinquíais	habéis delinquido
delinquen	delinquían	han delinquido

Future	Pluperfect	Preterite
delinquiré	había delinquido	delinquí
delinquirás	habías delinquido	delinquiste
delinquirá	había delinquido	delinquió
delinquiremos	habíamos delinquido	delinquimos
delinquiréis	habíais delinquido	delinquisteis
delinquirán	habían delinquido	delinquieron

Future perfect	Past anterior
habré delinquido	hube delinquido

CONDITIONAL / SUBJUNCTIVE

Present	Present	Imperfect
delinquiría	delinca	delinqu-iera/iese
delinquirías	delincas	delinqu-ieras/ieses
delinquiría	delinca	delinqu-iera/iese
delinquiríamos	delincamos	delinqu-iéramos/ésemos
delinquiríais	delincáis	delinqu-ierais/eseis
delinquirían	delincan	delinqu-ieran/iesen

Perfect	Perfect	Pluperfect
habría delinquido	haya delinquido	hub-iera/iese delinquido

GERUND	PAST PARTICIPLE	IMPERATIVE
delinquiendo	delinquido	delinque, delinquid delinca (Vd), delincan (Vds)

Han delinquido en numerosas ocasiones. *They have committed numerous offences.*
No creo que delinca otra vez. *I don't think he will offend again.*
Muchos drogadictos delinquen. *Many drug addicts break the law.*
En la guerra ambas partes delinquían. *In the war, both sides broke the law.*

el delito *crime, offence*
el delito de incendio *arson*
el delito menor *minor offence*
el delito de sangre *violent crime*

la delincuencia *crime, delinquency*
el/la delictivo/a *criminal*
el delinquimiento *delinquency, guilt*
el/la delincuente *delinquent*

61 demoler *to demolish, pull down* (tr.)

INDICATIVE

Present	Imperfect	Perfect
demuelo	demolía	he demolido
demueles	demolías	has demolido
demuele	demolía	ha demolido
demolemos	demolíamos	hemos demolido
demoléis	demolíais	habéis demolido
demuelen	demolían	han demolido

Future	Pluperfect	Preterite
demoleré	había demolido	demolí
demolerás	habías demolido	demoliste
demolerá	había demolido	demolió
demoleremos	habíamos demolido	demolimos
demoleréis	habíais demolido	demolisteis
demolerán	habían demolido	demolieron

Future perfect	Past anterior
habré demolido	hube demolido

CONDITIONAL / SUBJUNCTIVE

Present	Present	Imperfect
demolería	demuela	demol-iera/iese
demolerías	demuelas	demol-ieras/ieses
demolería	demuela	demol-iera/iese
demoleríamos	demolamos	demol-iéramos/iésemos
demoleríais	demoláis	demol-ierais/ieseis
demolerían	demuelan	demol-ieran/iesen

Perfect	Perfect	Pluperfect
habría demolido	haya demolido	hub-iera/iese demolido

GERUND / PAST PARTICIPLE / IMPERATIVE

GERUND	PAST PARTICIPLE	IMPERATIVE
demoliendo	demolido	demuele, demoled
		demuela (Vd), demuelan (Vds)

Voy a demoler el edificio. *I am going to pull down the building.*
Está demoliendo la cocina. *He's demolishing the kitchen.*
Demolieron la catedral. *They demolished the cathedral.*
Los godos demolieron el Imperio Romano. *The Goths brought down the Roman Empire.*
Su ambición es demoler la organización. *His ambition is to demolish the organization.*

demoledor(a) *powerful, devastating*
el argumento demoledor *powerful argument*
la demolición *demolition*

el ataque demoledor *shattering attack*
la ovación demoledora *overwhelming ovation, thunderous applause*

62 demostrar *to prove, demonstrate* (tr.)

INDICATIVE

Present	Imperfect	Perfect
demuestro	demostraba	he demostrado
demuestras	demostrabas	has demostrado
demuestra	demostraba	ha demostrado
demostramos	demostrábamos	hemos demostrado
demostráis	demostrabais	habéis demostrado
demuestran	demostraban	han demostrado

Future	Pluperfect	Preterite
demostraré	había demostrado	demostré
demostrarás	habías demostrado	demostraste
demostrará	había demostrado	demostró
demostraremos	habíamos demostrado	demostramos
demostraréis	habíais demostrado	demostrasteis
demostrarán	habían demostrado	demostraron

Future perfect	Past anterior
habré demostrado	hube demostrado

CONDITIONAL SUBJUNCTIVE

Present	Present	Imperfect
demostraría	demuestre	demostr-ara/ase
demostrarías	demuestres	demostr-aras/ases
demostraría	demuestre	demostr-ara/ase
demostraríamos	demostremos	demostr-áramos/ásemos
demostraríais	demostréis	demostr-arais/aseis
demostrarían	demuestren	demostr-aran/asen

Perfect	Perfect	Pluperfect
habría demostrado	haya demostrado	hub-iera/iese demostrado

GERUND PAST PARTICIPLE IMPERATIVE

demostrando	demostrado	demuestra, demostrad
		demuestre (Vd), demuestren (Vds)

Tengo una prueba para demostrarlo. *I've got something to prove it.*
Magallanes demostró que la tierra es redonda. *Magellan proved that the earth is round.*
Te demostraré el teorema. *I shall demonstrate the theorem.*
Nos demostró cómo funciona. *He showed us how it works.*
No puedes demostrarme nada. *You can't prove anything against me.*

la demostración *demonstration, show; proof* **demostrativo** *demonstrative*
la demostración de fuerza *show of force* **demostrable** *demonstrable, provable*
la demostración comercial *trade exhibition* **la demostrabilidad** *provability*
demostrar que... *to show that...*

63 dentar to indent; to cut teeth (tr./intr.)

INDICATIVE

Present	Imperfect	Perfect
diento	dentaba	he dentado
dientas	dentabas	has dentado
dienta	dentaba	ha dentado
dentamos	dentábamos	hemos dentado
dentáis	dentabais	habéis dentado
dientan	dentaban	han dentado

Future	Pluperfect	Preterite
dentaré	había dentado	denté
dentarás	habías dentado	dentaste
dentará	había dentado	dentó
dentaremos	habíamos dentado	dentamos
dentaréis	habías dentado	dentasteis
dentarán	habían dentado	dentaron

Future perfect	Past anterior
habré dentado	hube dentado

CONDITIONAL · SUBJUNCTIVE

Present	Present	Imperfect
dentaría	diente	dent-ara/ase
dentarías	dientes	dent-aras/ases
dentaría	diente	dent-ara/ase
dentaríamos	dentemos	dent-áramos/ásemos
dentaríais	dentéis	dent-arais/aseis
dentarían	dientan	dent-aran/asen

Perfect	Perfect	Pluperfect
habría dentado	haya dentado	hub-iera/iese dentado

GERUND · PAST PARTICIPLE · IMPERATIVE

GERUND	PAST PARTICIPLE	IMPERATIVE
dentando	dentado	dienta, dentad
		diente (Vd), dienten (Vds)

Quiero dentar la hoja de papel. *I want to make a perforated edge on the paper.*
¿Lo habéis dentado? *Have you indented it?*
¿Ha dentado el bebé? *Has the baby cut any teeth?*

dentado/a *toothed, jagged, indented*
dental *dental*
la dentadura *dentures, teeth*
dentadura postiza *false teeth*

dentellado/a *serrated, indented*
el diente *tooth*
un sello sin dentar *imperforate stamp*

64 derretir *to melt, thaw* (tr.)

INDICATIVE

Present	Imperfect	Perfect
derrito	derretía	he derretido
derrites	derretías	has derretido
derrite	derretía	ha derretido
derretimos	derretíamos	hemos derretido
derretís	derretíais	habéis derretido
derriten	derretían	han derretido

Future	Pluperfect	Preterite
derretiré	había derretido	derretí
derretirás	habías derretido	derretiste
derretirá	había derretido	derritió
derretiremos	habíamos derretido	derretimos
derretiréis	habíais derretido	derretisteis
derretirán	habían derretido	derritieron

Future perfect	Past anterior
habré derretido	hube derretido

CONDITIONAL

SUBJUNCTIVE

Present	Present	Imperfect
derretiría	derrita	derrit-iera/iese
derretirías	derritas	derrit-ieras/ieses
derretiría	derrita	derrit-iera/iese
derretiríamos	derritamos	derrit-iéramos/iésemos
derretiríais	derritáis	derrit-ierais/ieseis
derretirían	derritan	derrit-ieran/iesen

Perfect	Perfect	Pluperfect
habría derretido	haya derretido	hub-iera/iese derretido

GERUND

PAST PARTICIPLE

IMPERATIVE

GERUND	PAST PARTICIPLE	IMPERATIVE
derritiendo	derretido	derrite, derretid
		derrita (Vd), derritan (Vds)

Derrite la mantequilla primero. *First melt the butter.*
Se me ha derretido el helado. *My ice-cream has melted.*
El sol derretirá la nieve. *The sun will thaw the snow.*
Don Juan derrite a las señoras. *Don Juan makes the ladies fall in love with him.*
Se derrite por Pedro. *She is crazy about Pedro.*
Miguel me derrite con sus bromas. *Miguel exasperates me with his jokes.*
Acabo de derretir mi billete de 500 €. *I've just changed my 500 euro note.*

derretido *melted, thawed*　　　　**derretirse** *to liquefy*
derretido al vapor *reduced to steam*　　**derretirse por una** *to be crazy about somebody*
el derretimiento *melting, thawing;*
　(fig.) *squandering*

65 desalentar *make breathless, discourage* (tr.)

INDICATIVE

Present	Imperfect	Perfect
desaliento	desalentaba	he desalentado
desalientas	desalentabas	has desalentado
desalienta	desalentaba	ha desalentado
desalentamos	desalentábamos	hemos desalentado
desalentáis	desalentabais	habéis desalentado
desalientan	desalentaban	han desalentado

Future	Pluperfect	Preterite
desalentaré	había desalentado	desalenté
desalentarás	habías desalentado	desalentaste
desalentará	había desalentado	desalentó
desalentaremos	habíamos desalentado	desalentamos
desalentaréis	había desalentado	desalentasteis
desalentarán	habían desalentado	desalentaron

Future perfect	Past anterior
habré desalentado	hube desalentado

CONDITIONAL — SUBJUNCTIVE

Present	Present	Imperfect
desalentaría	desaliente	desalent-ara/ase
desalentarías	desalientes	desalent-aras/ases
desalentaría	desaliente	desalent-ara/ase
desalentaríamos	desalentemos	desalent-áramos/ásemos
desalentaríais	desalentéis	desalent-arais/aseis
desalentarían	desalienten	desalent-aran/asen

Perfect	Perfect	Pluperfect
habría desalentado	haya desalentado	hub-iera/iese desalentado

GERUND — PAST PARTICIPLE — IMPERATIVE

GERUND	PAST PARTICIPLE	IMPERATIVE
desalentando	desalentado	desalienta, desalentad
		desaliente (Vd), desalienten (Vds)

El correr me desalienta. *Running makes me breathless.*
Se desalientan subiendo las escaleras. *Going upstairs makes them breathless.*
La muerte de su mujer le desalentó mucho. *His wife's death affected him badly.*
No desalientes a Pedro. *Don't discourage Pedro.*
Se desalientan porque han perdido el partido. *They are discouraged because they have lost the match.*

desalentarse *to lose heart, get discouraged*　　**desalentador(a)** *discouraging*
el desaliento *discouragement, depression*　　**desalentadamente** *dispiritedly, faintly*
desalentado/a *discouraged*

66 descender *to descend, go down* (tr./intr.)

INDICATIVE

Present	Imperfect	Perfect
desciendo	descendía	he descendido
desciendes	descendías	has descendido
desciende	descendía	ha descendido
descendemos	descendíamos	hemos descendido
descendéis	descendíais	habéis descendido
descienden	descendían	han descendido

Future	Pluperfect	Preterite
descenderé	había descendido	descendí
descenderás	habías descendido	descendiste
descenderá	había descendido	descendió
descenderemos	habíamos descendido	descendimos
descenderéis	habíais descendido	descendisteis
descenderán	habían descendido	descendieron

Future perfect	Past anterior
habré descendido	hube descendido

CONDITIONAL   SUBJUNCTIVE

Present	Present	Imperfect
descendería	descienda	descend-iera/iese
descenderías	desciendas	descend-ieras/ieses
descendería	descienda	descend-iera/iese
descenderíamos	descendamos	descend-iéramos/iésemos
descenderíais	descendáis	descend-ierais/ieseis
descenderían	desciendan	descend-ieran/iesen

Perfect	Perfect	Pluperfect
habría descendido	haya descendido	hub-iera/iese descendido

GERUND   PAST PARTICIPLE   IMPERATIVE

GERUND	PAST PARTICIPLE	IMPERATIVE
descendiendo	descendido	desciende, descended
		descienda (Vd), desciendan (Vds)

Desciende las escaleras. *She goes down the stairs.*
Ha descendido el nivel del agua. *The level of water has gone down.*
Anoche descendió la temperatura. *The temperature dropped last night.*
¿Le descenderá la temperatura? *Will his temperature come down?*
La tribu desciende del Tibet. *The tribe comes from Tibet.*
El Cid no desciende de linaje de reyes. *El Cid does not come from a line of kings.*
'Verbo' desciende de 'verbum'. *'Verbo' derives from 'verbum'.*

el descenso *descent, going down, drop, fall*
el/la descendiente *descendant*
el descendimiento *lowering, descent*

descendente *descending*
la descendencia *origin, offspring, descendants*

67 descolgar *to take down, unhook* (tr.)

INDICATIVE

Present	Imperfect	Perfect
descuelgo	descolgaba	he descolgado
descuelgas	descolgabas	has descolgado
descuelga	descolgaba	ha descolgado
descolgamos	descolgábamos	hemos descolgado
descolgáis	descolgabais	habéis descolgado
descuelgan	descolgaban	han descolgado

Future	Pluperfect	Preterite
descolgaré	había descolgado	descolgué
descolgarás	habías descolgado	descolgaste
descolgará	había descolgado	descolgó
descolgaremos	habíamos descolgado	descolgamos
descolgaréis	habíais descolgado	descolgasteis
descolgarán	habían descolgado	descolgaron

Future perfect	Past anterior
habré descolgado	hube descolgado

CONDITIONAL / SUBJUNCTIVE

Present	Present	Imperfect
descolgaría	descuelgue	descolg-ara/ase
descolgarías	descuelgues	descolg-aras/ases
descolgaría	descuelgue	descolg-ara/ase
descolgaríamos	descolguemos	descolg-áramos/ásemos
descolgaríais	descolguéis	descolg-arais/aseis
descolgarían	descuelguen	descolg-aran/asen

Perfect	Perfect	Pluperfect
habría descolgado	haya descolgado	hub-iera/iese descolgado

GERUND	PAST PARTICIPLE	IMPERATIVE
descolgando	descolgado	descuelga, descolgad
		descuelgue (Vd), descuelguen (Vds)

Descuelga el cuadro. *Take down the picture.*
Voy a descolgar las cortinas. *I am going to take the curtains down.*
Descuelga el teléfono. *Pick up the phone.*
Se han descolgado las nubes. *Suddenly a few clouds appeared.*
Siempre se descuelga con una estupidez. *He always comes out with a silly remark.*

descolgarse *to lower, come down; turn up unexpectedly*
quedar descolgado *to be left behind*

descolgado/a *unhooked, off the hook*
descolgarse con... *to come out with...*

68 desconcertar *to upset, disconcert* (tr.)

INDICATIVE

Present	Imperfect	Perfect
desconcierto	desconcertaba	he desconcertado
desconciertas	desconcertabas	has desconcertado
desconcierta	desconcertaba	ha desconcertado
desconcertamos	desconcertábamos	hemos desconcertado
desconcertáis	desconcertabais	habéis desconcertado
desconciertan	desconcertaban	han desconcertado

Future	Pluperfect	
desconcertaré	había desconcertado	desconcerté
desconcertarás	habías desconcertado	desconcertaste
desconcertará	había desconcertado	desconcertó
desconcertaremos	habíamos desconcertado	desconcertamos
desconcertaréis	habías desconcertado	desconcertasteis
desconcertarán	habían desconcertado	desconcertaron

Future perfect	Past anterior
habré desconcertado	hube desconcertado

CONDITIONAL / SUBJUNCTIVE

Present	Present	Imperfect
desconcertaría	desconcierte	desconcert-ara/ase
desconcertarías	desconciertes	desconcert-aras/ases
desconcertaría	desconcierte	desconcert-ara/ase
desconcertaríamos	desconcertemos	desconcert-áramos/ásemos
desconcertarías	desconcertéis	desconcert-arais/aseis
desconcertarían	desconcierten	desconcert-aran/asen

Perfect	Perfect	Pluperfect
habría desconcertado	haya desconcertado	hub-iera/iese desconcertado

GERUND	PAST PARTICIPLE	IMPERATIVE
desconcertando	desconcertado	desconcierta, desconcertad desconcierte (Vd), desconcierten (Vds)

Este niño me desconcierta. *This boy upsets me.*
Le desconcertó verme con Miguel. *It disconcerted him to see me with Miguel.*
Se me ha desconcertado el estómago. *I've got an upset stomach.*
Desconcierta hasta el más sosegado. *It would upset anybody.*

desconcertado *disconcerted*　　　　**el desconcierto** *disorder, trouble, chaos*
desconcertador *disconcerning*
desconcertante *embarrassing, puzzling*

69 descontar *to discount, take away* (tr.)

INDICATIVE

Present	Imperfect	Perfect
descuento	descontaba	he descontado
descuentas	descontabas	has decontado
descuenta	descontaba	ha descontado
descontamos	descontábamos	hemos decontado
descontáis	descontabais	habéis descontado
descuentan	descontaban	han descontado

Future	Pluperfect	Preterite
descontaré	había descontado	desconté
descontarás	habías descontado	descontaste
descontará	había descontado	descontó
descontaremos	habíamos descontado	descontamos
descontaréis	habíais descontado	descontasteis
descontarán	habían descontado	descontaron

Future perfect	Past anterior
habré descontado	hube descontado

CONDITIONAL   SUBJUNCTIVE

Present	Present	Imperfect
descontaría	descuente	descont-ara/ase
descontarías	descuentes	descont-aras/ases
descontaría	descuente	descont-ara/ase
descontaríamos	descontemos	descont-áramos/ásemos
descontaríais	descontéis	descont-arais/aseis
descontarían	descuenten	descont-aran/asen

Perfect	Perfect	Pluperfect
habría descontado	haya descontado	hub-iera/iese descontado

GERUND   PAST PARTICIPLE   IMPERATIVE

GERUND	PAST PARTICIPLE	IMPERATIVE
descontando	descontado	descuenta, descontad
		descuente (Vd),
		descuenten (Vds)

Me ha descontado el 10%. *I've got a 10% discount.*
Te descontaré el precio de la botella. *I will not charge you for the price of the bottle.*
Si descuentas diez me quedan veinte. *If you take away ten I am left with twenty.*
Han descontado los intereses. *They have discounted the interest.*

por descontado *obviously, of course*   **¡Descuéntalo!** *Forget it!*
dar por descontado *to take for granted*   **(con) descuento** *(at a) discount*

70 despedir *to dismiss, see off* (tr.)

INDICATIVE

Present	**Imperfect**	**Perfect**
despido	despedía	he despedido
despides	despedías	has despedido
despide	despedía	ha despedido
despedimos	despedíamos	hemos despedido
despedís	despedíais	habéis despedido
despiden	despedían	han despedido

Future	**Pluperfect**	**Preterite**
despediré	había despedido	despedí
despedirás	habías despedido	despediste
despedirá	había despedido	despidió
despediremos	habíamos despedido	despedimos
despediréis	habíais despedido	despedisteis
despedirán	habían despedido	despidieron

Future perfect	**Past anterior**
habré despedido	hube despedido

CONDITIONAL / SUBJUNCTIVE

Present	**Present**	**Imperfect**
despediría	despida	despid-iera/iese
despedirías	despidas	despid-ieras/ieses
despediría	despida	despid-iera/iese
despediríamos	despidamos	despid-iéramos/iésemos
despediríais	despidáis	despid-ierais/ieseis
despedirían	despidan	despid-ieran/iesen

Perfect	**Perfect**	**Pluperfect**
habría despedido	haya despedido	hub-iera/iese despedido

GERUND	PAST PARTICIPLE	IMPERATIVE
despidiendo	despedido	despide, despedid
		despida (Vd), despidan (Vds)

Ya puedes despedirte de ello. *You'd better forget it.*
Van a despedir a los obreros. *They are going to dismiss the workers.*
Les despidieron en el acto. *They were fired on the spot.*
Me pienso despedir yo misma. *I'm going to quit.*
Fuimos a la estación a despedirles. *We went to the station to see them off.*
¡Estás despedido! *You're fired!*
Voy a despedirme de Juan. *I'm going to say goodbye to Juan.*
Me despediré luego. *I shall say goodbye later.*
Se despidieron *They said goodbye to each other.*

despedirse *to say goodbye*
el despido *sack, dismissal, sacking*
la despedida *farewell*
la despedida de soltero *stag party*

la despedida de aguas *drainage*
despedir el espíritu *to give up the ghost*

71 despertar *to awake, wake* (tr.)

INDICATIVE

Present	Imperfect	Perfect
despierto	despertaba	he despertado
despiertas	despertabas	has despertado
despierta	despertaba	ha despertado
despertamos	despertábamos	hemos despertado
despertáis	despertabais	habéis despertado
despiertan	despertaban	han despertado

Future	Pluperfect	Preterite
despertaré	había despertado	desperté
despertarás	habías despertado	despertaste
despertará	había despertado	despertó
despertaremos	habíamos despertado	despertamos
despertaréis	habíais depertado	despertasteis
despertarán	habían despertado	despertaron

Future perfect	Past anterior
habré despertado	hube despertado

CONDITIONAL SUBJUNCTIVE

Present	Present	Imperfect
despertaría	despierte	despert-ara/ase
despertarías	despiertes	despert-aras/ases
despertaría	despierte	despert-ara/ase
despertaríamos	despertemos	despert-áramos/ásemos
despertarías	despertéis	despert-arais/aseis
despertarían	despierten	despert-aran/asen

Perfect	Perfect	Pluperfect
habría despertado	haya despertado	hub-iera/iese despertado

GERUND	PAST PARTICIPLE	IMPERATIVE
despertando	despertado	despierta, despertad
		despierte (Vd), despierten (Vds)

Nos despertó la tormenta. *The storm awoke us.*
¿Les despertamos? *Shall we wake them?*
Me despierto a las 7. *I wake at 7 a.m.*
Te despertaré a las 6. *I'll wake you at 6.*
Ya se despertará a la realidad. *She'll wake up to reality.*
Por fin despertó de su error. *At last he realized his mistake.*
Elena despierta memorias. *Elena awakens memories.*

despertarse *to wake up*
el despertador *alarm clock*
el despertar de la primavera *the awakening of Spring*
soñar despierto *to daydream*

el despertamiento *awakening, revival, rebirth*
despierto/a *awake, wide awake, sharp, alert*

72 desplegar *to unfold, spread* (tr.)

INDICATIVE

Present	Imperfect	Perfect
despliego	desplegaba	he desplegado
despliegas	desplegabas	has desplegado
despliega	desplegaba	ha desplegado
desplegamos	desplegábamos	hemos desplegado
desplegáis	desplegabais	habéis desplegado
despliegan	desplegaban	han desplegado

Future	Pluperfect	Preterite
desplegaré	había desplegado	desplegué
desplegarás	habías desplegado	desplegaste
desplegará	había desplegado	desplegó
desplegaremos	habíamos desplegado	desplegamos
desplegaréis	habíais despleado	desplegasteis
desplegarán	habían desplegado	desplegaron

Future perfect	Past anterior
habré desplegado	hube desplegado

CONDITIONAL   SUBJUNCTIVE

Present	Present	Imperfect
desplegaría	despliegue	despleg-ara/ase
desplegarías	despliegues	despleg-aras/ases
desplegaría	despliegue	despleg-ara/ase
desplegaríamos	despleguemos	despleg-áramos/ásemos
desplegaríais	despleguéis	despleg-arais/aseis
desplegarían	desplieguen	despleg-aran/asen

Perfect	Perfect	Pluperfect
habría desplegado	haya desplegado	hub-iera/iese desplegado

GERUND   PAST PARTICIPLE   IMPERATIVE

GERUND	PAST PARTICIPLE	IMPERATIVE
desplegando	desplegado	despliega, desplegad
		despliegue (Vd), desplieguen (Vds)

Despliego un pañuelo. *I unfold a scarf.*
Paqui desplegó el periódico. *Paqui unfolded the newspaper.*
Desplegarán la bandera. *They will unfurl the flag.*
Vamos a desplegar las velas del barco. *We are going to unfurl the sails of the boat.*
sindesplegar los labios. *without uttering a word*
Desplegó mucha astucia. *He deployed much cunning.*
Desplegaremos las alas. *We shall spread our wings.*

el despliegue *display, deployment, exhibition, show*
desplegado *displayed*
la desplegadura *unfolding, spreading*
desplegar en abanico *to fan out*

desplegadamente *openly*
a velas desplegadas *with the sails set*
con banderas desplegadas *with the flags unfurled*

73 desterrar *to exile, banish* (tr.)

INDICATIVE

Present	Imperfect	Perfect
destierro	desterraba	he desterrado
destierras	desterrabas	has desterrado
destierra	desterraba	ha desterrado
desterramos	desterrábamos	hemos desterrado
desterráis	desterrabais	habéis desterrado
destierran	desterraban	han desterrado

Future	Pluperfect	Preterite
desterraré	había desterrado	desterré
desterrarás	habías desterrado	desterraste
desterrará	había desterrado	desterró
desterraremos	habíamos desterrado	desterramos
desterraréis	habíais desterrado	desterrasteis
desterrarán	habían desterrado	desterraron

Future perfect	Past anterior
habré desterrado	hube desterrado

CONDITIONAL · SUBJUNCTIVE

Present	Present	Imperfect
desterraría	destierre	desterr-ara/ase
desterrarías	destierres	desterr-aras/ases
desterraría	destierre	desterr-ara/ase
desterraríamos	desterremos	desterr-áramos/ásemos
desterraríais	desterréis	desterr-arais/aseis
desterrarían	destierren	desterr-aran/asen

Perfect	Perfect	Pluperfect
habría desterrado	haya desterrado	hub-iera/iese desterrado

GERUND	PAST PARTICIPLE	IMPERATIVE
desterrando	desterrado	destierra, desterrad
		destierre (Vd), destierren (Vds)

Hay que desterrar esas ideas. *Those ideas have to be banished.*
El gobierno ha desterrado el uso de las armas de fuego. *The government has banned the use of firearms.*
El rey desterró al Cid. *The king exiled el Cid.*
Deberíamos desterrar las armas nucleares. *We ought to banish nuclear arms.*
Desterramos toda sospecha. *We banish all suspicions from our minds.*

la tierra *soil, earth*
desterrar *to remove soil from (mines)*
el/la desterrado/a *exile, outlaw, outcast*

el destierro *exile, banishment*
en el destierro *in exile*

74 destruir *to destroy, ruin* (tr.)

INDICATIVE

Present	Imperfect	Perfect
destruyo	destruía	he destruido
destruyes	destruías	has destruido
destruye	destruía	ha destruido
destruimos	destruíamos	hemos destruido
destruís	destruíais	habéis destruido
destruyen	destruían	han destruido

Future	Pluperfect	Preterite
destruiré	había destruido	destruí
destruirás	habías destruido	destruiste
destruirá	había destruido	destruyó
destruiremos	habíamos destruido	destruimos
destruiréis	habíais destruido	destruisteis
destruirán	habían destruido	destruyeron

Future perfect	Past anterior
habré destruido	hube destruido

CONDITIONAL / SUBJUNCTIVE

Present	Present	Imperfect
destruiría	destruya	destru-yera/yese
destruirías	destruyas	destru-yeras/yeses
destruiría	destruya	destru-yera/yese
destruiríamos	destruyamos	destru-yéramos/yésemos
destruiríais	destruyáis	destru-yerais/yeseis
destruirían	destruyan	destru-yeran/yesen

Perfect	Perfect	Pluperfect
habría destruido	haya destruido	hub-iera/iese destruido

GERUND / PAST PARTICIPLE / IMPERATIVE

GERUND	PAST PARTICIPLE	IMPERATIVE
destruyendo	destruido	destruye, destruid
		destruya (Vd), destruyan (Vds)

No destruyas ese trabajo. *Do not destroy that work.*
La bomba destruyó la estación. *The bomb destroyed the station.*
He destruido la información. *I have destroyed the information.*
Lo van a destruir con explosivos. *They are going to blow it up.*
Ha sido destruido por un incendio. *It has been gutted by fire.*

destruirse *to cancel (math.)*
destruíble *destroyable*
destructor(a) *destroyer, destructive*
la destrucción *wreck, destruction*

destruyente *destructive*
destructible *destructible*
destructivamente *destructively*
la destructibilidad *destructiveness*

75 devolver *to return, give back* (tr.)

INDICATIVE

Present	Imperfect	Perfect
devuelvo	devolvía	he devuelto
devuelves	devolvías	has devuelto
devuelve	devolvía	ha devuelto
devolvemos	devolvíamos	hemos devuelto
devolvéis	devolvíais	habéis devuelto
devuelven	devolvían	han devuelto

Future	Pluperfect	Preterite
devolveré	había devuelto	devolví
devolverás	habías devuelto	devolviste
devolverá	había devuelto	devolvió
devolveremos	habíamos devuelto	devolvimos
devolveréis	habíais devuelto	devolvisteis
devolverán	habían devuelto	devolvieron

Future perfect	Past anterior
habré devuelto	hube devuelto

CONDITIONAL   SUBJUNCTIVE

Present	Present	Imperfect
devolvería	devuelva	devolv-iera/iese
devolverías	devuelvas	devolv-ieras/ieses
devolvería	devuelva	devolv-iera/iese
devolveríamos	devolvamos	devolv-iéramos/iésemos
devoleríais	devolváis	devolv-ierais/ieseis
devolverían	devuelvan	devolv-ieran/iesen

Perfect	Perfect	Pluperfect
habría devuelto	haya devuelto	hub-iera/iese devuelto

GERUND   PAST PARTICIPLE   IMPERATIVE

GERUND	PAST PARTICIPLE	IMPERATIVE
devolviendo	devuelto	devuelve, devolved
		devuelva (Vd), devuelvan (Vds)

Te devolveré tu libro mañana. *I'll return your book tomorrow.*
Le devolvió su regalo. *He returned his present.*
Me devolvieron el dinero. *They gave me back the money.*
El espejo devuelve la imagen. *The mirror reflects the image.*
Han devuelto el castillo a su antiguo esplendor. *They have restored the castle to its former glory.*

la devolución *return, refund*
la devolución de impuestos *tax refunds*
devolver mal por bien *to return bad for good*
devolver dinero *to refund money*
devolutivo/a *returnable*

devolver una visita *to return a visit*
devolver la pelota *to pass the buck*
devolver *to vomit, be sick (med.)*
la devolución de las inversiones
    return on investments

76 diferir *to postpone; to differ* (tr./intr.)

INDICATIVE

Present	Imperfect	Perfect
difiero	difería	he diferido
difieres	diferías	has diferido
difiere	difería	ha diferido
diferimos	diferíamos	hemos diferido
diferís	diferíais	habéis diferido
difieren	diferían	han diferido

Future	Pluperfect	Preterite
diferiré	había diferido	diferí
diferirás	habías diferido	diferiste
diferirá	había diferido	difirió
diferiremos	habíamos diferido	diferimos
diferiréis	habíais diferido	diferisteis
diferirán	habían diferido	difirieron

Future perfect	Past anterior
habré diferido	hube diferido

CONDITIONAL / SUBJUNCTIVE

Present	Present	Imperfect
diferiría	difiera	difir-iera/iese
diferirías	difieras	difir-ieras/ieses
diferiría	difiera	difir-iera/iese
diferiríamos	difiramos	difir-iéramos/iésemos
diferiríais	difiráis	difir-ierais/ieseis
diferirían	difieran	difir-ieran/iesen

Perfect	Perfect	Pluperfect
habría diferido	haya diferido	hub-iera/iese diferido

GERUND	PAST PARTICIPLE	IMPERATIVE
difiriendo	diferido	difiere, diferid
		difiera (Vd), difieran (Vds)

Han diferido la boda hasta el otoño. *The wedding has been postponed until the autumn.*
Vamos a diferir la reunión por unos días. *Let's defer the meeting for a few days.*
Nos conviene diferir la venta. *We should postpone the sale.*
Esta obra difiere de las anteriores. *This work is different from the previous ones.*

diferente *different*
la diferencia *difference*
a diferencia de... *unlike...*
diferir en *to be different in*

diferir de *to be different from*
diferentemente *differently*
diferible *deferrable*

77 digerir *to digest, absorb* (tr.)

INDICATIVE

Present	Imperfect	Perfect
digiero	digería	he digerido
digieres	digerías	has digerido
digiere	digería	ha digerido
digerimos	digeríamos	hemos digerido
digerís	digeríais	habéis digerido
digieren	digerían	han digerido

Future	Pluperfect	Preterite
digeriré	había digerido	digerí
digerirás	habías digerido	digeriste
digerirá	había digerido	digirió
digeriremos	habíamos digerido	digerimos
digeriréis	habías digerido	digeristeis
digerirán	habían digerido	digirieron

Future perfect	Past anterior
habré digerido	hube digerido

CONDITIONAL · SUBJUNCTIVE

Present	Present	Imperfect
digeriría	digiera	digir-iera/iese
digerirías	digieras	digir-ieras/ieses
digeriría	digiera	digir-iera/iese
digeriríamos	digiramos	digir-iéramos/iésemos
digeriríais	digiráis	digir-ierais/ieseis
digerirían	digieran	digir-ieran/iesen

Perfect	Perfect	Pluperfect
habría digerido	haya digerido	hub-iera/iese digerido

GERUND · PAST PARTICIPLE · IMPERATIVE

GERUND	PAST PARTICIPLE	IMPERATIVE
digiriendo	digerido	digiere, digerid
		digiera (Vd), digieran (Vds)

Tiene una úlcera y no puede digerir bien. *He has an ulcer and cannot digest well.*
No pude digerir la cena. *I couldn't digest the supper.*
Ya lo he digerido. *I have already assimilated it.*
Me cuesta digerir su argumento. *I find his argument hard to digest.*
Necesito leerlo tres veces para digerirlo. *I need to read it three times in order to assimilate it.*
Lo digeriremos mañana. *We shall absorb it tomorrow.*
No puedo digerir a Dalí. *I cannot stand Dalí.*

digerible *digestible*	**indigesto** *indigestible*
digestible *digestible*	**digestivo/a** *digestive*
la digestión *digestion*	**digestibilidad** *digestibility*
el digesto *digest*	**el digestor** *digester*

78 disolver *to dissolve, melt, break up* (tr.)

INDICATIVE

Present	Imperfect	Perfect
disuelvo	disolvía	he disuelto
disuelves	disolvías	has disuelto
disuelve	disolvía	ha disuelto
disolvemos	disolvíamos	hemos disuelto
disolvéis	disolvíais	habéis disuelto
disuelven	disolvían	han disuelto

Future	Pluperfect	Preterite
disolveré	había disuelto	disolví
disolverás	habías disuelto	disolviste
disolverá	había disuelto	disolvió
disolveremos	habíamos disuelto	disolvimos
disolveréis	habíais disuelto	disolvisteis
dosolverán	habían disuelto	disolvieron

Future perfect	Past anterior
habré disuelto	hube disuelto

CONDITIONAL / SUBJUNCTIVE

Present	Present	Imperfect
disolvería	disuelva	disolv-iera/iese
disolverías	disuelvas	disolv-ieras/ieses
disolvería	disuelva	disolv-iera/iese
disolveríamos	disolvamos	disolv-iéramos/iésemos
disolveríais	disolváis	disolv-ierais/ieseis
disolverían	disuelvan	disolv-ieran/iesen

Perfect	Perfect	Pluperfect
habría disuelto	haya disuelto	hub-iera/iese disuelto

GERUND / PAST PARTICIPLE / IMPERATIVE

GERUND	PAST PARTICIPLE	IMPERATIVE
disolviendo	disuelto	disuelve, disolved
		disuelva (Vd), disuelvan (Vds)

Se disuelve en agua. *It dissolves in water.*
Se ha disuelto el matrimonio. *The marriage had been dissolved.*
Tejero quería disolver las Cortes. *Tejero wanted to dissolve las Cortes.*
La policía disolvió la manifestación. *The police broke up the demonstration.*
Quería disolver la reunión. *He wanted to break up the meeting.*
El parlamento se disuelve en agosto. *Parliament breaks up in August.*

el disolvente *solvent, dissolvent*   **disoluble** *soluble*
el disolvedor *dissolver*   **disoluto/a** *dissolute, dissipated*
la disolución *solution, annulment, dissolution*

79 distinguir *to distinguish* (tr.)

INDICATIVE

Present	Imperfect	Perfect
distingo	distinguía	he distinguido
distingues	distinguías	has distinguido
distingue	distinguía	ha distinguido
distinguimos	distinguíamos	hemos distinguido
distinguís	distinguíais	habéis distinguido
distinguen	distinguían	han distinguido

Future	Pluperfect	Preterite
distinguiré	había distinguido	distinguí
distinguirás	habías distinguido	distinguiste
distiguirá	había distinguido	distinguió
distinguiremos	habíamos distinguido	distinguimos
distinguiréis	habíais distinguido	distinguisteis
distinguirán	habían distinguido	distinguieron

Future perfect	Past anterior
habré distinguido	hube distinguido

CONDITIONAL

SUBJUNCTIVE

Present	Present	Imperfect
distinguiría	distinga	distingu-iera/iese
distinguirías	distingas	distingu-ieras/ieses
distinguiría	distinga	distingu-iera/iese
distinguiríamos	distingamos	distingu-iéramos/iésemos
distinguiríais	distingáis	distingu-ierais/ieseis
distinguirían	distingan	distingu-ieran/iesen

Perfect	Perfect	Pluperfect
habría distinguido	haya distinguido	hub-iera/iese distinguido

GERUND	PAST PARTICIPLE	IMPERATIVE
distinguiendo	distinguido	distingue, distinguid
		distinga (Vd), distingan (Vds)

No distingo mi jersey. *I can't tell which is my jumper.*
La sabría distinguir entre 1.000. *I could distinguish it from amongst a thousand.*
¿Distingues los dos aspectos? *Can you distinguish between the two aspects?*
No les puedo distinguir. *I can't tell them apart.*
Leonor sabe distinguir. *Leonor is a discriminating person.*
Rodrigo les distingue con su amistad. *Rodrigo honours them with his friendship.*
Sé distinguir. *I know the difference. I can tell.*

la distinción *distinction, difference*
distinguible *distinguishible*
distinguido/a *well-known, refined, distinguished*

distintivo/a *distinctive*
distinto/a *distinct, clear; different; several*

80 divertir *to amuse, distract; to divert* (tr.)

INDICATIVE

Present	Imperfect	Perfect
divierto	divertía	he divertido
diviertes	divertías	has divertido
divierte	divertía	ha divertido
divertimos	divertíamos	hemos divertido
divertís	divertíais	habéis divertido
divierten	divertían	han divertido

Future	Pluperfect	Preterite
divertiré	había divertido	divertí
divertirás	habías divertido	divertiste
divertirá	había divertido	divirtió
divertiremos	habíamos divertido	divertimos
divertiréis	habíais divertido	divertisteis
divertirán	habían divertido	divirtieron

Future perfect	Past anterior
habré divertido	hube divertido

CONDITIONAL / SUBJUNCTIVE

Present	Present	Imperfect
divertiría	divierta	divirt-iera/iese
divertirías	diviertas	divirt-ieras/ieses
divertiría	divierta	divirt-iera/iese
divertiríamos	divirtamos	divirt-iéramos/iésemos
divertirías	divirtáis	divirt-ierais/ieseis
divertirían	diviertan	divirt-ieran/iesen

Perfect	Perfect	Pluperfect
habría divertido	haya divertido	hub-iera/iese divertido

GERUND / PAST PARTICIPLE / IMPERATIVE

GERUND	PAST PARTICIPLE	IMPERATIVE
divirtiendo	divertido	divierte, divertid
		divierta (Vd), diviertan (Vds)

El payaso divierte a los niños. *The clown amuses the children.*
Le divierte hacer eso. *It amuses him to do that.*
¡Divierte el tráfico! *Divert the traffic!*
Intenta divertir a Juan. *Try to distract Juan.*

divertirse *to enjoy oneself, have a good time*
la diversión *diversion, entertainment, amusement*
diversivo/a *diversive*

divertido/a *amusing, entertaining, merry*
el divertimiento *diversion, amusement, distraction*

81 doler *to ache, hurt; to mourn* (intr.)

INDICATIVE

Present	Imperfect	Perfect
duelo	dolía	he dolido
dueles	dolías	has dolido
duele	dolía	ha dolido
dolemos	dolíamos	hemos dolido
doléis	dolíais	habéis dolido
duelen	dolían	han dolido

Future	Pluperfect	Preterite
doleré	había dolido	dolí
dolerás	habías dolido	doliste
dolerá	había dolido	dolió
doleremos	habíamos dolido	dolimos
doleréis	habíais dolido	dolisteis
dolerán	habían dolido	dolieron

Future perfect	Past anterior
habré dolido	hube dolido

CONDITIONAL

SUBJUNCTIVE

Present	Present	Imperfect
dolería	duela	dol-iera/iese
dolerías	duelas	dol-ieras/ieses
dolería	duela	dol-iera/iese
doleríamos	dolamos	dol-iéramos/iésemos
doleríais	doláis	dol-ierais/ieseis
dolerían	duelen	dol-ieran/iesen

Perfect	Perfect	Pluperfect
habría dolido	haya dolido	hub-iera/iese dolido

GERUND	PAST PARTICIPLE	IMPERATIVE
doliendo	dolido	duele, doled
		duela (Vd), duelan (Vds)

¿Te duele mucho? *Does it hurt much?*
Me duelen los brazos. *My arms ache.*
Le duele la cabeza. *He has got a headache.*
No nos ha dolido nada. *It did not hurt us a bit.*
Aún le duele la pérdida. *He is still mourning the loss.*
No me duele el dinero. *I don't mind about the money.*
¡Ahí le duele! *You have put your finger on it! That's the point!*
¡Duélete de mí! *Pity me!*

la dolencia *ailment, complaint*
doliente *suffering, sad*
el dolo *fraud*
el dolor *pain, ache*

el dolor de cabeza *headache*
dolorido/a *sore, tender*
dolerse *to grieve, regret*

82 dormir *to sleep* (tr./intr.)

INDICATIVE

Present	Imperfect	Perfect
duermo	dormía	he dormido
duermes	dormías	has dormido
duerme	dormía	ha dormido
dormimos	dormíamos	hemos dormido
dormís	dormíais	habéis dormido
duermen	dormían	han dormido

Future	Pluperfect	Preterite
dormiré	había dormido	dormí
dormirás	habías dormido	dormiste
dormirá	había dormido	durmió
dormiremos	habíamos dormido	dormimos
dormiréis	habías dormido	dormisteis
dormirán	habían dormido	durmieron

Future perfect	Past anterior
habré dormido	hube dormido

CONDITIONAL / SUBJUNCTIVE

Present	Present	Imperfect
dormiría	duerma	durm-iera/iese
dormirías	duermas	durm-ieras/ieses
dormiría	duerma	durm-iera/iese
dormiríamos	durmamos	durm-iéramos/iésemos
dormiríais	durmáis	durm-ierais/ieseis
dormirían	duerman	durm-ieran/iesen

Perfect	Perfect	Pluperfect
habría dormido	haya dormido	hub-iera/iese dormido

GERUND	PAST PARTICIPLE	IMPERATIVE
durmiendo	dormido	duerme, dormid
		duerma (Vd), duerman (Vds)

Me gusta dormir. *I love sleeping.*
Pedro duerme ocho horas al día. *Pedro sleeps eight hours a day.*
La reina Leonor durmió aquí. *Queen Eleanor slept here.*
Dormiremos en un hotel. *We'll sleep in a hotel.*
He dormido como un santo/bendito. *I have slept peacefully.*
Durmieron a pierna suelta. *They slept soundly.*
Va a dormir la mona esta mañana. *She is going to sleep off her hangover this morning.*

la dormida *sleep*
el dormidero = sestil *sleeping place (for animals), roost*
la dormidera *opium poppy*
el/la dormilón/dormilona *sleepyhead*
el dormitorio *bedroom*

83 echar *to throw, pour; throw out* (tr./intr.)

INDICATIVE

Present	Imperfect	Perfect
echo	echaba	he echado
echas	echabas	has echado
echa	echaba	ha echado
echamos	echábamos	hemos echado
echáis	echabais	habéis echado
echan	echaban	han echado

Future	Pluperfect	Preterite
echaré	había echado	eché
echarás	habías echado	echaste
echará	había echado	echó
echaremos	habíamos echado	echamos
echaréis	habíais echado	echasteis
echarán	habían echado	echaron

Future perfect	Past anterior
habré echado	hube echado

CONDITIONAL / SUBJUNCTIVE

Present	Present	Imperfect
echaría	eche	ech-ara/ase
echarías	eches	ech-aras/ases
echaría	eche	ech-ara/ase
echaríamos	echemos	ech-áramos/ásemos
echaríais	echéis	ech-arais/aseis
echarían	echen	ech-aran/asen

Perfect	Perfect	Pluperfect
habría echado	haya echado	hub-iera/iese echado

GERUND / PAST PARTICIPLE / IMPERATIVE

GERUND	PAST PARTICIPLE	IMPERATIVE
echando	echado	echa, echad
		eche (Vd), echen (Vds)

Echa azúcar al café. *Put some sugar in the coffee.*
¿Te echo un poco de agua? *Shall I pour some water for you?*
Cuando protesté me echaron. *When I protested they threw me out.*
Echó el cuerpo atrás. *He leaned his body backwards.*
El bebé ha echado un diente. *The baby has cut a tooth.*
He echado raíces aquí. *I have put down roots here.*
Voy a echar la choza abajo. *I'm going to knock down the hut.*
La lluvia echó a perder la fruta. *The rain spoiled the fruit.*

echarse a *to start (doing something)*
echar a suertes *to draw lots*
echar a correr *to start running*
echarse *to lie down*

echar a perder *to waste*
la echadora de cartas *fortune teller*
la echada *throw, cast, boast*
echar de menos *to miss, feel nostalgia for*

84 elegir to select, choose (tr.)

INDICATIVE

Present	Imperfect	Perfect
elijo	elegía	he elegido
eliges	elegías	has elegido
elige	elegía	ha elegido
elegimos	elegíamos	hemos elegido
elegís	elegíais	habéis elegido
eligen	elegían	han elegido

Future	Pluperfect	Preterite
elegiré	había elegido	elegí
elegirás	habías elegido	elegiste
elegirá	había elegido	eligió
elegiremos	habíamos elegido	elegimos
elegiréis	habíais elegido	elegisteis
elegirán	habían elegido	eligieron

Future perfect	Past anterior
habré elegido	hube elegido

CONDITIONAL · SUBJUNCTIVE

Present	Present	Imperfect
elegiría	elija	elig-iera/iese
elegirías	elijas	elig-ieras/ieses
elegiría	elija	elig-iera/iese
elegiríamos	elijamos	elig-iéramos/iésemos
elegirías	elijáis	elig-ierais/ieseis
elegirían	elijan	elig-ieran/iesen

Perfect	Perfect	Pluperfect
habría elegido	haya elegido	hub-iera/iese elegido

GERUND	PAST PARTICIPLE	IMPERATIVE
eligiendo	elegido	elige, elegid
		elija (Vd), elijan (Vds)

Te toca elegir. *It's your turn to choose.*
¿Has elegido ya? *Have you chosen yet?*
Siempre elijo chocolate. *I always choose chocolate.*
Le eligieron entre los dos. *He was selected by both of them.*
¡Elige el que quieras! *Choose what you want!*
Me eligieron por votación. *I was voted in.*
Han elegido el camino más difícil. *They have chosen the most difficult path.*

elegible *eligible, selectable* **el/la elector(a)** *voter, elector*
elegido *chosen, selected* **la potencia electoral** *voting power*
la elección *choice, selection, option* **la elegibilidad** *eligibility*
las elecciones generales *general election* **las elecciones parciales** *by-election*

85 empezar *to begin, start* (tr./intr.)

INDICATIVE

Present	Imperfect	Perfect
empiezo	empezaba	he empezado
empiezas	empezabas	has empezado
empieza	empezaba	ha empezado
empezamos	empezábamos	hemos empezado
empezáis	empezabais	habéis empezado
empiezan	empezaban	han empezado

Future	Pluperfect	Preterite
empezaré	había empezado	empecé
empezarás	habías empezado	empezaste
empezará	había empezado	empezó
empezaremos	habíamos empezado	empezamos
empezaréis	habíais empezado	empezasteis
empezarán	habían empezado	empezaron

Future perfect	Past anterior
habré empezado	hube empezado

CONDITIONAL / SUBJUNCTIVE

Present	Present	Imperfect
empezaría	empiece	empez-ara/ase
empezarías	empieces	empez-aras/ases
empezaría	empiece	empez-ara/ase
empezaríamos	empecemos	empez-áramos/ásemos
empezaríais	empecéis	empez-arais/aseis
empezarían	empiecen	empez-aran/asen

Perfect	Perfect	Pluperfect
habría empezado	haya empezado	hub-iera/iese empezado

GERUND / PAST PARTICIPLE / IMPERATIVE

GERUND	PAST PARTICIPLE	IMPERATIVE
empezando	empezado	empieza, empezad empiece (Vd), empiecen (Vds)

El curso empieza en octubre. *The course starts in October.*
¡No empieces el trabajo! *Don't start the work!*
Ayer empezó a hacer calor. *Yesterday it started to get hot.*
Empecé diciendo que... *I started by saying that...*
Bueno, para empezar... *Well, to start with...*
Empezará a regir mañana. *It will come into force tomorrow.*
Voy a empezar a disparar. *I am going to open fire.*
Empiezan la excavación el lunes. *They start excavating on Monday.*

el empiece *starting, beginning*
empezado *under way*
para empezar *first of all, to start with*

el empiezo *beginning, start*
empezar por *to begin by*

86 encender *to light, turn on* (tr.)

INDICATIVE

Present	Imperfect	Perfect
enciendo	encendía	he encendido
enciendes	encendías	has encendido
enciende	encendía	ha encendido
encendemos	encendíamos	hemos encendido
encendéis	encendíais	habéis encendido
encienden	encendían	han encendido

Future	Pluperfect	Preterite
encenderé	había encendido	encendí
encenderás	habías encendido	encendiste
encenderá	había encendido	encendió
encenderemos	habíamos encendido	encendimos
encenderéis	habíais encendido	encendisteis
encenderán	habían encendido	encendieron

Future perfect	Past anterior
habré encendido	hube encendido

CONDITIONAL   SUBJUNCTIVE

Present	Present	Imperfect
encendería	encienda	encend-iera/iese
encenderías	enciendas	encend-ieras/ieses
encendería	encienda	encend-iera/iese
encenderíamos	encendamos	encend-iéramos/iésemos
encenderíais	encendáis	encend-ierais/ieseis
encenderían	enciendan	encend-ieran/iesen

Perfect	Perfect	Pluperfect
habría encendido	haya encendido	hub-iera/iese encendido

GERUND	PAST PARTICIPLE	IMPERATIVE
encendiendo	encendido	enciende, encended
		encienda (Vd), enciendan (Vds)

¡**Enciende una cerilla!** *Light a match!*
Encendió la luz. *She turned on the light.*
¿**Has encendido el horno?** *Have you switched on the oven?*
Ya habían encendido la radio. *They had already switched on the radio.*
Se encienden las luces a las seis. *It's lighting-up time at six.*
Se encendió con la noticia. *He got very excited by the news.*
Es tímida y se enciende enseguida. *She is shy and blushes easily.*

el encendedor *lighter*
encendido a mano *hand firing*
encenderse *to catch fire*
estar encendido *to be alight, on fire*

encendidamente *passionately, ardently*
encender un fósforo *to strike a match*
encender fuego *to light a fire*

87 encerrar *to shut in, lock up* (tr.)

INDICATIVE

Present	Imperfect	Perfect
encierro	encerraba	he encerrado
encierras	encerrabas	has encerrado
encierra	encerraba	ha encerrado
encerramos	encerrábamos	hemos encerrado
encerráis	encerrabais	habéis encerrado
encierran	encerraban	han encerrado

Future	Pluperfect	Preterite
encerraré	había encerrado	encerré
encerrarás	habías encerrado	encerraste
encerrará	había encerrado	encerró
encerraremos	habíamos encerrado	encerramos
encerraréis	habíais encerrado	encerrasteis
encerrarán	habían encerrado	encerraron

Future perfect	Past anterior
habré encerrado	hube encerrado

CONDITIONAL / SUBJUNCTIVE

Present	Present	Imperfect
encerraría	encierre	encerr-ara/ase
encerrarías	encierres	encerr-aras/ases
encerraría	encierre	encerr-ara/ase
encerraríamos	encerremos	encerr-áramos/ásemos
encerraríais	encerréis	encerr-arais/aseis
encerrarían	encierren	encerr-aran/asen

Perfect	Perfect	Pluperfect
habría encerrado	haya encerrado	hub-iera/iese encerrado

GERUND	PAST PARTICIPLE	IMPERATIVE
encerrando	encerrado	encierra, encerrad
		encierre (Vd), encierren (Vds)

El libro encierra toda la historia. *The book contains the whole story.*
Se encerró en el baño. *She shut herself in the bathroom.*
¿Has encerrado las gallinas? *Have you locked the hens in?*
Encerraremos los documentos en una caja fuerte. *We'll lock the documents in a safe.*
Les encerraron en un calabozo. *They were locked in jail.*
Camille fue encerrada en un manicomio. *Camille was put in a madhouse.*
Me encerraré en el silencio. *I shall maintain a total silence.*

el encerradero *fold, pen*
el encierro *closing, confinement, shutting in, locking*
el encierre *penning*

encerrado/a *contained*
el encerramiento *enclosure*

88 encomendar *to entrust, commend* (tr./intr.)

INDICATIVE

Present	Imperfect	Perfect
encomiendo	encomendaba	he encomendado
encomiendas	encomendabas	has encomendado
encomienda	encomendaba	ha encomendado
encomendamos	encomendábamos	hemos encomendado
encomendáis	encomendabais	habéis encomendado
encomiendan	encomendaban	han encomendado

Future	Pluperfect	Preterite
encomedaré	había encomendado	encomendé
encomendarás	habías encomendado	encomendaste
encomedará	había encomendado	encomendó
encomendaremos	habíamos encomendado	encomendamos
encomendaréis	habíais encomendado	encomendasteis
encomendarán	habían encomendado	encomendaron

Future perfect	Past anterior
habré encomendado	hube encomendado

CONDITIONAL | SUBJUNCTIVE

Present	Present	Imperfect
encomedaría	encomiende	encomend-ara/ase
encomendarías	encomiendes	encomend-aras/ases
encomedaría	encomiende	encomend-ara/ase
encomendaríamos	encomendemos	encomend-áramos/ásemos
encomendarías	encomendéis	encomend-arais/aseis
encomendarían	encomienden	encomend-aran/asen

Perfect	Perfect	Pluperfect
habría encomendado	haya encomendado	hub-iera/iese encomendado

GERUND | PAST PARTICIPLE | IMPERATIVE

GERUND	PAST PARTICIPLE	IMPERATIVE
encomendando	encomendado	encomienda, encomendad
		encomiende (Vd),
		encomienden (Vds)

Encomendó el niño a su madre. *She entrusted the child to her mother.*
Se ha encomendado un traje nuevo. *He has ordered a new suit.*
Me encomiendo a Dios. *I put my trust in God.*
Lo encomendó contra reembolso. *He sent a parcel cash on delivery.*
Encomiéndame a tu mujer. *Send my regards to your wife.*

la encomienda *confession, holding commission, patronage*
las encomiendas *regards, respects*
encomendado/a *entrusted*

encomendarse a *to put one's trust in*
encomendable *commendable*
el encomendamiento *charge, task*

89 encontrar *to find, meet* (tr./intr.)

INDICATIVE

Present	Imperfect	Perfect
encuentro	encontraba	he encontrado
encuentras	encontrabas	has encontrado
encuentra	encontraba	ha encontrado
encontramos	encontrábamos	hemos encontrado
encontráis	encontrabais	habéis encontrado
encuentran	encontraban	han encontrado

Future	Pluperfect	Preterite
encontraré	había encontrado	encontré
encontrarás	habías encontrado	encontraste
encontrará	había encontrado	encontró
encontraremos	habíamos encontrado	encontramos
encontraréis	habíais encontrado	encontrasteis
encontrarán	habían encontrado	encontraron

Future perfect	Past anterior
habré encontrado	hube encontrado

CONDITIONAL / SUBJUNCTIVE

Present	Present	Imperfect
encontraría	encuentre	encontr-ara/ase
encontrarías	encuentres	encontr-aras/ases
encontraría	encuentre	encontr-ara/ase
encontraríamos	encontremos	encontr-áramos/ásemos
encontraríais	encontréis	encontr-arais/aseis
encontrarían	encuentren	encontr-aran/asen

Perfect	Perfect	Pluperfect
habría encontrado	haya encontrado	hub-iera/iese encontrado

GERUND	PAST PARTICIPLE	IMPERATIVE
encontrando	encontrado	encuentra, encontrad
		encuentre (Vd), encuentren (Vds)

¿Qué tal lo encuentras? *How do you find it?*
Lo encuentro bastante fácil. *I find it rather easy.*
No lo encontramos. *We can't find it.*
Me voy a encontrar con Sara en la biblioteca. *I'm going to meet Sara in the library.*
¿Qué tal te encuentras? *How are you?*
No sé lo que le encuentran. *I don't know what they see in him.*
Me encontré con un obstáculo. *I ran into an obstacle.*
Se encuentra enferma. *She is ill.*
¡Te la vas a encontrar! *You are going to get it!*

hacerse el encontradizo *to bump into someone*
encontrado/a *contrary, conflicting*
encontrón, encontronazo *crash, collision*

encontrarse con uno *to meet, come across someone*
el encuentro *encounter*
el encuentro fortuito *meeting by chance*

90 enmendar *to correct; to compensate* (tr.)

INDICATIVE

Present	Imperfect	Perfect
enmiendo	enmendaba	he enmendado
enmiendas	enmendabas	has enmendado
enmienda	enmendaba	ha enmendado
enmendamos	enmendábamos	hemos enmendado
enmendáis	enmendabais	habéis enmendado
enmiendan	enmendaban	han enmendado

Future	Pluperfect	Preterite
enmendaré	había enmendado	enmendé
enmendarás	habías enmendado	enmendaste
enmendará	había enmendado	enmendó
enmendaremos	habíamos enmendado	enmendamos
enmendaréis	habíais enmendado	enmendasteis
enmendarán	habían enmendado	enmendaron

Future perfect	Past anterior
habré enmendado	hube enmendado

CONDITIONAL / SUBJUNCTIVE

Present	Present	Imperfect
enmendaría	enmiende	enmend-ara/ase
enmendarías	enmiendes	enmend-aras/ases
enmendaría	enmiende	enmend-ara/ase
enmendaríamos	enmendemos	enmend-áramos/ásemos
enmendaríais	enmendéis	enmend-arais/aseis
enmendarían	enmienden	enmend-aran/asen

Perfect	Perfect	Pluperfect
habría enmendado	haya enmendado	hub-iera/iese enmendado

GERUND	PAST PARTICIPLE	IMPERATIVE
enmendando	enmendado	enmienda, enmendad
		enmiende (Vd),
		enmienden (Vds)

No se puede enmendar. *It cannot be revised.*
Enmendaré el documento. *I shall amend the document.*
No hemos enmendado los errores. *We haven't corrected the errors.*
Te enmendaremos por ello. *We shall compensate you for it.*
El avión tuvo que enmendar el rumbo. *The plane had to correct its course.*

enmendarse *to reform*
la enmendación *emendation, correction*
la enmienda *emendation, reform, indemnity, correction, amendment*

la Quinta Enmienda *the Fifth Amendment*
la enmienda constitucional *amendment to the constitution*

91 entender *to understand* (tr./intr.)

INDICATIVE

Present	Imperfect	Perfect
entiendo	entendía	he entendido
entiendes	entendías	has entendido
entiende	entendía	ha entendido
entendemos	entendíamos	hemos entendido
entendéis	entendíais	habéis entendido
entienden	entendían	han entendido

Future	Pluperfect	Preterite
entenderé	había entendido	entendí
entenderás	habías entendido	entendiste
entenderá	había entendido	entendió
entenderemos	habíamos entendido	entendimos
entenderéis	habías entendido	entendisteis
entenderán	habían entendido	entendieron

Future perfect	Past anterior
habré entendido	hube entendido

CONDITIONAL / SUBJUNCTIVE

Present	Present	Imperfect
entendería	entienda	entend-iera/iese
entenderías	entiendas	entend-ieras/ieses
entendería	entienda	entend-iera/iese
entenderíamos	entendamos	entend-iéramos/iésemos
entenderíais	entendáis	entend-ierais/ieseis
entenderían	entiendan	entend-ieran/iesen

Perfect	Perfect	Pluperfect
habría entendido	haya entendido	hub-iera/iese entendido

GERUND / PAST PARTICIPLE / IMPERATIVE

GERUND	PAST PARTICIPLE	IMPERATIVE
entendiendo	entendido	entiende, entended
		entienda (Vd), entiendan (Vds)

No, no lo entiendo. *No, I do not understand it.*
Te lo pienso hacer entender. *I'll make you understand.*
Nos hicimos entender. *We made ourselves understood.*
No entiendo ni una palabra. *It's all Greek to me.*
¿Qué entiendes por eso? *What do you mean by that?*

las entendederas *brain (col.)*
el/la entendedor(a) *understanding person*
el/la entendido/a *knowledgeable person, expert*

el entendimiento *understanding, comprehension, intelligence*
a mi entender *in my opinion*

92 entenderse *to be understood, known* (r.)

Present	**Imperfect**	**Perfect**
me entiendo	me entendía	me he entendido
te entiendes	te entendías	te has entendido
se entiende	se entendía	se ha entendido
nos entendemos	nos entendíamos	nos hemos entendido
os entendéis	os entendíais	os habéis entendido
se entienden	se entendían	se han entendido

Future	**Pluperfect**	**Preterite**
me entenderé	me había entendido	me entendí
te entenderás	te habías entendido	te entendiste
se entenderá	se había entendido	se entendió
nos entenderemos	nos habíamos entendido	nos entendimos
os entenderéis	os habíais entendido	os entendisteis
se entenderán	se habían entendido	se entendieron

Future perfect	**Past anterior**
habré entendido	hube entendido

CONDITIONAL · SUBJUNCTIVE

Present	**Present**	**Imperfect**
me entendería	me entienda	me entend-iera/iese
te entenderías	te entiendas	te entend-ieras/ieses
se entendería	se entienda	se entend-iera/iese
nos entenderíamos	nos entendamos	nos entend-iéramos/iésemos
os entenderíais	os entendáis	os entend-ierais/ieseis
se entenderían	se entiendan	se entend-ieran/iesen

Perfect	**Perfect**	**Pluperfect**
me habría entendido	me haya entendido	me hub-iera/iese entendido

GERUND	PAST PARTICIPLE	IMPERATIVE
entendiéndose	entendido	entiéndete, entendeos
		entiéndase (Vd),
		entiéndanse (Vds)

Se entiende. *It is understood.*
¿Qué se entiende por eso? *What is meant by that?*
Se entiende que no es bueno. *It is known to be no good.*
Yo me entiendo. *I know what I'm doing.*
Creo que él se entiende. *I think he knows what he is on about.*
No me entiendo bien con los ordenadores. *I'm not very good with computers.*
¿Te entiendes con él? *Do you get on with him?*
Me he entendido con mi jefe. *I've come to an arrangement with my boss.*
Paula y Marcia se entienden bien. *Paula and Marcia get on well together.*
Para el precio, entiéndete con el gerente. *Discuss the price with the manager.*

93 enterrar *to bury* (tr.)

INDICATIVE

Present	Imperfect	Perfect
entierro	enterraba	he enterrado
entierras	enterrabas	has enterrado
entierra	enterraba	ha enterrado
enterramos	enterrábamos	hemos enterrado
enterráis	enterrabais	habéis enterrado
entierran	enterraban	han enterrado

Future	Pluperfect	Preterite
enterraré	había enterrado	enterré
enterrarás	habías enterrado	enterraste
enterrará	había enterrado	enterró
enterraremos	habíamos enterrado	enterramos
enterraréis	habíais enterrado	enterrasteis
enterrarán	habían enterrado	enterraron

Future perfect	Past anterior
habré enterrado	hube enterrado

CONDITIONAL · SUBJUNCTIVE

Present	Present	Imperfect
enterraría	entierre	enterr-ara/ase
enterrarías	entierres	enterr-aras/ases
enterraría	entierre	enterr-ara/ase
enterraríamos	enterremos	enterr-áramos/ásemos
enterraríais	enterréis	enterr-arais/aseis
enterrarían	entierren	enterr-aran/asen

Perfect	Perfect	Pluperfect
habría enterrado	haya enterrado	hub-iera/iese enterrado

GERUND	PAST PARTICIPLE	IMPERATIVE
enterrando	enterrado	entierra, enterrad
		entierre (Vd), entierren (Vds)

Queremos que la entierren en su pueblo. *We want her to be buried in her village.*
La enterraron el sábado. *She was buried on Saturday.*
Le van a enterrar dentro de tres días. *He is going to be buried in three days.*
Lo enterraré para siempre. *I shall never mention it or think about it again.*
El abuelo nos enterrará a todos. *Grandfather will outlive us all.*
Se enterró en vida. *He retired to a quiet place.*

el enterradero *burial ground*
la uña enterrada *ingrowing nail*
el enterrador *grave digger*
enterrado/a *buried*

el enterramiento *burial, interment*
el entierro *burial, funeral*
el tesoro enterrado *treasure trove*

94 enviar *to send* (tr.)

INDICATIVE

Present	Imperfect	Perfect
envío	enviaba	he enviado
envías	enviabas	has enviado
envía	enviaba	ha enviado
enviamos	enviábamos	hemos enviado
enviáis	enviabais	habéis enviado
envían	enviaban	han enviado

Future	Pluperfect	Preterite
enviaré	había enviado	envié
enviarás	habías enviado	enviaste
enviará	había enviado	envió
enviaremos	habíamos enviado	enviamos
enviaréis	habíais enviado	enviasteis
enviarán	habían enviado	enviaron

Future perfect	Past anterior
habré enviado	hube enviado

CONDITIONAL | SUBJUNCTIVE

Present	Present	Imperfect
enviaría	envíe	envi-ara/ase
enviarías	envíes	envi-aras/ases
enviaría	envíe	envi-ara/ase
enviaríamos	enviemos	envi-áramos/ásemos
enviaríais	enviéis	envi-arais/aseis
enviarían	envíen	envi-aran/asen

Perfect	Perfect	Pluperfect
habría enviado	haya enviado	hub-iera/iese enviado

GERUND	PAST PARTICIPLE	IMPERATIVE
enviando	enviado	envía, enviad
		envíe (Vd), envíen (Vds)

Te enviaré un recado. *I'll send you a message.*
Hemos enviado un regalo a mi madre. *We have sent my mother a present.*
Me lo envía Juan. *Juan is sending it for me.*
Angy me envió a recoger su paquete. *Angy sent me to collect her parcel.*
Voy a enviar un parte. *I'm going to file a dispatch.*
Enviaron a Carlos de paseo. *They sent Carlos packing.*

el envío *dispatch*
los gastos de envío *transport charges, postage and packing*
el envión *push*
el/la enviado/a *envoy*

el enviado especial *special correspondent*
la enviada *sending, shipment, consignment*

95 envolver *to wrap up, surround* (tr.)

INDICATIVE

Present	Imperfect	Perfect
envuelvo	envolvía	he envuelto
envuelves	envolvías	has envuelto
envuelve	envolvía	ha envuelto
envolvemos	envolvíamos	hemos envuelto
envolvéis	envolvíais	habéis envuelto
envuelven	envolvían	han envuelto

Future	Pluperfect	Preterite
envolveré	había envuelto	envolví
envolverás	habías envuelto	envolviste
envolverá	había envuelto	envolvió
envolveremos	habíamos envuelto	envolvimos
envolveréis	habíais envuelto	envolvisteis
envolverán	habían envuelto	envolvieron

Future perfect	Past anterior
habré envuelto	hube envuelto

CONDITIONAL / SUBJUNCTIVE

Present	Present	Imperfect
envolvería	envuelva	envolv-iera/iese
envolverías	envuelvas	envolv-ieras/ieses
envolvería	envuelva	envolv-iera/iese
envolveríamos	envolvamos	envolv-iéramos/iésemos
envolveríais	envolváis	envolv-ierais/ieseis
envolverían	envuelvan	envolv-ieran/iesen

Perfect	Perfect	Pluperfect
habría envuelto	haya envuelto	hub-iera/iese envuelto

GERUND	PAST PARTICIPLE	IMPERATIVE
envolviendo	envuelto	envuelve, envolved
		envuelva (Vd), envuelvan (Vds)

¿**Te lo envuelvo?** *Shall I wrap it up for you?*
Lo envolvió en un periódico. *She wrapped it up in a newspaper.*
La niebla envuelve la ciudad. *Fog envelops the town.*
Envolvieron a Miguel. *Miguel was involved in it.*
El misterio envuelve la situación. *Mystery surrounds the situation.*

la envoltura *cover, wrapper, wrapping, case*
el envolvedero *cover, wrapper, wrapping*
envuelto/a *wrapped*
envolvente *surrounding*

el envolvimiento *wrapping, involvement*
el envoltorio, envoltijo *package, wrapping, bundle*

96 erguir *to stand up straight, raise* (tr.)

INDICATIVE

Present	Imperfect	Perfect
irgo/yergo	erguía	he erguido
irgues/yergues	erguías	has erguido
irgue/yergue	erguía	ha erguido
erguimos	erguíamos	hemos erguido
erguís	erguíais	habéis erguido
yerguen	erguían	han erguido

Future	Pluperfect	Preterite
erguiré	había erguido	erguí
erguirás	habías erguido	erguiste
erguirá	había erguido	irguió
erguiremos	habíamos erguido	erguimos
erguiréis	habíais erguido	erguisteis
erguirán	habían erguido	irguieron

Future perfect	Past anterior
habré erguido	hube erguido

CONDITIONAL / SUBJUNCTIVE

Present	Present	Imperfect
erguiría	yerga/irga	irgu-iera/iese
erguirías	yergas/irgas	irgu-ieras/ieses
erguiría	yerga/irga	irgu-iera/iese
erguiríamos	irgamos	irgu-iéramos/iésemos
erguiríais	irgáis	irgu-ierais/ieseis
erguirían	irgan	irgu-ieran/iesen

Perfect	Perfect	Pluperfect
habría erguido	haya erguido	hub-iera/iese erguido

GERUND	PAST PARTICIPLE	IMPERATIVE
irguiendo	erguido	yergue/irgue, erguid
		yerga/irga (Vd), yergan/irgan (Vds)

Le gusta erguirse para parecer más alto. *He likes to stand up straight to look taller.*
¡Irgue/yergue la cabeza! *Raise your head!*
El caballo irguió las orejas. *The horse pricked up his ears.*
Se irguieron de repente. *They stood up suddenly.*
¡Vamos a erguir la cabeza! *Let's hold our heads high!*

erguido/a *erect, straight, proud*   **el erguimiento** *erection, straightening up*
la erección *erection, raising*   **estar muy erguido** *to swell with pride*
erecto/a *standing, straight*

97 errar *to err, miss* (tr./intr.)

INDICATIVE

Present	Imperfect	Perfect
yerro	erraba	he errado
yerras	errabas	has errado
yerra	erraba	ha errado
erramos	errábamos	hemos errado
erráis	errabais	habéis errado
yerran	erraban	han errado

Future	Pluperfect	Preterite
erraré	había errado	erré
errarás	habías errado	erraste
errará	había errado	erró
erraremos	habíamos errado	erramos
erraréis	habíais errado	errasteis
errarán	habían errado	erraron

Future perfect	Past anterior
habré errado	hube errado

CONDITIONAL

SUBJUNCTIVE

Present	Present	Imperfect
erraría	yerre	err-ara/ase
errarías	yerres	err-aras/ases
erraría	yerre	err-ara/ase
erraríamos	erremos	err-áramos/ásemos
erraríais	erréis	err-arais/aseis
errarían	yerren	err-aran/asen

Perfect	Perfect	Pluperfect
habría errado	haya errado	hub-iera/iese errado

GERUND	PAST PARTICIPLE	IMPERATIVE
errando	errado	yerra, errad
		yerre (Vd), yerren (Vds)

Perdóname si he errado. *Please forgive me if I was at fault.*
Erramos por el parque. *We wandered in the park.*
He errado en mi elección. *I have made a mistake in my choice.*
Errar es humano. *To err is human.*
Caperucita Roja erró el camino. *Little Red Riding Hood lost her way.*
Enrique erró el golpe. *Enrique missed the target.*

el error *error*	**el error de entrega** *misdelivery*
errante *wandering, travelling, errant*	**el error de imprenta** *misprint*
estrella errante *wandering star*	**errático/a** *erratic*
el error de escritura *graphic error*	**erróneo** *faulty, wrong*

98 **escribir** *to write, spell* (tr.)

INDICATIVE

Present	Imperfect	Perfect
escribo	escribía	he escrito
escribes	escribías	has escrito
escribe	escribía	ha escrito
escribimos	escribíamos	hemos escrito
escribís	escribíais	habéis escrito
escriben	escribían	han escrito

Future	Pluperfect	Preterite
escribiré	había escrito	escribí
escribirás	habías escrito	escribiste
escribirá	había escrito	escribió
escribiremos	habíamos escrito	escribimos
escribiréis	habíais escrito	escribisteis
escribirán	habían escrito	escribieron

Future perfect	Past anterior
habré escrito	hube escrito

CONDITIONAL   SUBJUNCTIVE

Present	Present	Imperfect
escribiría	escriba	escrib-iera/iese
escribirías	escribas	escrib-ieras/ieses
escribiría	escriba	escrib-iera/iese
escribiríamos	escribamos	escrib-iéramos/iésemos
escribiríais	escribáis	escrib-ierais/ieseis
escribirían	escriban	escrib-ieran/iesen

Perfect	Perfect	Pluperfect
habría escrito	haya escrito	hub-iera/iese escrito

GERUND   PAST PARTICIPLE   IMPERATIVE

GERUND	PAST PARTICIPLE	IMPERATIVE
escribiendo	escrito	escribe, escribid
		escriba (Vd), escriban (Vds)

Leonor escribe artículos para El País. *Leonor writes for El País.*
Paquí lo escribirá todo a máquina. *Paquí will type everything.*
Elvira escribe muy bien. *Elvira writes beautifully.*
'Burro' se escribe con b. *'Burro' is spelt with a b.*
¿Cómo se escribe? *How do you spell it?*

escribir a máquina *to type*   **el escribiente** *copyist*
escribir *to write longhand*   **el/la escritor(a)** *writer*
el escriba *scribe*   **la escritura** *writing*
el escribano *clerk*   **el escritorio** *desk*

99 estar *to be* (intr.) (aux.)

INDICATIVE

Present	Imperfect	Perfect
estoy	estaba	he estado
estás	estabas	has estado
está	estaba	ha estado
estamos	estábamos	hemos estado
estáis	estabais	habéis estado
están	estaban	han estado

Future	Pluperfect	Preterite
estaré	había estado	estuve
estarás	habías estado	estuviste
estará	había estado	estuvo
estaremos	habíamos estado	estuvimos
estaréis	habíais estado	estuvisteis
estarán	habían estado	estuvieron

Future perfect	Past anterior
habré estado	hube estado

CONDITIONAL · SUBJUNCTIVE

Present	Present	Imperfect
estaría	esté	estuv-iera/iese
estarías	estés	estuv-ieras/ieses
estaría	esté	estuv-iera/iese
estaríamos	estemos	estuv-iéramos/iésemos
estaríais	estéis	estuv-ierais/ieseis
estarían	estén	estuv-ieran/iesen

Perfect	Perfect	Pluperfect
habría estado	haya estado	hub-iera/iese estado

GERUND	PAST PARTICIPLE	IMPERATIVE
estando	estado	está, estad
		esté (Vd), estén (Vds)

Estamos en Burgos. *We are in Burgos.*
El Prado está en Madrid. *The Prado is in Madrid.*
Estuve en Berlín en 1982. *I was in Berlin in 1982.*
Estoy leyendo un libro. *I am reading a book.*
Estoy enamorada de Peter. *I'm in love with Peter.*
¿Cómo estás? *How are you?*
Está más viejo. *He looks older.*
Enseguida estará. *It will be ready soon.*

¡Estáte quieto! *Keep still!*
¿Estamos? *Agreed?*
Estoy de vacaciones *I am on holiday.*
Estoy contento/a. *I'm happy.*

Está enfermo. *He's ill.*
Está cansada. *She is tired.*
Está dormida. *She is asleep.*

100 evacuar *to evacuate* (tr.)

INDICATIVE

Present	Imperfect	Perfect
evacuo	evacuaba	he evacuado
evacuas	evacuabas	has evacuado
evacua	evacuaba	ha evacuado
evacuamos	evacuábamos	hemos evacuado
evacuáis	evacuabais	habéis evacuado
evacuan	evacuaban	han evacuado

Future	Pluperfect	Preterite
evacuaré	había evacuado	evacué
evacuarás	habías evacuado	evacuaste
evacuará	había evacuado	evacuó
evacuaremos	habíamos evacuado	evacuamos
evacuaréis	habíais evacuado	evacuasteis
evacuarán	habían evacuado	evacuaron

Future perfect	Past anterior
habré evacuado	hube evacuado

CONDITIONAL

SUBJUNCTIVE

Present	Present	Imperfect
evacuaría	evacue	evacu-ara/ase
evacuarías	evacues	evacu-aras/ases
evacuaría	evacue	evacu-ara/ase
evacuaríamos	evacuemos	evacu-áramos/ásemos
evacuaríais	evacuéis	evacu-arais/aseis
evacuarían	evacuen	evacu-aran/asen

Perfect	Perfect	Pluperfect
habría evacuado	haya evacuado	hub-iera/iese evacuado

GERUND

PAST PARTICIPLE

IMPERATIVE

GERUND	PAST PARTICIPLE	IMPERATIVE
evacuando	evacuado	evacua, evacuad
		evacue (Vd), evacuen (Vds)

Hay que evacuar el edificio. *We must evacuate the building.*
Están evacuando a los heridos. *They are taking the wounded out.*
Evacuaré el recipiente mañana. *I shall empty the container tomorrow.*
Está evacuando cenizas. *He is raking out ashes.*
Peter va a evacuar la máquina. *Peter is going to drain the engine.*

la evacuación *evacuation*
el/la evacuado/a *evacuee*
el evacuatorio *public lavatory*
el evacuante *diuretic, evacuant*

el evacuador *evacuator; wasteway,*
escape, spillway
evacuativo/a *evacuative, purge,*
purgative

101 **fregar** *to wash up, scrub* (tr.)

INDICATIVE

Present	Imperfect	Perfect
friego	fregaba	he fregado
friegas	fregabas	has fregado
friega	fregaba	ha fregado
fregamos	fregábamos	hemos fregado
fregáis	fregabais	habéis fregado
friegan	fregaban	han fregado

Future	Pluperfect	Preterite
fregaré	había fregado	fregué
fregarás	habías fregado	fregaste
fregará	había fregado	fregó
fregaremos	habíamos fregado	fregamos
fregaréis	habíais fregado	fregasteis
fregarán	habían fregado	fregaron

Future perfect	Past anterior
habré fregado	hube fregado

CONDITIONAL · SUBJUNCTIVE

Present	Present	Imperfect
fregaría	friegue	freg-ara/ase
fregarías	friegues	freg-aras/ases
fregaría	friegue	freg-ara/ase
fregaríamos	freguemos	freg-áramos/ásemos
fregaríais	freguéis	freg-arais/aseis
fregarían	frieguen	freg-aran/asen

Perfect	Perfect	Pluperfect
habría fregado	haya fregado	hub-iera/iese fregado

GERUND	PAST PARTICIPLE	IMPERATIVE
fregando	fregado	friega, fregad
		friegue (Vd), frieguen (Vds)

¿**Has fregado los platos?** *Have you done the washing-up?*
Me toca fregar mañana. *Tomorrow is my turn to do the washing-up.*
Tienes que fregar el suelo. *You are to mop the floor.*
Están fregando las paredes. *They are scrubbing the walls.*
¡No me friegues! *Stop bothering me!*
Está fregando a los niños. *He is pestering the children.*
Había fregación en la sala. *There was some friction in the room.*

la fregada *nuisance, misfortune*
el/la fregadero/a *sink, scullery;*
 nuisance, annoyance
el fregador *sink, dishcloth, scourer*

el fregasuelos *mop, cleaner*
la fregona *mop, cleaner, skivvy*
el friegaplatos *dishwasher*
el fregado, la fregadura *scrubbing*

102 freír to fry (tr.)

INDICATIVE

Present	Imperfect	Perfect
frío	freía	he frito
fríes	freías	has frito
fríe	freía	ha frito
freímos	freíamos	hemos frito
freís	freíais	habéis frito
fríen	freían	han frito

Future	Pluperfect	Preterite
freiré	había frito	freí
freirás	habías frito	freíste
freirá	había frito	frió
freiremos	habíamos frito	freímos
freiréis	habías frito	freísteis
freirán	habían frito	frieron

Future perfect	Past anterior	
habré frito	hube frito	

CONDITIONAL · SUBJUNCTIVE

Present	Present	Imperfect
freiría	fría	fr-iera/iese
freirías	frías	fr-ieras/ieses
freiría	fría	fr-iera/iese
freiríamos	friamos	fr-iéramos/iésemos
freirías	friáis	fr-ierais/ieseis
freirían	frían	fr-ieran/iesen

Perfect	Perfect	Pluperfect
habría frito	haya frito	hub-iera/iese frito

GERUND	PAST PARTICIPLE	IMPERATIVE
friendo	freído/frito	fríe, freíd
		fría (Vd), frían (Vds)

Voy a freír las patatas. *I am going to fry the potatoes.*
¿Has frito la carne? *Have you fried the meat?*
No lo has frito bastante. *You have not fried it enough.*
Al freír será el reír. *The proof of the pudding is in the eating.*
¡Vete a freír espárragos! *Go to hell!*
Me frío de calor. *I am extremely hot.*
Se la he frito a Carlos. *I have deceived Carlos.*
¡Me tienes frito! *I am fed up with you!*

la freidera *frying pan, fryer*	**frito/a** *fried*
la fritada *fried dish*	**las fritillas** *fritters*
la freiduría de pescado *fried fish shop*	**el/la freidor(a)** *one who fries*

103 gobernar *to govern, rule* (tr./intr.)

INDICATIVE

Present	Imperfect	Perfect
gobierno	gobernaba	he gobernado
gobiernas	gobernabas	has gobernado
gobierna	gobernaba	ha gobernado
gobernamos	gobernábamos	hemos gobernado
gobernáis	gobernabais	habéis gobernado
gobiernan	gobernaban	han gobernado

Future	Pluperfect	Preterite
gobernaré	había gobernado	goberné
gobernarás	habías gobernado	gobernaste
gobernará	había gobernado	gobernó
gobernaremos	habíamos gobernado	gobernamos
gobernaréis	habíais gobernado	gobernasteis
gobernarán	habían gobernado	gobernaron

Future perfect	Past anterior
habré gobernado	hube gobernado

CONDITIONAL / SUBJUNCTIVE

Present	Present	Imperfect
gobernaría	gobierne	gobern-ara/ase
gobernarías	gobiernes	gobern-aras/ases
gobernaría	gobierne	gobern-ara/ase
gobernaríamos	gobernemos	gobern-áramos/ásemos
gobernaríais	gobernéis	gobern-arais/aseis
gobernarían	gobiernen	gobern-aran/asen

Perfect	Perfect	Pluperfect
habría gobernado	haya gobernado	hub-iera/iese gobernado

GERUND	PAST PARTICIPLE	IMPERATIVE
gobernando	gobernado	gobierna, gobernad
		gobierne (Vd), gobiernen (Vds)

La madre gobierna esta familia. *It is the mother who rules this family.*
Franco gobernó desde 1939. *Franco ruled from 1939.*
Le gobierna su mujer. *His wife rules him.*
No sabe gobernar. *She doesn't know how to behave.*
¿Sabes gobernar el barco? *Do you know how to steer the ship?*

la gobernanta *governess*
el gobernante *ruler, governor*
el gobierno *government; steering, helm*
el gobierno doméstico *housekeeping*
el gobernador *ruler*

la gobernación *governing*
El Ministerio de la Gobernación
Home Office
El Ministro de la Gobernación
Home Secretary

104 haber to have (tr.) (aux.)

INDICATIVE

Present	Imperfect	Perfect
he	había	he habido
has	habías	has habido
ha	había	ha habido
hemos	habíamos	hemos habido
habéis	habíais	habéis habido
han	habían	han habido

Future	Pluperfect	Preterite
habré	había habido	hube
habrás	habías habido	hubiste
habrá	había habido	hubo
habremos	habíamos habido	hubimos
habréis	habíais habido	hubisteis
habrán	habían habido	hubieron

Future perfect	Past anterior	
habré habido	hube habido	

CONDITIONAL / SUBJUNCTIVE

Present	Present	Imperfect
habría	haya	hub-iera/iese
habrías	hayas	hub-ieras/ieses
habría	haya	hub-iera/iese
habríamos	hayamos	hub-iéramos/iésemos
habríais	hayáis	hub-ierais/ieseis
habrían	hayan	hub-ieran/iesen

Perfect	Perfect	Pluperfect
habría habido	haya habido	hub-iera/iese habido

GERUND	PAST PARTICIPLE	IMPERATIVE
habiendo	habido	hé, habed
		haya (Vd), hayan (Vds)

Hemos comido. *We have eaten.*
Habíamos comido. *We had eaten.*
Habremos comido. *We shall have eaten.*
Hay dos libros en la mesa. *There are two books on the table.*
Hay un libro en la silla. *There is a book on the chair.*
¿Habrá tiempo? *Will there be time?*
Tomaré lo que haya. *I'll have whatever is going.*
La baja de temperatura habida ayer. *The fall in temperature recorded yesterday.*
He de hacerlo. *I have to do it.*
Ha de llegar mañana. *He's due to arrive tomorrow.*
Han de ser las 2. *It must be 2 o'clock.*
Hay que hacerlo. *It has to be done.*
¿Qué hay? *What's up?*
No lo hay. *There isn't any.*
No hay de qué. *Don't mention it.*

105 hablar *to speak, talk* (tr./intr.)

INDICATIVE

Present	Imperfect	Perfect
hablo	hablaba	he hablado
hablas	hablabas	has hablado
habla	hablaba	ha hablado
hablamos	hablábamos	hemos hablado
habláis	hablabais	habéis hablado
hablan	hablaban	han hablado

Future	Pluperfect	Preterite
hablaré	había hablado	hablé
hablarás	habías hablado	hablaste
hablará	había hablado	habló
hablaremos	habíamos hablado	hablamos
hablaréis	habíais hablado	hablasteis
hablarán	habían hablado	hablaron

Future perfect	Past anterior
habré hablado	hube hablado

CONDITIONAL / SUBJUNCTIVE

Present	Present	Imperfect
hablaría	hable	habl-ara/ase
hablarías	hables	habl-aras/ases
hablaría	hable	habl-ara/ase
hablaríamos	hablemos	habl-áramos/ásemos
hablaríais	habléis	habl-arais/aseis
hablarían	hablen	habl-aran/asen

Perfect	Perfect	Pluperfect
habría hablado	haya hablado	hub-iera/iese hablado

GERUND	PAST PARTICIPLE	IMPERATIVE
hablando	hablado	habla, hablad
		hable (Vd), hablen (Vds)

¿Hablan español? *Do you speak Spanish?*
¿Hablaste con Juan? *Did you talk to Juan?*
¿Quién habla? *Who's calling? (on phone)*
Eso es hablar por hablar. *That's just wasted breath.*
Susanita habla por los codos. *Susanita talks nineteen to the dozen.*
Se habla inglés. *English spoken.*
¡Ni hablar! *Nonsense! Out of the question!*

el habla *speech*
hablador(a) *talkative, chatterbox, gossipy*
las habladas *boasting, bragging*
las habladurías *gossip, nasty talk*

el/la hablante *talking, speaker*
el hablista *good speaker*
la hablilla *rumour, tittle-tattle*
hablantín = hablanchín *talkative*

106 hacer *to do, make* (tr./intr.)

INDICATIVE

Present	Imperfect	Perfect
hago	hacía	he hecho
haces	hacías	has hecho
hace	hacía	ha hecho
hacemos	hacíamos	hemos hecho
hacéis	hacíais	habéis hecho
hacen	hacían	han hecho

Future	Pluperfect	Preterite
haré	había hecho	hice
harás	habías hecho	hiciste
hará	había hecho	hizo
haremos	habíamos hecho	hicimos
haréis	habíais hecho	hicisteis
harán	habían hecho	hicieron

Future perfect	Past anterior
habré hecho	hube hecho

CONDITIONAL / SUBJUNCTIVE

Present	Present	Imperfect
haría	haga	hic-iera/iese
harías	hagas	hic-ieras/ieses
haría	haga	hic-iera/iese
haríamos	hagamos	hic-iéramos/iésemos
haríais	hagáis	hic-ierais/ieseis
harían	hagan	hic-ieran/iesen

Perfect	Perfect	Pluperfect
habría hecho	haya hecho	hub-iera/iese hecho

GERUND	PAST PARTICIPLE	IMPERATIVE
haciendo	hecho	haz, haced
		haga (Vd), hagan (Vds)

Estoy haciendo café. *I'm making some coffee.*
No sabe qué hacer. *She doesn't know what to do.*
¿Qué haces ahí? *What are you doing there?*
Se hace enfermero. *He's becoming a nurse.*
Se hizo cortar el pelo. *She had her hair cut.*
Hace calor. *It's hot.*
Hace dos años. *Two years ago.*
Vivo aquí desde hace un mes. *I've been living here for a month.*
¡La has hecho buena! *A fine mess you've made!*

hacendoso/a *industrious, hard working*
el hecho *fact, deed*
hecho/a *agreed, finished, done, made*

hacedero/a *practicable, feasible*
el/la hacedor(a) *maker*
hacerse *to become, turn; pretend*

107 helar *to freeze, chill* (tr./intr.)

INDICATIVE

Present	Imperfect	Perfect
hielo	helaba	he helado
hielas	helabas	has helado
hiela	helaba	ha helado
helamos	helábamos	hemos helado
heláis	helabais	habéis helado
hielan	helaban	han helado

Future	Pluperfect	Preterite
helaré	había helado	helé
helarás	habías helado	helaste
helará	había helado	heló
helaremos	habíamos helado	helamos
helaréis	habíais helado	helasteis
helarán	habían helado	helaron

Future perfect	Past anterior
habré helado	hube helado

CONDITIONAL · SUBJUNCTIVE

Present	Present	Imperfect
helaría	hiele	hel-ara/ase
helarías	hieles	hel-aras/ases
helaría	hiele	hel-ara/ase
helaríamos	helemos	hel-áramos/ásemos
helaríais	heléis	hel-arais/aseis
helarían	hielen	hel-aran/asen

Perfect	Perfect	Pluperfect
habría helado	haya helado	hub-iera/iese helado

GERUND	PAST PARTICIPLE	IMPERATIVE
helando	helado	hiela, helad
		hiele (Vd), hielen (Vds)

Va a helar. *It's going to freeze.*
¿Helará mañana? *Is there going to be a frost tomorrow?*
Voy a helar la fruta. *I'm going to freeze the fruit.*
¿Se helarán las plantas? *Will the plants freeze?*
Estoy helada. *I'm frozen.*
Se ha helado el agua. *The water has frozen.*
Me fui porque me estaba helando. *I left because I was frozen.*

la helada *frost*
la helada tardía *late frost*
el helado *ice-cream*

el hielo *ice*
la heladería *ice-cream shop*
el helero *glacier*

108 herir *to wound, hurt, harm* (tr.)

INDICATIVE

Present	Imperfect	Perfect
hiero	hería	he herido
hieres	herías	has herido
hiere	hería	ha herido
herimos	heríamos	hemos herido
herís	heríais	habéis herido
hieren	herían	han herido

Future	Pluperfect	Preterite
heriré	había herido	herí
herirás	habías herido	heriste
herirá	había herido	hirió
heriremos	habíamos herido	herimos
heriréis	habíais herido	heristeis
herirán	habían herido	hirieron

Future perfect	Past anterior	
habré herido	hube herido	

CONDITIONAL / SUBJUNCTIVE

Present	Present	Imperfect
heriría	hiera	hir-iera/iese
herirías	hieras	hir-ieras/ieses
heriría	hiera	hir-iera/iese
heriríamos	hiramos	hir-iéramos/iésemos
heriríais	hiráis	hir-ierais/ieseis
herirían	hieran	hir-ieran/iesen

Perfect	Perfect	Pluperfect
habría herido	haya herido	hub-iera/iese herido

GERUND	PAST PARTICIPLE	IMPERATIVE
hiriendo	herido	hiere, herid
		hiera (Vd), hieran (Vds)

Ha sido herido en el brazo. *He has been wounded in the arm.*
Se ha herido la pierna. *She has hurt her leg.*
El cristal le hirió en la cabeza. *The glass injured him in the head.*
El accidente hirió su confianza. *The accident dented his confidence.*
Esos ruidos me hieren los oídos. *Those noises hurt my ears.*
Ese color me hiere la vista. *That colour hurts my eyes.*

la herida wound
herido/a wounded
hiriente wounding, cutting

109 **hervir** *to boil* (intr.)

INDICATIVE

Present	Imperfect	Perfect
hiervo	hervía	he hervido
hierves	hervías	has hervido
hierve	hervía	ha hervido
hervimos	hervíamos	hemos hervido
hervís	hervíais	habéis hervido
hierven	hervían	han hervido

Future	Pluperfect	Preterite
herviré	había hervido	herví
hervirás	habías hervido	herviste
hervirá	había hervido	hirvió
herviremos	habíamos hervido	hervimos
herviréis	habíais hervido	hervisteis
hervirán	habían hervido	hirvieron

Future perfect	Past anterior
habré hervido	hube hervido

CONDITIONAL

SUBJUNCTIVE

Present	Present	Imperfect
herviría	hierva	hirv-iera/iese
hervirías	hiervas	hirv-ieras/ieses
herviría	hierva	hirv-iera/iese
herviríamos	hirvamos	hirv-iéramos/iésemos
herviríais	hirváis	hirv-ierais/ieseis
hervirían	hiervan	hirv-ieran/iesen

Perfect	Perfect	Pluperfect
habría hervido	haya hervido	hub-iera/iese hervido

GERUND	PAST PARTICIPLE	IMPERATIVE
hirviendo	hervido	hierve, hervid
		hierva (Vd), hiervan (Vds)

Hierve el agua. *Boil the water.*
Herviré las verduras antes de cenar. *I'll boil the vegetables before supper.*
Lo herviremos a fuego lento. *We'll simmer it.*
Hervir y dejar reposar. *Boil and allow to settle.*
Me hierve la sangre. *I get very worked up.*
La alfombra hervía de pulgas. *The carpet was swarming with fleas.*
La tienda hervía de gente. *The shop was very crowded.*

el hervor *boiling; passion*
levantar al hervor *bring to the boil*
hervir a borbotones *to boil fast*

el hervidor *kettle, boiler*
el hervidero *boiling, bubbling; hot spring*

110 huir *to run away, escape* (tr./intr.)

INDICATIVE

Present	Imperfect	Perfect
huyo	huía	he huido
huyes	huías	has huido
huye	huía	ha huido
huimos	huíamos	hemos huido
huís	huíais	habéis huido
huyen	huían	han huido

Future	Pluperfect	Preterite
huiré	había huido	huí
huirás	habías huido	huiste
huirá	había huido	huyó
huiremos	habíamos huido	huimos
huiréis	habíais huido	huisteis
huirán	habían huido	huyeron

Future perfect	Past anterior
habré huido	hube huido

CONDITIONAL / SUBJUNCTIVE

Present	Present	Imperfect
huiría	huya	hu-yera/yese
huirías	huyas	hu-yeras/yeses
huiría	huya	hu-yera/yese
huiríamos	huyamos	hu-yéramos/yésemos
huirías	huyáis	hu-yerais/yeseis
huirían	huyan	hu-yeran/yesen

Perfect	Perfect	Pluperfect
habría huido	haya huido	hub-iera/iese huido

GERUND / PAST PARTICIPLE / IMPERATIVE

GERUND	PAST PARTICIPLE	IMPERATIVE
huyendo	huido	huye, huid
		huya (Vd), huyan (Vds)

Siempre huye del peligro. *He always runs away from danger.*
Huyen de la guerra. *They are running away from the war.*
El prisionero huyó de la cárcel. *The prisoner escaped from jail.*
El pájaro huirá del nido. *The bird will flee the nest.*
Huyeron a la desbandada. *They escaped in a mad rush.*

¡Huye! *Run!*
la huida *flight, escape*
huidizo *shy, elusive, receding*

huido/a *fugitive, runaway*
huidero *fleeting, short lived, transitory*

111 impedir *to impede, hinder, prevent* (tr.)

INDICATIVE

Present	Imperfect	Perfect
impido	impedía	he impedido
impides	impedías	has impedido
impide	impedía	ha impedido
impedimos	impedíamos	hemos impedido
impedís	impedíais	habéis impedido
impiden	impedían	han impedido

Future	Pluperfect	Preterite
impediré	había impedido	impedí
impedirás	habías impedido	impediste
impedirá	había impedido	impidió
impediremos	habíamos impedido	impedimos
impediréis	habíais impedido	impedisteis
impedirán	habían impedido	impidieron

Future perfect	Past anterior
habré impedido	hube impedido

CONDITIONAL | SUBJUNCTIVE

Present	Present	Imperfect
impediría	impida	impid-iera/iese
impedirías	impidas	impid-ieras/ieses
impediría	impida	impid-iera/iese
impediríamos	impidamos	impid-iéramos/iésemos
impediríais	impidáis	impid-ierais/ieseis
impedirían	impidan	impid-ieran/iesen

Perfect	Perfect	Pluperfect
habría impedido	haya impedido	hub-iera/iese impedido

GERUND	PAST PARTICIPLE	IMPERATIVE
impidiendo	impedido	impide, impedid
		impida (Vd), impidan (Vds)

Sus obligaciones le impiden venir. *His obligations prevent him from coming.*
Quiso impedirme hablar. *He tried to stop me from talking.*
Tratamos de impedir el accidente. *We tried to prevent the accident.*
Me veo impedida para ir. *I'm prevented from going.*
Me impidió hacerlo. *He stopped me from doing it.*
Hay que impedir el tráfico. *We have to block the traffic.*

impedido/a *crippled, disabled*
impeditivo *preventative*
el impedimento *impediment, obstacle*
los impedimentos *handicaps, impairments, impediments*

impedimento común *common bar, general ban*
la impedimenta *impedimenta*

112 **invertir** *to turn upside down; to invest* (tr.)

INDICATIVE

Present	Imperfect	Perfect
invierto	invertía	he invertido
inviertes	invertías	has invertido
invierte	invertía	ha invertido
invertimos	invertíamos	hemos invertido
invertís	invertíais	habéis invertido
invierten	invertían	han invertido

Future	Pluperfect	Preterite
invertiré	había invertido	invertí
invertirás	habías invertido	invertiste
invertirá	había invertido	invirtió
invertiremos	habíamos invertido	invertimos
invertiréis	habíais invertido	invertisteis
invertirán	habían invertido	invirtieron

Future perfect	Past anterior	
habré invertido	hube invertido	

CONDITIONAL · SUBJUNCTIVE

Present	Present	Imperfect
invertiría	invierta	invirt-iera/ises
invertirías	inviertas	invirt-ieras/ieses
invertiría	invierta	invirt-iera/iese
invertiríamos	invirtamos	invirt-iéramos/iésemos
invertirías	invirtáis	invirt-ierais/ieseis
invertirían	inviertan	invirt-ieran/iesen

Perfect	Perfect	Pluperfect
habría invertido	haya invertido	hub-iera/iese invertido

GERUND	PAST PARTICIPLE	IMPERATIVE
invirtiendo	invertido	invierte, invertid
		invierta (Vd), inviertan (Vds)

He invertido los papeles. *I've turned the papers upside down.*
Invierte el vaso. *Turn the glass upside down.*
Invertiremos la marcha. *We'll reverse.*
He invertido mi capital en acciones. *I have invested my capital in shares.*
Pienso invertir las ganancias en el negocio. *I'll plough back the profits into the business.*
Invirtieron dos días en el viaje. *They spent two days on the journey.*
No sé en qué invierte sus horas libres. *I don't know what he does with spare time.*

inverso *inverse, inverted*
invertido/a *reversed, upside down*
a la inversa *the other way round*
la inversión *reversal; investment*

la inversión de capitales *capital investment*
el inversionista *investor*

113 investir *to invest, confer* (tr.)

INDICATIVE

Present	Imperfect	Perfect
invisto	investía	he investido
invistes	investías	has investido
inviste	investía	ha investido
investimos	investíamos	hemos investido
investís	investíais	habéis investido
invisten	investían	han investido

Future	Pluperfect	Preterite
investiré	había investido	investí
investirás	habías investido	investiste
investirá	había investido	invistió
investiremos	habíamos investido	investimos
investiréis	habíais investido	investisteis
investirán	habían investido	invistieron

Future perfect	Past anterior
habré investido	hube investido

CONDITIONAL / SUBJUNCTIVE

Present	Present	Imperfect
investiría	invista	invist-iera/iese
investirías	invistas	invist-ieras/ieses
investiría	invista	invist-iera/iese
investiríamos	invistamos	invist-iéramos/iésemos
investiríais	invistáis	invist-ierais/ieseis
investirían	invistan	invist-ieran/iesen

Perfect	Perfect	Pluperfect
habría investido	haya investido	hub-iera/iese investido

GERUND	PAST PARTICIPLE	IMPERATIVE
invistiendo	investido	inviste, investid
		invista (Vd), invistan (Vds)

Ha sido investida de Doctor Honoris Causa. *She has had a Doctor Honoris Causa conferred on her.*
Le invistieron en 1938. *He was invested in 1938.*
Te voy a investir de poderes. *I shall invest you with powers.*
Te investiré una misión. *I shall entrust you with a mission.*
Quiere ser investido con derechos legales. *He wants to be invested with legal rights.*

investido/a *invested*	**investido de autoridad** *authorized*
el investido *conferee*	**la investidura** *investiture*

114 ir *to go* (intr.)

INDICATIVE

Present	Imperfect	Perfect
voy	iba	he ido
vas	ibas	has ido
va	iba	ha ido
vamos	íbamos	hemos ido
váis	ibais	habéis ido
van	iban	han ido

Future	Pluperfect	Preterite
iré	había ido	fui
irás	habías ido	fuiste
irá	había ido	fue
iremos	habíamos ido	fuimos
iréis	habíais ido	fuisteis
irán	habían ido	fueron

Future perfect	Past anterior
habré ido	hube ido

CONDITIONAL

SUBJUNCTIVE

Present	Present	Imperfect
iría	vaya	fu-era/ese
irías	vayas	fu-eras/eses
iría	vaya	fu-era/ese
iríamos	vayamos	fu-éramos/ésemos
iríais	vayáis	fu-erais/eseis
irían	vayan	fu-eran/esen

Perfect	Perfect	Pluperfect
habría ido	haya ido	hub-iera/iese ido

GERUND	PAST PARTICIPLE	IMPERATIVE
yendo	ido	ve, id
		vaya (Vd), vayan (Vds)

Voy a Madrid cada semana. *I go to Madrid every week.*
Fuimos al cine. *We went to the cinema.*
Iremos a la playa. *We'll go to the beach.*
Va en tren hasta Sevilla. *She goes to Seville by train.*
Va para médico. *He is going to become a doctor.*
Voy de compras. *I'm going shopping.*
Ni me va ni me viene. *I couldn't care less.*
Va mucho en ello. *A lot depends on it.*
¿Cómo te va? *How are things?*
¿Me va bien esto? *Does this suit me?*

¡Qué va! *Rubbish! Not at all!*   **la ida** *going, departure*
¡Vaya! *Well!, there!, I say!, I never!*   **de ida y vuelta** *return*

115 jugar to play (tr./intr.)

INDICATIVE

Present	Imperfect	Perfect
juego	jugaba	he jugado
juegas	jugabas	has jugado
juega	jugaba	ha jugado
jugamos	jugábamos	hemos jugado
jugáis	jugabais	habéis jugado
juegan	jugaban	han jugado

Future	Pluperfect	Preterite
jugaré	había jugado	jugué
jugarás	habías jugado	jugaste
jugará	había jugado	jugó
jugaremos	habíamos jugado	jugamos
jugaréis	habíais jugado	jugasteis
jugarán	habían jugado	jugaron

Future perfect	Past anterior
habré jugado	hube jugado

CONDITIONAL · SUBJUNCTIVE

Present	Present	Imperfect
jugaría	juegue	jug-ara/ase
jugarías	juegues	jug-aras/ases
jugaría	juegue	jug-ara/ase
jugaríamos	juguemos	jug-áramos/ásemos
jugaríais	juguéis	jug-arais/aseis
jugarían	jueguen	jug-aran/asen

Perfect	Perfect	Pluperfect
habría jugado	haya jugado	hub-iera/iese jugado

GERUND	PAST PARTICIPLE	IMPERATIVE
jugando	jugado	juega, jugad
		juegue (Vd), jueguen (Vds)

Juega al tenis. *He plays tennis.*
Jugamos al ajedrez. *We play chess.*
El partido se juega hoy. *The match is being played today.*
Lo jugó todo. *He gambled it all away.*
Se han jugado 600 €. *They staked 600 euros.*
¡Me la han jugado! *They've played a trick on me!*
Solamente está jugando contigo. *He is trifling with you.*
¿Quién juega? *Whose move is it?*

la jugada *game, play*	**el juego sucio** *foul play*
hacer una jugada *to make a move*	**el juego limpio** *fair play*
el juego *game*	**poner en juego** *to set in motion*
jugarse *to gamble, bet*	**juguetón/juguetona** *playful*

116 lavarse *to wash oneself* (r.)

INDICATIVE

Present	Imperfect	Perfect
me lavo	me lavaba	me he lavado
te lavas	te lavabas	te has lavado
se lava	se lavaba	se ha lavado
nos lavamos	nos lavábamos	nos hemos lavado
os laváis	os lavabais	os habéis lavado
se lavan	se lavaban	se han lavado

Future	Pluperfect	Preterite
me lavaré	me había lavado	me lavé
te lavarás	te habías lavado	te lavaste
se lavará	se había lavado	se lavó
nos lavaremos	nos habíamos lavado	nos lavamos
os lavaréis	os habíais lavado	os lavasteis
se lavarán	se habían lavado	se lavaron

Future perfect	Past anterior
me habré lavado	me hube lavado

CONDITIONAL   SUBJUNCTIVE

Present	Present	Imperfect
me lavaría	me lave	me lav-ara/ase
te lavarías	te laves	te lav-aras/ases
se lavaría	se lave	se lav-ara/ase
nos lavaríamos	nos lavemos	nos lav-áramos/ásemos
os lavaríais	os lavéis	os lav-arais/aseis
se lavarían	se laven	se lav-aran/asen

Perfect	Perfect	Pluperfect
me habría lavado	me haya lavado	me hub-iera/iese lavado

GERUND   PAST PARTICIPLE   IMPERATIVE

GERUND	PAST PARTICIPLE	IMPERATIVE
lavándose	lavado	lávate, lavaos
		lávese (Vd), lávense (Vds)

Me lavo las manos antes de comer. *I wash my hands before meals.*
Sara se lava el pelo tres veces por semana. *Sara washes her hair three times a week.*
Nos lavamos la ropa en el jardin. *We wash our clothes in the garden.*
Te lavarás aunque no quieras. *You'll wash whether you like it or not.*
Yo me lavo las manos de esto. *I wash my hands of this.*

lavable *washable*
el lavabo *sink, washbasin, toilet*
el lavadero *laundry*
la lavadora *washing machine*
la lavandería *launderette*

el lavaplatos *dishwater*
el lavavajillas *dishwasher (machine)*
la lavativa *enema, nuisance, bore*
lavar en seco *dry clean*

117 leer *to read* (tr./intr.)

INDICATIVE

Present	Imperfect	Perfect
leo	leía	he leído
lees	leías	has leído
lee	leía	ha leído
leemos	leíamos	hemos leído
leéis	leíais	habéis leído
leen	leían	han leído

Future	Pluperfect	Preterite
leeré	había leído	leí
leerás	habías leído	leíste
leerá	había leído	leyó
leeremos	habíamos leído	leímos
leeréis	habíais leído	leísteis
leerán	habían leído	leyeron

Future perfect	Past anterior
habré leído	hube leído

CONDITIONAL / SUBJUNCTIVE

Present	Present	Imperfect
leería	lea	le-yera/yese
leerías	leas	le-yeras/yeses
leería	lea	le-yera/yese
leeríamos	leamos	le-yéramos/yésemos
leeríais	leáis	le-yerais/yeseis
leerían	lean	le-yeran/yesen

Perfect	Perfect	Pluperfect
habría leído	haya leído	hub-iera/iese leído

GERUND	PAST PARTICIPLE	IMPERATIVE
leyendo	leído	lee, leed
		lea (Vd), lean (Vds)

Estoy leyendo una novela policíaca. *I'm reading a detective novel.*
Leo todas las noches. *I read every night.*
¿Te gusta leer? *Do you like reading?*
Elvira sabe leer en la boca. *Elvira can lip-read.*
Debes leer entre las líneas. *You ought to read between the lines.*
No te va a leer la mano. *She isn't going to read your palm.*

al que leyere estas líneas *to the reader*
la lectura *reading*
dar una lectura *to deliver a lecture*
el/la lector(a) *reader*

el lector de fichas *card reader*
la lectura de marcas *mark sensing*
 (computing)
la lección *lesson, class*

118 limpiar *to clean, cleanse* (tr.)

INDICATIVE

Present	Imperfect	Perfect
limpio	limpiaba	he limpiado
limpias	limpiabas	has limpiado
limpia	limpiaba	ha limpiado
limpiamos	limpiábamos	hemos limpiado
limpiáis	limpiabais	habéis limpiado
limpian	limpiaban	han limpiado

Future	Pluperfect	Preterite
limpiaré	había limpiado	limpié
limpiarás	habías limpiado	limpiaste
limpiará	había limpiado	limpió
limpiaremos	habíamos limpiado	limpiamos
limpiaréis	habíais limpiado	limpiasteis
limpiarán	habían limpiado	limpiaron

Future perfect	Past anterior
habré limpiado	hube limpiado

CONDITIONAL | SUBJUNCTIVE

Present	Persent	Imperfect
impiaría	limpie	limpi-ara/ase
limpiarías	limpies	limpi-aras/ases
limpiaría	limpie	limpi-ara/ase
limpiaríamos	limpiemos	limpi-áramos/ásemos
limpiarías	limpiéis	limpi-arais/aseis
limpiarían	limpien	limpi-aran/asen

Perfect	Perfect	Pluperfect
habría limpiado	haya limpiado	hub-iera/iese limpiado

GERUND | PAST PARTICIPLE | IMPERATIVE

limpiando	limpiado	limpia, limpiad
		limpie (Vd), limpien (Vds)

Tenemos que limpiar los cristales. *We have to clean the windows.*
Limpia el suelo. *Mop the floor.*
Se ha limpiado los zapatos. *She has cleaned her shoes.*
Miguel lo limpió ayer. *Miguel cleaned it yesterday.*
La policía quiere limpiar el juego. *The police want to clean out gambling.*
Limpiar en seco. *Dry clean only.*
Me limpiaron el bolso en el metro. *I had my bag stolen on the underground.*

la limpieza *cleaning, housework*	**el limpiametales** *metal polish*
limpio/a *clean*	**el limpiaplicador** *cotton-bud*
el limpiacristales *window cleaner*	**el limpiaparabrisas** *windscreen wiper*

119 llegar *to arrive, reach* (tr./intr.)

INDICATIVE

Present	Imperfect	Perfect
llego	llegaba	he llegado
llegas	llegabas	has llegado
llega	llegaba	ha llegado
llegamos	llegábamos	hemos llegado
llegáis	llegabais	habéis llegado
llegan	llegaban	han llegado

Future	Pluperfect	Preterite
llegaré	había llegado	llegué
llegarás	habías llegado	llegaste
llegará	había llegado	llegó
llegaremos	habíamos llegado	llegamos
llegaréis	habíais llegado	llegasteis
llegarán	habían llegado	llegaron

Future perfect	Past anterior
habré llegado	hube llegado

CONDITIONAL / SUBJUNCTIVE

Present	Present	Imperfect
llegaría	llegue	lleg-ara/ase
llegarías	llegues	lleg-aras/ases
llegaría	llegue	lleg-ara/ase
llegaríamos	lleguemos	lleg-áramos/ásemos
llegaríais	lleguéis	lleg-arais/aseis
llegarían	lleguen	lleg-aran/asen

Perfect	Perfect	Pluperfect
habría llegado	haya llegado	hub-iera/iese llegado

GERUND	PAST PARTICIPLE	IMPERATIVE
llegando	llegado	llega, llegad
		llegue (Vd), lleguen (Vds)

Llegaremos a las nueve. *We'll arrive at nine.*
Llegué a Madrid el martes. *I arrived in Madrid on Tuesday.*
No llegan a 40. *There are less than 40.*
No llega el cable. *The cable doesn't reach.*
Llegaron a las manos. *They came to blows.*
No me llega el dinero. *I don't have enough money.*
Por fin llegó a hacerlo. *In the end he managed to do it.*
Llegará a ser el jefe. *He'll end up as the boss.*

la llegada *arrival*
llegar a un acuerdo *to reach an agreement*
llegar a las armas *to resort to arms*

Está al llegar. *She is about to arrive.*
Miguel llegará lejos. *Miguel will go far.*

120 llorar *to cry, weep* (tr./intr.)

INDICATIVE

Present	Imperfect	Perfect
lloro	lloraba	he llorado
lloras	llorabas	has llorado
llora	lloraba	ha llorado
lloramos	llorábamos	hemos llorado
lloráis	llorabais	habéis llorado
lloran	lloraban	han llorado

Future	Pluperfect	Preterite
lloraré	había llorado	lloré
llorarás	habías llorado	lloraste
llorará	había llorado	lloró
lloraremos	habíamos llorado	lloramos
lloraréis	habías llorado	llorasteis
llorarán	habían llorado	lloraron

Future perfect	Past anterior
habré llorado	hube llorado

CONDITIONAL SUBJUNCTIVE

Present	Present	Imperfect
lloraría	llore	llor-ara/ase
llorarías	llores	llor-aras/ases
lloraría	llore	llor-ara/ase
lloraríamos	lloremos	llor-áramos/ásemos
lloraríais	lloréis	llor-arais/aseis
llorarían	lloren	llor-aran/asen

Perfect	Perfect	Pluperfect
habría llorado	haya llorado	hub-iera/iese llorado

GERUND	PAST PARTICIPLE	IMPERATIVE
llorando	llorado	llora, llorad
		llore (Vd), lloren (Vds)

Lloro cuando estoy triste. *I cry when I'm sad.*
¡No llores! *Don't cry!*
Estamos llorando la pérdida de su libertad. *We are crying for their lost freedom.*
Niño que no llora, no mama. *If you don't ask you don't get.*
Ximena lloraba a lágrima viva. *Ximena was crying her eyes out.*
Marta llora como una fuente. *Marta weeps buckets.*

el rey llorado *the late lamented king*　　**el lloro** *weeping, crying*
el/la llorateas *crybaby*　　**llorón/llorona** *weeping, tearful*
lloriquear *to whimper*　　**lloroso** *tearful*

121 llover *to rain* (tr./intr.)

INDICATIVE

Present	Imperfect	Perfect
llueve	llovía	ha llovido

Future	Pluperfect	Preterite
lloverá	había llovido	llovió

Future perfect	Past anterior	
habría llovido	hubo llovido	

CONDITIONAL | ## SUBJUNCTIVE

Present	Present	Imperfect
llovería	llueva	llov-iera/iese

Perfect	Perfect	Pluperfect
habría llovido	haya llovido	hub-iera/iese llovido

GERUND	PAST PARTICIPLE	IMPERATIVE
lloviendo	llovido	

¿Llueve mucho? *Does it rain much?*
Está lloviendo. *It's raining.*
¿Lloverá mañana? *Will it rain tomorrow?*
como llovido del cielo *unexpected, godsend*
llueva o no *come what may, rain or shine*
Siempre que llueve escampa. *Every cloud has a silver lining.*
Nos llovieron regalos encima. *We were showered with gifts.*
Llueve a cántaros/cubos/mares/chuzos. *It's raining cats and dogs.*

la lluvia *rain*
lluvioso/a *rainy, wet*
la llovizna *drizzle*

lloviznar *to drizzle*
lloviznoso *drizzly*

122 **medir** *to measure* (tr.)

INDICATIVE

Present	Imperfect	Perfect
mido	medía	he medido
mides	medías	has medido
mide	medía	ha medido
medimos	medíamos	hemos medido
medís	medíais	habéis medido
miden	medían	han medido

Future	Pluperfect	Preterite
mediré	había medido	medí
medirás	habías medido	mediste
medirá	había medido	midió
mediremos	habíamos medido	medimos
mediréis	habíais medido	medisteis
medirán	habían medido	midieron

Future perfect	Past anterior
habré medido	hube medido

CONDITIONAL	SUBJUNCTIVE	
Present	**Present**	**Imperfect**
mediría	mida	mid-iera/iese
medirías	midas	mid-ieras/ieses
mediría	mida	mid-iera/iese
mediríamos	midamos	mid-iéramos/iésemos
mediríais	midáis	mid-ierais/ieseis
medirían	midan	mid-ieran/iesen

Perfect	Perfect	Pluperfect
habría medido	haya medido	hub-iera/iese medido

GERUND	PAST PARTICIPLE	IMPERATIVE
midiendo	medido	mide, medid
		mida (Vd), midan (Vds)

Mide la tela. *Measure the cloth.*
¿Cómo se mide el cariño? *How can one measure love?*
¿Cuánto mide la habitación? *What are the measurements of the room?*
No lo has medido bien. *You haven't measured it properly.*
Le mide con la vista. *He sizes him up.*
Bush se midió con Hassan. *Bush tested himself against Hassan.*

la medida *measurement*	**medir un terreno** *to survey*
en cierta medida *up to a point*	**el traje a la medida** *made-to-measure suit*
a medida que... *as.../according...*	**medida preventiva** *preventive measure*
pesos y medidas *weights and measures*	**la medición** *measurement*

123 mentir *to lie* (intr.)

INDICATIVE

Present	Imperfect	Perfect
miento	mentía	he mentido
mientes	mentías	has mentido
miente	mentía	ha mentido
mentimos	mentíamos	hemos mentido
mentís	mentíais	habéis mentido
mienten	mentían	han mentido

Future	Pluperfect	Preterite
mentiré	había mentido	mentí
mentirás	habías mentido	mentiste
mentirá	había mentido	mintió
mentiremos	habíamos mentido	mentimos
mentiréis	habíais mentido	mentisteis
mentirán	habían mentido	mintieron

Future perfect	Past anterior
habré mentido	hube mentido

CONDITIONAL / SUBJUNCTIVE

Present	Present	Imperfect
mentiría	mienta	mint-iera/ises
mentirías	mientas	mint-ieras/ieses
mentiría	mienta	mint-iera/iese
mentiríamos	mintamos	mint-iéramos/iésemos
mentiríais	mintáis	mint-ierais/ieseis
mentirían	mientan	mint-ieran/iesen

Perfect	Perfect	Pluperfect
habría mentido	haya mentido	hub-iera/iese mentido

GERUND	PAST PARTICIPLE	IMPERATIVE
mintiendo	mentido	miente, mentid
		mienta (Vd), mientan (Vds)

No mientas. *Don't tell lies.*
Mentí para salir del apuro. *I lied to avoid embarrassment.*
Mintió para conseguir el empleo. *He lied to get the job.*
Mentiremos para que no se enfade. *We'll lie so that he doesn't get angry.*

la mentira *lie, falsehood*
la mentira piadosa *white lie*
la mentirijilla *little lie*
mentiroso/a *liar*

el/la mentirosillo/a *fibber*
el mentidero *gossip shop*
mentido/a *deceiving, false*

124 merendar *to have tea/a snack* (tr./intr.)

INDICATIVE

Present	Imperfect	Perfect
meriendo	merendaba	he merendado
meriendas	merendabas	has merendado
merienda	merendaba	ha merendado
merendamos	merendábamos	hemos merendado
merendáis	merendabais	habéis merendado
meriendan	merendaban	han merendado

Future	Pluperfect	Preterite
merendaré	había merendado	merendé
merendarás	habías merendado	merendaste
merendará	había merendado	merendó
merendaremos	habíamos merendado	merendamos
merendaréis	habíais merendado	merendasteis
merendarán	habían merendado	merendaron

Future perfect	Past anterior
habré merendado	hube merendado

CONDITIONAL · SUBJUNCTIVE

Present	Present	Imperfect
merendaría	meriende	merend-ara/ase
merendarías	meriendes	merend-aras/ases
merendaría	meriende	merend-ara/ase
merendaríamos	merendemos	merend-áramos/ásemos
merendaríais	merendéis	merend-arais/aseis
merendarían	merienden	merend-aran/asen

Perfect	Perfect	Pluperfect
habría merendado	haya merendado	hub-iera/iese merendado

GERUND · PAST PARTICIPLE · IMPERATIVE

GERUND	PAST PARTICIPLE	IMPERATIVE
merendando	merendado	merienda, merendad
		meriende (Vd), merienden (Vds)

Meriendo a las cinco. *I have a snack at five.*
Merendamos pan y chocolate. *We have bread and chocolate for tea.*
Merendó jamón. *He had ham (as a late-afternoon snack).*
¿Qué quieres merendar? *What do you want for your tea?*
Meriendo lo que escribe Miguel. *I look at what Miguel is writing.*
Merienda las cartas de Daniel. *She is peeping at Daniel's cards.*
Se ha merendado su fortuna. *She has squandered her fortune.*

el merendero *picnic spot*
la merienda *tea, afternoon tea, afternoon snack*
merienda cena *early supper (before 8 pm in Spain)*

ir de merienda *to go for a picnic*
juntar meriendas *to join fortunes*

125 moler *to grind, crush, mill* (tr.)

INDICATIVE

Present	Imperfect	Perfect
muelo	molía	he molido
mueles	molías	has molido
muele	molía	ha molido
molemos	molíamos	hemos molido
moléis	molíais	habéis molido
muelen	molían	han molido

Future	Pluperfect	Preterite
moleré	había molido	molí
molerás	habías molido	moliste
molerá	había molido	molió
moleremos	habíamos molido	molimos
moleréis	habíais molido	molisteis
molerán	habían molido	molieron

Future perfect	Past anterior
habré molido	hube molido

CONDITIONAL   SUBJUNCTIVE

Present	Present	Imperfect
molería	muela	mol-iera/iese
molerías	muelas	mol-ieras/ieses
molería	muela	mol-iera/iese
moleríamos	molamos	mol-iéramos/iésemos
moleríais	moláis	mol-ierais/ieseis
molerían	muelan	mol-ieran/iesen

Perfect	Perfect	Pluperfect
habría molido	haya molido	hub-iera/iese molido

GERUND   PAST PARTICIPLE   IMPERATIVE

GERUND	PAST PARTICIPLE	IMPERATIVE
moliendo	molido	muele, moled
		muela (Vd), muelan (Vds)

Me gusta moler el café. *I like grindling my own coffee.*
¿Quieres moler las especias? *Will you grind the spices?*
Molerán la aceituna mañana. *They will crush the olives tomorrow.*
¿Cuándo vas a moler la carne? *When are you going to mince the meat?*
Le molió a palos. *He gave him a beating.*
Estoy molida. *I'm exhausted.*
Me muele con sus comentarios. *He annoys/bores me with his comments.*

el moledor *grinder, roller, bore; grinding, crushing*
la molienda *milling; a nuisance*
el/la molinero/a *miller*

el molino de agua *water mill*
el molino de viento *wind mill*
el molinillo de café *coffee grinder*
el molinillo de carne *mincer*

126 morder *to bite, nip* (tr.)

INDICATIVE

Present	Imperfect	Perfect
muerdo	mordía	he mordido
muerdes	mordías	has mordido
muerde	mordía	ha mordido
mordemos	mordíamos	hemos mordido
mordéis	mordíais	habéis mordido
muerden	mordían	han mordido

Future	Pluperfect	Preterite
morderé	había mordido	mordí
morderás	habías mordido	mordiste
morderá	había mordido	mordió
morderemos	habíamos mordido	mordimos
morderéis	habíais mordido	mordisteis
morderán	habían mordido	mordieron

Future perfect	Past anterior
habré mordido	hube mordido

CONDITIONAL · SUBJUNCTIVE

Present	Present	Imperfect
mordería	muerda	mord-iera/iese
morderías	muerdas	mord-ieras/ieses
mordería	muerda	mord-iera/iese
morderíamos	mordamos	mord-iéramos/iésemos
morderíais	mordáis	mord-ierais/ieseis
morderían	muerdan	mord-ieran/iesen

Perfect	Perfect	Pluperfect
habría mordido	haya mordido	hub-iera/iese mordido

GERUND · PAST PARTICIPLE · IMPERATIVE

GERUND	PAST PARTICIPLE	IMPERATIVE
mordiendo	mordido	muerde, morded
		muerda (Vd), muerdan (Vds)

El niño me ha mordido el dedo. *The boy has bitten my finger.*
Eva mordió la manzana. *Eve bit the apple.*
Este perro no muerde. *This dog doesn't bite.*
Se ha mordido el labio. *He has bitten his lip.*
Estoy que muerdo. *I'm furious.*
Está que muerde. *He is hopping mad.*
¡Hombre, que no muerde! *Don't be shy!*
Perro que ladra no muerde. *A barking dog does not bite.*

la mordedura *bite*
el mordisco *bite, nibble*
mordiscar *to nibble, gnaw*

la mordida *bite; bribe*
morder sobre *to bite into*
mordedor(a) *biting*

127 morir *to die* (intr.)

INDICATIVE

Present	Imperfect	Perfect
muero	moría	he muerto
mueres	morías	has muerto
muere	moría	ha muerto
morimos	moríamos	hemos muerto
morís	moríais	habéis muerto
mueren	morían	han muerto

Future	Pluperfect	Preterite
moriré	había muerto	morí
morirás	habías muerto	moriste
morirá	había muerto	murió
moriremos	habíamos muerto	morimos
moriréis	habíais muerto	moristeis
morirán	habían muerto	murieron

Future perfect	Past anterior
habré muerto	hube muerto

CONDITIONAL   SUBJUNCTIVE

Present	Present	Imperfect
moriría	muera	mur-iera/iese
morirías	mueras	mur-ieras/ieses
moiría	muera	mur-iera/iese
moriríamos	muramos	mur-iéramos/iésemos
moriríais	muráis	mur-ierais/ieseis
morirían	mueran	mur-ieran/iesen

Perfect	Perfect	Pluperfect
habría muerto	haya muerto	hub-iera/iese muerto

GERUND	PAST PARTICIPLE	IMPERATIVE
muriendo	muerto	muere, morid
		muera (Vd), mueran (Vds)

Muchos niños mueren de hambre. *Many children die of hunger.*
Jan murió de cáncer. *Jan died of cancer.*
Mi abuelo murió hace diez años. *My grandfather died ten years ago.*
Fredes resultó muerta en el acto. *Fredes died instantly.*
Moría el día. *Night was falling.*
Sara está muerta de hambre. *Sara is starving.*
Paula se murió de risa. *Paula couldn't stop laughing.*
Daniel se muere por el fútbol. *Daniel is mad on football.*

la muerte *death*
muerto/a *dead*
Fue muerto a tiros. *He was shot dead.*
hacerse el muerto/a *to play dead*
la naturaleza muerta *still-life*

¡Muera el tirano! *Down with the tyrant!*
mortal *fatal, mortal*
la mortalidad *mortality*

128 mover *to move* (tr./intr.)

INDICATIVE

Present	Imperfect	Perfect
muevo	movía	he movido
mueves	movías	has movido
mueve	movía	ha movido
movemos	movíamos	hemos movido
movéis	movíais	habéis movido
mueven	movían	han movido

Future	Pluperfect	Preterite
moveré	había movido	moví
moverás	habías movido	moviste
moverá	había movido	movió
moveremos	habíamos movido	movimos
moveréis	habíais movido	movisteis
moverán	habían movido	movieron

Future perfect	Past anterior
habré movido	hube movido

CONDITIONAL	SUBJUNCTIVE	
Present	Present	Imperfect
movería	mueva	mov-iera/iese
moverías	muevas	mov-ieras/ieses
movería	mueva	mov-iera/iese
moveríamos	movamos	mov-iéramos/iésemos
moveríais	mováis	mov-ierais/ieseis
moverían	muevan	mov-ieran/iesen

Perfect	Perfect	Pluperfect
habría movido	haya movido	hub-iera/iese movido

GERUND	PAST PARTICIPLE	IMPERATIVE
moviendo	movido	mueve, moved
		mueva (Vd), muevan (Vds)

¿Podemos mover la mesa? *Can we move the table?*
Te toca mover. *It's your move.*
No me he movido del sitio. *I've not moved from my place.*
Tenemos que movernos. *We have to get a move on.*
Movió un jaleo tremendo. *He caused a big row.*
Deja de moverte. *Stop fidgeting.*
¡Muévete! *Hurry up!*

el movimiento *movement, motion*
la movida *move; affair, happening*
la movida madrileña *the Madrid scene*
móvil *mobile*

la movilidad *mobility*
la movilización *mobilization*
movible *changeable, mobile*
el movimiento de intercambio *turnover*

129 mudar *to change, alter* (tr./intr.)

INDICATIVE

Present	Imperfect	Perfect
mudo	mudaba	he mudado
mudas	mudabas	has mudado
muda	mudaba	ha mudado
mudamos	mudábamos	hemos mudado
mudáis	mudabais	habéis mudado
mudan	mudaban	han mudado

Future	Pluperfect	Preterite
mudaré	había mudado	mudé
mudarás	habías mudado	mudaste
mudará	había mudado	mudó
mudaremos	habíamos mudado	mudamos
mudaréis	habíais mudado	mudasteis
mudarán	habían mudado	mudaron

Future perfect	Past anterior
habré mudado	hube mudado

CONDITIONAL · SUBJUNCTIVE

Present	Present	Imperfect
mudaría	mude	mud-ara/ase
mudarías	mudes	mud-aras/ases
mudaría	mude	mud-ara/ase
mudaríamos	mudemos	mud-áramos/ásemos
mudarías	mudéis	mud-arais/aseis
mudarían	muden	mud-aran/asen

Perfect	Perfect	Pluperfect
habría mudado	haya mudado	hub-iera/iese mudado

GERUND	PAST PARTICIPLE	IMPERATIVE
mudando	mudado	muda, mudad
		mude (Vd), muden (Vds)

Peter se ducha antes de mudar de ropa. *Peter has a shower before he changes his clothes.*
He mudado de opinión. *I've changed my mind.*
Los pollitos mudarán las plumas pronto. *The chicks will shed their feathers soon.*
Lo he mudado de sitio. *I've put it somewhere else.*
Nos mudamos de ciudad. *We are moving to another town.*
Mi hermana se ha mudado de casa. *My sister has moved house.*
A Carlos se le está mudando la voz. *Carlos's voice is starting to break.*

mudar de color *to change colour*
mudarse (de casa) *to move house*
la muda *change, alteration, change of clothing*

la mudanza *change, move of house*
mudable *changeable, fickle, inconstant*

130 negar *to refuse, deny* (tr./intr.)

INDICATIVE

Present	Imperfect	Perfect
niego	negaba	he negado
niegas	negabas	has negado
niega	negaba	ha negado
negamos	negábamos	hemos negado
negáis	negabais	habéis negado
niegan	negaban	han negado

Future	Pluperfect	Preterite
negaré	había negado	negué
negarás	habías negado	negaste
negará	había negado	negó
negaremos	habíamos negado	negamos
negaréis	habías negado	negasteis
negarán	habían negado	negaron

Future perfect	Past anterior
habré negado	hube negado

CONDITIONAL   SUBJUNCTIVE

Present	Present	Imperfect
negaría	niegue	neg-ara/ase
negarías	niegues	neg-aras/ases
negaría	niegue	neg-ara/ase
negaríamos	neguemos	neg-áramos/ásemos
negarías	neguéis	neg-arais/aseis
negarían	nieguen	neg-aran/asen

Perfect	Perfect	Pluperfect
habría negado	haya negado	hub-iera/iese negado

GERUND   PAST PARTICIPLE   IMPERATIVE

negando	negado	niega, negad
		niegue (Vd), nieguen (Vds)

Le niegan todo lo que pide. *They refuse him everything.*
Me negó la mano. *He refused to shake hands with me.*
Nos negaron la entrada. *They wouldn't let us in.*
No creo que se niegue. *I don't think he'll refuse.*
Jacky se negó a hacerlo. *Jacky refused to do it.*

la negación *negation, refusal, denial*
negado/a *inept, stupid*
la negativa *negative, refusal, denial*

negarse a *to refuse to*
negativamente *negatively*
negable *deniable*

131 oír *to hear, listen* (tr./intr.)

INDICATIVE

Present	Imperfect	Perfect
oigo	oía	he oído
oyes	oías	has oído
oye	oía	ha oído
oímos	oíamos	hemos oído
oís	oíais	habéis oído
oyen	oían	han oído

Future	Pluperfect	Preterite
oiré	había oído	oí
oirás	habías oído	oíste
oirá	había oído	oyó
oiremos	habíamos oído	oímos
oiréis	habíais oído	oísteis
oirán	habían oído	oyeron

Future perfect	Past anterior
habré oído	hube oído

CONDICIONAL / CONDITIONAL — SUBJUNCTIVE

Present	Present	Imperfect
oiría	oiga	o-yera/yese
oirías	oigas	o-yeras/yeses
oiría	oiga	o-yera/yese
oiríamos	oigamos	o-yéramos/yésemos
oiríais	oigáis	o-yerais/yeseis
oirían	oigan	o-yeran/yesen

Perfect	Perfect	Pluperfect
habría oído	haya oído	hub-iera/iese oído

GERUND	PAST PARTICIPLE	IMPERATIVE
oyendo	oído	oye, oíd
		oiga (Vd), oigan (Vds)

He oído hablar de ti. *I have heard about you.*
Me gusta oír la radio. *I like to listen to the radio.*
Le oí abrir la ventana. *I heard him opening the window.*
Oigo música por las mañanas. *I listen to music in the morning.*
Tal y como lo oyes. *Just like I'm telling you.*
Lo oyó como quien oye llover. *He turned a deaf ear to it.*
¡Oiga, por favor! *Excuse me, please!*

el oído *ear, sense of hearing* **oye, oiga Vd** *listen, excuse me*
el oído interno *inner ear* **oir, ver y callar** *to mind your own business*
de oídas *by hearsay* **dar oídos** *to lend an ear, to listen*

132 oler *to smell* (tr./intr.)

INDICATIVE

Present	Imperfect	Perfect
huelo	olía	he olido
hueles	olías	has olido
huele	olía	ha olido
olemos	olíamos	hemos olido
oléis	olíais	habéis olido
huelen	olían	han olido

Future	Pluperfect	Preterite
oleré	había olido	olí
olerás	habías olido	oliste
olerá	había olido	olió
oleremos	habíamos olido	olimos
oleréis	habíais olido	olisteis
olerán	habían olido	olieron

Future perfect	Past anterior
habré olido	hube olido

CONDITIONAL	SUBJUNCTIVE	
Present	Present	Imperfect
olería	huela	ol-iera/iese
olerías	huelas	ol-ieras/ieses
olería	huela	ol-iera/iese
oleríamos	olamos	ol-iéramos/iésemos
oleríais	oláis	ol-ierais/ieseis
olerían	huelan	ol-ieran/iesen

Perfect	Perfect	Pluperfect
habría olido	haya olido	hub-iera/iese olido

GERUND	PAST PARTICIPLE	IMPERATIVE
oliendo	olido	huele, oled
		huela (Vd), huelan (Vds)

Huele a madreselva. *It smells of honeysuckle.*
Siempre huelen mal. *They always smell bad.*
¿Quieres oler mi perfume? *Do you want to smell my perfume?*
Ya se ha olido lo que estamos haciendo. *He has already guessed what we are doing.*
Esto me huele a excusa. *I have a feeling that this is just an excuse.*
Huelen todo. *They pry into everything.*
Huele que apesta. *It stinks.*

el olor *smell*
el olfato *sense of smell*
inodoro *odourless*
olfativo *olfactory*

oloroso/a = aromático/a *fragrant, sweet smelling*
olfatear *to sniff*

133 partir *to divide; to leave, set off* (tr./intr.)

INDICATIVE

Present	Imperfect	Perfect
parto	partía	he partido
partes	partías	has partido
parte	partía	ha partido
partimos	partíamos	hemos partido
partís	partíais	habéis partido
parten	partían	han partido

Future	Pluperfect	Preterite
partiré	había partido	partí
partirás	habías partido	partiste
partirá	había partido	partió
partiremos	habíamos partido	partimos
partiréis	habíais partido	partisteis
partirán	habían partido	partieron

Future perfect	Past anterior	
habré partido	hube partido	

CONDITIONAL / SUBJUNCTIVE

Present	Present	Imperfect
partiría	parta	part-iera/iese
partirías	partas	part-ieras/ieses
partiría	parta	part-iera/iese
partiríamos	partamos	part-iéramos/iésemos
partiríais	partáis	part-ierais/ieseis
partirían	partan	part-ieran/iesen

Perfect	Perfect	Pluperfect
habría partido	haya partido	hub-iera/iese partido

GERUND	PAST PARTICIPLE	IMPERATIVE
partiendo	partido	parte, partid
		parta (Vd), partan (Vds)

Vamos a partir la diferencia. *Let's split the difference.*
He partido la naranja en dos. *I have cut the orange in two.*
Paqui partió de Chicago el viernes pasado. *Paqui left Chicago last Friday.*
El avión parte de Ibiza. *The plane departs from Ibiza.*
¡Te voy a partir la cara! *I'll split your head open!*
a partir del lunes *starting from Monday*

la partida *departure, register; game (of cards)*
la partida de nacimiento *birth certificate*
la partida de matrimonio *marriage certificate*
la partida de defunción *death certificate*
la partitura *musical score*
el partido *(political) party; game, match*
repartir *to distribute*

134 pedir *to ask, request* (tr.)

INDICATIVE

Present	Imperfect	Perfect
pido	pedía	he pedido
pides	pedías	has pedido
pide	pedía	ha pedido
pedimos	pedíamos	hemos pedido
pedís	pedíais	habéis pedido
piden	pedían	han pedido

Future	Pluperfect	Preterite
pediré	había pedido	pedí
pedirás	habías pedido	pediste
pedirá	había pedido	pidió
pediremos	habíamos pedido	pedimos
pediréis	habíais pedido	pedisteis
pedirán	habían pedido	pidieron

Future perfect	Past anterior
habré pedido	hube pedido

CONDITIONAL

SUBJUNCTIVE

Present	Present	Imperfect
pediría	pida	pid-iera/iese
pedirias	pidas	pid-ieras/ieses
pediría	pida	pid-iera/iese
pediríamos	pidamos	pid-iéramos/iésemos
pediríais	pidáis	pid-ierais/ieseis
pedirían	pidan	pid-ieran/iesen

Perfect	Perfect	Pluperfect
habría pedido	haya pedido	hub-iera/iese pedido

GERUND	PAST PARTICIPLE	IMPERATIVE
pidiendo	pedido	pide, pedid
		pida (Vd), pidan (Vds)

¿Te puedo pedir un favor? *Can I ask you a favour?*
Me pidió que le comprara un coche. *He asked me to buy him a car.*
¿Cuánto piden por esto? *How much are they asking for this?*
Les pediremos perdón. *We shall ask them to forgive us.*
La pared está pidiendo una mano de pintura. *The wall could do with a coat of paint.*
Ese gris pide un color rosa. *That grey needs a pink.*
El triunfo pide una celebración. *The victory calls for a celebration.*

la petición *request, plea*
a petición de... *at the request of...*
pedigüeño/a *insistent, demanding*
pedilón/pedilona *demanding*

el pedido *order*
el pedidor *petitioner*
el pedimento *petition*

135 pensar *to think* (tr./intr.)

INDICATIVE

Present	Imperfect	Perfect
pienso	pensaba	he pensado
piensas	pensabas	has pensado
piensa	pensaba	ha pensado
pensamos	pensábamos	hemos pensado
pensáis	pensabais	habéis pensado
piensan	pensaban	han pensado

Future	Pluperfect	Preterite
pensaré	había pensado	pensé
pensarás	habías pensado	pensaste
pensará	había pensado	pensó
pensaremos	habíamos pensado	pensamos
pensaréis	habíais pensado	pensasteis
pensarán	habían pensado	pensaron

Future perfect	Past anterior
habré pensado	hube pensado

CONDITIONAL · SUBJUNCTIVE

Present	Present	Imperfect
pensaría	piense	pens-ara/ase
pensarías	pienses	pens-aras/ases
pensaría	piense	pens-ara/ase
pensaríamos	pensemos	pens-áramos/ásemos
pensaríais	penséis	pens-arais/aseis
pensarían	piensen	pens-aran/asen

Perfect	Perfect	Pluperfect
habría pensado	haya pensado	hub-iera/iese pensado

GERUND	PAST PARTICIPLE	IMPERATIVE
pensando	pensado	piensa, pensad piense (Vd), piensen (Vds)

¿En qué piensas? *What are you thinking about?*
Pensaba en las vacaciones. *I was thinking about the holidays.*
Luis piensa que Francisca es amable. *Luis thinks that Francisca is nice.*
No sé qué pensar de Lola. *I don't know what to think about Lola.*
Mi ropa da que pensar. *My clothes set people thinking.*
¡Ni lo pienses! *Not a bit of it!*
Te voy a dar que pensar. *I'm going to give you food for thought.*

el pensamiento *thought; the mind*
el/la pensador(a) *thinker*
pensado/a *thought of*
pensante *thinking*

pensativo/a *thoughtful, pensive*
sin pensar *without thinking*
pensar mal de *to think ill of*

136 perder *to lose* (tr./intr.)

INDICATIVE

Present	Imperfect	Perfect
pierdo	perdía	he perdido
pierdes	perdías	has perdido
pierde	perdía	ha perdido
perdemos	perdíamos	hemos perdido
perdéis	perdíais	habéis perdido
pierden	perdían	han perdido

Future	Pluperfect	Preterite
perderé	había perdido	perdí
perderás	habías perdido	perdiste
perderá	había perdido	perdió
perderemos	habíamos perdido	perdimos
perderéis	habíais perdido	perdisteis
perderán	habían perdido	perdieron

Future perfect	Past anterior
habré perdido	hube perdido

CONDITIONAL / SUBJUNCTIVE

Present	Present	Imperfect
perdería	pierda	perd-iera/iese
perderías	pierdas	perd-ieras/ieses
perdería	pierda	perd-iera/iese
perderíamos	perdamos	perd-iéramos/iésemos
perderíais	perdáis	perd-ierais/ieseis
perderían	pierdan	perd-ieran/iesen

Perfect	Perfect	Pluperfect
habría perdido	haya perdido	hub-iera/iese perdido

GERUND	PAST PARTICIPLE	IMPERATIVE
perdiendo	perdido	pierde, perded
		pierda (Vd), pierdan (Vds)

Sara ha perdido 5 kg. *Sara has lost 5 kg.*
Elena va a perder la costumbre. *Elena is going to lose the habit.*
Daniel no se pierde nada. *Daniel doesn't miss a thing.*
Leonor no pierde un momento. *Leonor doesn't waste a moment.*
Se ha echado a perder. *It has gone to waste.*
Lo doy por perdido. *I give up.*

la pérdida *loss, waste*
perdido/a *lost*
perdidamente enamorado/a *passionately in love*

estar pedido por *to be crazy about*
perdidoso *losing, easily lost*
la perdición *ruin, undoing, waste*
el perdido *scoundrel*

137 poblar *to populate, stock* (tr./intr.)

INDICATIVE

Present	Imperfect	Perfect
pueblo	poblaba	he poblado
pueblas	poblabas	has poblado
puebla	poblaba	ha poblado
poblamos	poblábamos	hemos poblado
pobláis	poblabais	habéis poblado
pueblan	poblaban	han poblado

Future	Pluperfect	Preterite
poblaré	había poblado	poblé
poblarás	habías poblado	poblaste
poblará	había poblado	pobló
poblaremos	habíamos poblado	poblamos
poblaréis	habíais poblado	poblasteis
poblarán	habían poblado	poblaron

Future perfect	Past anterior
habré poblado	hube poblado

CONDITIONAL

SUBJUNCTIVE

Present	Present	Imperfect
poblaría	pueble	pobl-ara/ase
poblarías	puebles	pobl-aras/ases
poblaría	pueble	pobl-ara/ase
poblaríamos	poblemos	pobl-áramos/ásemos
poblaríais	pobléis	pobl-arais/aseis
poblarían	pueblen	pobl-aran/asen

Perfect	Perfect	Pluperfect
habría poblado	haya poblado	hub-iera/iese poblado

GERUND	PAST PARTICIPLE	IMPERATIVE
poblando	poblando	puebla, poblad
		pueble (Vd), pueblen (Vds)

Los ingleses poblaron Australia. *The English populated Australia.*
Vamos a poblar la colina de pinos. *We are going to plant pines on the hill.*
Pobló la colmena con abejas importadas. *He stocked the hive with imported bees.*
Me gustaría conocer los peces que pueblan el fondo del mar. *I would like to study the fish that inhabit the bottom of the sea.*
El arbusto se ha poblado. *The bush has come into leaf.*
Estas tribus se pueblan mucho. *These tribes have many children.*

poblarse *to fill, come into leaf*
la población *population, town, village*
el poblachón *dump*
poblado/a *inhabited*

el poblador *settler*
el pueblo *village, town; people, nation*
el pueblecito *little village*

138 poder *to be able to, can* (tr./intr.)

INDICATIVE

Present	Imperfect	Perfect
puedo	podía	he podido
puedes	podías	has podido
puede	podía	ha podido
podemos	podíamos	hemos podido
podéis	podíais	habéis podido
pueden	podían	han podido

Future	Pluperfect	Preterite
podré	había podido	pude
podrás	habías podido	pudiste
podrá	había podido	pudo
podremos	habíamos podido	pudimos
podréis	habíais podido	pudisteis
podrán	habían podido	pudieron

Future perfect	Past anterior
habré podido	hube podido

CONDITIONAL SUBJUNCTIVE

Present	Present	Imperfect
podría	pueda	pud-iera/iese
podrías	puedas	pud-ieras/ieses
podría	pueda	pud-iera/iese
podríamos	podamos	pud-iéramos/iésemos
podríais	podáis	pud-ierais/ieseis
podrían	puedan	pud-ieran/iesen

Perfect	Perfect	Pluperfect
habría podido	haya podido	hub-iera/iese podido

GERUND PAST PARTICIPLE IMPERATIVE

GERUND	PAST PARTICIPLE	IMPERATIVE
pudiendo	podido	puede, poded
		pueda (Vd), puedan (Vds)

¿Puedes venir un momento? *Can you come for a moment?*
Puede que esté en Burgos. *She may be in Burgos.*
No podemos ir a Pamplona. *We can't go to Pamplona.*
No se puede comer. *It is not fit to eat.*
¿Se puede? *May I come in?*
No puedo con él. *I can't deal with him any more.*
¡No puedo más! *I've had enough!*
a más no poder *for all it's worth/to the limit/as much as possible*

el poder *power, strength, law*   **poderoso/a** *powerful*
los plenos poderes *full powers*   **poderosamente** *powerfully*
el poderío *power; might*

139 poner *to put* (tr.)

INDICATIVE

Present	Imperfect	Perfect
pongo	ponía	he puesto
pones	ponías	has puesto
pone	ponía	ha puesto
ponemos	poníamos	hemos puesto
ponéis	poníais	habéis puesto
ponen	ponían	han puesto

Future	Pluperfect	Preterite
pondré	había puesto	puse
pondrás	habías puesto	pusiste
pondrá	había puesto	puso
pondremos	habíamos puesto	pusimos
pondréis	habíais puesto	pusisteis
pondrán	habían puesto	pusieron

Future perfect	Past anterior
habré puesto	hube puesto

CONDITIONAL | SUBJUNCTIVE

Present	Present	Imperfect
pondría	ponga	pus-iera/iese
pondrías	pongas	pus-ieras/ieses
pondría	ponga	pus-iera/iese
pondríamos	pongamos	pus-iéramos/iésemos
pondríais	pongáis	pus-ierais/ieseis
pondrían	pongan	pus-ieran/iesen

Perfect	Perfect	Pluperfect
habría puesto	haya puesto	hub-iera/iese puesto

GERUND	PAST PARTICIPLE	IMPERATIVE
poniendo	puesto	pon, poned
		ponga (Vd), pongan (Vds)

Quiero poner la silla ahí. *I want to put the chair there.*
Pedro está poniendo la mesa. *Pedro is laying the table.*
Frank puso la radio más alta. *Frank turned the radio up.*
La gallina ha puesto un huevo. *The hen has laid an egg.*
Me pone miedo. *It scares me.*
¿Que ponen en el cine? *What's on at the cinema?*
Ana se ha puesto pantalones. *Ana is wearing trousers.*
Elena se ha puesto roja. *Elena has gone red.*
Leonor se puso seria. *Leonor became serious.*
¡Paqui, no te pongas así! *Please, Paqui, don't be like that!*

ponerse *to put on (clothes); to become, turn* **el poner en escena** *staging (theatre)*
el ponedero *nestling box* **el poner en marcha** *launch*
la puesta de sol *sunset*

140 preferir *to prefer* (tr.)

INDICATIVE

Present	Imperfect	Perfect
prefiero	prerfería	he preferido
prefieres	prerferías	has preferido
prefiere	prefería	ha preferido
preferimos	preferíamos	hemos preferido
preferís	preferíais	habéis preferido
prefieren	preferían	han preferido

Future	Pluperfect	Preterite
preferiré	había preferido	preferí
preferirás	habías preferido	preferiste
preferirá	había preferido	prefirió
preferiremos	habíamos preferido	preferimos
preferiréis	habíais preferido	preferisteis
preferirán	habían preferido	prefirieron

Future perfect	Past anterior
habré preferido	hube preferido

CONDITIONAL | SUBJUNCTIVE

Present	Present	Imperfect
preferiría	prefiera	prefir-iera/iese
preferirías	prefieras	prefir-ieras/ieses
preferiría	prefiera	prefir-iera/iese
preferiríamos	prefiramos	prefir-iéramos/iésemos
preferiríais	prefiráis	prefir-ierais/ieseis
preferirían	prefieran	prefir-ieran/iesen

Perfect	Perfect	Pluperfect
habría preferido	haya preferido	hub-iera/iese preferido

GERUND | PAST PARTICIPLE | IMPERATIVE

GERUND	PAST PARTICIPLE	IMPERATIVE
prefiriendo	preferido	prefiere, preferid
		prefiera (Vd), prefieran (Vds)

¿Cuál prefieres? *Which one do you prefer?*
Prefiero el azul. *I prefer the blue one.*
Preferiría ir a casa. *I would rather go home.*
Han preferido ir en taxi. *They have preferred to go by taxi.*
¿Qué prefieres? *What will you have?*

la preferencia *preference*
preferencial *preferential*
preferente *preferential, preferred*
preferible *preferable*

mostrar preferencia por *to show preference to*
preferido/a *favourite*
la clase preferida *club class*
preferiblemente *preferably*

141 probar *to prove, try (on), taste* (tr./intr.)

INDICATIVE

Present	Imperfect	Perfect
pruebo	probaba	he probado
pruebas	probabas	has probado
prueba	probaba	ha probado
probamos	probábamos	hemos probado
probáis	probabais	habéis probado
prueban	probaban	han probado

Future	Pluperfect	Preterite
probaré	había probado	probé
probarás	habías probado	probaste
probará	había probado	probó
probaremos	habíamos probado	probamos
probaréis	habíais probado	probasteis
probarán	habían probado	probaron

Future perfect	Past anterior
habré probado	hube probado

CONDITIONAL / SUBJUNCTIVE

Present	Present	Imperfect
probaría	pruebe	prob-ara/ase
probarías	pruebes	prob-aras/ases
probaría	pruebe	prob-ara/ase
probaríamos	probemos	prob-áramos/ásemos
probaríais	probéis	prob-arais/aseis
probarían	prueben	prob-aran/asen

Perfect	Perfect	Pluperfect
habría probado	haya probado	hub-iera/iese probado

GERUND	PAST PARTICIPLE	IMPERATIVE
probando	probado	prueba, probad
		pruebe (Vd), prueben (Vds)

Prueba el postre, está buenísimo. *Try the dessert, it's very good.*
Está probado que la tierra es redonda. *It has been proved that the earth is round.*
¿Puedo probarme la falda? *Can I try the skirt on?*
No puede probar la máquina. *He can't test the machine.*
¿Probamos? *Shall we have a go?*
No me prueba bien el café. *Coffee doesn't agree with me.*
Mark no lo prueba nunca. *Mark never touches it.*
No me prueba el verde. *Green doesn't suit me.*

el probador *fitting room*
el/la probador(a) *taster (wine, tea)*
probado/a *tasted, proven*
la probanza *proof, evidence*

probatorio *convincing*
la probeta *test tube*
la prueba *proof, evidence*

142 prohibir *to forbid, ban, prohibit* (tr.)

INDICATIVE

Present	Imperfect	Perfect
prohíbo	prohibía	he prohibido
prohíbes	prohibías	has prohibido
prohíbe	prohibía	ha prohibido
prohibimos	prohibíamos	hemos prohibido
prohibís	prohibíais	habéis prohibido
prohíben	prohibían	han prohibido

Future	Pluperfect	Preterite
prohibiré	había prohibido	prohibí
prohibirás	habías prohibido	prohibiste
prohibirá	había prohibido	prohibió
prohibiremos	habíamos prohibido	prohibimos
prohibiréis	habíais prohibido	prohibisteis
prohibirán	habían prohibido	prohibieron

Future perfect	Past anterior	
habré prohibido	hube prohibido	

CONDITIONAL / SUBJUNCTIVE

Present	Present	Imperfect
prohibiría	prohíba	prohib-iera/iese
prohibirías	prohíbas	prohib-ieras/ieses
prohibiría	prohíba	prohib-iera/iese
prohibiríamos	prohibamos	prohib-iéramos/iésemos
prohibiríais	prohibáis	prohib-ierais/ieseis
prohibirían	prohíban	prohib-ieran/iesen

Perfect	Perfect	Pluperfect
habría prohibido	haya prohibido	hub-iera/iese prohibido

GERUND / PAST PARTICIPLE / IMPERATIVE

GERUND	PAST PARTICIPLE	IMPERATIVE
prohibiendo	prohibido	prohíbe, prohibid
		prohíba (Vd), prohíban (Vds)

Se prohíbe aparcar. *No parking.*
Prohibido fumar. *No smoking.*
La ley lo prohíbe. *It is forbidden by law.*
Se ha prohibido el uso de teléfonos móviles aquí. *Mobile phones are banned here.*
Me prohibieron entrar en su casa. *They forbade me to enter their house.*
Prohibida la entrada a menores de 18. *Under 18s not admitted.*

la prohibición *ban, prohibition*
la prohibición total *total ban*
levantar la prohibición (de) *to lift the ban (on)*

prohibitivo *prohibitive*
el precio de gasolina es prohibitivo
petrol is prohibitively expensive

143 quebrar *to break, smash* (tr./intr.)

INDICATIVE

Present	Imperfect	Perfect
quiebro	quebraba	he quebrado
quiebras	quebrabas	has quebrado
quiebra	quebraba	ha quebrado
quebramos	quebrábamos	hemos quebrado
quebráis	quebrabais	habéis quebrado
quiebran	quebraban	han quebrado

Future	Pluperfect	Preterite
quebraré	había quebrado	quebré
quebrarás	habías quebrado	quebraste
quebrará	había quebrado	quebró
quebraremos	habíamos quebrado	quebramos
quebraréis	habíais quebrado	quebrasteis
quebrarán	habían quebrado	quebraron

Future perfect	Past anterior
habré quebrado	hube quebrado

CONDITIONAL   SUBJUNCTIVE

Present	Present	Imperfect
quebraría	quiebre	quebr-ara/ase
quebrarías	quiebres	quebr-aras/ases
quebraría	quiebre	quebr-ara/ase
quebraríamos	quebremos	quebr-áramos/ásemos
quebraríais	quebréis	quebr-arais/aseis
quebrarían	quiebren	quebr-aran/asen

Perfect	Perfect	Pluperfect
habría quebrado	haya quebrado	hub-iera/iese quebrado

GERUND   PAST PARTICIPLE   IMPERATIVE

GERUND	PAST PARTICIPLE	IMPERATIVE
quebrando	quebrado	quiebra, quebrad
		quiebre (Vd), quiebren (Vds)

Se ha quebrado un hueso. *He has broken a bone.*
No quiebres el estante. *Don't break the shelf.*
La compañía ha quebrado. *The company has gone bankrupt.*
Carmen ha quebrado con Pepe. *Carmen has broken up with Pepe.*
Quiebra ese azul. *Make that blue softer.*
Está empezando a quebrar. *She is getting wrinkles.*
No tiene quiebra. *It can't go wrong.*

la quiebra *break, loss, bankruptcy*
quebrazón *crushing, smashing*
la quebrada *gorge, gap, pass*
el quebrado *fraction (maths)*

quebradizo/a *brittle, fragile*
quebrado/a *rough, bankrupt*
quebrado/a de color *pale*
el quebradero de cabeza *headache, worry*

144 querer *to love; to want* (tr.)

INDICATIVE

Present	Imperfect	Perfect
quiero	quería	he querido
quieres	querías	has querido
quiere	quería	ha querido
queremos	queríamos	hemos querido
queréis	queríais	habéis querido
quieren	querían	han querido

Future	Pluperfect	Preterite
querré	había querido	quise
querrás	habías querido	quisiste
querrá	había querido	quiso
querremos	habíamos querido	quisimos
querréis	habíais querido	quisisteis
querrán	habían querido	quisieron

Future perfect	Past anterior
habré querido	hube querido

CONDITIONAL

SUBJUNCTIVE

Present	Present	Imperfect
querría	quiera	quis-iera/iese
querrías	quieras	quis-ieras/ieses
querría	quiera	quis-iera/iese
querríamos	queramos	quis-iéramos/iésemos
querríais	queráis	quis-ierais/ieseis
querrían	quieran	quis-ieran/iesen

Perfect	Perfect	Pluperfect
habría querido	haya querido	hub-iera/iese querido

GERUND	PAST PARTICIPLE	IMPERATIVE
queriendo	querido	quiere, quered
		quiera (Vd), quieran (Vds)

Te quiero mucho. *I love you a lot.*
¿Quieres pan? *Do you want some bread?*
Ven cuando quieras. *Come whenever you want.*
¿Cuánto quieres por el coche? *How much do you want for the car?*
Lo hizo queriendo. *He did it deliberately.*
Quiero decir... *I mean...*
Querer es poder. *Where there's a will there's a way.*
¿Quiere cerrar la puerta? *Would you mind shutting the door?*

No quiero. *I refuse.*
el/la querido/a *loved, beloved, lover*
el queridongo *lover (pejorative)*

la querencia *lair, haunt, favourite spot*
el querendón *affectionate, spoiled child, favourite pet*
sin querer *without meaning to*

145 recomendar *to recommend* (tr.)

INDICATIVE

Present	Imperfect	Perfect
recomiendo	recomendaba	he recomendado
recomiendas	recomendabas	has recomendado
recomienda	recomendaba	ha recomendado
recomendamos	recomendábamos	hemos recomendado
recomendáis	recomendabais	habéis recomendado
recomiendan	recomendaban	han recomendado

Future	Pluperfect	Preterite
recomendaré	había recomendado	recomendé
recomendarás	habías recomendado	recomendaste
recomendará	había recomendado	recomendó
recomendaremos	habíamos recomendado	recomendamos
recomendaréis	habíais recomendado	recomendasteis
recomendarán	habían recomendado	recomendaron

Future perfect	Past anterior
habré recomendado	hube recomendado

CONDITIONAL · SUBJUNCTIVE

Present	Present	Imperfect
recomendaría	recomiende	recomend-ara/ase
recomendarías	recomiendes	recomend-aras/ases
recomendaría	recomiende	recomend-ara/ase
recomendaríamos	recomendemos	recomend-áramos/ásemos
recomendaríais	recomendéis	recomend-arais/aseis
recomendarían	recomienden	recomend-aran/asen

Perfect	Perfect	Pluperfect
habría recomendado	haya recomendado	hub-iera/iese recomendado

GERUND · PAST PARTICIPLE · IMPERATIVE

GERUND	PAST PARTICIPLE	IMPERATIVE
recomendando	recomendado	recomienda, recomendad
		recomiende (Vd), recomienden (Vds)

Te recomiendo el helado de mango. *I can recommend the mango ice-cream.*
Nos recomendaron a su hijo. *They entrusted their son to us.*
¿Me recomiendas un dentista? *Can you recommend a dentist?*

recomendable *recommendable*
la recomendación *recommendation, suggestion; reference*
recomendante *recommending; recommender, endorser*

recomendatorio/a *recommendatory*
recomendablemente *commendably*
recomendado/a *registered*

146 recordar *to remind, remember* (tr./intr.)

INDICATIVE

Present	Imperfect	Perfect
recuerdo	recordaba	he recordado
recuerdas	recordabas	has recordado
recuerda	recordaba	ha recordado
recordamos	recodábamos	hemos recordado
recordáis	recordabais	habéis recordado
recuerdan	recordaban	han recordado

Future	Pluperfect	Preterite
recordaré	había recordado	recordé
recordarás	habías recordado	recordaste
recordará	había recordado	recordó
recordaremos	habíamos recordado	recordamos
recordaréis	habíais recordado	recordasteis
recordarán	habían recordado	recordaron

Future perfect	Past anterior
habré recordado	hube recordado

CONDITIONAL   SUBJUNCTIVE

Present	Present	Imperfect
recordaría	recuerde	record-ara/ase
recordarías	recuerdes	record-aras/ases
recordaría	recuerde	record-ara/ase
recordaríamos	recordemos	record-áramos/ásemos
recordaríais	recordéis	record-arais/aseis
recordarían	recuerden	record-aran/asen

Perfect	Perfect	Pluperfect
habría recordado	haya recordado	hub-iera/iese recordado

GERUND	PAST PARTICIPLE	IMPERATIVE
recordando	recordado	recuerda, recordad
		recuerde (Vd), recuerden (Vds)

Eduardo te recordará siempre. *Eduardo will always remember you.*
No lo recuerdo. *I don't remember it.*
Esto me recuerda a Quevedo. *This reminds me of Quevedo.*
Recuérdale que me debe 20 €. *Remind him that he owes me 20 euros.*
Que yo recuerde... *As far as I can remember...*
Si mal no recuerdo... *If my memory serves me right...*
Creo recordar... *I seem to remember...*

el récord *record*
en un tiempo récord *in record time*
batir el récord *to break a record*
recordable *memorable*
la recordación *recollection*

digno de recordar *memorable*
recordativo *reminiscent*
el recuerdo *memory, memento, souvenir, regards*
los recuerdos *good wishes, regards*

147 referir *to refer, relate* (tr.)

INDICATIVE

Present	Imperfect	Perfect
refiero	refería	he referido
refieres	referías	has referido
refiere	refería	ha referido
referimos	referíamos	hemos referido
referís	referíais	habéis referido
refieren	referían	han referido

Future	Pluperfect	Preterite
referiré	había referido	referí
referirás	habías referido	referiste
referirá	había referido	refirió
referiremos	habíamos referido	referimos
referiréis	habíais referido	referisteis
referirán	habían referido	refirieron

Future perfect	Past anterior
habré referido	hube referido

CONDITIONAL SUBJUNCTIVE

Present	Present	Imperfect
referiría	refiera	refir-iera/iese
referirías	refieras	refir-ieras/ieses
referiría	refiera	refir-iera/iese
referiríamos	refiramos	refir-iéramos/iésemos
referiríais	refiráis	refir-ierais/ieseis
referirían	refieran	refir-ieran/iesen

Perfect	Perfect	Pluperfect
habría referido	haya referido	hub-iera/iese referido

GERUND PAST PARTICIPLE IMPERATIVE

GERUND	PAST PARTICIPLE	IMPERATIVE
refiriendo	referido	refiere, referid
		refiera (Vd), refieran (Vds)

Me estaba refiriendo a Goya. *I was referring to Goya.*
Han referido la obra a Cervantes. *They have referred the work to Cervantes.*
¿Te refieres a Leonor de Castilla? *Are you referring to Eleanor of Castile?*
Por lo que es refiere a eso... *As for that...*
En lo que se refiere a su hablo... *As regards his work...*

la referencia *reference, allusion*
el referéndum *referendum*
referente *referring, relating*

el referí (LA) *referee, umpire*
referible *referable*
referido/a *related, said, above mentioned*

148 reforzar *to reinforce, strengthen* (tr.)

INDICATIVE

Present	Imperfect	Perfect
refuerzo	reforzaba	he reforzado
refuerzas	reforzabas	has reforzado
refuerza	reforzaba	ha reforzado
reforzamos	reforzábamos	hemos reforzado
reforzáis	reforzabais	habéis reforzado
refuerzan	reforzaban	han reforzado

Future	Pluperfect	Preterite
reforzaré	había reforzado	reforcé
reforzarás	habías reforzado	reforzaste
reforzará	había reforzado	reforzó
reforzaremos	habíamos reforzado	reforzamos
reforzaréis	habíais reforzado	reforzasteis
reforzarán	habían reforzado	reforzaron

Future perfect	Past anterior
habré reforzado	hube reforzado

CONDITIONAL — SUBJUNCTIVE

Present	Present	Imperfect
reforzaría	refuerce	reforz-ara/ase
reforzarías	refuerces	reforz-aras/ases
reforzaría	refuerce	reforz-ara/ase
reforzaríamos	reforcemos	reforz-áramos/ásemos
reforzaríais	reforcéis	reforz-arais/aseis
reforzarían	refuercen	reforz-aran/asen

Perfect	Perfect	Pluperfect
habría reforzado	haya reforzado	hub-iera/iese reforzado

GERUND — PAST PARTICIPLE — IMPERATIVE

GERUND	PAST PARTICIPLE	IMPERATIVE
reforzando	reforzado	refuerza, reforzad
		refuerce (Vd), refuercen (Vds)

Tengo que reforzar la mesa. *I have to reinforce the table.*
¿Has reforzado la guarnición del libro? *Have you reinforced the book-binding?*
No refuerces el nudo. *Don't reinforce the knot.*
Reforzaron las paredes. *They reinforced the walls.*

el reforzador *booster, intensifier*
el refuerzo *strengthening, reinforcement, brace*
los refuerzos *reinforcements*

reforzado/a *reinforced, strengthened, magnified*
el reforzamiento *reinforcement, strengthening*

149 regar *to water, irrigate* (tr.)

INDICATIVE

Present	Imperfect	Perfect
riego	regaba	he regado
riegas	regabas	has regado
riega	regaba	ha regado
regamos	regábamos	hemos regado
regáis	regabais	habéis regado
riegan	regaban	han regado

Future	Pluperfect	Preterite
regaré	había regado	regué
regarás	habías regado	regaste
regará	había regado	regó
regaremos	habíamos regado	regamos
regaréis	habíais regado	regasteis
regarán	habían regado	regaron

Future perfect	Past anterior
habré regado	hube regado

CONDITIONAL — SUBJUNCTIVE

Present	Present	Imperfect
regaría	riegue	reg-ara/ase
regarías	riegues	reg-aras/ases
regaría	riegue	reg-ara/ase
regaríamos	reguemos	reg-áramos/ásemos
regaríais	reguéis	reg-arais/aseis
regarían	rieguen	reg-aran/asen

Perfect	Perfect	Pluperfect
habría regado	haya regado	hub-iera/iese regado

GERUND	PAST PARTICIPLE	IMPERATIVE
regando	regado	riega, regad
		riegue (Vd), rieguen (Vds)

Riego las plantas con una regadera. *I water the plants with a watering can.*
Peter está regando con la manga. *Peter is watering with the hose.*
¿Has regado las lechugas? *Have you watered the lettuces?*
Ángel riega el plato con vino. *Ángel has wine with his meal.*
Cele iba regando monedas. *Cele was scattering coins all over the place.*
Nos está regando. *She is having us on.*

la regata *irrigation channel; boat race*
el riego *watering, irrigation*
el riego por aspersión *watering by sprinkler*
la regadura *irrigation*
la tierra de regadío *irrigable, irrigated land*
la regadera *watering can*

150 reír *to laugh* (tr./intr.)

INDICATIVE

Present	Imperfect	Perfect
río	reía	he reído
ríes	reías	has reído
ríe	reía	ha reído
reímos	reíamos	hemos reído
reís	reíais	habéis reído
ríen	reían	han reído

Future	Pluperfect	Preterite
reiré	había reído	reí
reirás	habías reído	reíste
reirá	había reído	rió
reiremos	habíamos reído	reímos
reiréis	habíais reído	reísteis
reirán	habían reído	rieron

Future perfect	Past anterior	
habré reído	hube reído	

CONDITIONAL   SUBJUNCTIVE

Present	Present	Imperfect
reiría	ría	ri-era/ese
reirías	rías	ri-eras/eses
reiría	ría	ri-era/ese
reiríamos	riamos	ri-éramos/ésemos
reiríais	riáis	ri-erais/eseis
reirían	rían	ri-eran/esen

Perfect	Perfect	Pluperfect
habría reído	haya reído	hub-iera/iese reído

GERUND   PAST PARTICIPLE   IMPERATIVE

GERUND	PAST PARTICIPLE	IMPERATIVE
riendo	reído	ríe, reíd
		ría (Vd), rían (Vds)

Nos reímos mucho con Juan. *We laugh a lot with Juan.*
Se ríe mucho de Juan. *He laughs a lot at Juan.*
Pedro nos hace reír siempre. *Pedro always makes us laugh.*
Le ríen los ojos. *His eyes sparkle.*
Fue para reírse. *It was utterly absurd.*
Mi jersey se ríe por los codos. *My jumper is coming apart at the elbows.*
Al freír será el reír. *You'll get your come-uppance.*

la risa *laughter*	**la sonrisa** *smile*
risueño/a *smiling*	**risiblemente** *laughably*
soltar la risa *to burst out laughing*	**la risica/risita/risilla** *giggle*
risible *risible, ludicrous*	**la risotada** *guffaw, boisterous laughter*

151 remendar *to mend* (tr.)

INDICATIVE

Present	Imperfect	Perfect
remiendo	remendaba	he remendado
remiendas	remendabas	has remendado
remienda	remendaba	ha remendado
remendamos	remendábamos	hemos remendado
remendáis	remendabais	habéis remendado
remiendan	remendaban	han remendado

Future	Pluperfect	Preterite
remendaré	había remendado	remendé
remendarás	habías remendado	remendaste
remendará	había remendado	remendó
remendaremos	habíamos remendado	remendamos
remendaréis	habíais remendado	remendasteis
remendarán	habían remendado	remendaron

Future perfect	Past anterior
habré remendado	hube remendado

CONDITIONAL | SUBJUNCTIVE

Present	Present	Imperfect
remendaría	remiende	remend-ara/ase
remendarías	remiendes	remend-aras/ases
remendaría	remiende	remend-ara/ase
remendaríamos	remendemos	remend-áramos/ásemos
remendarías	remendéis	remend-arais/aseis
remendarían	remienden	remend-aran/asen

Perfect	Perfect	Pluperfect
habría remendado	haya remendado	hub-iera/iese remendado

GERUND	PAST PARTICIPLE	IMPERATIVE
remendando	remendado	remienda, remendad
		remiende (Vd), remienden (Vds)

Peter va a remendar la silla. *Peter is going to mend the chair.*
¿Has remendado la camisa? *Have you mended the shirt?*
Mi abuela remienda calcetines. *My grandmother darns socks.*
Tengo que remendar los errores. *I have to correct the mistakes.*

el remendón *cobbler*
el zapatero remendón *shoe repairer*
remendado/a *mended*
a remiendos *piecemeal, in bits*

el/la remendista *mender*
el remiendo *patch, darn; mending, patching*
echar un remiendo a *to patch*

152 renegar *to deny, renounce, detest* (tr./intr.)

INDICATIVE

Present	Imperfect	Perfect
reniego	renegaba	he renegado
reniegas	renegabas	has renegado
reniega	renegaba	ha renegado
renegamos	renegábamos	hemos renegado
renegáis	renegabais	habéis renegado
reniegan	renegaban	han renegado

Future	Pluperfect	Preterite
renegaré	había renegado	renegué
renegarás	habías renegado	renegaste
renegará	había renegado	renegó
renegaremos	habíamos renegado	renegamos
renegaréis	habíais renegado	renegasteis
renegarán	habían renegado	renegaron

Future perfect	Past anterior
habré renegado	hube renegado

CONDITIONAL | SUBJUNCTIVE

Present	Present	Imperfect
renegaría	reniegue	reneg-ara/ase
renegarías	reniegues	reneg-aras/ases
renegaría	reniegue	reneg-ara/ase
renegaríamos	reneguemos	reneg-áramos/ásemos
renegaríais	reneguéis	reneg-arais/aseis
renegarían	renieguen	reneg-aran/asen

Perfect	Perfect	Pluperfect
habría renegado	haya renegado	hub-iera/iese renegado

GERUND | PAST PARTICIPLE | IMPERATIVE

renegando	renegado	reniega, renegad
		reniegue (Vd), renieguen (Vds)

Pedro reniega haberlo dicho. *Pedro vigorously denies having said that.*
Renegó de la religión cristiana y se hizo mahometano. *He renounced Christianity and became a Moslem.*
Sara reniega del profesorado. *Sara detests the teachers.*
Bob renegó de su propio hijo. *Bob disowned his own son.*
Renegaremos de su amistad. *We shall break completely with him.*

renegado/a *renegade, cantankerous*   **el reniego** *curse, grumble, complaint,*
renegón/renegona *grumbling, grouchy,*   *blasphemy*
  cantankerous

153 reñir *to quarrel, scold* (tr./intr.)

INDICATIVE

Present	Imperfect	Perfect
riño	reñía	he reñido
riñes	reñías	has reñido
riñe	reñía	ha reñido
reñimos	reñíamos	hemos reñido
reñís	reñíais	habéis reñido
riñen	reñían	han reñido

Future	Pluperfect	Preterite
reñiré	había reñido	reñí
reñirás	habías reñido	reñiste
reñirá	había reñido	riñó
reñiremos	habíamos reñido	reñimos
reñiréis	habíais reñido	reñisteis
reñirán	habían reñido	riñeron

Future perfect	Past anterior
habré reñido	hube reñido

CONDITIONAL · SUBJUNCTIVE

Present	Present	Imperfect
reñiría	riña	riñ-era/ese
reñirías	riñas	riñ-eras/eses
reñiría	riña	riñ-era/ese
reñiríamos	riñamos	riñ-éramos/ésemos
reñiríais	riñáis	riñ-erais/eseis
reñirían	riñan	riñ-eran/esen

Perfect	Perfect	Pluperfect
habría reñido	haya reñido	hub-iera/iese reñido

GERUND · PAST PARTICIPLE · IMPERATIVE

GERUND	PAST PARTICIPLE	IMPERATIVE
riñendo	reñido	reñe, reñid
		riña (Vd), riñan (Vds)

Elena riñe a los niños. *Elena scolds the children.*
No me riñas. *Don't tell me off.*
Le reñiré por romperlo. *I shall reprimand him for breaking it.*
Marta ha reñido con Pedro. *Marta has fallen out with Pedro.*
Se pasan la vida riñendo. *They are always quarrelling.*
Riñeron por cuestión de dinero. *They quarrelled over money.*

reñidamente *bitterly, hard, stubbornly*
reñidor(a) *quarrelsome*
reñido/a *bitter, hard fought*

la riña *quarrel, argument, fight, brawl*
el reñidero de gallos *cockpit*

154 repetir *to repeat* (tr./intr.)

INDICATIVE

Present	Imperfect	Perfect
repito	repetía	he repetido
repites	repetías	has repetido
repite	repetía	ha repetido
repetimos	repetíamos	hemos repetido
repetís	repetíais	habéis repetido
repiten	repetían	han repetido

Future	Pluperfect	Preterite
repetiré	había repetido	repetí
repetirás	habías repetido	repetiste
repetirá	había repetido	repitió
repetiremos	habíamos repetido	repetimos
repetiréis	habíais repetido	repetisteis
repetirán	habían repetido	repitieron

Future perfect	Past anterior
habré repetido	hube repetido

CONDITIONAL · SUBJUNCTIVE

Present	Present	Imperfect
repetiría	repita	repit-iera/iese
repetirías	repitas	repit-ieras/ieses
repetiría	repita	repit-iera/iese
repetiríamos	repitamos	repit-iéramos/iésemos
repetiríais	repitáis	repit-ierais/ieseis
repetirían	repitan	repit-ieran/iesen

Perfect	Perfect	Pluperfect
habría repetido	haya repetido	hub-iera/iese repetido

GERUND	PAST PARTICIPLE	IMPERATIVE
repitiendo	repetido	repite, repetid
		repita (Vd), repitan (Vds)

¿Quieres repetir la explicación, por favor? *Can you repeat the explanation, please?*
Repiten que es imposible. *They repeat that it is impossible.*
No lo volveré a repetir. *I shall not say it again.*
La audiencia pidió que repitieran. *The audience asked for an encore.*
Los niños repiten lo que hacen los mayores. *Children imitate adults.*
¡Ojalá no se repita eso! *I hope this will not happen again!*

la repetición *repetition, recurrence, encore*
repetidamente *repeatedly*
repetido/a *repeated*
repetidas veces *many times, over and over again*

el repetidor *booster, repeater*
repetir de un plato *to have a second helping*

155 requerir *to require, need* (tr.)

INDICATIVE

Present	Imperfect	Perfect
requiero	requería	he requerido
requieres	requerías	has requerido
requiere	requería	ha requerido
requerimos	requeríamos	hemos requerido
requerís	requeríais	habéis requerido
requieren	requerían	han requerido

Future	Pluperfect	Preterite
requeriré	había requerido	requerí
reguerirás	habías requerido	requeriste
requerirá	había requerido	requirió
requeriremos	habíamos requerido	requerimos
requeriréis	habíais requerido	requeristeis
requerirán	habían requerido	requirieron

Future perfect	Past anterior
habré requerido	hube requerido

CONDITIONAL · SUBJUNCTIVE

Present	Present	Imperfect
requeriría	requiera	requir-iera/iese
requerirías	requieras	requir-ieras/ieses
requeriría	requiera	requir-iera/iese
requeriríamos	requiramos	requir-iéramos/iésemos
requeriríais	requiráis	requir-ierais/ieseis
requerirían	requieran	requir-ieran/iesen

Perfect	Perfect	Pluperfect
habría requerido	haya requerido	hub-iera/iese requerido

GERUND	PAST PARTICIPLE	IMPERATIVE
requiriendo	requerido	requiere, requerid
		requiera (Vd), requieran (Vds)

Esto requiere mucho cuidado. *This requires a lot of care.*
El hablo requería atención. *The job needed attention.*
¿Requerirás las gafas? *Will you need your glasses?*
Se requiere experiencia para el trabajo. *Experience is required for the job.*
Calixto requiere de amores a Melibea. *Calixto woos Melibea*

el requerimiento *request, demand, summons, notification*
el requeriente *one who requires/demands*
el requisito *requirement*
el requiriente *petitioner, process-server*

la requisa *levy*
el requerimiento de pago *demand for payment*
el requerimiento al pago *request for payment*

156 retemblar *to shake, tremble* (intr.)

INDICATIVE

Present	Imperfect	Perfect
retiemblo	retemblaba	he retemblado
retiemblas	retemblabas	has retemblado
retiembla	retemblaba	ha retemblado
retemblamos	retemblábamos	hemos retemblado
retembláis	retemblabais	habéis retemblado
retiemblan	retemblaban	han retemblado

Future	Pluperfect	Preterite
retemblaré	había retemblado	retemblé
retemblarás	habías retemblado	retemblaste
retemblará	había retemblado	retembló
retemblaremos	habíamos retemblado	retemblamos
retemblaréis	habíais retemblado	retemblasteis
retemblarán	habían retemblado	retemblaron

Future perfect	Past anterior
habré retemblado	hube retemblado

CONDITIONAL — SUBJUNCTIVE

Present	Present	Imperfect
retemblaría	retiemble	retembl-ara/ase
retemblarías	retiembles	retembl-aras/ases
retemblaría	retiemble	retembl-ara/ase
retemblaríamos	retemblemos	retembl-áramos/ásemos
retemblaríais	retembléis	retembl-arais/aseis
retemblarían	retiemblen	retembl-aran/asen

Perfect	Perfect	Pluperfect
habría retemblado	haya retemblado	hub-iera/iese retemblado

GERUND — PAST PARTICIPLE — IMPERATIVE

GERUND	PAST PARTICIPLE	IMPERATIVE
retemblando	retemblado	retiembla, retemblad
		retiemble (Vd), retiemblen

La casa retiembla cuando pasa el tren. *The house shakes every time a train goes by.*
Retembló todo el piso. *The whole of the floor trembled.*
Los truenos nos hacían retemblar. *The thunder made us shudder.*
Retiemblo de miedo. *I shake with fear.*
Retemblaron al verle. *They shuddered when they saw him.*
La casa retembló con la explosión. *The house shook with the explosion.*

157 reventar *to burst, explode* (tr./intr.)

INDICATIVE

Present	Imperfect	Perfect
reviento	reventaba	he reventado
revientas	reventabas	has reventado
revienta	reventaba	ha reventado
reventamos	reventábamos	hemos reventado
reventáis	reventabais	habéis reventado
revientan	reventaban	han reventado

Future	Pluperfect	Preterite
reventaré	había reventado	reventé
reventarás	habías reventado	reventaste
reventará	había reventado	reventó
reventaremos	habíamos reventado	reventamos
reventaréis	habíais reventado	reventasteis
reventarán	habían reventado	reventaron

Future perfect	Past anterior
habré reventado	hube reventado

CONDITIONAL

SUBJUNCTIVE

Present	Present	Imperfect
reventaría	reviente	revent-ara/ase
reventarías	revientes	revent-aras/ases
reventaría	reviente	revent-ara/ase
reventaríamos	reventemos	revent-áramos/ásemos
reventarías	reventéis	revent-arais/aseis
reventarían	revienten	revent-aran/asen

Perfect	Perfect	Pluperfect
habría reventado	haya reventado	hub-iera/iese reventado

GERUND	PAST PARTICIPLE	IMPERATIVE
reventando	reventado	revienta, reventad
		reviente (Vd), revienten (Vds)

Se ha reventado el globo. *The balloon has burst.*
Casi reventé de ira. *I almost exploded with anger.*
Reventamos de risa. *We burst out laughing*
Me revienta hacer eso. *I hate doing that.*
Les revienta de aburrimiento. *It bores them to tears.*
Reviento por un chocolate. *I'm dying for a chocolate.*
Elvira está que revienta. *Elvira is full to bursting.*

el/la reventador(a) *trouble maker*
el reventón *burst, explosion*
dar un reventón *to burst, explode*

el reventadero *rough ground, tough job*
reventado/a *burst, flat (tyre)*

158 rodar *to roll* (tr./intr.)

INDICATIVE

Present	Imperfect	Perfect
ruedo	rodaba	he rodado
ruedas	rodabas	has rodado
rueda	rodaba	ha rodado
rodamos	rodábamos	hemos rodado
rodáis	rodabais	habéis rodado
ruedan	rodaban	han rodado

Future	Pluperfect	Preterite
rodaré	había rodado	rodé
rodarás	habías rodado	rodaste
rodará	había rodado	rodó
rodaremos	habíamos rodado	rodamos
rodaréis	habíais rodado	rodasteis
rodarán	habían rodado	rodaron

Future perfect	Past anterior
habré rodado	hube rodado

CONDITIONAL

SUBJUNCTIVE

Present	Present	Imperfect
rodaría	ruede	rod-ara/ase
rodarías	ruedes	rod-aras/ases
rodaría	ruede	rod-ara/ase
rodaríamos	rodemos	rod-áramos/ásemos
roderíais	rodéis	rod-arais/aseis
rodarían	rueden	rod-aran/asen

Perfect	Perfect	Pluperfect
habría rodado	haya rodado	hub-iera/iese rodado

GERUND	PAST PARTICIPLE	IMPERATIVE
rodando	rodado	rueda, rodad
		ruede (Vd), rueden (Vds)

¡**Rueda la pelota!** *Roll the ball!*
El coche rodó cuesta abajo. *The car rolled downhill.*
El motor lleva rodando toda la mañana. *The engine has been running all morning.*
Va a rodar una película. *She is going to shoot a film.*
Ha rodado medio mundo. *She has travelled halfway round the world.*
Le quiere rodar a patadas. *He wants to knock him over.*
Lo he echado todo a rodar. *I have spoiled everything.*
Va rodando de aquí para allá. *He drifts from place to place.*

la rodada *wheel track, route*
el rodadero *cliff, precipice*
rodado/a *on wheels*
la rodaja *slice, small wheel, small disc*
el ruedo *rotation, bullring, arena*

la rueda *wheel*
la rueda de atrás *rear wheel*
la rueda de recambio *spare wheel*
la rueda de prensa *press conference*

159 rogar *to beg, ask for* (tr.)

INDICATIVE

Present	Imperfect	Perfect
ruego	rogaba	he rogado
ruegas	rogabas	has rogado
ruega	rogaba	ha rogado
rogamos	rogábamos	hemos rogado
rogáis	rogabais	habéis rogado
ruegan	rogaban	han rogado

Future	Pluperfect	Preterite
rogaré	había rogado	rogué
rogarás	habías rogado	rogaste
rogará	había rogado	rogó
rogaremos	habíamos rogado	rogamos
rogaréis	habíais rogado	rogasteis
rogarán	habían rogado	rogaron

Future perfect	Past anterior
habré rogado	hube rogado

CONDITIONAL · SUBJUNCTIVE

Present	Present	Imperfect
rogaría	ruegue	rog-ara/ase
rogarías	ruegues	rog-aras/ases
rogaría	ruegue	rog-ara/ase
rogaríamos	roguemos	rog-áramos/ásemos
rogaríais	roguéis	rog-arais/aseis
rogarían	rueguen	rog-aran/asen

Perfect	Perfect	Pluperfect
habría rogado	haya rogado	hub-iera/iese rogado

GERUND	PAST PARTICIPLE	IMPERATIVE
rogando	rogado	ruega, rogad
		ruegue (Vd), rueguen (Vds)

Por favor, te lo ruego. *Please, I beg of you.*
Les rogué que lo hicieran. *I begged them to do it.*
Te ruego que lo hagas. *I ask you to do it.*
Se lo he rogado muchas veces. *I have pleaded with him many a time.*
Se ruega no fumar. *Please do not smoke.*
No se hace de rogar. *You do not have to ask him twice.*

la rogación *request, pleading*
la rogatoria *request, pleading* (LA)
ruegos y preguntas *any other business*

el ruego *request, entreaty*
a ruego de... *at the request of...*
rogador/rogadora/rogante *pleader*

160 saber to know, know how to; to taste of (tr./intr.)

INDICATIVE

Present	Imperfect	Perfect
sé	sabía	he sabido
sabes	sabías	has sabido
sabe	sabía	ha sabido
sabemos	sabíamos	hemos sabido
sabéis	sabíais	habéis sabido
saben	sabían	han sabido

Future	Pluperfect	Preterite
sabré	había sabido	supe
sabrás	habías sabido	supiste
sabrá	había sabido	supo
sabremos	habíamos sabido	supimos
sabréis	habíais sabido	supisteis
sabrán	habían sabido	supieron

Future perfect	Past anterior
habré sabido	hube sabido

CONDITIONAL   SUBJUNCTIVE

Present	Present	Imperfect
sabría	sepa	sup-iera/iese
sabrías	sepas	sup-ieras/ieses
sabría	sepa	sup-iera/iese
sabríamos	sepamos	sup-iéramos/iésemos
sabríais	sepáis	sup-ierais/ieseis
sabrían	sepan	sup-ieran/iesen

Perfect	Perfect	Pluperfect
habría sabido	haya sabido	hub-iera/iese sabido

GERUND   PAST PARTICIPLE   IMPERATIVE

GERUND	PAST PARTICIPLE	IMPERATIVE
sabiendo	sabido	sabe, sabed
		sepa (Vd), sepan (Vds)

¿Sabes dónde está Sara? *Do you know where Sara is?*
No, no sé. *No, I don't know.*
Yo sí sé, está en la biblioteca. *I do, she's in the library.*
¿Sabes nadar? *Can you swim?*
Te hago saber... *I'm informing you...*
¡Yo qué sé! *How should I know!*
Que yo sepa... *As far as I know...*
Esto sabe a vainilla. *This tastes of vanilla.*

hacer saber algo a uno *to let someone know something*
el sabelotodo *know-all*
el sabio *expert, learned, sensible, wise*

el/la sabihondo/a *self-proclaimed expert*
sabiduría *wisdom*
a sabiendas *in the know, knowing*
un no sé que *a certain something*

161 salir *to go out, leave* (intr.)

INDICATIVE

Present	Imperfect	Perfect
salgo	salía	he salido
sales	salías	has salido
sale	salía	ha salido
salimos	salíamos	hemos salido
salís	salíais	habéis salido
salen	salían	han salido

Future	Pluperfect	Preterite
saldré	había salido	salí
saldrás	habías salido	saliste
saldrá	había salido	salió
saldremos	habíamos salido	salimos
saldréis	habíais salido	salisteis
saldrán	habían salido	salieron

Future perfect	Past anterior
habré salido	hube salido

CONDITIONAL

SUBJUNCTIVE

Present	Present	Imperfect
saldría	salga	sal-iera/iese
saldrías	salgas	sal-ieras/ieses
saldría	salga	sal-iera/iese
saldríamos	salgamos	sal-iéramos/iésemos
saldríais	salgáis	sal-ierais/ieseis
saldrían	salgan	sal-ieran/iesen

Perfect	Perfect	Pluperfect
habría salido	haya salido	hub-iera/iese salido

GERUND	PAST PARTICIPLE	IMPERATIVE
saliendo	salido	sal, salid
		salga (Vd), salgan (Vds)

¿Salimos esta noche? *Shall we go out tonight?*
Saldremos el domingo por la mañana. *We'll leave on Sunday morning.*
La sidra sale de las manzanas. *Cider comes from apples.*
Salen juntos desde hace dos años. *They have been going out together for two years.*
¿De dónde has salido? *Where did you spring from?*
Salimos del apuro. *We managed to get out of the jam.*
El vestido le sale muy caro. *The dress works out very expensive.*
Me salió mal el proyecto. *The plan went badly for me.*

la salida *exit, way out, departure*
la salida de tono *inept remark*
la salida de artistas *stage door*
la salida de urgencias *emergency exit*

salido/a *gone, projecting, protuberant; on heat*
saliente *projecting, prominent*

162 segar to mow, cut (tr./intr.)

INDICATIVE

Present	Imperfect	Perfect
siego	segaba	he segado
siegas	segabas	has segado
siega	segaba	ha segado
segamos	segábamos	hemos segado
segáis	segabais	habéis segado
siegan	segaban	han segado

Future	Pluperfect	Preterite
segaré	había segado	segué
segarás	habías segado	segaste
segará	había segado	segó
segaremos	habíamos segado	segamos
segaréis	habíais segado	segasteis
segarán	habían segado	segaron

Future perfect	Past anterior
habré segado	hube segado

CONDITIONAL · SUBJUNCTIVE

Present	Present	Imperfect
segaría	siegue	seg-ara/ase
segarías	siegues	seg-aras/ases
segaría	siegue	seg-ara/ase
segaríamos	seguemos	seg-áramos/ásemos
segarías	seguéis	seg-arais/aseis
segarían	sieguen	seg-aran/asen

Perfect	Perfect	Pluperfect
habría segado	haya segado	hub-iera/iese segado

GERUND	PAST PARTICIPLE	IMPERATIVE
segando	segado	siega, segad
		siegue (Vd), sieguen (Vds)

Siegan el césped los lunes. *They mow the lawn on Mondays.*
Van a segar el trigo. *They are going to harvest the corn.*
El accidente le segó la juventud. *The accident cut him off in his prime.*
Ha segado mis esperanzas. *She has ruined my hopes.*

segable *ready to cut*
la segadera *sickle*
el/la segador(a) *harvester, reaper*
la segadora *mower*

la segadora de césped *lawnmower*
la segadora-trilladora
 (cosechadora) *combine harvester*
la siega *harvesting, reaping, mowing*

163 sembrar *to sow* (tr.)

INDICATIVE

Present	Imperfect	Perfect
siembro	sembraba	he sembrado
siembras	sembrabas	has sembrado
siembra	sembraba	ha sembrado
sembramos	sembrábamos	hemos sembrado
sembráis	sembrabais	habéis sembrado
siembran	sembraban	han sembrado

Future	Pluperfect	Preterite
sembraré	había sembrado	sembré
sembrarás	habías sembrado	sembraste
sembrará	había sembrado	sembró
sembraremos	habíamos sembrado	sembramos
sembraréis	habíais sembrado	sembrasteis
sembrarán	habían sembrado	sembraron

Future perfect	Past anterior
habré sembrado	hube sembrado

CONDITIONAL | SUBJUNCTIVE

Present	Present	Imperfect
sembraría	siembre	sembr-ara/ase
sembrarías	siembres	sembr-aras/ases
sembraría	siembre	sembr-ara/ase
sembraríamos	sembremos	sembr-áramos/ásemos
sembraríais	sembréis	sembr-arais/aseis
sembrarían	siembren	sembr-aran/asen

Perfect	Perfect	Pluperfect
habría sembrado	haya sembrado	hub-iera/iese sembrado

GERUND | PAST PARTICIPLE | IMPERATIVE

sembrando	sembrado	siembra, sembrad
		siembre (Vd), siembren (Vds)

Voy a sembrar lechuga. *I am going to plant some lettuce.*
¿Estás sembrando patatas? *Are you sowing potatoes?*
Siembran todo en la primavera. *They sow everything in spring.*
Sembraremos flores y verduras juntas. *We'll sow flowers and vegetables together.*
El que siembra recoge. *One reaps what one has sown.*

sembrar a voleo *to scatter seeds*
la sembradera *seed drill*
el sembrado *sown field*

el/la sembrador(a) *sower*
la sembradura *sowing*
la siembra *sowing time, sowing*

164 sentarse *to sit down* (r.)

INDICATIVE

Present	Imperfect	Perfect
me siento	me sentaba	me he sentado
te sientas	te sentabas	te has sentado
se sienta	se sentaba	se ha sentado
nos sentamos	nos sentábamos	nos hemos sentado
os sentáis	os sentabais	os habéis sentado
se sientan	se sentaban	se han sentado

Future	Pluperfect	Preterite
me sentaré	me había sentado	me senté
te sentarás	te habías sentado	te sentaste
se sentará	se había sentado	se sentó
nos sentaremos	nos habíamos sentado	nos sentamos
os sentaréis	os habíais sentado	os sentasteis
se sentarán	se habían sentado	se sentaron

Future perfect	Past anterior
me habré sentado	me hube sentado

CONDITIONAL

SUBJUNCTIVE

Present	Present	Imperfect
me sentaría	me siente	me sent-ara/ase
te sentarías	te sientes	te sent-aras/ases
se sentaría	se siente	se sent-ara/ase
nos sentaríamos	nos sentemos	nos sent-áramos/ásemos
os sentaríais	os sentéis	os sent-arais/aseis
se sentarían	se sienten	se sent-aran/asen

Perfect	Perfect	Pluperfect
me habría sentado	me haya sentado	me hub-iera/iese sentado

GERUND

PAST PARTICIPLE

IMPERATIVE

sentándose	sentado	siéntate, sentaos
		siéntese (Vd), siéntense (Vds)

Luis Antonio se sentó a comer. *Luis Antonio sat down to eat.*
Paqui y yo nos sentamos al fuego. *Paqui and I sit by the fire.*
¡Peter, sentémonos aquí! *Peter, let's sit here!*
¡Siéntese usted! *Please, do sit down!*
sentar *to suit, agree with*
El sol me sienta bien. *The sun agrees with me.*
No me sientan bien los pimientos. *Peppers don't agree with me.*
Ese corte de pelo te sienta mal. *That haircut doesn't suit you.*

el asiento *seat*
el sentadero *seat*
de una sentada *at one sitting*

sentado/a *seated, sitting*
sentador(a) *smart, elegant*
dar por sentado *to take for granted*

165 sentir *to feel, regret* (tr./intr.)

INDICATIVE

Present	Imperfect	Perfect
siento	sentía	he sentido
sientes	sentías	has sentido
siente	sentía	ha sentido
sentimos	sentíamos	hemos sentido
sentís	sentíais	habéis sentido
sienten	sentían	han sentido

Future	Pluperfect	Preterite
sentiré	había sentido	sentí
sentirás	habías sentido	sentiste
sentirá	había sentido	sintió
sentiremos	habíamos sentido	sentimos
sentiréis	habíais sentido	sentisteis
sentirán	habían sentido	sintieron

Future perfect	Past anterior
habré sentido	hube sentido

CONDITIONAL | SUBJUNCTIVE

Present	Present	Imperfect
sentiría	sienta	sint-iera/iese
sentirías	sientas	sint-ieras/ieses
sentiría	sienta	sint-iera/iese
sentiríamos	sintamos	sint-iéramos/iésemos
sentiríais	sintáis	sint-ierais/ieseis
sentirían	sientan	sint-ieran/iesen

Perfect	Perfect	Pluperfect
habría sentido	haya sentido	hub-iera/iese sentido

GERUND | PAST PARTICIPLE | IMPERATIVE

GERUND	PAST PARTICIPLE	IMPERATIVE
sintiendo	sentido	siente, sentid
		sienta (Vd), sientan (Vds)

Siento ganas de comer. *I feel like eating.*
Siente un dolor en el pecho. *He feels a pain in his chest.*
No sentíamos el frío. *We didn't feel the cold.*
Sentiré no haberlo hecho antes. *I shall regret not having done it before.*
El tiempo pasó sin sentir. *Time went by very quickly.*
Me siento como en mi casa. *I feel at home here.*
Lo siento muchísimo. *I'm very sorry.*

los sentimientos *feelings, emotions*
la sensación *sensation, feeling*
sensiblero/a *sentimental*
sentimental *sentimental, emotional*

el sentimentalismo *sentimentalism*
la sensiblería *sentimentality*
sensible *sensitive*

166 ser *to be* (intr.) (aux.)

INDICATIVE

Present	Imperfect	Perfect
soy	era	he sido
eres	eras	has sido
es	era	ha sido
somos	éramos	hemos sido
sois	erais	habéis sido
son	eran	han sido

Future	Pluperfect	Preterite
seré	había sido	fui
serás	habías sido	fuiste
será	había sido	fue
seremos	habíamos sido	fuimos
seréis	habíais sido	fuisteis
serán	habían sido	fueron

Future perfect	Past anterior
habré sido	hube sido

CONDITIONAL / SUBJUNCTIVE

Present	Present	Imperfect
sería	sea	fu-era/ese
serías	seas	fu-eras/eses
sería	sea	fu-era/ese
seríamos	seamos	fu-éramos/ésemos
seríais	seáis	fu-erais/eseis
serían	sean	fu-eran/esen

Perfect	Perfect	Pluperfect
habría sido	haya sido	hub-iera/iese sido

GERUND	PAST PARTICIPLE	IMPERATIVE
siendo	sido	se, sed
		sea (Vd), sean (Vds)

¿Quién es? *Who is he? Who is she? Who is it?*
Soy María. *I am María.*
Es mi hermano Miguel Ángel. *This is my brother, Miguel Angel.*
¿Eres española? *Are you Spanish?*
Sí, soy española, soy de Burgos. *Yes, I am, I'm from Burgos.*
Mi padre es granjero. *My father is a farmer.*
Santiago es egoísta y tonto. *Santiago is selfish and silly.*
Son las cuatro. *It is four o'clock.*

es decir *i.e., that is to say*   **un ser** *being, essence*
o sea... *in other words, or rather...*   **los seres vivos** *living things*

167 servir *to serve; be of use* (tr./intr.)

INDICATIVE

Present	Imperfect	Perfect
sirvo	servía	he servido
sirves	servías	has servido
sirve	servía	ha servido
servimos	servíamos	hemos servido
servís	servíais	habéis servido
sirven	servían	han servido

Future	Pluperfect	Preterite
serviré	había servido	serví
servirás	habías servido	serviste
servirá	había servido	sirvió
serviremos	habíamos servido	servimos
serviréis	habíais servido	servisteis
servirán	habían servido	sirvieron

Future perfect	Past anterior
habré servido	hube servido

CONDITIONAL / SUBJUNCTIVE

Present	Present	Imperfect
serviría	sirva	sirv-iera/iese
servirías	sirvas	sirv-ieras/ieses
serviría	sirva	sirv-iera/iese
serviríamos	sirvamos	sirv-iéramos/iésemos
serviríais	sirváis	sirv-ierais/ieseis
servirían	sirvan	sirv-ieran/iesen

Perfect	Perfect	Pluperfect
habría servido	haya servido	hub-iera/iese servido

GERUND	PAST PARTICIPLE	IMPERATIVE
sirviendo	servido	sirve, servid
		sirva (Vd), sirvan (Vds)

No piensa servir a la patria. *He will not serve his country.*
Las monjas sirven a Dios. *Nuns serve God.*
¿Nos servirá vino? *Will he serve us with wine?*
¿Ya le sirven, señora? *Are you being served, madam?*
¿En qué puedo servirle? *How can I help you?*
¡Para servirle! *At your service!*
Simón no sirve para nada. *Simón is good for nothing.*

el servicio *service*
el servicio a domicilio *home delivery*
servicial *helpful, obliging*
el/la servidor(a) *servant, employee*
la servidumbre *servitude*

servicialmente *obligingly*
servible *usable, useful, serviceable*
el serviciador *tax collector, toll collector*

168 situar *to put, situate, locate* (tr.)

INDICATIVE

Present	Imperfect	Perfect
sitúo	situaba	he situado
sitúas	situabas	has situado
sitúa	situaba	ha situado
situamos	situábamos	hemos situado
situáis	situabais	habéis situado
sitúan	situaban	han situado

Future	Pluperfect	Preterite
situaré	había situado	situé
situarás	habías situado	situaste
situará	había situado	situó
situaremos	habíamos situado	situamos
situaréis	habíais situado	situasteis
situarán	habían situado	situaron

Future perfect	Past anterior
habré situado	hube situado

CONDITIONAL · SUBJUNCTIVE

Present	Present	Imperfect
situaría	sitúe	situ-ara/ase
situarías	sitúes	situ-aras/ases
situaría	sitúe	situ-ara/ase
situaríamos	situemos	situ-áramos/ásemos
situaríais	situéis	situ-arais/aseis
situarían	sitúen	situ-aran/asen

Perfect	Perfect	Pluperfect
habría situado	haya situado	hub-iera/iese situado

GERUND	PAST PARTICIPLE	IMPERATIVE
situando	situado	sitúa, situad
		sitúe (Vd), sitúen (Vds)

Sitúan la obra en el siglo XVI. *They place the play in the 16th century.*
Han situado Troya en Turquía. *Troy has been placed in Turkey.*
Marcos situó fondos en el extranjero. *Marcos placed money in accounts abroad.*
Nos situaremos en frente de la tienda. *We'll place ourselves opposite the shop.*
Situaré una pensión para mi sobrina. *I shall settle an income on my niece.*

la situación *situation*
el sitio *place, location, siege*
situado/a *located, placed*

sito/a *situated, located, lying*
estar situado/a *to be well placed,*
  financially secure

169 soler *to be in the habit of* (intr.)

INDICATIVE

Present	Imperfect	Perfect
suelo	solía	he solido
sueles	solías	has solido
suele	solía	ha solido
solemos	solíamos	hemos solido
soléis	solíais	habéis solido
suelen	solían	han solido

Future	Pluperfect	Preterite
(not used)	había solido	solí
	habías solido	soliste
	había solido	solió
	habíamos solido	solimos
	habíais solido	solisteis
	habían solido	solieron

Future perfect	Past anterior	
(not used)	hube solido	

CONDITIONAL / SUBJUNCTIVE

Present	Present	Imperfect
(not used)	suela	sol-iera/iese
	suelas	sol-ieras/ieses
	suela	sol-iera/iese
	solamos	sol-iéramos/iésemos
	soláis	sol-ierais/ieseis
	suelan	sol-ieran/iesen

Perfect	Perfect	Pluperfect
(not used)	haya solido	hub-iera/iese solido

GERUND	PAST PARTICIPLE	IMPERATIVE
soliendo	solido	(not used)

Suele pasar por aquí. *He usually comes this way.*
Solíamos ir todos los años. *We used to go every year.*
No suelen beber cerveza. *They don't normally drink beer.*
¿Sueles venir tarde? *Do you normally get there late?*
¿Soléis venir los martes? *Do you normally come on Tuesdays?*

170 soltar *to loosen, undo, let go of* (tr.)

INDICATIVE

Present	Imperfect	Perfect
suelto	soltaba	he soltado
sueltas	soltabas	has soltado
suelta	soltaba	ha soltado
soltamos	soltábamos	hemos soltado
soltáis	soltabais	habéis soltado
sueltan	soltaban	han soltado

Future	Pluperfect	Preterite
soltaré	había soltado	solté
soltarás	habías soltado	soltaste
soltará	había soltado	soltó
soltaremos	habíamos soltado	soltamos
soltaréis	habíais soltado	soltasteis
soltarán	habían soltado	soltaron

Future perfect	Past anterior
habré soltado	hube soltado

CONDITIONAL / SUBJUNCTIVE

Present	Present	Imperfect
soltaría	suelte	solt-ara/ase
soltarías	sueltes	solt-aras/ases
soltaría	suelte	solt-ara/ase
soltaríamos	soltemos	solt-áramos/ásemos
soltaríais	soltéis	solt-arais/aseis
soltarían	suelten	solt-aran/asen

Perfect	Perfect	Pluperfect
habría soltado	haya soltado	hub-iera/iese soltado

GERUND	PAST PARTICIPLE	IMPERATIVE
soltando	soltado	suelta, soltad
		suelte (Vd), suelten (Vds)

No sueltes la cuerda. *Don't let go of the rope.*
David soltó el globo. *David let go of the balloon.*
Paqui soltó el nudo. *Paqui undid the knot.*
Soltaremos al pájaro la semana que viene. *We'll free the bird next week.*
Franco no soltaba el puesto por nada. *Franco would not give up the job for anything.*
Se me soltó un grito. *I let out a yell.*
Me suelto con cada tontería... *I come out with such silly ideas...*
¡Suéltame! *Let go of me!*

la soltura *looseness, slackness*
la soltura de vientre *diarrhoea*

Habla árabe con soltura. *She speaks Arabic fluently.*

171 sonar *to ring, sound* (tr./intr.)

INDICATIVE

Present	Imperfect	Perfect
sueno	sonaba	he sonado
suenas	sonabas	has sonado
suena	sonaba	ha sonado
sonamos	sonábamos	hemos sonado
sonáis	sonabais	habéis sonado
suenan	sonaban	han sonado

Future	Pluperfect	Preterite
sonaré	había sonado	soné
sonarás	habías sonado	sonaste
sonará	había sonado	sonó
sonaremos	habíamos sonado	sonamos
sonaréis	habíais sonado	sonasteis
sonarán	habían sonado	sonaron

Future perfect	Past anterior
habré sonado	hube sonado

CONDITIONAL · SUBJUNCTIVE

Present	Present	Imperfect
sonaría	suene	son-ara/ase
sonarías	suenes	son-aras/ases
sonaría	suene	son-ara/ase
sonaríamos	sonemos	son-áramos/ásemos
sonaríais	sonéis	son-arais/aseis
sonarían	suenen	son-aran/asen

Perfect	Perfect	Pluperfect
habría sonado	haya sonado	hub-iera/iese sonado

GERUND · PAST PARTICIPLE · IMPERATIVE

GERUND	PAST PARTICIPLE	IMPERATIVE
sonando	sonado	suena, sonad
		suene (Vd), suenen (Vds)

Sonaremos la alarma. *We'll ring the alarm.*
Han sonado las diez. *It has struck ten.*
Esta frase no me suena bien. *This sentence doesn't sound right to me.*
Suena a hueco. *It sounds hollow.*
Me sonaban las tripas. *My tummy was rumbling.*
Me suena ese nombre. *That name rings a bell.*

sonado/a *famous, talked about, talked of*
la sonaja *little bell, jingle stick*
el sonajero *rattle*
sonarse (las narices) *blow one's nose*

sonante *audible, resounding*
la sonata *sonata*
contante y sonante *ready cash*
se suena que... *it is rumoured that...*

172 soñar *to dream* (tr./intr.)

INDICATIVE

Present	Imperfect	Perfect
sueño	soñaba	he soñado
sueñas	soñabas	has soñado
sueña	soñaba	ha soñado
soñamos	soñábamos	hemos soñado
soñais	soñabais	habéis soñado
sueñan	soñaban	han soñado

Future	Pluperfect	Preterite
soñaré	había soñado	soñé
soñarás	habías soñado	soñaste
soñará	había soñado	soñó
soñaremos	habíamos soñado	soñamos
soñaréis	habíais soñado	soñasteis
soñarán	habían soñado	soñaron

Future perfect	Past anterior
habré soñado	hube soñado

CONDITIONAL   SUBJUNCTIVE

Present	Present	Imperfect
soñaría	sueñe	soñ-ara/ase
soñarías	sueñes	soñ-aras/ases
soñaría	sueñe	soñ-ara/ase
soñaríamos	soñemos	soñ-áramos/ásemos
soñaríais	soñéis	soñ-arais/aseis
soñarían	sueñen	soñ-aran/asen

Perfect	Perfect	Pluperfect
habría soñado	haya soñado	hub-iera/iese soñado

GERUND   PAST PARTICIPLE   IMPERATIVE

GERUND	PAST PARTICIPLE	IMPERATIVE
soñando	soñado	sueña, soñad
		sueñe (Vd), sueñen (Vds)

Sueño todas las noches. *I dream every night.*
Anoche soñé con Daniel. *Last night I dreamt about Daniel*
Soñaba con un Rolex. *She dreamed about having a Rolex.*
Soñaron lo mismo. *They had the same dream.*
Charo sueña despierta. *Charo daydreams.*
Elvira sueña en voz alta. *Elvira talks in her sleep.*
¡Ni lo sueñes! *Not on your life!*

el sueño *dream*
la vida es sueño *life is a dream*
soñado/a *ideal, dreamed of*
el/la soñador(a) *dreamer, dreamy, idealist,*
  romantic

la soñolencia *somnolencia*
soñoliento/a *sleepy, drowsy,*
  somnolent
tener sueño *be sleepy*
echar un sueño *take a nap*

173 subir *to go up, rise, climb* (tr./intr.)

INDICATIVE

Present	Imperfect	Perfect
subo	subía	he subido
subes	subías	has subido
sube	subía	ha subido
subimos	subíamos	hemos subido
subís	subíais	habéis subido
suben	subían	han subido

Future	Pluperfect	Preterite
subiré	había subido	subí
subirás	habías subido	subiste
subirá	había subido	subió
subiremos	habíamos subido	subimos
subiréis	habíais subido	subisteis
subirán	habían subido	subieron

Future perfect	Past anterior
habré subido	hube subido

CONDITIONAL / SUBJUNCTIVE

Present	Present	Imperfect
subiría	suba	sub-iera/iese
subirías	subas	sub-ieras/ieses
subiría	suba	sub-iera/iese
subiríamos	subamos	sub-iéramos/iésemos
subiríais	subáis	sub-ierais/ieseis
subirían	suban	sub-ieran/iesen

Perfect	Perfect	Pluperfect
habría subido	haya subido	hub-iera/iese subido

GERUND	PAST PARTICIPLE	IMPERATIVE
subiendo	subido	sube, subid
		suba (Vd), suban (Vds)

Subimos las escaleras corriendo. *We ran upstairs.*
Subí hasta el último piso. *I went up to the top floor.*
Han subido los precios. *Prices have gone up.*
Me subiré a una escalera. *I'll climb a ladder.*
Vamos a subir al tren. *Let's get on the train.*
Se le ha subido el vino a la cabeza. *The wine has gone to her head.*
Pedro sube el tono cuando se enfada. *Pedro raises his voice when he gets angry.*

la subida *rise, ascent, climb; increase*
la subienda *shoal*
de subida *on the increase*

subido/a *strong (smell), high (price), loud (noise), tall (plant), bright (colour)*

174 sugerir *to suggest, hint* (tr.)

INDICATIVE

Present	Imperfect	Perfect
sugiero	sugería	he sugerido
sugieres	sugerías	has sugerido
sugiere	sugería	ha sugerido
sugerimos	sugeríamos	hemos sugerido
sugerís	sugeríais	habéis sugerido
sugieren	sugerían	han sugerido

Future	Pluperfect	Preterite
sugeriré	había sugerido	sugerí
sugerirás	habías sugerido	sugeriste
sugerirá	había sugerido	sugirió
sugeriremos	habíamos sugerido	sugerimos
sugeriréis	habíais sugerido	sugeristeis
sugerirán	habían sugerido	sugirieron

Future perfect	Past anterior
habré sugerido	hube sugerido

CONDITIONAL / SUBJUNCTIVE

Present	Present	Imperfect
sugeriría	sugiera	sugir-iera/iese
sugerirías	sugieras	sugir-ieras/ieses
sugenriría	sugiera	sugir-iera/iese
sugeriríamos	sugiramos	sugir-iéramos/iésemos
sugeriríais	sugiráis	sugir-ierais/ieseis
sugerirían	sugieran	sugir-ieran/iesen

Perfect	Perfect	Pluperfect
habría sugerido	haya sugerido	hub-iera/iese sugerido

GERUND	PAST PARTICIPLE	IMPERATIVE
sugiriendo	sugerido	sugiere, sugerid
		sugiera (Vd), sugieran (Vds)

Te sugiero el verde. *I suggest the green one.*
El accidente me sugirió el tema del libro. *The accident gave me the idea for the book.*
Se lo sugerimos a Carlos. *We prompted Carlos to do it.*
Sugiero que lo hagas. *I suggest that you do it.*

la sugerencia *suggestion*
sugerente *full of suggestion, evocative*
sugerible *suggestive*
sugestionable *suggestive, impressionable, easily influenced*

la sugestión *suggestion, hint*
sugestivo/a *suggestive, expressive; interesting, attractive*

175 tapar *to cover, hide* (tr.)

INDICATIVE

Present	Imperfect	Perfect
tapo	tapaba	he tapado
tapas	tapabas	has tapado
tapa	tapaba	ha tapado
tapamos	tapábamos	hemos tapado
tapáis	tapabais	habéis tapado
tapan	tapaban	han tapado

Future	Pluperfect	Preterite
taparé	había tapado	tapé
taparás	habías tapado	tapaste
tapará	había tapado	tapó
taparemos	habíamos tapado	tapamos
taparéis	habíais tapado	tapasteis
taparán	habían tapado	taparon

Future perfect	Past anterior
habré tapado	hube tapado

CONDITIONAL SUBJUNCTIVE

Present	Present	Imperfect
taparía	tape	tap-ara/ase
taparías	tapes	tap-aras/ases
taparía	tape	tap-ara/ase
taparíamos	tapemos	tap-áramos/ásemos
taparíais	tapéis	tap-arais/aseis
taparían	tapen	tap-aran/asen

Perfect	Perfect	Pluperfect
habría tapado	haya tapado	hub-iera/iese tapado

GERUND PAST PARTICIPLE IMPERATIVE

GERUND	PAST PARTICIPLE	IMPERATIVE
tapando	tapado	tapa, tapad
		tape (Vd), tapen (Vds)

Tapa la botella. *Put the top on the bottle.*
¿Has tapado la cazuela? *Have you put the lid on the pan?*
Guille es tímido y se tapa la cara. *Guille is shy and covers his face.*
La valla nos tapa el viento. *The fence protects us from the wind.*
¡Tápate la boca! *Shut your mouth!*
No me tapes la luz. *Don't stand in my light.*

la tapa *lid, cap, top*
la tapadera *lid, cover*
el tapón *plug, stopper, cap*

el tapete *rug, table cloth, tapestry*
el tapagujeros *stopgap, stand-in*

176 temblar *to tremble, shake* (intr.)

INDICATIVE

Present	Imperfect	Perfect
tiemblo	temblaba	he temblado
tiemblas	temblabas	has temblado
tiembla	temblaba	ha temblado
temblamos	temblábamos	hemos temblado
tembláis	temblabais	habéis temblado
tiemblan	temblaban	han temblado

Future	Pluperfect	Preterite
temblaré	había temblado	temblé
temblarás	habías temblado	temblaste
temblará	había temblado	tembló
temblaremos	habíamos temblado	temblamos
temblaréis	habíais temblado	temblasteis
temblarán	habían temblado	temblaron

Future perfect	Past anterior
habré temblado	hube temblado

CONDITIONAL / SUBJUNCTIVE

Present	Present	Imperfect
temblaría	tiemble	tembl-ara/ase
temblarías	tiembles	tembl-aras/ases
temblaría	tiemble	tembl-ara/ase
temblaríamos	temblemos	tembl-áramos/ásemos
temblaríais	tembléis	tembl-arais/aseis
temblarían	tiemblen	tembl-aran/asen

Perfect	Perfect	Pluperfect
habría temblado	haya temblado	hub-iera/iese temblado

GERUND	PAST PARTICIPLE	IMPERATIVE
temblando	temblado	tiembla, temblad
		tiemble (Vd), tiemblen (Vds)

Mafalda está temblando. *Mafalda is trembling.*
El chico temblaba de miedo. *The boy was shaking with fear.*
Temblamos de emoción. *We trembled with emotion.*
Carlos tiembla como un azogado. *Carlos trembles like a leaf.*
Tiembla de frío. *She is shivering with cold.*
Dejamos la botella temblando. *We made the bottle look pretty silly.*

la tembladera *violent shaking*
el tembleque *shaking fit*
el temblor de tierra *earthquake*
temblante *trembling, shaking*

el temblor *trembling*
la temblequera *fear, cowardice*
tembloroso *trembling, shaking*

177 temer *to fear, dread* (tr./intr.)

INDICATIVE

Present	Imperfect	Perfect
temo	temía	he temido
temes	temías	has temido
teme	temía	ha temido
tememos	temíamos	hemos temido
teméis	temíais	habéis temido
temen	temían	han temido

Future	Pluperfect	Preterite
temeré	había temido	temí
temerás	habías temido	temiste
temerá	había temido	temió
temeremos	habíamos temido	temimos
temeréis	habíais temido	temisteis
temerán	habían temido	temieron

Future perfect	Past anterior
habré temido	hube temido

CONDITIONAL | SUBJUNCTIVE

Present	Present	Imperfect
temería	tema	tem-iera/iese
temerías	temas	tem-ieras/ieses
temería	tema	tem-iera/iese
temeríamos	temamos	tem-iéramos/iésemos
temeríais	temáis	tem-ierais/ieseis
temerían	teman	tem-ieran/iesen

Perfect	Perfect	Pluperfect
habría temido	haya temido	hub-iera/iese temido

GERUND | PAST PARTICIPLE | IMPERATIVE

GERUND	PAST PARTICIPLE	IMPERATIVE
temiendo	temido	teme, temed
		tema (Vd), teman (Vds)

Temen a los ladrones. *They are afraid of thieves.*
¿Temes a tu padre? *Are you afraid of your father?*
Teme que vaya a volver. *She is afraid he'll come back.*
No temas. *Don't be afraid.*

el temor *fear, dread, apprehension*
temible *frightening, fearsome*
temeroso/a *timid; dreadful, fearful*
temerosamente *timorously, timidly*

la temeridad *temerity, boldness, daring*
temerario *bold, imprudent*
temerariamente *rashly, foolhardily*

178 tender *to spread, lay out; tend* (tr./intr.)

INDICATIVE

Present	Imperfect	Perfect
tiendo	tendía	he tendido
tiendes	tendías	has tendido
tiende	tendía	ha tendido
tendemos	tendíamos	hemos tendido
tendéis	tendíais	habéis tendido
tienden	tendían	han tendido

Future	Pluperfect	Preterite
tenderé	había tendido	tendí
tenderás	habías tendido	tendiste
tenderá	había tendido	tendió
tenderemos	habíamos tendido	tendimos
tenderéis	habíais tendido	tendisteis
tenderán	habían tendido	tendieron

Future perfect	Past anterior
habré tendido	hube tendido

CONDITIONAL

SUBJUNCTIVE

Present	Present	Imperfect
tendería	tienda	tend-iera/iese
tenderías	tiendas	tend-ieras/ieses
tendería	tienda	tend-iera/iese
tenderíamos	tendamos	tend-iéramos/iésemos
tenderíais	tendáis	tend-ierais/ieseis
tenderían	tiendan	tend-ieran/iesen

Perfect	Perfect	Pluperfect
habría tendido	haya tendido	hub-iera/iese tendido

GERUND	PAST PARTICIPLE	IMPERATIVE
tendiendo	tendido	tiende, tended
		tienda (Vd), tiendan (Vds)

Tiende el mantel. *Spread out the tablecloth.*
Grego está tendiendo la ropa. *Grego is hanging the clothes out.*
Lo tendió de un golpe. *He floored him with one blow.*
Susana tiende a exagerar. *Susana tends to exaggerate.*
El color tiende más al verde que al azul. *The colour seems to be more green than blue.*
Pablo tiende al pesimismo. *Pablo is prone to pessimism.*
Las plantas tienden a la luz. *Plants turn towards the light.*

tenderse *to lie down, stretch out*	**la tendencia** *tendency, trend, drift*
el tendal *spread, jumble, disorder*	**el tendero(a)** *shopkeeper*
la tendalera *disorder*	**el tendedero** *clothes line*
tienda *shop; tent*	
tendido *lying down, flat*	

179 tener *to have, possess* (tr./intr.)

INDICATIVE

Present	Imperfect	Perfect
tengo	tenía	he tenido
tienes	tenías	has tenido
tiene	tenía	ha tenido
tenemos	teníamos	hemos tenido
tenéis	teníais	habéis tenido
tienen	tenían	han tenido

Future	Pluperfect	Preterite
tendré	había tenido	tuve
tendrás	habías tenido	tuviste
tendrá	había tenido	tuvo
tendremos	habíamos tenido	tuvimos
tendréis	habíais tenido	tuvisteis
tendrán	habían tenido	tuvieron

Future perfect	Past anterior
habré tenido	hube tenido

CONDITIONAL / SUBJUNCTIVE

Present	Present	Imperfect
tendría	tenga	tuv-iera/iese
tendrías	tengas	tuv-ieras/ieses
tendría	tenga	tuv-iera/iese
tendríamos	tengamos	tuv-iéramos/iésemos
tendríais	tengáis	tuv-ierais/ieseis
tendrían	tengan	tuv-ieran/iesen

Perfect	Perfect	Pluperfect
habría tenido	haya tenido	hub-iera/iese tenido

GERUND	PAST PARTICIPLE	IMPERATIVE
teniendo	tenido	ten, tened
		tenga (Vd), tengan (Vds)

Miguel tiene un piso en Burgos. *Miguel owns a flat in Burgos.*
¿Tienes coche? *Have you got a car?*
No teníamos sitio. *We didn't have room.*
Tengo una reunión mañana. *I've got a meeting tomorrow.*
¿Qué tienes? *What's the matter with you?*
Tenemos que marcharnos. *We have to go.*
No tiene nada que ver contigo. *It's got nothing to do with you.*
Leonor tiene prisa. *Leonor is in a hurry.*

Tiene calor. *She's hot.*
Tenemos hambre. *We're hungry.*
Tienes sueño. *You're sleepy.*
Ten cuidado. *Be careful.*

la tenencia *holding, tenancy*
el tenedor *holder, fork*
la teneduría *bookkeeping*
el/la tenedor/a de acciones
  shareholder

180 tentar *to feel, try; to tempt* (tr.)

INDICATIVE

Present	Imperfect	Perfect
tiento	tentaba	he tentado
tientas	tentabas	has tentado
tienta	tentaba	ha tentado
tentamos	tentábamos	hemos tentado
tentáis	tentabais	habéis tentado
tientan	tentaban	han tentado

Future	Pluperfect	Preterite
tentaré	había tentado	tenté
tentarás	habías tentado	tentaste
tentará	había tentado	tentó
tentaremos	habíamos tentado	tentamos
tentaréis	habíais tentado	tentasteis
tentarán	habían tentado	tentaron

Future perfect	Past anterior
habré tentado	hube tentado

CONDITIONAL · SUBJUNCTIVE

Present	Present	Imperfect
tentaría	tiente	tent-ara/ase
tentarías	tientes	tent-aras/ases
tentaría	tiente	tent-ara/ase
tentaríamos	tentemos	tent-áramos/ásemos
tentaríais	tentéis	tent-arais/aseis
tentarían	tienten	tent-aran/asen

Perfect	Perfect	Pluperfect
habría tentado	haya tentado	hub-iera/iese tentado

GERUND	PAST PARTICIPLE	IMPERATIVE
tentando	tentado	tienta, tentad
		tiente (Vd), tienten (Vds)

Voy a tentar hacerlo. *I'm going to do it.*
El ciego iba tentando su camino. *The blind man was feeling his way.*
Hemos tentado todos los remedios. *We've tried all the remedies.*
No me tienta la idea. *The idea doesn't tempt me.*
No le tientes a fumar. *Don't encourage him to smoke.*
Me tienta un vino. *I fancy a glass of wine.*
No tientes al diablo. *Don't look for trouble.*

el tentáculo *tentacle, feeler*
la tentación *temptation*
el/la tentador(a) *tempter, temptress*
la tentativa *attempt*
la tentativa de asesinato *attempted murder*
tentativo/a *tentative*

181 teñir *to dye, stain* (tr.)

INDICATIVE

Present	Imperfect	Perfect
tiño	teñía	he teñido
tines	teñías	has teñido
tiñe	tenía	ha teñido
teñimos	teníamos	hemos teñido
teñís	teníais	habéis teñido
tiñen	teñían	han teñido

Future	Pluperfect	Preterite
teñiré	había teñido	teñí
teñirás	habías teñido	teñiste
teñirá	había teñido	tiñó
teñiremos	habíamos teñido	teñimos
teñiréis	habíais teñido	teñisteis
teñirán	habían teñido	tiñeron

Future perfect	Past anterior	
habré teñido	hube teñido	

CONDITIONAL / SUBJUNCTIVE

Present	Present	Imperfect
teñiría	tiña	tiñ-era/ese
teñirías	tiñas	tiñ-eras/eses
teñiría	tiña	tiñ-era/ese
teñiríamos	tiñamos	tiñ-éramos/ésemos
teñiríais	tiñáis	tiñ-erais/eseis
teñirían	tiñan	tiñ-eran/esen

Perfect	Perfect	Pluperfect
habría teñido	haya teñido	hub-iera/iese teñido

GERUND	PAST PARTICIPLE	IMPERATIVE
tiñendo	teñido	tiñe, teñid
		tiña (Vd), tiñan (Vds)

He teñido la falda de azul. *I've dyed the skirt blue.*
La toalla ha teñido la camiseta. *The colour of the towel has come out on the T-shirt.*
¿Te tiñes el pelo? *Do you dye your hair?*
Tiñeron todo de color negro. *They dyed everything black.*
Pedro está teñido de amor. *Pedro is love-struck.*
Su pintura está teñida con melancolía. *His paintings have got melancholic tinges.*

tinto/a *dyed; tinged*
el tinto *red wine*
teñido/a *dyed, tinted, stained*

el tinte *dye, dyeing*
la tintura *dyeing*
la tintorería *dry cleaner's*

182 tocar *to touch; to play* (tr./intr.)

INDICATIVE

Present	Imperfect	Perfect
toco	tocaba	he tocado
tocas	tocabas	has tocado
toca	tocaba	ha tocado
tocamos	tocábamos	hemos tocado
tocáis	tocabais	habéis tocado
tocan	tocaban	han tocado

Future	Pluperfect	Preterite
tocaré	había tocado	toqué
tocarás	habías tocado	tocaste
tocará	había tocado	tocó
tocaremos	habíamos tocado	tocamos
tocaréis	habíais tocado	tocasteis
tocarán	habían tocado	tocaron

Future perfect	Past anterior
habré tocado	hube tocado

CONDITIONAL | SUBJUNCTIVE

Present	Present	Imperfect
tocaría	toque	toc-ara/ase
tocarías	toques	toc-aras/ases
tocaría	toque	toc-ara/ase
tocaríamos	toquemos	toc-áramos/ásemos
tocaríais	toquéis	toc-arais/aseis
tocarían	toquen	toc-aran/asen

Perfect	Perfect	Pluperfect
habría tocado	haya tocado	hub-iera/iese tocado

GERUND | PAST PARTICIPLE | IMPERATIVE

GERUND	PAST PARTICIPLE	IMPERATIVE
tocando	tocado	toca, tocad
		toque (Vd), toquen (Vds)

Puedo tocar el fondo. *I can touch the bottom.*
¡No me toques! *Don't touch me!*
Toca el timbre. *Ring the bell.*
Toco el piano. *I play the piano.*
A ti te tocaba hablar. *It was your turn to speak.*
Le tocó la lotería. *He won the lottery.*
Por lo que a mí me toca... *As far as I'm concerned...*
Está tocado. *He is crazy.*

tocarle a uno *to fall to somebody, to be somebody's turn*
el toque *touch*
el tocador *dressing table*
el/la tocador(a) *player, performer*

la toca *headdress, bonnet*
el tocado *headdress, hair-do*
tocante *with regards to*
el tocadiscos *record player*

183 tomar *to take, have* (tr./intr.)

INDICATIVE

Present	Imperfect	Perfect
tomo	tomaba	he tomado
tomas	tomabas	has tomado
toma	tomaba	ha tomado
tomamos	tomábamos	hemos tomado
tomáis	tomabais	habéis tomado
toman	tomaban	han tomado

Future	Pluperfect	Preterite
tomaré	había tomado	tomé
tomarás	habías tomado	tomaste
tomará	había tomado	tomó
tomaremos	habíamos tomado	tomamos
tomaréis	habíais tomado	tomasteis
tomarán	habían tomado	tomaron

Future perfect	Past anterior
habré tomado	hube tomado

CONDITIONAL / SUBJUNCTIVE

Present	Present	Imperfect
tomaría	tome	tom-ara/ase
tomarías	tomes	tom-aras/ases
tomaría	tome	tom-ara/ase
tomaríamos	tomemos	tom-áramos/ásemos
tomaríais	toméis	tom-arais/aseis
tomarían	tomen	tom-aran/asen

Perfect	Perfect	Pluperfect
habría tomado	haya tomado	hub-iera/iese tomado

GERUND	PAST PARTICIPLE	IMPERATIVE
tomando	tomado	toma, tomad
		tome (Vd), tomen (Vds)

Tomamos unos vinos. *We had a few glasses of wine.*
Tomé la primera calle a la derecha. *I took the first turning on the right.*
Nos tomaremos unas vacaciones en junio. *We'll take a holiday in June.*
Tomaron a Guille por un policía. *They took Guille to be a policeman.*
Te toman por loco. *They think you are mad.*
¡Toma! *Fancy that!, Here you are!, There!*

la toma *taking, capture; plug, socket*	**Está tomado.** *He is drunk.*
la toma de aire *air intake*	**el tomadero** *handle, tap, outlet*
la toma de corriente *power point*	**la tomadura** *hoax, rip-off*
tomar el sol *to sunbathe*	**la tomadura de pelo** *practical joke*

184 torcer *to twist, turn, bend* (tr.)

INDICATIVE

Present	Imperfect	Perfect
tuerzo	torcía	he torcido
tuerces	torcías	has torcido
tuerce	torcía	ha torcido
torcemos	torcíamos	hemos torcido
torcéis	torcíais	habéis torcido
tuercen	torcían	han torcido

Future	Pluperfect	Preterite
torceré	había torcido	torcí
torcerás	habías torcido	torciste
torcerá	había torcido	torció
torceremos	habíamos torcido	torcimos
torceréis	habíais torcido	torcisteis
torcerán	habían torcido	torcieron

Future perfect	Past anterior
habré torcido	hube torcido

CONDITIONAL · SUBJUNCTIVE

Present	Present	Imperfect
torcería	tuerza	torc-iera/iese
torcerías	tuerzas	torc-ieras/ieses
torcería	tuerza	torc-iera/iese
torceríamos	torzamos	torc-iéramos/iésemos
torceríais	torzáis	torc-ierais/ieseis
torcerían	tuerzan	torc-ieran/iesen

Perfect	Perfect	Pluperfect
habría torcido	haya torcido	hub-iera/iese torcido

GERUND · PAST PARTICIPLE · IMPERATIVE

GERUND	PAST PARTICIPLE	IMPERATIVE
torciendo	torcido	tuerce, torced
		tuerza (Vd), tuerzan (Vds)

El coche torció a la izquierda. *The car turned left.*
Quiere torcer la madera. *He wants to bend the wood.*
Torcieron la barra de hierro. *They bent the iron bar.*
Tom no da el brazo a torcer. *You can't twist Tom's arm.*
Se ha torcido la leche. *The milk has gone sour.*

el torcimiento *twisting, sprain*
la torcedura *sprain, twisting*
la torcida *wick*

torcido/a *twisted, crooked*
torcidamente *crookedly, deviously*
el retorcijón *sudden twist*

185 tostar *to toast, roast, tan* (tr.)

INDICATIVE

Present	Imperfect	Perfect
tuesto	tostaba	he tostado
tuestas	tostabas	has tostado
tuesta	tostaba	ha tostado
tostamos	tostábamos	hemos tostado
tostáis	tostabais	habéis tostado
tuestan	tostaban	han tostado

Future	Pluperfect	Preterite
tostaré	había tostado	tosté
tostarás	habías tostado	tostaste
tostará	había tostado	tostó
tostaremos	habíamos tostado	tostamos
tostaréis	habíais tostado	tostasteis
tostarán	habían tostado	tostaron

Future perfect	Past anterior
habré tostado	hube tostado

CONDITIONAL | SUBJUNCTIVE

Present	Present	Imperfect
tostaría	tueste	tost-ara/ase
tostarías	tuestes	tost-aras/ases
tostaría	tueste	tost-ara/ase
tostaríamos	tostemos	tost-áramos/ásemos
tostaríais	tostéis	tost-arais/aseis
tostarían	tuesten	tost-aran/asen

Perfect	Perfect	Pluperfect
habría tostado	haya tostado	hub-iera/iese tostado

GERUND | PAST PARTICIPLE | IMPERATIVE

tostando	tostado	tuesta, tostad
		tueste (Vd), tuesten (Vds)

Tuesta el pan. *Make some toast, please.*
Lo tostó demasiado. *He toasted it too much.*
¿Has tostado el café? *Have you roasted the coffee?*
Nos tostaremos al sol. *We'll get brown in the sun.*

la tostada *piece of toast*
dar una tostada a uno *to put one over on someone*
tostado/a *toasted, with a tan, brown*

el tostador *toaster*
el tostón *crouton; roast suckling pig*
dar el tostón *to be a bore*
la tostadura *toasting, roasting*

186 trabajar *to work* (tr./intr.)

INDICATIVE

Present	Imperfect	Perfect
trabajo	trabajaba	he trabajado
trabajas	trabajabas	has trabajado
trabaja	trabajaba	ha trabajado
trabajamos	trabajábamos	hemos trabajado
trabajáis	trabajabais	habéis trabajado
trabajan	trabajaban	han trabajado

Future	Pluperfect	Preterite
trabajaré	había trabajado	trabajé
trabajarás	habías trabajado	trabajaste
trabajará	había trabajado	trabajó
trabajaremos	habíamos trabajado	trabajamos
trabajaréis	habíais trabajado	trabajasteis
trabajarán	habían trabajado	trabajaron

Future perfect	Past anterior
habré trabajado	hube trabajado

CONDITIONAL / SUBJUNCTIVE

Present	Present	Imperfect
trabajaría	trabaje	trabaj-ara/ase
trabajarías	trabajes	trabaj-aras/ases
trabajaría	trabaje	trabaj-ara/ase
trabajaríamos	trabajemos	trabaj-áramos/ásemos
trabajaríais	trabajéis	trabaj-arais/aseis
trabajarían	trabajen	trabaj-aran/asen

Perfect	Perfect	Pluperfect
habría trabajado	haya trabajado	hub-iera/iese trabajado

GERUND	PAST PARTICIPLE	IMPERATIVE
trabajando	trabajado	trabaja, trabajad
		trabaje (Vd), trabajen (Vds)

¿Dónde trabajas? *Where do you work?*
Trabajo en un banco. *I work in a bank.*
Trabajaron en un hospital. *They worked in a hospital.*
Trabajaré a tiempo parcial. *I'll work part time.*
Me cuesta trabajo entenderlo. *It is hard for me to understand it.*
Angela se tomó el trabajo de venir. *Angela took the trouble to come.*

el trabajo *work, labour*
el/la trabajador(a) *worker*
trabajador(a) *hard-working*
trabajado *worn out*

trabajoso/a *hard, laborious*
los trabajos forzados *hard labour*
ahorrarse el trabajo *to save oneself the trouble*

187 traducir *to translate* (tr.)

INDICATIVE

Present	Imperfect	Perfect
traduzco	traducía	he traducido
traduces	traducías	has traducido
traduce	traducía	ha traducido
traducimos	traducíamos	hemos traducido
traducís	traducíais	habéis traducido
traducen	traducían	han traducido

Future	Pluperfect	Preterite
traduciré	había traducido	traduje
traducirás	habías traducido	tradujiste
traducirá	había traducido	tradujo
traduciremos	habíamos traducido	tradujimos
traduciréis	habíais traducido	tradujisteis
traducirán	habían traducido	tradujeron

Future perfect	Past anterior
habré traducido	hube traducido

CONDITIONAL   SUBJUNCTIVE

Present	Present	Imperfect
traduciría	traduzca	traduj-era/ese
traducirías	traduzcas	traduj-eras/eses
traduciría	traduzca	traduj-era/ese
traduciríamos	traduzcamos	traduj-éramos/ésemos
traduciríais	traduzcáis	traduj-erais/eseis
traducirían	traduzcan	traduj-eran/esen

Perfect	Perfect	Pluperfect
habría traducido	haya traducido	hub-iera/iese traducido

GERUND   PAST PARTICIPLE   IMPERATIVE

GERUND	PAST PARTICIPLE	IMPERATIVE
traduciendo	traducido	traduce, traducid
		traduzca (Vd), traduzcan (Vds)

Voy a traducir el documento. *I'm going to translate the document.*
Lo traduje al inglés. *I translated it into English.*
Traduce del inglés al español. *He translates from English into Spanish.*
Quiero que traduzcas el contrato. *I want you to translate the contract.*

la traducción *translation*   **traducible** *translatable*
el/la traductor(a) *translator*

188 traer *to bring* (tr.)

INDICATIVE

Present	Imperfect	Perfect
traigo	traía	he traído
traes	traías	has traído
trae	traía	ha traído
traemos	traíamos	hemos traído
traéis	traíais	habéis traído
traen	traían	han traído

Future	Pluperfect	Preterite
traeré	había traído	traje
traerás	habías traído	trajiste
traerá	había traído	trajo
traeremos	habíamos traído	trajimos
traeréis	habíais traído	trajisteis
traerán	habían traído	trajeron

Future perfect	Past anterior
habré traído	hube traído

CONDITIONAL | SUBJUNCTIVE

Present	Present	Imperfect
traería	traiga	traj-era/ase
traerías	traigas	traj-eras/eses
traería	traiga	traj-era/ese
traeríamos	traigamos	traj-éramos/ésemos
traeríais	traigáis	traj-erais/eseis
traerían	traigan	traj-eran/esen

Perfect	Perfect	Pluperfect
habría traído	haya traído	hub-iera/iese traído

GERUND	PAST PARTICIPLE	IMPERATIVE
trayendo	traído	trae, traed
		traiga (Vd), traigan (Vds)

Traigo el pan. *I bring the bread.*
¿Puedes traer el vino? *Can you bring the wine?*
¿Han traído el libro? *Have you brought the book?*
El periódico no trae la noticia. *The newspaper does not carry the news.*
Manolito me trae de cabeza. *Manolito causes problems.*
Carlos nos trae locos. *Carlos drives us mad.*
Su padre se las trae. *Her father is very severe.*

traer a la memoria *to recall*
  (to memory)
la traída *carrying*
la traída de aguas *water supply*
traído/a *worn, worn out, old*

traerse algo entre manos *to plot*
el/la traedor(a) *porter, carrier, bearer,*
  bringer
la traedura *bringing, conduction, carrying*
traedizo/a *carried, brought, transported*

189 tratar *to treat, deal; to try* (tr.)

INDICATIVE

Present	Imperfect	Perfect
trato	trataba	he tratado
tratas	tratabas	has tratado
trata	trataba	ha tratado
tratamos	tratábamos	hemos tratado
tratáis	tratabais	habéis tratado
tratan	trataban	han tratado

Future	Pluperfect	Preterite
trataré	había tratado	traté
tratarás	habías tratado	trataste
tratará	había tratado	trató
trataremos	habíamos tratado	tratamos
trataréis	habíais tratado	tratasteis
tratarán	habían tratado	trataron

Future perfect	Past anterior
habré tratado	hube tratado

CONDITIONAL · SUBJUNCTIVE

Present	Present	Imperfect
trataría	trato	trat-ara/ase
tratarías	trates	trat-aras/ases
trataría	trate	trat-ara/ase
trataríamos	tratemos	trat-áramos/ásemos
trataríais	tratéis	trat-arais/aseis
tratarían	traten	trat-aran/asen

Perfect	Perfect	Pluperfect
habría tratado	haya tratado	hub-iera/iese tratado

GERUND · PAST PARTICIPLE · IMPERATIVE

GERUND	PAST PARTICIPLE	IMPERATIVE
tratando	tratado	trata, tratad
		trate (Vd), traten (Vds)

Me tratan muy bien aquí. *They treat me very well here.*
Van a tratarle con un nuevo fármaco. *They are going to treat him with a new drug.*
Está acostumbrado a tratar con criminales. *He's used to dealing with criminals.*
Está tratando con el enemigo. *He is negotiating with the enemy.*
Hay que tratar los huevos con cuidado. *Eggs have to be handled carefully.*
Este libro trata de la historia española. *This book is about Spanish history.*
Trató de entrar pero no pudo. *He tried to get in but he couldn't.*
¿De qué se trata? *What's it about?/What's the trouble?*
Se trata de la nueva piscina. *It's a matter of the new swimming pool.*
¿Nos tratamos de 'tú'? *Shall we address each other as 'tú'?*

el tratado *agreement, treaty; treatise*
el tratamiento *treatment, handling, management; style of address*
el trato *relationship, dealings; manner*
de fácil trato *easy to get on with*

entrar en tratos con *to enter into negotiations with*
en tratante (en) *dealer, trader (in)*

190 tronar *to thunder, shoot* (tr./intr.)

INDICATIVE

Present	Imperfect	Perfect
trueno	tronaba	he tronado
truenas	tronabas	has tronado
truena	tronaba	ha tronado
tronamos	tronábamos	hemos tronado
tronáis	tronabais	habéis tronado
truenan	tronaban	han tronado

Future	Pluperfect	Preterite
tronaré	había tronado	troné
tronarás	habías tronado	tronaste
tronará	había tronado	tronó
tronaremos	habíamos tronado	tronamos
tronaréis	habíais tronado	tronasteis
tronarán	habían tronado	tronaron

Future perfect	Past anterior
habré tronado	hube tronado

CONDITIONAL · SUBJUNCTIVE

Present	Present	Imperfect
tronaría	truene	tron-ara/ase
tronarías	truenes	tron-aras/ases
tronaría	truene	tron-ara/ase
tronaríamos	tronemos	tron-áramos/ásemos
tronaríais	tronéis	tron-arais/aseis
tronarían	truenen	tron-aran/asen

Perfect	Perfect	Pluperfect
habría tronado	haya tronado	hub-iera/iese tronado

GERUND	PAST PARTICIPLE	IMPERATIVE
tronando	tronado	truena, tronad
		truene (Vd), truenen (Vds)

Truena mucho. *It thunders a lot.*
Tronó durante toda la tormenta. *It was thundering during all of the storm.*
Tronaron a los prisioneros de guerra. *The prisoners of war were executed.*
El día de la Fiesta de la Hispanidad truenan los cañones como saludo. *They fire the cannons as a salute on Columbus Day.*
por lo que pueda tronar *just in case*
Se tronó. *He was ruined.*
Estoy que trueno. *I'm furious.*
Está que truena con su mujer. *He's fallen out with his wife.*

el tronazón *thunderstorm*
la tronada *thunderstorm*
el trueno *thunder*
el tronido *thunderclap*

tronado/a *broken down, useless*
estar tronado *to be broke*
tronante *thundering, thunderous*

191 valer *to cost, be worth* (tr./intr.)

INDICATIVE

Present	Imperfect	Perfect
valgo	valía	he valido
vales	valías	has valido
vale	valía	ha valido
valemos	valíamos	hemos valido
valéis	valíais	habéis valido
valen	valían	han valido

Future	Pluperfect	Preterite
valdré	había valido	valí
valdrás	habías valido	valiste
valdrá	había valido	valió
valdremos	habíamos valido	valimos
valdréis	habíais valido	valisteis
valdrán	habían valido	valieron

Future perfect	Past anterior
habré valido	hube valido

CONDITIONAL · SUBJUNCTIVE

Present	Present	Imperfect
valdría	valga	val-iera/iese
valdrías	valgas	val-ieras/ieses
valdría	valga	val-iera/iese
valdríamos	valgamos	val-iéramos/iésemos
valdríais	valgáis	val-ierais/ieseis
valdrían	valgan	val-ieran/iesen

Perfect	Perfect	Pluperfect
habría valido	haya valido	hub-iera/iese valido

GERUND	PAST PARTICIPLE	IMPERATIVE
valiendo	valido	vale, valed
		valga (Vd), valgan (Vds)

¿Cuánto vale? *How much is it?*
Vale €9. *It costs 9 euros.*
Es viejo pero todavía vale. *It's old but it still serves.*
Valía mucho dinero. *It was worth a lot of money.*
No vale nada. *It is worthless.*
No vale un higo. *It's not worth a brass farthing.*
Vale lo que pesa. *It's worth its weight in gold.*
Más vale así. *It's better this way.*
Más vale tarde que nunca. *Better late than never.*
No vale la pena. *It is not worth it.*

el valor *worth, price, value*
la valía *worth, value*
la valoración *valuation*

el vale *coupon, voucher*
el valimiento *value; benefit; favour*
valioso/a *valuable*

192 vencer *to defeat, overcome* (tr./intr.)

INDICATIVE

Present	Imperfect	Perfect
venzo	vencía	he vencido
vences	vencías	has vencido
vence	vencía	ha vencido
vencemos	vencíamos	hemos vencido
vencéis	vencíais	habéis vencido
vencen	vencían	han vencido

Future	Pluperfect	Preterite
venceré	había vencido	vencí
vencerás	habías vencido	venciste
vencerá	había vencido	venció
venceremos	habíamos vencido	vencimos
venceréis	habíais vencido	vencisteis
vencerán	habían vencido	vencieron

Future perfect	Past anterior
habré vencido	hube vencido

CONDITIONAL / SUBJUNCTIVE

Present	Present	Imperfect
vencería	venza	venc-iera/iese
vencerías	venzas	venc-ieras/ieses
vencería	venza	venc-iera/iese
venceríamos	venzamos	venc-iéramos/iésemos
venceríais	venzáis	venc-ierais/ieseis
vencerían	venzan	venc-ieran/iesen

Perfect	Perfect	Pluperfect
habría vencido	haya vencido	hub-iera/iese vencido

GERUND	PAST PARTICIPLE	IMPERATIVE
venciendo	vencido	vence, venced
		venza (Vd), venzan (Vds)

Nos han vencido. *They have defeated us.*
El Cid venció a los moros. *El Cid defeated the Moors.*
Venceremos. *We shall win.*
Le venció el sueño. *Sleep overcame him.*
Vence en elegancia. *He is the most elegant.*
No te dejes vencer. *Don't give in.*
Se ha vencido el plazo. *Time is up.*
Me doy por vencido/a. *I give in.*

vencedor(a) *victorious*   **la victoria** *victory*
el vencimiento *breaking, collapsing*   **pagar vencido** *to pay in arrears*
vencido/a *defeated*

193 vender *to sell* (tr.)

INDICATIVE

Present	Imperfect	Perfect
vendo	vendía	he vendido
vendes	vendías	has vendido
vende	vendía	ha vendido
vendemos	vendíamos	hemos vendido
vendéis	vendíais	habéis vendido
venden	vendían	han vendido

Future	Pluperfect	Preterite
venderé	había vendido	vendí
venderás	habías vendido	vendiste
venderá	había vendido	vendió
venderemos	habíamos vendido	vendimos
venderéis	habíais vendido	vendisteis
venderán	habían vendido	vendieron

Future perfect	Past anterior
habré vendido	hube vendido

CONDITIONAL / SUBJUNCTIVE

Present	Present	Imperfect
vendería	venda	vend-iera/iese
venderías	vendas	vend-ieras/ieses
vendería	venda	vend-iera/iese
venderíamos	vendamos	vend-iéramos/iésemos
venderíais	vendáis	vend-ierais/ieseis
venderían	vendan	vend-ieran/iesen

Perfect	Perfect	Pluperfect
habría vendido	haya vendido	hub-iera/iese vendido

GERUND / PAST PARTICIPLE / IMPERATIVE

GERUND	PAST PARTICIPLE	IMPERATIVE
vendiendo	vendido	vende, vended
		venda (Vd), vendan (Vds)

Vende coches. *He sells cars.*
Vamos a vender la casa. *We're going to sell the house.*
He vendido mis libros viejos. *I've sold my old books.*
Se venden manzanas. *Apples for sale.*
Venden café al por mayor. *They sell coffee wholesale.*
Vendemos al por menor. *We retail.*
Te lo vendo al contado. *I'll sell it to you for cash.*
Enrique se vende caro. *Enrique plays hard to get.*

se vende *for sale*
la venta *sale, selling; country inn*
el precio de venta *sale price*
la venta a domicilio *door-to-door sale*

el/la vendedor(a) *salesman*
vender a comisión *to sell on commission*

194 venir *to come, arrive* (intr.)

INDICATIVE

Present	Imperfect	Perfect
vengo	venía	he venido
vienes	venías	has venido
viene	venía	ha venido
venimos	veníamos	hemos venido
venís	veníais	habéis venido
vienen	venían	han venido

Future	Pluperfect	Preterite
vendré	había venido	vine
vendrás	habías venido	viniste
vendrá	había venido	vino
vendremos	habíamos venido	vinimos
vendréis	habíais venido	vinisteis
vendrán	habían venido	vinieron

Future perfect	Past anterior
habré venido	hube venido

CONDITIONAL / SUBJUNCTIVE

Present	Present	Imperfect
vendría	venga	vin-iera/iese
vendrías	vengas	vin-ieras/ieses
vendría	venga	vin-iera/iese
vendríamos	vengamos	vin-iéramos/iésemos
vendríais	vengáis	vin-ierais/ieseis
vendrían	vengan	vin-ieran/iesen

Perfect	Perfect	Pluperfect
habría venido	haya venido	hub-iera/iese venido

GERUND	PAST PARTICIPLE	IMPERATIVE
viniendo	venido	ven, venid
		venga (Vd), vengan (Vds)

Venimos a comer. *We've come for lunch.*
¡Ven acá! *Come over here!*
Vinieron a vernos. *They came to see us.*
Le hace venir a su oficina. *He summons him to his office.*
Vino a dar en la cárcel. *He ended up in jail.*
Los planes se vinieron abajo. *The plans collapsed.*
Todo se le viene encima. *Everything gets on top of him.*
Viene a ser lo mismo. *It amounts to the same thing.*

de ahí viene que... *hence...*
¡Venga! *Come on!*
¡Venga ya! *Come off it!*

la venida *coming, arrival*
el mes que viene *next month*
venidero/a *coming, posterity*

195 ver *to see* (tr./intr.)

INDICATIVE

Present	Imperfect	Perfect
veo	veía	he visto
ves	veías	has visto
ve	veía	ha visto
vemos	veíamos	hemos visto
veis	veíais	habéis visto
ven	veían	han visto

Future	Pluperfect	Preterite
veré	había visto	vi
verás	habías visto	viste
verá	había visto	vio
veremos	habíamos visto	vimos
veréis	habíais visto	visteis
verán	habían visto	vieron

Future perfect	Past anterior	
habré visto	hube visto	

CONDITIONAL · SUBJUNCTIVE

Present	Present	Imperfect
vería	vea	vi-era/ese
verías	veas	vi-eras/eses
vería	vea	vi-era/ese
veríamos	veamos	vi-éramos/ésemos
veríais	veáis	vi-erais/eseis
verían	vean	vi-eran/esen

Perfect	Perfect	Pluperfect
habría visto	haya visto	hub-iera/iese visto

GERUND	PAST PARTICIPLE	IMPERATIVE
viendo	visto	ve, ved
		vea (Vd), vean (Vds)

La vi en la tienda. *I saw her in the shops.*
No lo veo. *I can't see it.*
Le he visto ya. *I've already seen him.*
Vamos a ver una obra. *We're going to see a play.*
Ver y callar. *It's best to keep your mouth shut.*
¡A ver! *Let's see! Show me!*
Está por ver. *It remains to be seen.*
¡Para que veas! *So there!*

la vista *sight, eyesight, vision*
el vistazo *look, glance*
las vistillas *viewpoint, high place*
una cosa nunca vista *something unheard of*

vistoso/a *colourful*
el visto bueno *approval*
Está mal visto. *It is not done.*
Está muy visto. *It is very common.*

196 verter *to spill, pour* (tr./intr.)

INDICATIVE

Present	Imperfect	Perfect
vierto	vertía	he vertido
viertes	vertías	has vertido
vierte	vertía	ha vertido
vertemos	vertíamos	hemos vertido
vertéis	vertíais	habéis vertido
vierten	vertían	han vertido

Future	Pluperfect	Preterite
verteré	había vertido	vertí
verterás	habías vertido	vertiste
verterá	había vertido	vertió
verteremos	habíamos vertido	vertimos
verteréis	habíais vertido	vertisteis
verterán	habían vertido	vertieron

Future perfect	Past anterior
habré vertido	hube vertido

CONDITIONAL / SUBJUNCTIVE

Present	Present	Imperfect
vertería	vierta	vert-iera/iese
verterías	viertas	vert-ieras/ieses
vertería	vierta	vert-iera/iese
verteríamos	vertamos	vert-iéramos/iésemos
verteríais	vertáis	vert-ierais/ieseis
verterían	viertan	vert-ieran/iesen

Perfect	Perfect	Pluperfect
habría vertido	haya vertido	hub-iera/iese vertido

GERUND / PAST PARTICIPLE / IMPERATIVE

GERUND	PAST PARTICIPLE	IMPERATIVE
vertiendo	vertido	vierte, verted
		vierta (Vd), viertan (Vds)

Peter ha vertido la sopa sobre el mantel. *Peter has spilled the soup on the tablecloth.*
El río Arlanza vierte en el Duero. *The river Arlanza flows into the Duero.*
Vierte la sopa en la sopera. *Pour the soup into the tureen.*
Vamos a vertir el agua en el jardín. *We're going to pour the water into the garden.*

el vertedero *rubbish dump*
vertedor *bailer; overflow, outlet*
vertido/a *spilled*
vertible *spillable*

vertiente *side of a mountain, watershed, slope*
el vertedero público *landfill*
el vertido accidental de petróleo *accidental oil spill*

197 viajar *to travel* (intr.)

INDICATIVE

Present	Imperfect	Perfect
viajo	viajaba	he viajado
viajas	viajabas	has viajado
viaja	viajaba	ha viajado
viajamos	viajábamos	hemos viajado
viajáis	viajabais	habéis viajado
viajan	viajaban	han viajado

Future	Pluperfect	Preterite
viajaré	había viajado	viajé
viajarás	habías viajado	viajaste
viajará	había viajado	viajó
viajaremos	habíamos viajado	viajamos
viajaréis	habíais viajado	viajasteis
viajarán	habían viajado	viajaron

Future perfect	Past anterior
habré viajado	hube viajado

CONDITIONAL

SUBJUNCTIVE

Present	Present	Imperfect
viajaría	viaje	viaj-ara/ase
viajarías	viajes	viaj-aras/ases
viajaría	viaje	viaj-ara/ase
viajaríamos	viajemos	viaj-áramos/ásemos
viajaríais	viajéis	viaj-arais/aseis
viajarían	viajen	viaj-aran/asen

Perfect	Perfect	Pluperfect
habría viajado	haya viajado	hub-iera/iese viajado

GERUND	PAST PARTICIPLE	IMPERATIVE
viajando	viajado	viaja, viajad
		viaje (Vd), viajen (Vds)

Me gusta viajar. *I love travelling.*
Viajamos en tren. *We travelled by train.*
Francisca ha viajado mucho. *Francisca has travelled a lot.*
Leonor y Esperanza viajarán por Argentina. *Leonor and Esperanza will travel through Argentina.*

el viaje *journey, trip, tour*
el viaje de novios *honeymoon*
¡Buen viaje! *Bon voyage!*
el viaje de ida y vuelta *return journey*

el/la viajero/a *traveller*
el viajante de comercio *commercial traveller*

198 vivir *to live* (tr./intr.)

INDICATIVE

Present	Imperfect	Perfect
vivo	vivía	he vivido
vives	vivías	has vivido
vive	vivía	ha vivido
vivimos	vivíamos	hemos vivido
vivís	vivíais	habéis vivido
viven	vivían	han vivido

Future	Pluperfect	Preterite
viviré	había vivido	viví
vivirás	habías vivido	viviste
vivirá	había vivido	vivió
viviremos	habíamos vivido	vivimos
viviréis	habíais vivido	vivisteis
vivirán	habían vivido	vivieron

Future perfect	Past anterior
habré vivido	hube vivido

CONDITIONAL / SUBJUNCTIVE

Present	Present	Imperfect
viviría	viva	viv-iera/iese
vivirías	vivas	viv-ieras/ieses
viviría	viva	viv-iera/iese
viviríamos	vivamos	viv-iéramos/iésemos
viviríais	viváis	viv-ierais/ieseis
vivirían	vivan	viv-ieran/iesen

Perfect	Perfect	Pluperfect
habría vivido	haya vivido	hub-iera/iese vivido

GERUND	PAST PARTICIPLE	IMPERATIVE
viviendo	vivido	vive, vivid
		viva (Vd), vivan (Vds)

Vivimos en Burgos. *We live in Burgos.*
Viví en Pamplona en 1974. *I lived in Pamplona in 1974.*
Quiero vivir en paz. *I want to live in peace.*
Ana vive al día. *Ana lives from day to day.*
No tienen con qué vivir. *They haven't enough to live on.*
No me dejan vivir. *They don't give me any peace.*

vivo/a *living, alive; lively, vivid*	**la vivienda** *housing, dwelling*
la lengua viva *living language*	**¡Viva el rey!** *Long live the king!*
el buen vivir *the good life*	**el vivero** *tree nursery, seedbed*
los víveres *provisions, stores*	**la viveza** *liveliness, smartness*

199 volcar *to overturn* (tr./intr.)

INDICATIVE

Present	Imperfect	Perfect
vuelco	volcaba	he volcado
vuelcas	volcabas	has volcado
vuelca	volcaba	ha volcado
volcamos	volcábamos	hemos volcado
volcáis	volcabais	habéis volcado
vuelcan	volcaban	han volcado

Future	Pluperfect	Preterite
volcaré	había volcado	volqué
volcarás	habías volcado	volcaste
volcará	había volcado	volcó
volcaremos	habíamos volcado	volcamos
volcaréis	habíais volcado	volcasteis
volcarán	habían volcado	volcaron

Future perfect	Past anterior
habré volcado	hube volcado

CONDITIONAL / SUBJUNCTIVE

Present	Present	Imperfect
volcaría	vuelque	volc-ara/ase
volcarías	vuelques	volc-aras/ases
volcaría	vuelque	volc-ara/ase
volcaríamos	volquemos	volc-áramos/ásemos
volcaríais	volquéis	volc-arais/aseis
volcarían	vuelquen	volc-aran/asen

Perfect	Perfect	Pluperfect
habría volcado	haya volcado	hub-iera/iese volcado

GERUND / PAST PARTICIPLE / IMPERATIVE

GERUND	PAST PARTICIPLE	IMPERATIVE
volcando	volcado	vuelca, volcad
		vuelque (Vd), vuelquen (Vds)

El coche volcó en la curva. *The car turned over on the bend.*
Volcamos en el kilómetro 40. *We overturned at kilometre 40.*
El barco ha volcado. *The ship capsized.*
Se volcó el vaso. *The glass tipped over.*
Volcamos a Sara. *We made Sara dizzy.*
Pienso volcar a Elena. *I'm going to make Elena change her mind.*
Miguel se vuelca para conseguirlo. *Miguel does the utmost to get it.*
Miguel se vuelca por complacerte. *Miguel bends over backwards to satisfy you.*

el vuelco *overturning, upset, spill* **el volquete** *dumper, dumptruck*
dar un vuelco *to overturn, capsize*

200 **volver** *to turn, return, do again* (tr./intr.)

INDICATIVE

Present	Imperfect	Perfect
vuelvo	volvía	he vuelto
vuelves	volvías	has vuelto
vuelve	volvía	ha vuelto
volvemos	volvíamos	hemos vuelto
volvéis	volvíais	habéis vuelto
vuelven	volvían	han vuelto

Future	Pluperfect	Preterite
volveré	había vuelto	volví
volverás	habías vuelto	volviste
volverá	había vuelto	volvió
volveremos	habíamos vuelto	volvimos
volveréis	habíais vuelto	volvisteis
volverán	habían vuelto	volvieron

Future perfect	Past anterior
habré vuelto	hube vuelto

CONDITIONAL

SUBJUNCTIVE

Present	Present	Imperfect
volvería	vuelva	volv-iera/iese
volverías	vuelvas	volv-ieras/ieses
volvería	vuelva	volv-iera/iese
volveríamos	volvamos	volv-iéramos/iésemos
volveríais	volváis	volv-ierais/ieseis
volverían	vuelvan	volv-ieran/iesen

Perfect	Perfect	Pluperfect
habría vuelto	haya vuelto	hub-iera/iese vuelto

GERUND	PAST PARTICIPLE	IMPERATIVE
volviendo	vuelto	vuelve, volved
		vuelva (Vd), vuelvan (Vds)

Vuelve la hoja del libro. *Turn the page of the book.*
Volvió la mirada hacia Ana. *He turned his eyes towards Ana.*
Volveremos mañana. *We'll return tomorrow.*
Volvió a decirlo. *He said it again.*
Se desmayó, pero enseguida volvió en sí. *He fainted, but he soon came round.*
El ruido me vuelve loco. *Noise makes me mad.*
Se ha vuelto atrás. *He has gone back on his word.*

la vuelta *return, other side; tour*
dar una vuelta *to go for a short walk*
las vueltas *change*
dar vueltas *to turn, spin, revolve*

la vuelta de la marea *the turn of the tide*
la vuelta cerrada *sharp bend*
volverse *to turn round*

Spanish–English verb list

On the following pages you will find approximately 3000 Spanish verbs, with their meanings and the number, or numbers, of the model verb they follow. If the number is in **bold print**, the verb is one of the 200 modelled in full.

abajar *to go down* tr. *10*
abalanzar *to balance* tr. (r.) *31*
abalar *to move, shake* tr. (r.) *10*
abaldonar *to vilify, offend* tr. *10*
abalear *to separate, fire on, shoot at* tr. *10*
abalizar *to mark with buoys, take bearings* tr. *31*
aballar *to move* tr. *10*
aballestar *to haul, make taut* tr. *10*
abanar *to cool* tr. *10*
abanderar *to register under a flag, join* tr./intr. *10*
abandonar *to abandon, give up* tr./intr. *10*
abanicar *to fan* tr. (r.) *24*
abaratar *to make cheaper* tr./intr. *10*
abarcar *to encompass, embrace, contain* tr. *24*
abarrotar *to secure; fill, crowd* tr. *10*
abastar *to supply, provision* tr. (r.) *10*
abastecer *to supply, provide* tr. *47*
abatanar *to fill, bear* tr. *10*
abatar *to frighten* tr. (r.) *10*
abatir *to knock down, overthrow, demolish* tr./intr. *133*
abdicar *to abdicate* tr./intr. *24*
abducir *to abduct* tr. *45*
abellacar *to make/become vile* tr. (r.) *24*

aberrar *to err, be mistaken* intr. *10*
abetunar *to blacken* tr. *10*
abigarrar *to crowd* tr. *10*
abismar *to overwhelm, confuse* tr. (r.) *10*
abjurar *to abjure* tr. *10*
ablandar *to soften, pacify, improve* tr./intr. *10*
ablandecer *to soften* tr. *47*
abnegarse *to go without* r. *30, 116*
abobar *to bewilder, make stupid* tr. (r.) *10*
abocar *to bite; pour* tr./intr. *24*
abocetar *to sketch* tr. *10*
abochornar *to embarrass, wilt, wither* tr. (r.) *10*
abofetear *to slap* tr. *10*
abogar *to plead, defend, plead for* intr. *30*
abolir *to abolish* tr. *133*
abollar *to dent, bruise* tr. (r.) *10*
abombar *to make convex* tr./intr. (r.) *10*
abominar *to abominate* tr./intr. *10*
abonar *to subscribe* tr./intr. (r.) *10*
abordar *to board* tr./intr. *10*
aborrascarse *to become stormy* r. *24, 116*
aborrecer *to abhor, detest* tr. *54*
abortar *to abort, miscarry* tr./intr. *10*

abotijarse *to get bloated* r. 116

abotonar *to button; bud* tr./intr. (r.) *10*

abovedar *to vault, arch* tr. *10*

abozalar *to muzzle* tr. *10*

abrasar *to burn, fire* tr./intr. (r.) *10*

abrazar *to embrace, hug* tr. (r.) *31*

abrevar *to water, provide a drink* tr. *10*

abreviar *to shorten, reduce* tr. (r.) *10*

abrigar *to shelter, protect* tr. (r.) *30*

abrillantar *to polish, make glitter* tr. *10*

abrir *to open* (past participle: **abierto**) tr. (r.) *133*

abrochar *to button up, fasten* tr. *10*

abrogar *to repeat, abolish, annul* tr. *30*

abroncar *to annoy, irritate* tr. (r.) *24*

abrumar *to overwhelm, crush; embarrass* tr. (r.) *10*

absolver *to absolve* tr. *200*

absortar *to engross* tr. (r.) *10*

abstenerse *to abstain* r. *179*

abstraer *to abstract* tr./intr. (r.) *188*

abuenar *to calm, improve* tr. *10*

abullonar *to emboss, embroider* tr. *10*

abultar *to augment, enlarge, be bulky* tr./intr. *10*

abundar *to abound* tr./intr. *10*

abuñolar *to make fritters (of/with sth.)* tr. *2*

aburar *to burn, scorch* tr. *10*

aburguesarse *to become bourgeois* r. *116*

aburrarse *to become stupid* r. *116*

aburrir *to bore, annoy* tr. *133*

aburrirse *to be bored, get bored* r. *133*

abusar *to abuse* intr. *10*

acaballerar *to be/behave like a gentleman* tr. (r.) *10*

acabar *to finish, end* tr. (r.) *10*

acachetear *to slap in the face* tr. *10*

academizar *to academize* tr. *31*

acaecer *to happen* intr. (imp.) *54*

acalambrarse *to get a cramp* r. 116

acallar *to silence, pacify* tr. *10*

acalorar *to heat, warm up, get hot* tr. *10*

acamar *to fallen, be flattened* tr./intr. (r.) *10*

acamastronarse *to become artful* r. 116

acampanar *to shape (be shaped) like a bell* tr. *10*

acampar *to camp* tr./intr. (r.) *10*

acanalar *to striate, channel* tr. *10*

acanallar *to corrupt, become base* tr (r.) *10*

acantalear *to hail, rain very hard* intr.. *10*

acantear *to throw stones at, stone* tr. *10*

acantilar *to run aground, dredge* tr. (r.) *10*

acantonar *to quarter, billet, limit* tr. (r.) *10*

acaparar *to buy up, hoard, monopolize* tr. *10*

acapararse *to come to terms with* r. 116

acapillar *to capture, trap* tr. *10*

acapuchar *to shape into a hood* tr. *10*

acaramelar *to cover with caramel; get carried away* tr. (r.) *10*

acarar *to confront, face* tr. *10*

acardenalar *to bruise* tr. (r.) *10*

acarear *to confront, face* tr. *10*
acariciar *to caress, fondle* tr. *10*
acariciarse *to fondle oneself/each other* tr. (r.) *116*
acariñar *to treat lovingly* tr. *10*
acarminar *to dye red, redden* tr. *10*
acarralar *to skip a thread; wither* tr. (r.) *10*
acarrear *to transport, carry, incur* tr. (r.) *10*
acarroñar *to intimidate, become intimidated* tr. (r.) *10*
acartonar *to become like cardboard; wither* tr. (r.) *10*
acaserarse *to become fond of* r. *116*
acatar *to obey, respect, observe* tr. *10*
acatarrar *to catch a cold; annoy* tr. (r.) *10*
acaudalar *to amass, accumulate* tr. *10*
acaudillar *to lead, command, elect a leader* tr. (r.) *10*
acceder *to accede, agree* intr. *23*
accidentar *to have an accident, injure* tr. (r.) *10*
accionar *to put in motion, gesticulate* tr./intr. *10*
acechar *to lie in, wait for, observe, spy on* tr. *10*
acecinar *to cure meat by salting and smoking* tr. *10*
acecinarse *to become thin or lean with age* r. *116*
acedar *to sour, make bitter* tr. (r.) *10*
aceitar *to oil, smear with oil* tr. *10*
acelerar *to accelerate, speed* tr./intr. *10*
acemilar *to deal with mules* tr. *10*

acendrar *to purify, refine* tr. *10*
acensuar *to take the census, assess, tax* tr. *10*
acentuar *to stress, accent, mark with an accent* tr. *10*
acepar *to take root* intr. *10*
acepillar *to plane, brush, polish* tr. *10*
aceptar *to accept* tr. *10*
acequiar *to dig irrigation ditches* tr./intr. *10*
acerar *to make pavements/sidewalks* tr. *10*
acerar *to steel, turn into steel, strengthen* tr. *10*
acercar *to bring near* tr. *24*
acercarse *to approach* r. *24, 116*
acerrojar *to lock, bolt* tr. *10*
acertar *to guess, be right* tr./intr. **1**
acetrinar *to turn greenish* tr. (r.) *10*
acezar *to pant, gasp* intr. *31*
achacar *to impute, attribute* tr. *24*
achanchar *to check* tr. (r.) *10*
achantarse *to hide, conform* r. *116*
achaparrarse *to become chubby, grow stunted* r. *116*
acharolar *to vanish* tr. *10*
achatar *to flatten* tr. *10*
achicar *to diminish, bale out (a boat), lessen, reduce* tr. *24*
achicharrar *to scorch, burn, sizzle* tr. (r.) *10*
achinar *to intimidate, scare* tr. *10*
achirlar *to thin down* tr. *10*
achispar *to brighten up, make tipsy* tr. (r.) *10*
achocar *to hurl, injure* tr./intr. *24*
achocharse *to become senile, dote* r. *116*

achubascarse to cloud over and threaten rain r. *24, 116*

achuchar to crush, crumple, squeeze tr. *10*

achularse to become uncouth/rude/caddish r. *116*

achurar to gut, knife tr. *10*

achurrar to flatten tr. *10*

achurruscar to burn, scorch, squeeze tr. *24*

acibarar to make bitter, embitter tr. *10*

acicalar to dress up, make oneself smart tr. (r.) *10*

acicatear to incite, spur on tr. *10*

acidificar to acidify tr. *24*

aciguatar to watch, observe tr. *10*

aciguatarse to get fish poisoning r. *116*

aclamar to acclaim, hail tr. *10*

aclarar to clarify, explain, clear tr./intr. *10*

aclararse to rinse, clarify, clear r. *116*

aclimatar to acclimatize tr. *10*

aclimatizarse to acclimatize r. *116*

aclocarse to go broody r. *2, 24, 116*

acobardar to intimidate, become frightened tr./intr. *10*

acobijar to mulch tr. *10*

acocarse to become worm-ridden (fruit) r. *24, 116*

acocear to kick, maltreat tr. *10*

acocharse to crouch, duck r. *116*

acochinar to make dirty tr. *10*

acodalar to prop, shore tr. *10*

acodar to lean; layer tr. *10*

acodarse to lean (on elbow) r. *116*

acoderar to bring the broad side, bear tr. *10*

acodiciar to covet, long for, desire tr. *10*

acoger to welcome, shelter tr. *35*

acogollar to cover up tender plants, sprout, bud tr./intr. *10*

acogotar to kill, intimidate tr. *10*

acohombrar to bank, hill, earth up tr. *10*

acojinar to make cushions tr. *10*

acolar to unite tr. *10*

acolchar to pad, stuff, quilt tr. *10*

acollar to bank up with earth, caulk tr. *2*

acollarar to put a collar on tr. *10*

acollonar to scare, frighten tr. (r.) *10*

acomedirse to volunteer, oblige r. *122*

acometer to attack, undertake tr. *23*

acomodar to accommodate, suit tr./intr. *10*

acompañar to accompany, escort, go with tr. *10*

acompasar to measure, divide into bars tr. *10*

acomplejar to cause inhibitions, suffer from complexes tr. *10*

acomunarse to unite, confederate r. *116*

aconchar to push to safety, run aground, go to a safe place tr. *10*

acondicionar to condition, prepare tr. (r.) *10*

acongojar to anguish, be anguished tr. (r.) *10*

aconsejar to advise, counsel tr. *186*

acontecer to happen, come to pass intr. (imp.) *192*

acopar to trim, shape tr./intr. *10*

acopiar to gather, classify, collect tr. *10*

acoplar *to couple, join, mate* tr. (r.) 10

acoquinar *to intimidate, scare* tr. (r.) 10

acorar *to anguish, wither, wilt* tr. (r.) 10

acorazar *to armour, armourplate* tr. (r.) 31

acorchar *to line with cork* tr. 10

acordar *to agree, correspond* tr. 2

acordarse *to recollect, remember* r. 2, 116

acordonar *to fasten with a cord, tie* tr. 10

acornear *to gore, butt* tr. 10

acorralar *to pen, corner, intimidate* tr. 10

acorrer *to help, turn to the aid of* tr./intr. 23

acortar *to shorten, reduce, cut down* tr. (r.) 10

acosar *to harass, pursue, pester* tr. 10

acosijar *to overwhelm, oppress* tr. 10

acostar *to put to bed* tr./intr. 3

acostarse *to go to bed, lie down* r. 3

acostumbrar *to get used to, be accustomed to* tr./intr 10

acostumbrarse *to get used to* r. 116

acotar *to annotate, choose, select* tr. 10, *to survey, fix, prune, trim* tr. (r.) 10

acotejar *to make oneself comfortable* tr. (r.) 10

acrecentar *to increase* tr. (r.) 4

acrecer *to augment, be transferred* tr./intr. (r.) 54

acreditar *to credit* tr. (r.) 10

acrianzar *to raise, rear, bring up* tr. 31

acribar *to riddle, sift* tr. 10

acribillar *to riddle with bullets, harass* tr. 10

acriminar *to incriminate, impute* tr. 10

acriollarse *to adopt Spanish American ways* r. 116

acrisolar *to refine, purify* tr. 10

acristianar *to make Christian, Christianize* tr. 10

activar *to activate* tr. 10

actuar *to act, perform, bring an action* tr. 168

acuadrillar *to band together, get together* tr. (r.) 10

acuantiar *to assess the value or the quantity* tr. 10

acuartelar *to quarter, billet* tr. (r.) 10

acuartillar *to make into quarters* tr. 10

acuatizar *to land on water* intr. 31

acuchamarse *to become sad/ languid* r. 116

acuchillar *to cut, knife, slash* tr. 10

acuchucar *to squeeze, squash* tr. 24

acuciar *to hasten, urge, yearn for* tr. 10

acuclillarse *to squat* r. 116

acudir *to attend, assist* intr. 133

acuerpar *to support, defend* tr. 10

acuidarse *to be preoccupied with* r. 116

acuilmarse *to grieve* r. 116

acular *to back, back up* tr. (r.) 10

acullicar *to chew cocoa leaves* tr. 24

acumuchar *to accumulate, heap* tr. 10

acumular *to accumulate, amass* tr. 10

acunar *to cradle, rock* tr. 10

acuñar to wedge, coin, seal tr. *10*

acurrucarse to curl up, get cosy r. *24, 116*

acusar to accuse tr. (r.) *10*

adamar to become effeminate tr. (r.) *10*

adaptar to adapt, adjust tr. (r.) *10*

adatar to credit tr. *10*

adecenar to divide into tens tr. *10*

adecentar to make presentable, smarten tr. *33*

adecuar to adapt, fit tr. *10*

adehesar to convert land into pasture tr. *10*

adelantar to overtake, advance, progress tr./intr. *10*

adelantarse to go ahead, go forward r. *116*

adelgazar to lose weight tr./intr. (r.) *31*

adensar to thicken, condense tr. *10*

adentellar to bite tr. *10*

adentrar to go deeper into tr. *10*

aderezar to adorn, mend, get ready tr. *31*

adeudar to owe, go into debt, debit tr. (r.) *10*

adherir to adhere tr. (r.) *108*

adiamantar to set diamonds tr. *10*

adicionar to add, prolong tr. *10*

adiestrar to train, to coach tr. (r.) **5**

adietar to put on a diet, go on a diet tr. (r.) *10*

adinerar to convert into money, become rich tr. (r.) *10*

adivinar to guess, foretell tr. *10*

adjudicar to award, judge tr. (r.) *24*

adjuntar to enclose tr. *10*

administrar to manage tr. *10*

admirar to admire tr. (r.) *10*

admitir to admit, grant tr. *133*

adobar to season, marinate tr. *10*

adocenar to divide into dozens tr. *10*

adoctrinar to indoctrinate, instruct tr. *10*

adolecer to fall sick intr. (r.) *47*

adolorar to ache tr. *10*

adomiciliar to live (somewhere), have an address tr (r.) *10*

adonizarse to adorn oneself, beautify r. *31, 116*

adoptar to adopt tr. *10*

adoquinar to pave tr. *10*

adorar to adore, worship tr./intr. *10*

adormecer to put to sleep tr.(r.) *47*

adornar to adorn tr. *10*

adosar to place near tr. *10*

adquirir to acquire tr. **6**

adscribir to attach, ascribe tr. *98*

aducir to provide, quote tr. *45*

adueñarse to take possession r. *116*

adular to adulate, flatter tr. *10*

adulterar to adulterate, commit adultery tr./intr. (r.) *10*

adulzar to sweeten, soften tr. *31*

adulzorar to become sweet tr. *10*

adurir to burn tr. (r.) *133*

advenir to come, arrive intr. *194*

adverar to attest, authenticate tr. *10*

advertir to warn, advise; notice tr. **7**

afamar to make famous, become famous tr. (r.) *10*

afanar to press, hurry, steal tr. (r.) *10*

afear to make ugly, deform tr. *10*

afectar to affect, have an effect on tr. *10*

afeitarse to shave oneself tr. (r.) *116*

afeminar to make or become effeminate tr. (r.) *10*

aferrar to grapple tr./intr. (r.) *33*

afianzar *to fasten, hold on fast* tr. (r.) *31*

aficionar *to inspire, affection* tr. (r.) *10*

afijar *to affix, secure* tr. *10*

afilar *to sharpen, grown thin/ pointed* tr. (r.) *10*

afiliar *to join, affiliate* tr. (r.) *10*

afillar *to adopt* tr. *10*

afinar *to tune, perfect* tr./intr. (r.) *10*

afincar *to settle down, buy estate* intr. (r.) *24*

afirmar *to state, assure, affirm* tr. (r.) *10*

afligir *to afflict, grieve* tr. (r.) *84*

aflojar *to loosen, slacken* tr./intr. (r.) *10*

aflorar *to show, emerge* tr./intr. *10*

aflotar *to loosen, pay up, slacken* tr./intr. *10*

afluir *to flow, congregate* intr. *110*

afollar *to blow at* tr. (r.) *2*

afondar *to sink, submerge, touch the bottom* tr./intr. (r.) *10*

aforar *to rent* tr. *2*

aforrar *to line* tr. (r.) *10*

afortunar *to make happy* tr. *10*

afrentar *to affront, insult* tr. (r.) *10*

afrontar *to face, defy, confront* tr./intr. *10*

afufar *to escape* intr. (r.) *10*

afumarse *to get drunk* r. *116*

agachar *to lower, bend* tr. (r.) *10*

agañotar *to choke, strangle* tr. *10*

agarbar *to crouch, stoop* r. *10*

agarrar *to grasp, catch* tr. *10*

agarrotar *to choke, stiffen* tr. *10*

agasajar *to pamper, shower with gifts* tr. *10*

agaucharse *to become a gaucho* r. *116*

agazapar *to catch, stalk, crouch* tr. (r.) *10*

agenciar *to get, obtain, procure* tr./intr. (r.) *10*

agestarse *to make gestures, make faces* r. *116*

agigantar *to make or become enormous* tr. (r.) *10*

agilitar *to set in motion* tr. (r.) *10*

agilitarse *to limber up* tr. (r.) *10*

agitar *to shake, agitate* tr. (r.) *10*

aglomerar *to gather* tr. (r.) *10*

aglutinar *to join* tr. (r.) *10*

agobiar *to overwhelm, oppress* tr. (r.) *10*

agonizar *to be agony, annoy* tr./intr. *31*

agorar *to augur, predict* tr. *2*

agostar *to wither* tr./intr. (r.) *10*

agotar *to exhaust, use up* tr. (r.) *10*

agraciar *to grace, adorn, award* tr. *10*

agradar *to be pleasing, please* intr. *10*

agradarse *to please* intr. (r.) *116*

agradecer *to be grateful* tr. *54*

agrandar *to enlarge, increase* tr. (r.) *10*

agravar *to aggravate, make worse* tr. (r.) *10*

agraviar *to wrong, injure* tr. (r.) *10*

agredir *to attack* tr. *133*

agregar *to collate, collect, add* tr. *30*

agregarse *to add, collect* r. *30, 116*

agremiar *to unite, become a union/ syndicate* tr. (r.) *10*

agriar *to make sour* tr. (r.) *10*

agrietar *to split, crack* tr. (r.) *10*

agrumar *to curdle, clot* tr. (r.) *10*

agrupar *to group* tr. (r.) *10*

agruparse *to group* r. *116*

aguachar *to flood* tr. (r.) *10*

aguachinarse *to flood, get waterlogged* tr. (r.) 116

aguantar *to bear, endure* tr./intr. (r.) 10

aguar *to dilute* tr. (r.) 10

aguardar *to await, expect* tr./intr. 10

aguardarse *to expect, wait for* r. 116

aguerrir *to instruct (military)* tr. (r.) 133

aguijonear *to prick, goad, incite* tr. 10

aguzar *to sharpen, grind* tr. 31

ahijar *to adopt* tr./intr. 10

ahilar *to go in single file, line up* tr./intr. (r.) 10

ahitar *to surfeit, bloat* tr. (r.) 10

ahogarse *to drown* tr. (r.) 30, 116

ahondar *to deepen, go down* tr./intr. (r.) 10

ahorcar *to hang* tr. (r.) 10

ahormar *to mould, fit* tr. (r.) 10

ahornar *to put in the oven* tr. 10

ahorrar *to economize, save* tr. 10

ahorrarse *to save, economize* r. 116

ahuecar *to soften, fluff up, become vain* tr./intr. (r.) 24

ahumar *to smoke, cure in smoke* tr. (r.) 10

ahuyentar *to drive away, banish* tr. 10

aislar *to isolate* tr. (r.) 10

ajetrear *to bustle about, tire, fatigue* tr. (r.) 10

ajornalar *to hire by the day* tr. (r.) 10

ajuarar *to furnish* tr. 10

ajuiciar *to judge, become sensible* tr./intr. 10

ajumarse *to get drunk* r. 116

ajustar *to adjust, fit, adapt* tr./intr. 10

ajustarse *to conform* r. 116

alabar *to praise, sing* tr./intr. 10

aladrar *to plough* tr. 10

alambicar *to distill* tr. 24

alambrar *to fence with wire* tr. 10

alampar *to yearn, crave for* intr. (r.) 10

alardear *to show off, boast, brag* intr. 10

alargar *to lengthen, extend* tr. (r.) 30

alarmar *to alarm, call to arms, be alarmed* tr. (r.) 10

albear *to turn white; get up at dawn* intr. 10

albergar *to give shelter, take lodging* tr./intr. (r.) 30

alborear *to dawn* intr. (imp.) 10

alborotar *to stir up, agitate, make noise* tr./intr. (r.) 10

alborozar *to delight, feel elated* tr. (r.) 31

albuminar *to emulsify* tr. 10

alcahazar *to keep/put in a cage* tr. 31

alcahuetear *to procure, pimp* tr./intr. 10

alcalizar *to alkalize* tr. 31

alcantarillar *to provide drains* tr. 10

alcanzar *to attain, reach* tr./intr. (r.) 31

alcoholizar *to make alcohol, drink heavily* tr. (r.) 31

alcorzar *to coat with sugar icing* tr. 31

alear *to flutter/flap; recover* tr./intr. 10

alebrar *to cower, be sacred* intr. (r.) 33

alebrarse *to throw oneself flat on the ground* r. 116

aleccionar *to instruct, teach* tr. 10

alegamar *to fertilize with mud or silt* tr. 10

alegar to allege, contend, declare tr. 30

alegrar to make happy; stir up tr. 10

alegrarse to rejoice, be glad r. 116

alejar to remove, go far away tr. (r.) 10

alentar to encourage; breathe tr./intr. (r.) **8**

alertar to alert, sound the alarm tr. 10

alfombrar to carpet tr. 10

alforzar to pleat, tuck tr. 10

algodonar to cover/fill/work with cotton tr. 10

alhajar to bejewel, adorn with jewels tr. 10

alheñar to dye with henna tr. (r.) 10

aliar to join, ally tr. (r.) 10

alicatar to tile tr. 10

alienar to alienate, transfer, become alienated tr. (r.) 10

alifar to polish tr. 10

aligar to tie, bind tr. 30

aligerar to ligthen, relieve, make lighter tr./intr. 10

alimentar to feed tr./intr. (r.) 10

alimonarse to turn yellowish r. 116

alindar to adorn, make pretty; mark the limits, border tr./intr. (r.) 10

alinear to align, line up tr. (r.) 10

aliñar to season, put salad dressing on tr. 10

aliquebrarse to break a wing, be crestfallen r. 116, 143

alisar to smooth, sleek tr. (r.) 10

alistar to recruit, enlist, enrol tr./intr. (r.) 10

aliviar to lessen, lighten, relieve tr. (r.) 10

allanar to make flat, level tr. (r.) 10

allegar to gather, arrive tr./intr. 119

almacenar to store tr. 10

almadiar to get sea sick tr. (r.) 10

almagrar to colour with red ochre; defame tr. 10

almibarar to cover with syrup tr. 10

almidonar to starch tr. 10

almizclar to perfume with musk tr. 10

almorzar to have lunch/a late breakfast tr./intr. **9**

alocar to make mad tr. (r.) 24

alojar to lodge, give accommodation tr. (r.) 10

alongar to lengthen tr. (r.) 2, 30

aloquecerse to become mad r. 92

alorarse to become tanned from the sun and the wind r. 116

alquilar to rent, hire tr. (r.) 10

alquitranar to tar, coat with tar tr. 10

alterar to alter, change tr. (r.) 10

altercar to disagree intr. (r.) 24

alternar to alternate tr./intr. 10

altivar to become proud tr. (r.) 10

altivecer to become arrogant tr. (r.) 47

alucinar to hallucinate, delude tr. (r.) 10

alumbrar to illuminate tr./intr. 10

alumbrarse to be/get high/ tipsy, become lively (from drink); illuminate, enlighten r. 116

alzar to lift, elevate, pick up tr. 31

alzarse to raise, lift, pick up r. 31, 116

amaestrar to train, coach, tame tr. 10

amagar to stimulate, appear tr. (r.) 30

amainar *to lower, clam, lessen* tr./intr. *10*

amalgamar *to amalgamate, mix* tr. *10*

amamantar *to suckle, nurse* tr. *10*

amancebarse *to cahabit, live together* r. *116*

amancillar *to stain, defame* tr. *10*

amanecer *to dawn* intr. (imp.) *47*

amanerarse *to become mannered, act affectedly* r. *116*

amanojar *to bundle, bunch* tr. *10*

amansar *to tame* tr. (r.) *10*

amañar *to fake; get the knack of doing things* tr. (r.) *10*

amar *to love, be fond of* tr. **10**

amarar *to land on water* intr. *10*

amarecer *to mate* tr. *47*

amargar *to make bitter, embitter* tr. (r.) *30*

amarrar *to tie, moor, bind* tr. (r.) *10*

amartelar *to drive mad, fall deeply in love* tr. (r.) *10*

amartillar *to hammer* tr. *10*

amasar *to knead, mix, amass* tr. *10*

ambicionar *to desire, yearn* tr. *10*

ambular *to walk, stroll* intr. *10*

amedrantar *to frighten* tr. *10*

amelonarse *to fall madly in love* tr. *116*

amenazar *to threaten* tr. *31*

amenguar *to reduce* tr./intr. *12*

amigar *to bring together* tr. (r.) *30*

amilanar *to intimidate, scare* tr. (r.) *10*

aminorar *to diminish* tr. *10*

amnistiar *to grant amnesty* tr. *10*

amoblar *to furnish* tr. *2*

amodorrarse *to become drowsy, grow sleepy* r. *116*

amojonar *to delimit, mark* tr. *10*

amolar *to grind* tr. *2*

amoldar *to model, fashion* tr. *10*

amollar *to yield, ease off, give in* tr./intr. *10*

amonestar *to reprove, warn* tr. *10*

amontonar *to pile together* tr. *10*

amoratar *to turn blue/purple* tr. (r.) *10*

amorrar *to sulk, hang, pitch* tr./intr. *10*

amortajar *to shroud, lay out* tr. *10*

amortecer *to dull, dim, soften* tr. (r.) *47*

amortiguar *to muffle, soften, cushion* tr. *12*

amortizar *to pay off, amortize* tr. *31*

amoscarse *to get angry* r. *116*

amotinar *to mutiny* tr. *10*

amparar *to protect* tr. *10*

ampliar *to amplify* tr. *10*

amplificar *to amplify, enlarge* tr. *24*

amputar *to amputate* tr. *10*

amustiar *to wither* tr. *10*

analizar *to analyse* tr. *31*

anclar *to anchor* intr. *10*

andar *to walk, go* tr./intr. (r.) **11**

anegar *to drown, become flooded* tr. *130*

anestesiar *to anaesthetize* tr. *10*

anexar *to annex* tr. *10*

angostar *to narrow* tr./intr. (r.) *10*

anhelar *to wish, desire, yearn for* tr. *10*

anillar *to form into rings* tr. *10*

animar *to animate, enlighten* tr. (r.) *10*

aniquilar *to wipe out, annihilate* tr. (r.) *10*

anochecer *to get dark* intr. (imp.) *47*

anotar *to annotate, make notes* tr. 10

ansiar *to yearn for* tr. 10

anteponer *to place in front, prefer* tr. (r.) 139

antevenir *to precede* intr. 194

antever *to foresee* tr. 195

anticipar *to anticipate, advance, be early* tr. (r.) 10

antojarse *to feel like, fancy* r. 116

anublar *to cloud, dim, darken* tr. (r.) 10

anudar *to tie knots* tr. (r.) 10

anular *to cancel, make null and void* tr. 10

anularse *to annul, make void* r. 116

anunciar *to announce, foretell, proclaim* tr. 10

anunciarse *to announce, proclaim* r. 116

añadir *to add, pad* tr. 133

añorar *to pine for, miss* tr./intr. 10

apabullar *to crush, overwhelm* tr. 10

apacentar *to graze, feed* tr. 33

apaciguar *to pacify, calm down* tr. (r.) **12**

apadrinar *to sponsor* tr. (r.) 10

apagar *to turn off, put out* tr. 30

apagarse *to turn off* r. 30, 116

apalabrar *to come to an agreement* tr. (r.) 10

apalear *to beat* tr. 10

apañar *to pick, manage* tr. (r.) 10

aparar *to prepare* tr. 10

aparcar *to park* tr. 24

aparecer *to appear, show up* intr. 47

aparecerse *to appear, show up* r. 47, 116

aparentar *to feign, simulate, seem* tr. 10

apartar *to separate, sort* tr./intr. (r.) 10

apasionar *to incite, excite, be mad about* tr. (r.) 10

apear *to dismount, get off, lodge* tr. (r.) 10

apedrear *to stone* tr. 10

apelar *to appeal* intr. 10

apellidar *to call by the surname* tr. (r.) 10

apercibir *to provide, prepare, warn* tr. 133

apercibirse (de) *to became aware of* r. 133

apercollar *to seize by the collar or neck* tr. 2

apernar *to tackle* tr. 33

aperrear *to annoy, pester* tr. 10

apestar *to be infected, stink* tr./intr. (r.) 10

apetecer *to fancy, crave for* tr. 47

apiadar *to feel with, pity* tr. (r.) 10

apiñar *to crowd* tr. 10

apiparse *to gorge food* r. 116

aplacar *to placate* tr. 24

aplacer *to please* tr./intr. 47

aplacerse *to please* r. 47, 116

aplanar *to flatten* tr. (r.) 10

aplastar *to squash, crush* tr. (r.) 10

aplaudir *to applaud, clap* tr. (r.) 133

aplazar *to postpone* tr. 31

aplicar *to apply* tr. (r.) 24

apodar *to nickname* tr. 10

apoderarse *to take possession* r. 116

aporcar *to cover with earth* tr. 2, 24

aportar *to arrive at a port* intr. 2

aportarse *to bring* r. 2, 116

apostar *to bet, post* tr./intr. (r.) **13**

apoyar *to rest, lean* tr./intr. (r.) 10

apreciar to appreciate tr. 10

apreciarse to appreciate, appraise r. 116

aprender to learn tr. (r.) 23

apresurar to hurry, hasten tr. (r.) 10

apresurarse to hasten, hurry, rush r. 116

apretar to grip, press together tr./intr. (r.) **14**

aprobar to approve, pass tr./intr. **15**

aprovechar to take advantage of tr./intr. (r.) 10

aprovecharse to take advantage, avail oneself r. 116

apuñalar to slash, stab tr. 10

apuñar to grasp, clench the fist tr./intr. 10

apurar to grieve; hurry, finish tr. 10

apurarse to fret, grieve, worry r. 116

aquejar to afflict, worry tr. 10

arañar to scratch tr. (r.) 10

arar to plough tr. 10

arbitrar to referee, judge tr./intr. (r.) 10

archivar to file tr. 10

arder to burn intr. 23

argüir to argue, reason tr./intr. **16**

armar to arm tr. (r.) 10

arrancar to snatch, pull out, start (engines) tr./intr. 24

arrancarse to start, pull up, root out r. 24, 116

arrastrar to drag, pull along tr./intr. (r.) 10

arreciar to make stronger tr./intr. 10

arrecirse to become numb r. 134

arreglar to arrange, fix, repair tr. (r.) 10

arreglarse to settle, make one look one's best; get ready, manage r. 116

arrendar to let, lease, hire out tr. **17**

arrepentir to repent, regret tr. (r.) 108

arriesgar to risk tr. (r.) 30

arrimar to bring near tr. (r.) 10

arrojar to fling, hurl tr. 10

arrojarse to throw, hurl, fling r. 116

arropar to clothe, wrap up tr. (r.) 10

arrugar to wrinkle, crease, crumple tr. (r.) 30

articular to articulate, pronounce distinctly tr. 10

asaltar to assail, assault tr. 10

asar to roast tr. (r.) 10

ascender to ascend tr./intr. (r.) 136

asear to clean, tidy tr. (r.) 10

asegurar to assure, assert, insure tr. 10

asegurarse to affirm, insure r. 116

asentar to settle, set, make firm tr. **18**

asentir to assent, agree intr. **19**

aserrar to saw tr. 33

asestar to aim, deal, deliver tr. 33

asir to grasp, seize tr./intr. **20**

asistir to be present at, attend; assist tr./intr. (r.) 133

asolar to devastate tr. (r.) 2

asoldar to pay troops tr. (r.) 53

asomar to show, appear tr./intr. (r.) 10

asombrar to amaze, astonish tr. (r.) 10

asonar to sound intr. 2

aspirar to inhale, suck in, aspirate tr./intr. 10

asquear to be nauseated tr./intr. (r.) 10

asumir to assume, command tr. 133

asustarse to be frightened r. 116

atacar to attack tr. (r.) *24*

atañer to concern, appertain intr. (r.) *23*

atar to bind, tie tr. (r.) *10*

atardecer to draw towards evening, get dark intr. (imp.) *47*

atarear to give work tr. *10*

atascar to get stuck tr. (r.) *24*

ataviar to attire, adorn, deck tr. (r.) *10*

atender to attend, pay attention, serve tr./intr. (r.) **21**

atenderse to depend on, rely on, abide by r. *116*

atentar to attempt tr./intr. *33*

aterirse to become numb with cold tr. (r.) *133*

aterrar to terrorize tr./intr. *33*

atestar to cram tr. *33*

atestarse to pack, attest, stuff, testify r. *33, 116*

atraer to allure, attract, charm tr. *188*

atraerse to attract, allure r. *188*

atrancar to lock tr./intr. (r.) *24*

atrapar to trap, catch tr. *10*

atravesar to cross, go through tr. **22**

atravesarse to cross, go through r. *22, 116*

atreverse to dare, venture r. *23*

atribuir to attribute to tr. (r.) *110*

atronar to thunder tr. (r.) *2*

atropellar to trample/knock down tr. (r.) *10*

aturdir to daze, stun, bewilder tr. (r.) *133*

aullar to howl tr. *10*

aumentar to increase tr./intr. (r.) *10*

ausentarse to be absent r. *116*

autorizar to authorize tr. *31*

avanzar to advance tr./intr. (r.) *31*

avenir to reconcile tr. (r.) *194*

aventar to fan tr. (r.) *33*

avergonzar to shame, embarrass tr. *2, 31*

avergonzarse to be ashamed r. *2, 31, 116*

averiar to go wrong tr. (r.) *10*

averiguar to find out tr./intr. *12*

avisar to inform, (give) notice, warn tr. *10*

avivar to enliven tr./intr. (r.) *10*

ayudar to help, aid, assist tr. (r.) *10*

ayunar to fast intr. *10*

azolar to chop with an axe tr. *2*

azotar to beat, thrash tr. (r.) *10*

babear to dribble intr. *10*

bailar to dance tr. *10*

bajar to descend, go down tr./intr. *186*

bajarse to go down, descend r. *116*

baladrar to shout, whoop intr. *10*

balancear to sway, balance, rock intr./tr. (r.) *10*

balar to bleat intr. *10*

balbucear to hesitate (in speech), stammer intr. *10*

balbucir to stammer, stutter intr. *45*

baldar to cripple, maim tr. (r.) *10*

bandear to chase, wound tr./intr. *10*

bañar to bathe tr. *10*

bañarse to bathe oneself, take a bath r. *116*

barajar to shuffle cards, quarrel tr./intr. (r.) *10*

barbar to grow a beard intr. *10*

barbotar to mumble, mutter tr./intr. *10*

barnizar to varnish tr. *31*

barquear *to cross in a boat* tr./intr. 10

barrenar *to drill* tr. 10

barrer *to sweep* tr./intr. (r.) 23

barruntar *to guess, surmise* tr. 10

bartolear *to idle* intr. 10

basar *to base, support* tr. (r.) 10

bastar *to be enough* intr. (imp.) 10

bastardear *to degenerate, debase* tr./intr. 10

bastarse *to be sufficient, suffice* r. 116

bastonear *to cane* tr. 10

batallar *to fight, battle* intr. 10

batir *to beat, whip* tr./intr. (r.) 133

bautizar *to baptize, christen* tr. 31

beber *to drink* tr./intr. (r.) **23**

becar *to grant, award* tr. 24

bendecir *to bless* tr. 57

beneficiar *to benefit* tr. (r.) 10

berrear *to bleat, bellow, shriek* intr. 10

besar *to kiss* tr. (r.) 10

bestializarse *to become beast-like* r. 116

besuquear *to lavish kisses on* tr. 10

betunar *to polish* tr. 10

bichar *to spy on* tr. 10

bieldar *to winnow* tr. 10

bienquerer *to like, to be fond of* tr. 144

bienquistar *to reconcile* tr. (r.) 10

bienvivir *to live well* intr. 198

bifurcarse *to branch off, bifurcate* r. 24, 116

bigardear *to lead an aimless life* intr. 10

bilocarse *to be in two places, go mad* r. 24, 116

binar *to hoe, dig over* tr./intr. 10

biografiar *to write a biography* tr. 10

birlar *to throw, cheat, rob, filch* tr. 10

bisar *to repeat* tr. 10

bizarrear *to act gallantly* intr. 10

bizcochar *to bake* tr. 10

bizcornear *to squint* intr. 10

bizmar *to apply a poultice* tr. 10

bizquear *to squint* intr. 10

blandear *to soften* tr./intr. (r.) 10

blandir *to brandish, swing* tr./intr. (r.) 133

blanquear *to whiten, bleach, whitewash* tr./intr. 10

blanquecer *to blanch, whiten* tr. 54

blasfemar *to blaspheme, curse, swear* intr. 10

blasonar *to emblazon, boast, brag* tr./intr. 10

blindar *to armour* tr. 10

bloquear *to block, obstruct* tr. 10

bobear *to play the fool* intr. 10

bobinar *to wind, reel, coil* tr. 10

bocadear *to divide into bits/ mouthfuls* tr. 10

bocartear *to crush* tr. 10

bochar *to hit and move* tr. 10

bocinar *to blow a horn* intr. 10

bofarse *to sag, grown spongy* r. 116

bogar *to row* tr. 10

bombardear *to bombard* tr. 10

bonificar *to increase production* tr. 24

borbotar (= borboritar) *to bubble, boil* tr. 10

bordar *to embroider* tr. 10

bordear *to skirt, go round* tr./intr. 10

bornear *to twist* tr. 10

borrar *to cross out, erase* tr. 10

borrarse *to erase, delete* r. 116

borronear *to scribble, scrawl* tr. 10

bostezar *to yawn, gape* intr. *31*

botar *to launch (a boat), bounce* tr./intr. *10; to fling, cast away* tr. *10*

bramar *to bellow, roar* intr. *10*

bravear *to bluster, bully* intr. *10*

brear *to maltreat, annoy, vex* tr. *10*

bregar *to fight, brawl* tr./intr. *30*

bregarse *to struggle* r. *30, 116*

brillar *to shine* intr. *10*

brincar *to skip, jump, bounce* tr./intr. *24*

brindar *to toast, offer* tr./intr. (r.) *10*

bromear *to joke, jest* intr. (r.) *10*

broncear *to bronze, tan* tr. (r.) *10*

brotar *to sprout, bud* intr. *10*

brumar *to crash, oppress* tr. *10*

bruñir *to polish, buff* tr. *198*

bucear *to dive, swim under water* intr. *10*

bufar *to snort, puff* intr. (r.) *10*

bufonear *to jest, joke, act the buffoon* intr. (r.) *10*

bullir *to boil, bustle, budge, bubble* tr./intr. *198*

burbujear *to bubble* intr. *10*

burlar *to mock, dodge, make fun* tr./intr. *10*

burlarse *to ridicule, make fun* r. *116*

buscar *to look for* tr. **24**

cabalgar *to ride a horse* tr./intr. *30*

cabecear *to nod, shake/toss the head* intr. *10*

caber *to fit, have enough room* intr. **25**

caberse *to be contained, fit into* r. *25*

cabrearse *to annoy, bother* tr./intr. (r.) *116*

cacarear *to crow, cackle, brag, boast* tr./intr. *10*

cachar *to break into pieces* tr. *10*

caer *to fall* intr. **26**

caerse *to fall down, tumble* r. *26*

cagar *to defecate, soil, spoil* (vulg.) tr./intr. (r.) *30*

calar *to soak, drench* tr./intr. (r.) *10*

calaverear *to lead a wild/dissolute life* intr. *10*

calcar *to trace, copy* tr. *24*

calcular *to calculate* tr. *10*

caldear *to heat up, warm* tr. (r.) *10*

calentar *to warm, heat (up)* tr. **27**

calentarse *to get warm, get angry, become excited* r. *27, 116*

calificar *to assess, rate, rank* tr. (r.) *24*

callar *to shut up, be silent* tr./intr. *10*

callarse *to be/remain silent, keep quiet* r. *116*

callejear *to be (always) in the streets* intr. *10*

calmar *to calm, soothe, grow calm* tr./intr. (r.) *10*

calumniar *to slander, defame* tr. *10*

calzarse *to shoe, put on shoes* r. *31, 116*

cambiar *to change* tr./intr. (r.) *118*

camelar *to woo, use flattery to achieve something* tr. *10*

caminar *to walk* tr./intr. **28**

camochar *to trim, prune* tr. *10*

camorrear *to quarrel* intr. *10*

canalizar *to make channels, pipe* tr. *31*

cancelar *to cancel, strike out* tr. *10*

cancerar *to make cancerous, reprove* tr. (r.) *10*

canchar *to toast, roast* tr./intr. *10*

canchear *to clamber, shirk* intr. *10*

candar *to lock* tr. *10*

canecer to grow grey hair, go grey tr./intr. *47*

canillar to wind on a spool tr. *10*

canjear to exchange tr. *10*

cansar to be tired, get tired tr. *10*

cansarse to get tired, become weary r. *116*

cantalear to sing softly, hum intr. *10*

cantar to sing, chant tr./intr. (r.) **29**

cantonear to idle, wander about intr. *10*

capar to castrate tr. *10*

capitular to capitulate, surrender tr./intr. *10*

capotar to turn over intr. *10*

captar to win, capture tr. *10*

caracterizar to characterize tr. (r.) *31*

carbonizar to carbonize, char tr. (r.) *31*

carcajear to laugh heartily, guffaw intr. (r.) *10*

carcomer to gnaw, decay tr. (r.) *39*

carear to confront, face tr./intr. (r.) *10*

carecer to lack intr. *54*

cargar to burden, load tr./intr. (r.) *30*

cargarse to load, burden r. *30, 116*

carpintear to work as a carpenter intr. *10*

carrasquear to crackle, crunch intr. *10*

cartear to write letters to one another, correspond intr. (r.) *10*

casar to get married, marry tr./intr. (r.) *10*

casarse to get married, marry r. *116*

cascar to break, crack tr./intr. (r.) *24*

castigar to punish tr. **30**

castrar to castrate, dry, prune tr. (r.) *10*

catalogar to list, catalogue tr. *30*

catar to sample, taste tr. *10*

catear to seek, search for tr. *10*

categorizar to categorize tr. *31*

catonizar to censure severely intr. *31*

caucionar to bond, pledge, caution tr. *10*

causar to cause tr. *10*

cautelar to prevent, take precautions tr. (r.) *10*

cautivar to capture, captivate tr. *10*

cavar to dig, excavate tr./intr. *10*

cavilar to ponder, meditate, reflect upon tr./intr. *10*

cayapear to gang up on and attack intr. *10*

cazar to hunt, chase, catch tr. **31**

cazoletear to meddle intr. *10*

cebar to fatten tr./intr (r.) *10*

ceder to yield, surrender tr./intr. *23*

cegar to blind, block tr./intr. (r.) **32**

cejar to back up, withdraw intr. *10*

celar to supervise, watch out for tr./intr. *10*

celebrar to celebrate tr./intr. *10*

cellisquear to sleet intr. *10*

cenar to have supper tr. *10*

cencerrear to jingle, clang intr. *10*

censar to census, take a census of tr. *10*

censurar to censure, criticize, judge tr. *10*

centellar to sparkle, twinkle intr. *10*

centellear to flicker, sparkle, shimmer intr. *10*

centrar to centre tr. *10*

centuplicar to increase hundredfold tr. (r.) *24*

ceñir to gird tr. (r.) *134*

cepillar to brush tr. (r.) *10*

cepillarse to brush oneself, finish r.
116

cercar to fence, enclose, lay siege
tr. 24

cerner to sift, bolt tr./intr. (r.) 136

cernir to sift tr. 165

cerrar to close, shut, lock tr./intr. (r.)
33

certificar to certify, register (letters)
tr. 24

certificarse to certify, attest r. 24,
116

cesar to cease, stop intr. 10

chafar to crease, crumple tr. (r.) 10

chafarse to flatten r. 116

chamuscar to singe, scorch tr. (r.) 24

chapar to cover, plate tr. 10

chaparrear to rain heavily, pour intr.
10

chapucear to botch, bungle tr. 10

chapuzar to duck, dip under water
tr./intr. (r.) 31

charlar to chat, prattle intr. 10

chascar to click, crack, crunch
tr./intr. 24

chasquear to play a practical joke,
crackle tr./intr. (r.) 10

chequear to check, inspect tr. 10

chiflar to whistle, jeer, trim intr./tr.
(r.) 10

chillar to scream, shriek intr. 10

chinchar to annoy, irritate tr. 10

chingar to drink; annoy, bother
tr. (r.) 30

chirriar to squeak, sizzle, creak,
spatter intr. 10

chismear to gossip intr. 10

chispear to throw sparks, sparkle tr.
10

chistar to mumble, mutter intr. 10

chocar to collide, clash tr./intr. 24

chochear to be doddering intr. 10

chorrear to gush, spurt, jet intr. 10

chuchear to whisper intr. 10

chupar to lick, suck tr./intr. (r.) 10

churruscar to burn tr. (r.) 24

cicatrizar to scar tr./intr. (r.) 31

cifrar to cipher, code tr. (r.) 10

cimbrar to bend, beat tr./intr. (r.) 10

cimentar to cement tr. 33

cincar to galvanize tr. 24

cincelar to chisel, carve, engrave tr.
10

cinchar to slog, work hard tr./intr. 10

circular to move, circulate tr./intr. 10

circuncidar to circumcise, trim tr. 10

circundar to encircle tr. 10

circunferir to circumscribe, limit,
confine tr. 108

circunvalar to surround, encircle tr.
10

circunvolar to fly around,
circumnavigate tr. 199

ciscar to soil, make dirty tr. (r.) 24

citar to make an appointment,
quote tr. 10

civilizar to civilize, become civilized
tr. (r.) 31

cizañar to create enmity tr. 10

clamar to cry out, implore intr. 10

clamorear to clamour, wail tr./intr.
10

clarear to make clear, make lighter,
dawn tr./intr. (r.) 10

clasificar to classify, sort out tr. (r.)
24

claudicar to limp, give up intr. 24

clausurar to close, close up tr. 10

clavar to nail, fix tr. 10

clisar to stereotype tr. 10

clocar (= cloquear) *to cluck, cackle* intr. *24*

clorar *to chlorinate* tr. *10*

coagular *to coagulate, curdle* tr. (r.) *10*

coartar *to limit, restrain* tr. *10*

cobardear *to be a coward* tr. *10*

cobijar *to cover, shelter* tr. (r.) *10*

cobrar *to charge, get paid, collect* tr. (r.) *10*

cocer *to boil, cook* tr./intr. (r.) **34**

cocinar *to cook* tr./intr. (r.) *10*

codear *to nudge* tr./intr. (r.) *10*

coger *to take, pick up, catch* tr./intr. **35**

cogerse *to take* r. *35*

coincidir *to coincide, agree* intr. *133*

colar *to filter, strain* tr./intr. (r.) **36**

colear *to wag, move* tr./intr. (r.) *10*

colectar *to collect* tr. *10*

colegir *to gather, collect, deduce* tr. *84*

colgar *to hang, hang up* tr./intr. (r.) **37**

colgarse *to hang up* r. *37, 116*

colmar *to fill* tr. (r.) *10*

colocar *to place, put* tr. (r.) *24*

colocarse *to place, put* r. *24, 116*

colonizar *to colonize* tr. *31*

colorear *to give colour* tr./intr. *10*

comediar *to average, divide equally* tr. *10*

comedir *to govern, control* tr./intr. (r.) *134*

comedirse *to be moderate/ controlled* r. *134*

comentar *to comment, make comments* tr./intr. *10*

comenzar *to start, begin* tr./intr. **38**

comer *to eat/have lunch* tr./intr. (r.) **39**

comerciar *to trade, deal* intr. *10*

cometer *to commit, entrust* tr. *23*

comiscar *to nibble, peck at* tr. *24*

comisionar *to commission* tr. *10*

compadecer *to sympathize* tr. *47*

compadecerse *to have pity* r. *47*

compaginar *to arrange, fit* tr. (r.) *10*

comparar *to compare, check* tr. *10*

comparecer *to appear, make an appearance* intr. *47*

compartir *to share, divide* tr. *133*

compeler *to compel* tr. *23*

competir *to compete, contest* intr. **40**

complacer *to please* tr. (r.) *10*

completar *to complete* tr. *10*

complicar *to complicate* tr. (r.) *24*

componer *to compose* tr. (r.) *139*

componerse *to compose* r. *139*

comprar *to buy, purchase* tr. (r.) **41**

comprender *to understand* tr. *23*

comprimir *to compress* tr. *133*

comprobar *to check, confirm* tr. **42**

comprometer *to compromise* tr. *23*

compungir *to move to tears* tr. (r.) *84*

comunicar *to communicate* tr. (r.) *10*

concebir *to conceive, imagine* intr./tr. **43**

conceder *to concede, admit, grant* tr. *23*

concentrar *to concentrate* tr. (r.) *10*

concernir *to concern* tr./intr. *108*

concernirse *to concern, relate to* r. *108*

concertar *to arrange, agree* tr./intr. **44**

concertarse *to concert* r. *44, 116*

conciliar *to conciliate, reconcile* tr. (r.) *10*

concluir *to conclude* tr./intr. (r.) *110*

concordar *to agree* tr./intr. (r.) *2*

concretar *to sum up, make concrete* tr. (r.) *10*

conculcar *to trample, infringe* tr. *24*

concurrir *to meet, assemble* intr. *133*

concursar *to participate in a contest, take part; declare bankrupt* tr./intr. *10*

condecir *to harmonize, fit, match* intr. *57*

condecorar *to decorate, bestow* tr. *10*

condenar *to condemn, sentence* tr. (r.) *10*

condensar *to condense, compress* tr. (r.) *10*

condescender *to condescend* intr. *66*

condicionar *to condition, agree* tr./intr. *10*

condimentar *to season, flavour* tr. *10*

condolerse *to condole* r. *81*

condonar *to condone, pardon, excuse* tr. *10*

conducir *to drive, conduct, lead* tr./intr. **45**

conducirse *to drive, conduct, lead* r. *45*

conectar *to connect, plug in* tr. *10*

confabular *to discuss, confer* intr. (r.) *10*

confeccionar *to make, maufacture, prepare* tr. *10*

conferir *to confer* tr./intr. *108*

confesar *to confess, admit* tr. (r.) **46**

confiar *to trust* tr./intr. (r.) *10*

confinar *to confine, adjoin, seclude* tr./intr. (r.) *10*

confirmar *to confirm* tr. *10*

confirmarse *to confirm, verify* r. *116*

confiscar *to confiscate* tr. *24*

confitar *to coat with sugar* tr. *10*

conformar *to conform* tr. (r.) *10*

conformarse (con) *to put up with, resign* r. *10*

confortar *to comfort* tr. *10*

confrontar *to confront, border* tr./intr. (r.) *10*

confundir *to confound, mix up, muddle up* tr. (r.) *133*

congelar *to freeze, get/become frozen* tr. (r.) *10*

congeniar *to be compatible* intr. *10*

conglomerar *to conglomerate* tr. (r.) *10*

congraciar *to adulate, flatter* tr. (r.) *10*

congratular *to congratulate* tr. (r.) *10*

congregar *to assemble, congregate* tr. (r.) *10*

conjugar *to conjugate* tr. *115*

conjurar *to swear, entreat* tr./intr. (r.) *10*

conmemorar *to commemorate* tr. *10*

conmover *to excite emotion* tr. (r.) *128*

conocer *to know, be acquainted with* tr./intr. (r.) **47**

conocerse *to know oneself* r. *47*

conseguir *to achieve, get; manage to* tr. **48**

conseguirse *to achieve, attain, get, obtain* r. *48*

consentir *to consent, allow* tr./intr. (r.) **49**

conservar *to preserve* tr. (r.) *10*

considerar *to consider, examine, think over* tr. (r.) *10*

consignar *to write in, consign, deposit* tr. *10*

consistir *to consist, be composed of* intr. *133*

consolar *to console* tr. (r.) *2*

consonar *to harmonize* intr. *2*

constar *to be clear, consist, be composed* intr. *10*

constatar *to verify, prove* tr. *10*

constipar *to give a cold, catch a cold* tr. (r.) *10*

constituir *to constitute, make up* tr. (r.) *110*

constreñir *to constrain* tr. *134*

construir *to construct* tr. (r.) *110*

consultar *to ask for advice* tr./intr. *10*

consumar *to consummate* tr. *10*

consumir *to consume* tr. (r.) *133*

contactar *to contact* tr. *10*

contagiar *to infect, transmit* tr. *10*

contar *to count, tell, narrate* **50**

contender *to contend, compete* intr. (r.) *136*

contener *to contain, hold* tr. *179*

contenerse *to restrain oneself* r. *179*

contentar *to please, gratify* tr. (r.) *10*

contestar *to reply, answer* tr./intr. (r.) *10*

continuar *to continue, proceed* tr./intr. *168*

contradecir *to contradict* tr. (r.) *57*

contraer *to contract* tr. (r.) *188*

contrahacer *to imitate, copy* tr. (r.) *106*

contramarcar *to countermark* tr. *24*

contraponer *to compare, contrast* tr. (r.) *139*

contratar *to contrast, engage, hire* tr. *10*

contravenir *to contravene, violate* tr. *194*

contribuir *to contribute* tr./intr. *110*

controlar *to monitor, control, check* tr. *10*

controvertir *to argue* tr./intr. *108*

contundir *to bruise* tr. (r.) *133*

convalecer *to convalesce, recover* intr. *47*

convencer *to convince* tr. (r.) *192*

convenir *to agree, be convenient* intr. (r.) *194*

conversar *to converse, have a conversation* intr. *10*

convertir *to convert, change* tr. (r.) **51**

convidar *to invite* tr. *10*

convocar *to call together, summon* tr. *24*

convocarse *to convoke, call, summon* r. *24, 116*

coordinar *to coordinate* tr. *10*

copiar *to copy* tr. *10*

coquetear *to flirt* tr. *10*

coronar *to crown* tr. (r.) *10*

corregir *to correct, put right* tr. **52**

corregirse *to correct oneself* r. *52*

correr *to run, race, flow* tr./intr. (r.) *23*

correrse *to run, hurry, move, come* r. *23*

corresponder *to correspond* intr. (r.) *23*

corretar *to run around, chase* tr./intr. *10*

corroer *to erode, corrode* tr. (r.) *23*

corromper *to corrupt* tr./intr. (r.) *23*

cortar *to cut, cut off, cut out (eliminate)* tr./intr. *10*

cortarse *to cut oneself* r. *116*

cosechar *to harvest* tr./intr. *10*

coser *to sew* tr./intr. *23*

cosquillear *to tickle* tr. *10*

costar *to cost, be difficult* intr. *53*

costear *to pay for* tr. (r.) *10*

cotejar *to tally, check* tr. *10*

cotizar *to quote, contribute* tr. *31*

cotorrear *to chatter, prattle* tr. *10*

crear *to create, establish* tr. *10*

crecer *to grow, increase* intr. *54*

creer *to believe* tr./intr. (r.) *117*

criar *to breed, bring up, rear* tr. *10*

cribar *to sieve, bolt* tr. *10*

crispar *to put on edge, twitch* tr. (r.) *10*

criticar *to criticize* tr. *24*

croar *to croak* tr. *10*

cruzar *to cross* tr. *31*

cruzarse *to cross* (r.) *31, 116*

cubrir *to cover* (past participle: **cubierto**) tr. (r.) *133*

cubrirse *to cover oneself* (past participle: **cubierto**) r. *133*

cucar *to wink, mock* tr./intr. *24*

cuidar *to care for* tr./intr. (r.) *10*

cuidarse *to take care of oneself* r. *116*

culpar *to blame, accuse* tr. (r.) *10*

cultivar *to grow, cultivate* tr. *10*

cumplir *to fulfil, keep, reach (years)* tr./intr. (r.) *133*

curar *to cure* tr./intr. (r.) *10*

curtir *to tan, harden* tr. (r.) *133*

curvar *to curve, bend* tr. (r.) *10*

custodiar *to guard, take care of* tr. *10*

danzar *to dance* tr./intr. *31*

dañar *to damage* tr. *10*

dañarse *to get damaged/hurt* r. *116*

dar *to give* tr. (r.) **55**

debatir *to debate* tr. *133*

deber *to owe, must, ought to* tr. (r.) **56**

decaer *to decay, weaken* intr. *26*

decentar *to cut into* tr. (r.) *33*

decepcionar *to disappoint* tr. *10*

decidir *to decide, determine* tr./intr. (r.) *133*

decir *to say, tell* tr. (r.) **57**

declamar *to recite, declaim* tr./intr. *10*

declarar *to state, declare, admit* tr./intr. (r.) *10*

declinar *to decline, refuse, decay* tr./intr. *10*

decorar *to decorate* tr. *10*

decretar *to decree, give judgement on* tr. *10*

dedicar *to dedicate, address* tr. *24*

dedicarse *to devote oneself* r. *24, 116*

deducir *to deduce* tr. *45*

defecar *to defecate* tr./intr. *24*

defender *to defend* tr. **58**

defenderse *to defend* r. **58**

defenecer *to close* tr. *47*

deferir *to defer, delegate* tr./intr. **59**

deferirse *to pay deference* r. **59**

definir *to define, clarify* tr. *133*

deflagrar *to burn with sudden and sparkling combustion* intr. *30*

deformar *to deform, become deformed* tr. (r.) *10*

defraudar *to defraud, cheat, disappoint* tr. *10*

degenerar *to degenerate* intr. *10*

deglutir *to swallow* tr./intr. *133*
degollar *to behead* tr. *2*
degradar *to demote, degrade* tr. (r.) *10*
degustar *to taste, sample* tr. *10*
dejar *to allow, let, leave* tr. (r.) *186*
dejarse *to let, allow, leave, permit* r. *116*
delatar *to denounce, accuse* tr. *10*
delegar *to delegate* tr. *30*
deleitar *to delight, please* tr. (r.) *10*
deletrear *to spell, decipher* tr. *10*
deliberar *to deliberate, ponder, consider* tr./intr. *10*
delinquir *to break the law, offend* intr. **60**
delirar *to be delirious, rave* intr. *10*
demacrar *to emaciate, waste away* tr. (r.) *10*
demandar *to sue, crave, demand* tr. *10*
demarcar *to delimit, mark* tr. *24*
demediar *to divide in halves* tr. (r.) *10*
demoler *to demolish, pull down* tr. **61**
demorar *to delay, remain* tr./intr. (r.) *10*
demostrar *to prove, demonstrate* tr. **62**
demostrarse *to demonstrate, prove* r. *62, 116*
demudar *to change, alter, disguise* tr. (r.) *10*
denegar *to deny, refuse* tr. *130*
denigrar *to slander, defame* tr. *10*
denominar *to denominate, designate* tr. *10*
denostar *to revile, insult* tr. *62*
denotar *to denote, indicate* tr. *10*

densar *to condense* tr. *10*
dentar *to indent; cut teeth* tr./intr. **63**
denunciar *to denounce, accuse* tr. (r.) *10*
departir *to converse* intr. *133*
depender *to depend* intr. *23*
depilar *to remove hair* tr. (r.) *10*
deponer *to depose, lay aside, vomit* tr./intr. *139*
deportar *to deport, exile* tr. *10*
depositar *to store, place* tr. (r.) *10*
depreciar *to depreciate* tr. *10*
deprimir *to depress, humiliate* tr. (r.) *133*
depurar *to purify* tr. (r.) *10*
derivar *to derive* tr./intr. (r.) *10*
derogar *to ablish, derogate* tr. *159*
derramar *to spill* tr. (r.) *10*
derrengar *to strain, sprain* tr. (r.) *30, 33*
derretir *to melt, thaw* tr. (r.) **64**
derribar *to demolish, knock down, throw down* tr. *10*
derribarse *to fall down, overthrow* tr. *116*
derrocar *to hurtle, cast, overthrow* tr. (r.) *24*
derrochar *to waste, squander* tr. *10*
derrotar *to defeat* tr. (r.) *10*
derrumbar *to demolish, tear down* tr. (r.) *10*
derrumbarse *to demolish* r. *116*
desabrigar *to uncover* tr. (r.) *10*
desabrochar *to unfasten* tr. (r.) *10*
desacertar *to err* intr. *1*
desacordar *to be in discord* tr. (r.) *2*
desaferrar *to unfasten* tr. (r.) *33*
desafinar *to be/play out of tune* intr. (r.) *10*

desaforar *to encroach* tr. (r.) *2*
desagradecer *to be ungrateful* tr. *47*
desaguar *to drain, dissipate* tr./intr. (r.) *12*
desahogar *to comfort, alleviate* tr. (r.) *10*
desairar *to rebuff, upset, disregard* tr. *10*
desalentar *to discourage, make breathless* tr. (r.) **65**
desaliñar *to disarrange, make untidy* tr. (r.) *10*
desalmar *to weaken* tr. (r.) *10*
desalojar *to move out, vacate* tr./intr. *10*
desamoblar *to unfurnish* tr. *2*
desandar *to go back, retrace* tr. *11*
desanimar *to discourage* tr. (r.) *10*
desaparecer *to disappear, make disappear* tr./intr. *47*
desapretar *to loosen* tr. (r.) *33*
desaprobar *to disapprove of, condemn* tr. *15*
desarbolar *to strip, clear trees* tr. *10*
desarmar *to disarm* tr. (r.) *10*
desarrendarse *to shake off the bridle* r. *17, 116*
desarrollar *to develop* tr. (r.) *10*
desasentar *not to suit, move* tr./intr. (r.) *33*
desasir *to let go, get loose, disengage* tr. (r.) *20*
desasosegar *to disturb* tr. *30, 33*
desatender *to disregard* tr. *178*
desatentar *to perturb* tr. (r.) *180*
desavenir *to bring discord, disagree* tr. (r.) *194*
desaviar *to deprive, mislead* tr. (r.) *10*
desayunar *to have breakfast* intr. (r.) *10*

desayunarse *to breakfast, have breakfast* r. *116*
desazonar *to make tasteless* tr. (r.) *171*
desbaratar *to wreck, ruin* tr./intr. (r.) *10*
desbordar *to overflow* intr. (r.) *10*
descalzarse *to take off one's shoes* r. *31, 116*
descansar *to rest, get rest* tr./intr. (r.) *10*
descararse *to behave inpudently* r. *116*
descargar *to unload, free* tr./intr. (r.) *30*
descarriar *to misguide, lead astray* tr. (r.) *10*
descender *to descend, go down* tr./intr. **66**
descerrajar *to remove, fire* tr. *10*
descogollar *to strip, remove the core (from vegetables)* tr. *10*
descolgar *to take down, unhook* tr. (r.) **67**
descollar *to protrude* intr. (r.) *2*
descomedir *to be rude* intr. *134*
descomer *to defecate* intr. *23*
descomponer *to disarrange, disturb* tr. *139*
descomponerse *to decompose* r. *139*
desconcertar *to disconcert* tr. **68**
desconcertarse *to disconcert, disarrange* r. *68, 116*
desconectar *to switch off, disconnect* tr. (r.) *10*
desconfiar *to distrust, doubt, suspect* intr. *10*
desconocer *to be ignorant, not to know* tr. (r.) *47*

desconsentir *to dissent* tr. *165*

desconsolar *to discourage* tr. (r.) *2*

descontar *to discount, take away* tr. **69**

descontarse *to discount, deduct* r. *69, 116*

descontinuar *to discontinue* tr. *10*

desconvenir *to disagree, not to fit* intr. (r.) *194*

descornarse *to dehorn, rack one's brains* r. *2, 116*

describir *to delineate, describe* tr. *98*

describirse *to describe, sketch* r. *98*

descubrir *to discover* (past participle: **descubierto**) tr. (r.) *133*

descuidar *to neglect* tr./intr. *10*

descuidarse *to neglect, not to bother* r. *116*

desdecir *to degenerate, retract* intr. (r.) *57*

desdentar *to pull teeth* tr. *63*

desdentarse *to extract teeth, break ones's teeth* r. *63, 116*

desdeñar *to disdain, scorn* tr. (r.) *10*

desear *to desire, wish, want* tr. (r.) *10*

desecar *to dessicate* tr. (r.) *24*

desechar *to reject* tr. *83*

desembarcar *to disembark, go ashore* tr./intr. (r.) *24*

desembragar *to declutch, disengage gears* tr. *30*

desempedrar *to unpave* tr. *33*

desempedrarse *to remove stone; rush along* r. *33, 116*

desempeñar *to take out of pawn, discharge, play, perform, play a part in* tr. (r.) *10*

desencajar *to take apart* tr. (r.) *10*

desencantar *to disenchant, disillusion* tr. (r.) *29*

desencerrar *to let loose* tr. *33*

desencordar *to disentangle* tr. *2*

desenfadar *to make up, soothe, calm down* tr. (r.) *10*

desengrosar *to make thinner* tr./intr. *2*

desenredar *to disentangle* tr. (r.) *10*

desentablar *to break up* tr. *10*

desentender *to ignore* tr. *91*

desentenderse *to pay no attention to* r. *92*

desenterrar *to exhume, dig up* tr. *93*

desentonar *to be out of tune, not to fit, humble* tr./intr. (r.) *10*

desenvolver *to unroll, unwrap* tr. (r.) *95*

desertar *to desert* tr. (r.) *10*

deservir *to be disobliging* tr. *134*

desesperar *to despair* tr./intr. (r.) *10*

desfallecer *to weaken, become weak* tr./intr. *47*

desferrar *to free from irons* tr. *33*

desflocar *to unravel* tr. (r.) *2*

desfogar *to make a vent to allow fire to escape* tr./intr. (r.) *2*

desfogarse *to get in a passion* r. *2, 116*

desgajar *to rip, tear off* tr. (r.) *10*

desganar *to dissuade* tr. (r.) *10*

desganarse *to lose one's appetite, be bored* r. *116*

desgarrar *to split, rip, tear* tr. (r.) *10*

desgastar *to wear out* tr. (r.) *10*

desgobernar *to misgovern* tr. (r.) *103*

desgraciar *to deprive, make ungraceful* tr. *10*

desguarnecer *to remove, disarm* tr. *47*

deshacer to destroy, take apart, undo tr. (r.) 106

deshechar to destroy, waste tr. 83

deshelar to thaw tr. (r.) 107

desherbar to remove weeds tr. 33

desherrar to unshoe horses tr. (r.) 33

deshonrar to dishonour tr. 10

designar to designate, appoint tr. 10

desinflar to deflate tr. (r.) 10

desinteresarse to disinterest r. 116

desleír to dilute, dissolve tr. (r.) 150

deslendrar to clean the hair tr. 33

desliar to untie tr. (r.) 94

desligar to untie, undo tr. (r.) 30

deslizar to slide tr. (r.) 31

deslucir to tarnish tr. (r.) 45

deslumbrar to dazzle, blind tr. (r.) 10

desmandar to stray tr. (r.) 10

desmatar to clear shrubs/plants tr. 10

desmayar to faint, dismay, lose heart tr./intr. (r.) 10

desmejorar to deteriorate, get worse tr./intr. (r.) 10

desmelar to harvest honey tr. 33

desmembrar to dismember tr. (r.) 33

desmentir to deny, refute tr./intr. 123

desmenuzar to crumble, break into pieces tr. 31

desmerecer to be unworthy, deteriorate tr./intr. 47

desmigajar to crumble tr. (r.) 10

desmochar to top, cut, cut off the top tr. 10

desmoler to digest, wear out tr. 125

desmoronar to fall to pieces tr. (r.) 10

desnatar to skim tr. 10

desnevar to remove snow, thaw intr. 33

desnucar to break the neck tr. (r.) 182

desnudar to undress, strip tr. 10

desnudarse to get undressed r. 116

desobedecer to disobey tr. 47

desocupar to vacate, clear tr. (r.) 10

desoír to ignore, be deak to tr. 131

desolar to desolate, destroy tr. (r.) 2

desollar to flay, skin tr. 2

desordenar to disarrange, disorder tr (r.) 10

desorganizar to disorganize tr. (r.) 31

desosar to remove bones tr. 2

desovar to spawn intr. (r.) 2

despabilar to liven up, sharpen tr. (r.) 10

despachar to finish, send, hurry tr./intr. (r.) 10

despachurrar to squash, crush, smash tr. 10

despampanar to prune, let off steam tr./intr. (r.) 10

desparramar to scatter, sprinkle tr. (r.) 10

despavorir to be aghast intr. (r.) 133

despechar to spite tr. (r.) 10

despedazar to shred, tear to pieces tr. (r.) 31

despedir to dismiss, see off tr. (r.) **70**

despedirse to take leave, say goodbye r. 70

despedrar to clear, remove rubble tr. 33

despegar to unglue, take off tr./intr. 30

despegarse to unstick, unglue, detach r. 30, 116

despeinarse to dishevel, to let one's hair down r. 116

desperdiciar *to waste, miss* tr. *10*

desperezarse *to stretch oneself* r. *31, 116*

despernar *to cut off a leg* tr. (r.) *33*

despertar *to awake, waken* tr. **71**

despertarse *to wake up* r. *71, 116*

despilfarrar *to waste, squander* tr. (r.) *10*

despistar *to mislead* tr. (r.) *10*

desplacer *to displease, annoy* tr. *54*

desplazar *to displace* tr. *31*

desplegar *to unfold, spread* tr. (r.) **72**

despoblar *to depopulate* tr. (r.) *137*

despojar *to strip off* tr. (r.) *10*

despreciar *to despise, scorn* tr. *10*

desprender *to detach* tr. (r.) *23*

desquiciar *to disjoint, deprive* tr. (r.) *10*

destacar *to stand out, emphasize* tr./intr. (r.) *24*

destellar *to twinkle, sparkle* intr. *10*

destemplar *to disturb, lose control* tr. (r.) *10*

destentar *to free from temptation* tr. *33*

desteñir *to lose colour* tr./intr. (r.) *181*

desterrar *to exile, banish* tr. **73**

destinar *to destine* tr. *10*

destituir *to discharge, dismiss* tr. *110*

destorcer *to untwist* tr. (r.) *184*

destrocar *to re-exchange* tr. *182*

destruir *to destroy, ruin* tr. (r.) **74**

destruirse *to destroy, cancel* r. *74*

desusar *to disuse, go out of use* tr. (r.) *10*

desvalijar *to rob, swindle* tr. *10*

desvanecer *to make vanish, disappear* tr. *47*

desvanecerse *to vanish, disappear* r. *47*

desventar *to let out air* tr. *33*

desvergonzarse *to be impudent* r. *2, 31, 116*

desvestirse *to undress oneself* r. *133*

desviar *to divert, lead away* tr. (r.) *10*

desvivirse *to be very eager* r. *198*

detallar *to itemize, detail* tr. *10*

detener *to stop, detain* tr (r.) *179*

detenerse *to stop oneself* r. *179*

determinar *to determine* tr. (r.) *10*

devengar *to produce* (interest) tr. *30*

devenir *to happen, become* intr. *194*

devolver *to return, give back* tr. (r.) **75**

devolverse *to restore, give back* r. *75*

devorar *to devour* tr. (r.) *10*

dezmar *to diminish* tr. *33*

dialogar *to converse, speak* tr. *30*

dibujar *to sketch, draw* tr. *118*

dictar *to dictate, prescribe* tr. *10*

difamar *to defame, discredit* tr. *10*

diferenciar *to distinguish, differentiate* tr./intr. (r.) *10*

diferir *to postpone, differ* tr./intr. **76**

dificultar *to impede, hinder, consider unlikely* tr./intr. *10*

difundir *to difuse, spread* tr. (r.) *133*

digerir *to digest, absorb* tr. (r.) **77**

dignarse *to condescend* r. *116*

diluviar *to pour with rain, flood* intr. (imp.) *10*

dirigir *to direct* tr. (r.) *52*

discernir *to discern* tr. *108*

disciplinar *to discipline, control* tr. (r.) *10*

discordar *to discord* intr. *2*

disculpar *to apologize, excuse* tr. (r.) *10*

disculparse to apologize, excuse oneself r. 10

discurrir to reflect, ponder, devise tr./intr. 133

discutir to discuss, argue tr./intr. 133

disentir to dissent, differ intr. 165

diseñar to design, outline tr. (r.) 10

disertar to discuss, expound intr. 10

disfrutar to enjoy, make use of tr./intr. 10

disgregar to break up tr. (r.) 30

disgustar to annoy tr. (r.) 10

disgustarse to get annoyed r. 116

disimular to pretend, dissemble tr./intr. 10

disminuir to diminish tr./intr. (r.) 110

disolver to dissolve, melt, break up tr. (r.) **78**

disonar to be dissonant intr. 171

disparar to shoot tr. (r.) 10

disparatar to talk nonsense intr. 10

dispensar to dispense, distribute, excuse, exempt tr. 10

dispensarse to excuse, dispense, exempt r. 116

dispersar to disperse tr. 10

disponer to dispose, make use of tr./intr. (r.) 139

disputar to dispute, argue tr./intr. (r.) 10

distanciar to distance tr. (r.) 10

distinguir to distinguish tr. (r.) **79**

distraer to distract tr. (r.) 188

distribuir to distribute, allocate tr. (r.) 110

divertir to amuse, distract; divert tr. (r.) **80**

divertirse to enjoy oneself r. 80

dividir to divide tr. (r.) 133

divorciar to divorce tr. 10

divorciarse to get divorced r. 116

doblar to fold, double, turn tr./intr. (r.) 10

documentar to inform, prove with documents tr. (r.) 10

dolar to plane, cut tr. 2

doler to ache, hurt, mourn intr. **81**

dolerse to grieve r. 81

domar to tame, control tr. 10

dominar to dominate, rule, stand out tr./intr. (r.) 10

donar to donate tr. (r.) 10

dorar to cover with gold, fry golden brown tr. (r.) 10

dormir to sleep, put to sleep tr./intr. **82**

dormirse to fall asleep r. 82

dormitar to doze, be drowsy intr. (r.) 10

duchar to shower, take a shower tr. 10

ducharse to have a shower r. 116

dudar to doubt, hesitate tr./intr. 10

dulcificar to sweeten, soothe tr. (r.) 24

durar to last, endure intr. 10

echar to throw, pour; throw out tr./intr. (r.) **83**

echarse a to start doing something r. 83, 116

economizar to economize, save tr. 31

edificar to construct, buiild tr. 24

editar to publish tr. 10

educar to instruct, teach, bring up tr. 24

efectuar to carry out tr. (r.) 10

ejecutar to execute, perform, carry out tr. (r.) 10

ejercer to practise (a profession), exercise tr./intr. 192

ejercitar *to drill, train, exercise* tr. (r.) *10*

elaborar *to manufacture, make* tr. *10*

elegir *to select, choose* tr. (r.) **84**

elevar *to elevate, raise* tr. (r.) *10*

eliminar *to eliminate* tr. *10*

elogiar *to praise* tr. *10*

embaír *to deceive, mislead, impose on* tr. *133*

embalar *to pack* tr./intr. *10*

embarazar *to hamper; make pregnant* tr. (r.) *31*

embarcar *to board, go on board* tr. (r.) *24*

embargar *to impede, obstruct* tr. *30*

embarrar *to splash with mud* tr. (r.) *10*

embaucar *to deceive, cheat* tr. *24*

embeber *to soak in, soak up, shrink* tr./intr. (r.) *23*

embelesar *to fascinate, captivate* tr. (r.) *10*

embellecer *to beautify, embellish* tr. (r.) *47*

embestir *to assail* tr./intr. *134*

embobar *to stupefy, fascinate* tr. (r.) *10*

embobecer *to make foolish* tr. (r.) *47*

emborrachar *to intoxicate, get drunk* tr. (r.) *10*

emborronar *to scribble* tr. *10*

embravecer *to infuriate, enrage, become furious* tr./intr. *47*

embrollar *to mix up, muddle* tr. (r.) *10*

embromar *to tease, loiter* tr./intr. (r.) *10*

embrutecer *to brutalize, become brutal* tr. (r.) *47*

embustear *to lie, fib* intr. *10*

emitir *to emit* tr. (r.) *133*

emocionar *to move, touch* tr. (r.) *10*

empachar *to give/get indigestion* tr. (r.) *10*

empalmar *to join, couple* tr./intr. (r.) *10*

empañar *to mist, blur* tr. *10*

empapar *to soak* tr. (r.) *10*

emparejar *to match, pair off* tr./intr. (r.) *10*

emparentar *to become related by marriage* intr. *33*

empedernir *to become petrified, harden* tr. (r.) *133*

empedrar *to pave* tr. *33*

empeller (= empellar) *to push, shove* tr. *23*

empeñar *to pawn, pledge* tr. (r.) *10*

empequeñecer *to make smaller, reduce, diminish* tr. (r.) *47*

empezar *to begin, start* tr./intr. (r.) **85**

empezarse *to begin, start* r. *85, 116*

emplear *to employ, use* tr. (r.) *10*

emplumecer *to fledge, grow feathers* intr. *47*

empobrecer *to impoverish, become poorer* tr./intr. (r.) *47*

emporcar *to soil, stain* tr. (r.) *2, 24*

emprender *to undertake* tr. *23*

empujar *to push, shove* tr. *10*

enaltecer *to extol, praise* tr. *47*

enamorar *to inspire love in, fall in love, flirt* tr. (r.) *10*

enardecer *to kindle, get worked up* tr. (r.) *47*

encabezar *to lead, register, bestow the title* tr. (r.) *31*

encabronar *to enrage* tr. *10*

encajar *to fit in* tr. (r.) *10*

encallecer *to harden, become hardened* intr. *47*

encalvecer *to become bald* intr. *47*

encanecer *to grow grey, become grey* tr./intr. (r.) *47*

encantar *to enchant* tr. (r.) *10*

encañar *to channel; form stalks* tr./intr. *10*

encarar *to face* tr./intr. (r.) *10*

encarecer *to raise, praise* tr. (r.) *47*

encargar *to entrust, ask for in advance* tr. (r.) *30*

encargarse *(de) to take charge of* r. *30, 116*

encender *to light, turn on* tr. (r.) **86**

encerrar *to shut in, lock up* tr. (r.) **87**

enchapar *to veneer, plate* tr. *10*

enchufar *to connect, plug in* tr. (r.) *10*

enclocar *to cluck* intr. (r.) *2, 24*

encobar *to brood, sit on eggs* intr. *2*

encoger *to shrink* tr./intr. (r.) *35*

encojar *to lame, cripple* tr. (r.) *10*

encomendar *to entrust, commend* tr./intr. (r.) **88**

encontrar *to find, meet* tr./intr. **89**

encontrarse *to come across/upon, meet* r. *89, 116*

encorar *to cover with leather* tr./intr. (r.) *2*

encorarse *to heal* intr. (r.) *2, 116*

encordar *to string instruments* tr. *2*

encorvar *to curve, bend* tr. (r.) *10*

encostrar *to coat, form a crust* tr./intr. (r.) *10*

encovar *to put in a cellar* tr. (r.) *2*

encrespar *to curl, enrage* tr. (r.) *10*

encrudecer *to make rough/raw, irritate* tr. *54*

encruelecer *to incite to cruelty* tr. *47*

encubertar *to cover* tr. (r.) *63*

encubrir *to conceal (past participle: encubierto)* tr. *133*

endentar *to enrage* tr. *63*

endentecer *to teethe, cut teeth* intr. *47*

enderezar *to straighten, make straight* tr./intr. (r.) *31*

endeudarse *to get into debt* r. *116*

endorsar *to endorse* tr. *10*

endulzar *to sweeten* tr. (r.) *31*

endurecer *to harden, become hard* tr./intr. (r.) *47*

enemistar *to make enemies* tr. (r.) *10*

enfadar *to anger, irritate* tr. (r.) *10*

enfadarse *to become angry* r. *116*

enfermar *to make sick, become ill* tr./intr. (r.) *10*

enflaquecer *to make/become thin* tr./intr. *47*

enfocar *to focus* tr. *24*

enfrascar *to bottle up, put into bottles* tr. *24*

enfrascarse *to become entangled, become involved* r. *24, 116*

enfrentar *to face, confront* tr./intr. (r.) *10*

enfrentarse *to face, confront* r. *116*

enfriar *to cool, chill* tr./intr. (r.) *94*

enfriarse *to get cold* r. *94, 116*

enfurecer *to infuriate, make furious* tr. *47*

enfurecerse *to become furious* r. *47*

engaitar *to trick, deceive* tr. *10*

engañar *to deceive, mislead* tr. *10*

engañarse *to lie to oneself* r. *116*

engatusar *to inveigle, swindle, take in, beguile* tr. *10*

engendrar *to beget, engender* tr. (r.) *10*

engomar *to glue, gum* tr. *10*

engorar *to confuse* tr./intr. (r.) *2*

engordar *to put on weight, fatten, become fat* tr./intr. (r.) *10*

engorrar *to irritate, bother, annoy* tr. (r.) *10*

engrandecer *to enlarge, increase* tr. (r.) *47*

engrasar *to grease, oil* tr. (r.) *10*

engreír *to make vain or conceited* tr. *150*

engreírse *to become haughty* r. *150*

engrosar *to make thick, put on weight* tr./intr. (r.) *2*

engullir *to gulp down, bolt, gobble* tr. *198*

enhestar *to hoist, rise up* tr. *33*

enhestarse *to set upright* r. *33, 116*

enjabonar *to soap, wash with soap* tr. *10*

enjalbegar *to whitewash* tr. (r.) *30*

enjambrar *to swarm, multiply* tr./intr. *10*

enjaular *to put in a cage, confine* tr. *10*

enjuagar *to rinse* tr. (r.) *30*

enjugar *to dry, wipe* tr. (r.) *115*

enjuiciar *to examine, judge a case* tr. *10*

enlazar *to join, connect* tr. (r.) *31*

enloquecer *to drive insane, go mad* tr./intr. (r.) *47*

enlucir *to plaster, polish* tr. *187*

enmelar *to smear with honey* tr./intr. *33*

enmendar *to correct, compensate* tr. (r.) **90**

enmohecer *to make mouldy, mildrew, go rusty* tr. *47*

enmudecer *to silence, hush, become speechless* tr./intr. (r.) *47*

ennegrecer *to blacken, turn black* tr. *47*

ennoblecer *to ennoble, embellish* tr. *47*

ennoblecerse *to become noble* r. *47*

enojar *to annoy, irritate, vex* tr. (r.) *10*

enojarse *to become angry* r. *116*

enorgullecer *to make proud, become proud* tr. (r.) *47*

enrabiar *to anger* tr. (r.) *10*

enrarecer *to thin out, become scarce* tr./intr. *47*

enredar *to entangle, cause trouble/mischief* tr./intr. (r.) *10*

enripiar *to fill with gravel* tr. *10*

enriquecer *to enrich, get rich* tr./intr. (r.) *47*

enrodar *to wheel* tr. *2*

enrojecer *to make red, blush* tr/intr. (r.) *47*

enronquecer *to make/become hoarse* tr. (r.) *47*

enroscar *to curl, twist* tr. (r.) *24*

ensacar *to bag* tr. *24*

ensalzar *to glorify, praise* tr. (r.) *31*

ensanchar *to widen* tr./intr. (r.) *10*

ensangrentar *to stain with blood* tr. (r.) *33*

ensartar *to string, thread* tr. (r.) *10*

ensayar *to practise, rehearse, test* tr. (r.) *10*

enseñar *to teach, point out, show* tr. (r.) *10*

ensillar *to saddle* tr. *10*

ensolver *to include, reduce* tr. *200*

ensorbecer to make arrogant/proud tr. (r.) 47

ensordecer to deafen, become deaf tr./intr. (r.) 47

ensuciar to dirty, stain, soil tr./intr. (r.) 10

entablar to start, board tr. (r.) 10

entallecer to grow shoots tr. 47

entender to understand tr./intr. (r.) **91**

entenderse to be understood r. **92**

enterar to inform tr. (r.) 10

enterarse to find out r. 116

enternecer to make tender, move, touch tr. (r.) 47

enterrar to bury tr. (r.) **93**

entonar to intone, sing in tune, put on airs tr. (r.) 10

entontar to stupefy tr. (r.) 10

entontecer to make/become silly tr./intr. (r.) 47

entorpecer to dull, stupefy, obstruct tr. 47

entortar to make tortuous tr. 2

entortar to make crooked, make blind in one eye tr. 2

entrar to enter, come in, go in tr./intr. (r.) 10

entregar to deliver, hand over, give tr. (r.) 30

entregarse to surrender, give in r. 30, 116

entrelazar to interwave, interlace tr. 31

entrelucir to show, shine intr. 187

entremorir to burn out, flicker intr. (r.) 127

entrenar to train tr. (r.) 10

entreoír to half hear, hear vaguely tr. 131

entrepernar to cross one's legs intr. (r.) 33

entretener to entertain, make bearable tr. (r.) 179

entretenerse to amuse oneself r. 179

entrever to descry, surmise, catch a glimpse tr. 195

entrevistar to interview tr./intr. (r.) 10

entristecer to sadden, become sad tr. (r.) 47

entullecer to stop, become crippled tr./intr. 47

entumecer to numb, become numb, become swollen tr. 47

entumecerse to become numb r. 47

enunciar to state, enunciate tr. (r.) 10

envanecer to make conceited tr. (r.) 47

envasar to bottle, pack tr. 10

envejecer to age, become old tr. (r.) 47

envenenar to poison tr. (r.) 10

enverdecer to turn green intr. 47

envestir to clothe tr. 134

enviar to send tr. (r.) **94**

enviciar to corrupt; grow too much foliage tr./intr. (r.) 10

envidiar to envy, covet tr. 10

envilecer to debase, vilify, degrade tr. (r.) 47

envolver to wrap up, surround tr. (r.) **95**

envolverse to have an affair, become involved r. 95

enyesar to plaster tr. 10

enzarzar to cover with brambles; get involved tr. (r.) 31

epilogar *to summarize* tr. *30*

equilibrar *to balance* tr. (r.) *10*

equipar *to equip, furnish* tr. *10*

equiparar *to compare, match, make equal* tr. (r.) *10*

equivaler *to equal, amount to* intr. *191*

equivocar *to mistake, equivocate* tr./intr. *24*

equivocarse *to be mistaken* r. *24, 116*

erguir *to stand up straight, raise* tr. (r.) **96**

erguirse *to swell up with pride, stiffen* r. *96*

erigir *to erect, build, establish* tr. (r.) *52*

errar *to err, miss* tr./intr. (r.) **97**

errarse *to err, miss, roam, wander* r. *97, 116*

eructar *to belch, burp* intr. *10*

escabar *to remove weeds* tr. *10*

escacharrar *to break, ruin* tr. (r.) *10*

escalar *to climb* tr./intr. (r.) *10*

escarbar *to scratch, scrape, investigate* tr. *10*

escarchar *to ice, freeze, frost* tr./intr. *10*

escardar *to weed* tr. *10*

escarmentar *to learn by experience* tr./intr. (r.) *33*

escarmentarse *to correct, learn from mistakes* r. *33, 116*

escarnecer *to ridicule, mock* tr. (r.) *47*

esclarecer *to lighten, get light, dawn* tr./intr. *47*

escocer *to sting, annoy, vex* tr./intr. (r.) *34*

escocerse *to itch* r. *34*

escoger *to choose, select* tr. (r.) *35*

escogerse *to select for oneself* r. *35*

esconder *to hide* tr. (r.) *23*

escribir *to write, spell* tr. **98**

escribirse *to write to each other* r. *98*

escuchar *to listen, listen to* tr/intr. (r.) *10*

escupir *to spit* tr./intr. (r.) *133*

escurrir *to drain, drip* tr./intr. (r.) *133*

esforzar *to encourage* tr./intr. (r.) *2*

esforzarse *to make an effort* r. *2*

esmaltar *to enamel* tr. *10*

esmerar *to take great care, polish* tr. (r.) *10*

espabilar *to snuff, blink, wake up* tr./intr. (r.) *10*

espantar *to scare, frighten* tr. (r.) *10*

esparcir *to scatter, spread* tr. (r.) *45*

especular *to view, speculate* tr./intr. *10*

esperar *to hope, wait for* tr./intr. (r.) *10*

espesar *to thicken* tr. (r.) *10*

espiar *to spy, spy upon* tr./intr. (r.) *10*

espolvorear *to dust, sprinkle* tr. *10*

esquiar *to ski* intr. *10*

esquilar *to shear* tr. *10*

esquinar *to make/form a corner, quarrel* tr./intr. (r.) *10*

esquivar *to avoid* tr. (r.) *10*

establecer *to establish* tr. (r.) *47*

estafar *to swindle, defraud* tr. *10*

estallar *to explode, burst* tr. *10*

estancar *to come to a standstill* tr. (r.) *24*

estar *to be* intr. (aux.) **99**

estercolar *to spread manure* tr./intr. *10*

estilar *to be in fashion* tr./intr. (r.) *10*

estimar *to esteem, estimate, respect, value* tr. (r.) *10*

estipular *to stipulate* tr./intr. *10*

estirar *to stretch* tr. (r.) *10*

estofar *to stew, quilt* tr. *10*

estorbar *to be in the way, obstruct* tr. *10*

estornudar *to sneeze* intr. *10*

estrechar *to narrow, tighten* tr. (r.) *10*

estregar *to scour, rub* tr. *30, 33*

estrellar *to shine, crash* tr. (r.) *10*

estremecer *to shake, stagger, tremble* tr. (r.) *47*

estrenar *to use, appear for the first time* tr./intr. (r.) *10*

estreñir *to constipate* tr. (r.) *134*

estropear *to spoil, damage* tr. (r.) *10*

estrujar *to squeeze* tr. *10*

estudiar *to study* tr./intr. (r.) *10*

evacuar *to evacuate* tr. **100**

evadir *to evade* tr. (r.) *133*

evaluar *to evaluate* tr. (r.) *10*

evaporar *to evaporate, vanish* tr. (r.) *10*

evitar *to avoid* tr. (r.) *10*

evolucionar *to evolve, develop* intr. *10*

examinar *to examine* tr. *10*

examinarse *to sit an exam* r. *116*

exasperar *to irritate, exasperate* tr. (r.) *10*

exceder *to exceed, surpass* tr. (r.) *23*

exceptuar *to exclude, exempt* tr. *10*

excitar *to excite, stimulate* tr. (r.) *10*

excluir *to exclude, expel* tr. (r.) *110*

excusar *to excuse, apologize* tr. (r.) *10*

exhibir *to exhibit, display, show* tr. *133*

exigir *to demand, urge, require* tr. (r.) *84*

exiliar *to exile* tr. (r.) *10*

eximir *to exempt, free* tr. (r.) *133*

existir *to exist, be* intr. *133*

expedir *to forward, expedite* *134*

expedirse *to expedite, dispatch* tr. (r.) *134*

expeler *to expel, eject* tr. *23*

experimentar *to try, experiment* tr./intr. (r.) *10*

explicar *to explain* tr. (r.) *24*

explorar *to explore, investigate* tr. *10*

explotar *to exploit, explode* tr./intr. (r.) *10*

exponer *to expose, jeopardize* tr. (r.) *140*

expresar *to express, express oneself* tr. (r.) *10*

extender *to extend* tr. (r.) *136*

extenuar *to debilitate, weaken* tr. (r.) *10*

exterminar *to eradicate, exterminate* tr. (r.) *10*

extinguir *to extinguish, become extinct* tr. (r.) *110*

extraer *to draw out, remove, extract* tr. (r.) *188*

extraviar *to lose, lead astray* tr. (r.) *10*

fabricar *to fabricate, manufacture* tr. (r.) *24*

facilitar *to facilitate* tr. *10*

fallar *to judge, find, fail* tr./intr. (r.) *10*

fallecer *to expire, die* intr. *47*

falsear *to falsify, misrepresent* tr. *10*

falsificar *to falisfy, forge* tr. *24*

faltar *to be missing, lack* intr. (r.) *10*

fantasear to daydream, fancy tr./intr. 10

farfullar to gabble, do hastily tr./intr. 10

farolear to brag, boast, show off intr. 10

fascinar to fascinate, enchant tr. (r.) 10

fastidiar to annoy, irritate tr. (r.) 118

fatigar to tire, exhaust tr. (r.) 30

favorecer to favour, support tr./intr. (r.) 47

fecundar (= fecundizar) to fertilize tr. 10

felicitar to congratulate tr. (r.) 10

fenecer to finish, die, end tr./intr. 47

fermentar to ferment, be agitated tr./intr. 10

ferrarse to trim r. 33, 116

fertilizar to fertilize, enrich tr. 31

festejar to feast, entertain, celebrate tr. (r.) 10

fiar to confide, trust, guarantee tr./intr. (r.) 10

fichar to register, clock in tr. 10

figurar to figure, depict, draw, appear tr./intr. 10

figurarse to figure, imagine r. 116

fijar to fix, fasten, clinch, set tr. 10

fijarse to notice, settle, pay attention r. 116

filiar to take personal date, join tr. (r.) 10

filmar to film tr. 10

filtrar to filter, leak tr./intr. (r.) 10

finalizar to end, conclude tr./intr. 31

financiar to finance tr. 10

fingir to feign, pretend tr. (r.) 52

firmar to sign tr. 10

fisgar to snoop, pry on, mock tr./intr. (r.) 30

flamear to blaze, flame tr. 10

flaquear to weaken intr. 10

fletar to charter a ship, hire tr. (r.) 10

flirtear to flirt intr. 10

flojear to weaken, grown weak intr. 10

florecer to flower intr. (r.) 47

flotar to float intr. 10

fluctuar to fluctuate intr. 10

fluir to flow intr. 110

fomentar to encourage, promote tr. 10

forjar to forge, shape tr. 10

formar to form, shape tr./intr. (r.) 10

formular to formulate tr. 10

forrar to line, cover tr. (r.) 10

fortalecer to fortify, strengthen tr. (r.) 47

fortificar to strengthen tr. 24

forzar to compel, force tr. (r.) 2

fotocopiar to photocopy, make photocopies tr. 10

fotografiar to photograph, take photographs tr. 10

fracasar to fail intr. 10

fraccionar to break up, divide tr. (r.) 10

fraguar to forge, set, plan tr./intr. (r.) 12

franquear to free, liberate tr. (r.) 10

frecuentar to frequent, do again and again tr. 10

fregar to wash up, scrub tr. **101**

freír to fry tr. **102**

frenar to break, restrain tr./intr. 10

frisar to frizz; approach tr./intr. 10

frotar to rub tr. (r.) 10

fruncir to pleat, knit tr. (r.) 45

frustrar to frustrate tr. (r.) 10
fulminar to strike tr. 10
fumar to smoke tr./intr. (r.) 10
funcionar to function, run/work (machinery) intr. 10
fundar to found tr. (r.) 10
fundir to melt, cast tr. (r.) 133
fusionar to combine, merge, amalgamate tr. (r.) 10
fustigar to whip, lash tr. 30

galantear to woo, court tr. 10
galardonar to recompense, reward tr. 10
gallear to tread, cover, shout and threaten tr./intr. 10
galopar to gallop intr. 10
galvanizar to galvanize tr. 31
ganar to gain, earn, win tr./intr. (r.) 10
gansear to say/do stupid things tr. 10
garabatear to scribble tr./intr. 10
garantir to guarantee tr. 133
garantizar to guarantee, answer for tr. (r.) 31
garbear to put on airs, show off intr. 10
gastar to waste, use up, spend tr. (r.) 10
gatear to crawl tr./intr. 10
gemiquear to whine intr. 10
gemir to groan, grieve, moan, howl intr. 134
generalizar to generalize tr./intr. (r.) 31
generar to generate tr. 10
gestionar to negotiate tr. 10
gibar to bend, annoy, bother tr. 10
gimotear to whine, wail intr. 10

girar to turn round, spin tr./intr. 10
glorificar to glorify tr. (r.) 24
glosar to gloss, censure tr. 10
gobernar to govern, rule tr./intr. (r.) **103**
golfear to waste time intr. 10
golosear to nibble at delicacies intr. 10
golpear to crush, blow, hit tr./intr. (r.) 10
gorgoritear to trill, quaver intr. 10
gorjear to warble, gurgle intr. (r.) 10
gorrear to live parasitically, sponge intr. 10
gorronear to cadge, sponge intr. 10
gotear to drip intr. 10
gozar to enjoy, be happy tr./intr. (r.) 31
grabar to engrave, record tr. (r.) 10
graduar to graduate, grade tr. (r.) 10
grajear to caw, gurgle, chatter intr. 10
gramar to knead tr. 10
granar to seed intr. 10
granear to sow seeds, granulate tr. 10
granizar to hail, hurl tr./intr (imp.) 31
granjear to earn, get, gain tr. (r.) 10
gratificar to reward, recompense tr. 24
gravar to burden, tax tr. 10
gravitar to gravitate intr. 10
graznar to crow, croak, squawk intr. 10
grietarse to crack, split r. 116
grillarse to escape r. 116
gritar to shout, yell, scream, shriek tr./intr. (r.) 10
groar to croak intr. 10

gruñir to creak (door hinges, etc.); grunt, growl, snarl intr. (r.) *198*

guadañar to mow, scythe tr. *10*

guardar to keep, guard, save tr./intr. (r.) *10*

guarecer to shelter, hide tr. (r.) *47*

guarnecer to garnish, decorate tr. *47*

guasearse to joke, jest r. *116*

guerrear to wage war, fight intr. *10*

guiar to guide, lead, sprout tr./intr. (r.) *94*

guipar to notice, see tr. *10*

guisar to cook, prepare (food) tr. *10*

gustar to be pleasing, like, enjoy tr./intr. (r.) *10*

haber to have tr. (aux.) **104**

habitar to inhabit, reside, dwell tr./intr. *10*

habituar to accustom, get used to tr. (r.) *10*

hablar to speak, talk tr./intr. (r.) **105**

hacendar to transfer, own (property) tr. (r.) *33*

hacer to do, make tr./intr. **106**

hacerse to become r. *106*

halagar to flatter tr. *30*

halar to haul, pull tr./intr. *10*

hallar to find, locate, discover tr. *10*

hallarse to find, be (location) r. *116*

hamacar (= hamaquear) to rock, swing tr. *24*

hambrear to starve, hunger tr./intr. *10*

hartar to satiate, fill, bore tr. (r.) *10*

hastiar to bore, tire tr. *10*

hechizar to bewitch, charm tr. *31*

heder to stink intr. *136*

helar to freeze, chill tr./intr. **107**

henchir to fill tr. (r.) *134*

hender to split *136*

hendir to split, crack tr. (r.) *108*

heñir to knead tr. *134*

heredar to inherit tr. *10*

herir to wound, hurt, harm tr. (r.) **108**

hermanar to join, harmonize tr. (r.) *10*

hermosear to beautify, embellish tr. *10*

herrar to shoe a horse tr. *33*

hervir to boil intr. **109**

hidratar to hydrate tr. (r.) *10*

hidrogenar to hydrogenate tr. *10*

higienizar to make hygienic tr. *31*

hilar to spin tr. *10*

hilvanar to baste, tack, hem tr. *10*

hincar to prick, drive into tr. (r.) *24*

hinchar to fill with air, inflate, swell tr./intr. (r.) *10*

hipar to hiccup, have hiccups intr. *10*

hipnotizar to hypnotize tr. *31*

hipotecar to mortgage, take out a mortgage tr. *24*

historiar to record history tr. *10*

hojear to leaf through, glance, flake tr./intr. *10*

holgar to rest intr. (r.) *2*

hollar to trample on tr. *2*

homenajear to pay homage in tr. *10*

hondear to sound, sling tr./intr. *10*

honrar to honour, accept, pay tr. *10*

hornear to bake intr. *10*

horripilar to horrify, become terrified tr. (r.) *10*

hospedar to lodge tr. (r.) *10*

hospitalizar to hospitalize tr. *31*

hostigar to lash, whip, trouble tr. *30*

hostilizar to antagonize, harass tr. *31*

huir to run away, escape tr./intr. (r.) **110**

humear *to smoke, fumigate* tr./intr. *10*

humedecer *to dampen, humidify* tr. *47*

humillar *to humiliate, humble* tr. (r.) *10*

hundir *to sink* tr. (r.) *133*

hurgar *to poke* tr. *30*

hurtar *to rob, steal, pinch* tr. (r.) *10*

husmear *to snoop on, smell out, nose* tr./intr. (r.) *10*

idealizar *to idealize* tr. *31*

idear *to plan, think up, conceive* tr. *10*

identificar *to identify* tr. (r.) *24*

ignorar *to be ignorant of, ignore, not to know* tr. (r.) *10*

igualar *to make equal, equal* tr./intr. (r.) *10*

iluminar *to illuminate* tr. *10*

ilusionar *to fascinate, have illusions, hope* tr. (r.) *10*

ilustrar *to enlighten* tr. (r.) *10*

imaginar *to imagine, fancy, suppose* tr. (r.) *10*

imbuir *to imbue, infuse* tr. *110*

imitar *to imitate* tr. *10*

impacientar *to make/become impatient* tr. (r.) *10*

impartir *to grant, impart* tr. *133*

impedir *to impede, hinder, prevent* tr. (r.) **111**

impeler *to push, incite, urge* tr. *23*

imperar *to rule, prevail* intr. *10*

implantar *to implant, introduce* tr. *10*

implicar *to implicate, imply* tr./intr. (r.) *24*

implorar *to entreat, beg, implore* tr. *10*

imponer *to impose, dominate* tr. (r.) *139*

importar *to import, cost; be important, matter, mind* tr./intr. (r.) (imp.) *10*

importunar *to bother, pester, importune* tr. *10*

imposibilitar *to prevent, stop, make impossible* tr. *10*

impregnar *to impregnate* tr. *10*

impresionar *to impress, make an impression* tr. (r.) *10*

imprimir *to print, imprint, impress; fix in the mind* tr. (past participle: **impreso**) *133*

improbar *to disapprove, condemn* tr. *141*

improvisar *to improvise* tr. *10*

impugnar *to contradict, refute* tr. *10*

impulsar *to encourage, impel* tr. *10*

imputar *to impute, charge with* tr. *10*

inaugurar *to open, initiate* tr. *10*

incapacitar *to disable, incapacitate* tr. *10*

incendiar *to set on fire* tr. *10*

incendiarse *to catch fire* r. *116*

incensar *to perfume* tr. *33*

incidir *to fall, cut, influence* tr./intr. *133*

inclinar *to incline, bow, tilt* tr. (r.) *10*

incluir *to include, enclose* tr. (r.) *110*

incomodar *to inconvenience, bother* tr. (r.) *10*

incomunicar *to isolate, confine* tr. (r.) *10*

incordiar *to annoy, inconvenience* tr. *10*

incorporar *to incorporate* tr. (r.) *10*

incorporarse *to sit up* r. *116*

inculcar *to instill, inculcate, implant* tr. (r.) *24*

incumbir *to be incumbent, concern* tr./intr. (r.) *133*

incumplir *to fail* tr./intr. *133*

incurrir *to incur, become liable* intr. *133*

indagar *to investigate* tr. *30*

indemnizar *to compensate* tr. *31*

independizar *to emancipate, liberate* tr. (r.) *31*

indicar *to indicate, point out* tr. *24*

indignar *to irritate, make indignant* tr. (r.) *10*

indisponer *to indispose, become ill* tr. (r.) *140*

inducir *to induce, persuade* tr. (r.) *45*

indultar *to pardon* tr. *10*

inebriar *to intoxicate, make drunk* tr. *10*

infamar *to defame, slander* tr. (r.) *10*

infectar *to infect* tr. (r.) *10*

inferir *to infer* tr. *108*

infernar *to damn* tr. *33*

infestar *to infest, become infested* tr. (r.) *10*

inflamar *to inflame, burst into flame* tr. (r.) *10*

inflar *to inflate, become inflated/ proud* tr. (r.) *10*

influir *to influence, have influence* tr./intr. *110*

informarse *to inform, find out* tr./ intr. (r.) *116*

infundir *to pour in, fill* tr. *133*

ingeniar *to conceive, devise* tr. (r.) *10*

ingerir *to ingest* tr. *108*

ingresar *to join, go, enter* tr. (r.) *10*

inhibir *to inhibit, restrain* tr. (r.) *133*

iniciar *to begin, initiate* tr. (r.) *10*

injerir *to insert, introduce* tr. (r.) *108*

injertar *to graft* tr. *10*

inmolar *to sacrifice* tr. (r.) *10*

inmovilizar *to immobilize, tie up* tr. (r.) *31*

inmutar *to alter, change* tr. (r.) *10*

innovar *to innovate, make changes in* tr. *10*

inquietar *to disquiet, disturb* tr. (r.) *10*

inquirir *to inquire into, investigate* tr. *108*

inscribir *to inscribe, register, record* tr. (r.) *98*

insertar *to insert, include* tr. (r.) *10*

insidiar *to plot, set a trap* tr. *10*

insinuar *to insinuate* tr. (r.) *10*

insistir *to insist, persist* intr. *133*

insolar *to get sunstroke* tr. (r.) *10*

inspirar *to inspire, be inspired* tr. (r.) *10*

instalar *to install* tr. (r.) *10*

instar *to urge, press* tr./intr. (r.) *10*

instaurar *to establish, institute, set up* tr. *10*

instigar *to provoke* tr. *30*

instituir *to institute, found* tr. (r.) *110*

instruir *to instruct, teach, investigate* tr. (r.) *110*

insubordinar *to mutiny, rebel, incite* tr. (r.) *10*

insultar *to insult, abuse* tr. (r.) *10*

integrar *to integrate* tr. *10*

intentar *to intend, try* tr. *10*

interesar *to interest, care, concern* tr./intr. *10*

interesarse *to be interested in* r. 116
intermediar *to mediate* intr. 10
internar *to intern, confine, penetrate* tr./intr. (r.) 10
interponer *to interpose* tr. (r.) 139
interpretar *to interpret* tr. 10
interrogar *to interrogate, question* tr. 159
interrumpir *to interrupt, discontinue* tr. 133
intervenir *to intervene, participate* tr./intr. 194
intimar *to anounce, convey, become intimate* tr./intr. 10
intimidar *to intimidate, become intimidated* tr. (r.) 10
intoxicar *to poison, be poisoned* tr. (r.) 24
intrigar *to intrigue, plot* tr./intr. (r.) 30
introducir *to introduce, get into* tr. (r.) 45
intrisarse *to usurp* r. 116
intuir *to sense, perceive* tr. 110
inundar *to flood, inundate* tr. (r.) 10
inutilizar *to make useless, ruin* tr. (r.) 31
invadir *to invade* tr. 133
invalidar *to invalidate* tr. 10
inventar *to invent, discover* tr. 10
invernar *to pass the winter* intr. 33
invertir *to invert, turn upside down* tr. 112
investigar *to investigate* tr. 30
investir *to confer; invest* tr. 113
invitar *to invite* tr. 10
invocar *to appeal to* tr. 24
involucrar *to involve, implicate* tr. 10
inyectar *to inject* tr. 10

ir *to go* tr. **114**
irse *to go away* r. 114
ironizar *to ridicule* tr. 31
irritar *to irritate* tr. (r.) 10
irrumpir *to burst in* intr. 133
izar *to hoist, haul up, heave* tr. 31

jadear *to pant* intr. 10
jaquear *to check, harass* tr. 10
jeringar *to inject, syringe* r. 30
jubilar *to retire, pension off* tr. (r.) 10
jugar *to play* tr./intr. (r.) **115**
jugarse *to gamble* r. 115, 116
juntar *to connect, join, unite* tr. (r.) 10
juntarse *to meet* r. 116
jurar *to swear, take an oath* tr/intr. (r.) 10
justificar *to justify, be justified* tr. (r.) 30
juzgar *to judge* tr. (r.) 30

labrar *to farm; make a lasting impression* tr./intr. 10
lacrar *to seal* tr. 10
ladear *to tilt* tr./intr. (r.) 10
ladrar *to bark* tr./intr. 10
ladronear *to steal, shoplift* intr. 10
lamentar *to lament* tr./intr. (r.) 10
lamer *to lick* tr. (r.) 23
languidecer *to languish* intr. 47
lanzar *to hurl, fling, launch, throw* tr. (r.) 31
largar *to release, leave* tr. (r.) 30
lastimar *to hurt, damage, offend* tr. (r.) 10
lastir *to beat, palpitate, throb, annoy* tr./intr. 133
lavar *to wash* tr. (r.) 10

lavarse to wash oneself r. **116**
laxar to loosen, slacken tr. (r.) 10
leer to read tr./intr. (r.) **117**
legalizar to legalize tr. 31
legar to bequeath, leave tr. 10
legislar to legislate intr. 10
legitimar to legitimate, prove tr. 10
levantar to lift, raise tr. (r.) 10
levantarse to get up r. 116
liar to bundle, tie tr. (r.) 10
liberar to free, liberate tr. 10
librar to draw, issue, save, free
    tr./intr. (r.) 10
licenciar to discharge, release tr. (r.)
    10
licenciarse to graduate/get a degree
    r. 116
lidiar to fight (bullfight) tr./intr. 10
ligar to tie, bind, unite tr./intr. (r.) 30
lijar to sandpaper tr. 10
limar to polish, file, smooth tr. 10
limitar to limit, reduce tr./intr. (r.) 10
limpiar to clean, cleanse tr. (r.) **118**
lindar to adjoin, border intr. 10
liquidar to liquidate, sell off, become
    liquid tr. (r.) 10
lisonjear to flatter, compliment tr.
    10
llamar to call, name tr./intr. (r.) 10
llamarse to be called, be named r.
    116
llamear to flame, blaze intr. 10
llegar to arrive, reach tr./intr. (r.) **119**
llenar to fill, fill up tr./intr. (r.) 10
llevar to carry, wear, take away
    tr./intr. (r.) 10
llorar to cry, weep tr./intr. **120**
lloriquear to cry constantly, whine
    intr. (r.) 10

llover to rain tr./intr. (imp.) **121**
lloviznar to drizzle intr. (imp.) 10
localizar to locate, find tr. (r.) 31
lograr to achieve, get, attain, procure
    tr. (r.) 10
lubricar to lubricate tr. 24
luchar to fight, strive, struggle,
    wrestle intr. 10
lucir to display, show, exhibit
    tr./intr. 45
luir to redeem tr. (r.) 110
lujuriar to lust, be lustful/lecherous
    intr. 10
lustrar to polish; travel, roam
    tr./intr. 10

macerar to macerate, marinate,
    soak, mortify tr. (r.) 10
madrugar to get up early tr./intr.
    (r.) 30
madurar to ripen, become ripe
    tr./intr. (r.) 10
magullar to batter and bruise tr. (r.)
    10
malcriar to pamper, spoil tr. 10
maldecir to curse, damn tr./intr. (r.)
    57
malear to spoil, ruin tr. (r.) 10
malgastar to squander, waste,
    mis-spend tr. 10
malograr to waste, miss, fail tr. (r.)
    10
malquerer to dislike, hate tr. 144
malquistar to excite disputes,
    alienate tr. (r.) 10
malsonar to sound unpleasant 2
malvar to corrupt tr. 10
mamar to suck tr./intr. (r.) 10
manar to run, flow, spring tr./intr. 10

mancar to be wanting, maim, go lame tr./intr. (r.) 24

manchar to stain, blot tr. (r.) 10

mandar to order, command tr./intr. (r.) 10

manejar to drive (a car), handle, manage tr. (r.) 10

mangar to cadge, scrounge, pinch tr. 30

manifestar to manifest tr. (r.) 33

manipular to manipulate tr. 10

manir to keep meat until it becomes tender tr. 133

mantener to maintain, support, keep up tr. 179

mantenerse to support oneself r. 179

manufacturar to manufacture, make tr. (r.) 10

maquillarse to put on make up r. 116

maravillar to marvel, wonder tr. (r.) 10

marcar to mark, note, observe tr. (r.) 24

marchar to march, get under way, go intr. (r.) 10

marcharse to go away, leave, exit r. 116

marchitar to wither tr. (r.) 10

marear to navigate, become seasick tr. (r.) 10

martillear (= martillar) to hammer tr. 10

mascar (= masticar) to chew, masticate tr. 24

matar to kill tr. (r.) 10

mecer to rock tr. (r.) 192

mediar to get half way intr. 10

medir to measure tr./intr. **122**

medirse to measure, judge r. 122

medrar to grow intr. 10

mejorar to better, improve tr./intr. (r.) 10

melar to soften, take honey tr./intr. 33

mencionar to mention tr. (r.) 10

mendigar to beg tr./intr. 30

menear to shake tr. (r.) 10

menguar to diminish tr. (r.) 12

menstruar to menstruate intr. 10

mentar to mention, name tr. 33

mentir to lie tr./intr. **123**

mercadear to trade, deal intr. 10

merecer to deserve, merit tr./intr. (r.) 47

merendar to have tea/a snack tr./intr. **124**

mermar to decrease, diminish, reduce tr./intr. 10

meter to put, cause, get tr. (r.) 23

mezclar to mix tr. (r.) 10

migar to crumb tr. 30

mimar to spoil, pamper, indulge tr. 10

mirar to look at, watch tr./intr. (r.) 10

mitigar to allay, mitigate tr. 30

moblar to furnish tr. 2

moderar to moderate, control tr. (r.) 10

mohecer to make mouldy, rust, go rusty tr. 47

mojar to wet tr./intr. (r.) 10

mojarse to get wet, wet oneself r. 116

moldear to mould, cast tr. 10

moler to grind, crush, mill tr. **125**

molestar to bother, annoy tr. (r.) 10

mondar to clean, peel tr. (r.) 10
monear to clown around intr. 10
monologar to soliloquize intr. 30
montar to mount, go up, climb tr./ intr. (r.) 10
morder to bite, nip tr. (r.) **126**
mordiscar to nibble tr. 24
morir to die intr. (r.) **127**
mortificar to annoy, vex tr. (r.) 24
mostrar to show, point out tr. (r.) 62
mover to move tr./intr. (r.) **128**
mudar to change, alter tr./intr. **129**
mudarse to change one's clothes, move r. 116, 129
mugir to moo intr. 52
mullir to fluff up, soften tr. 10
multiplicar to multiply tr./intr. (r.) 24
murmurar to murmur, mutter tr./ intr. 10
mutilar to mutilate, cripple tr. 10

nacer to be born intr. (r.) 47
nacionalizar to nationalize, naturalize tr. (r.) 31
nadar to swim intr. 10
narrar to narrate, relate tr. 10
naturalizar to naturalize, nationalize tr. (r.) 31
naufragar to be shipwrecked, fail intr. 30
nausear to feel sick intr. 10
navegar to navigate, sail tr./intr. 30
necear to talk nonsense, act foolishly intr. 10
necesitar to need, be in need tr./ intr. 10
negar to refuse, deny tr./intr. (r.) **130**
negociar to negotiate tr./intr. 10
negrear (= **negrecer**) to turn black, blacken intr. 10

neutralizar to neutralize tr. (r.) 31
nevar to snow tr./intr. (imp.) 33
niñear to behave in a childish manner intr. 10
nivelar to level tr. (r.) 10
nombrar to name, appoint tr. 10
normalizar to make normal, standardize tr. (r.) 31
notar to notice, remark, mark tr. 10
noticiar to inform, notify tr. 10
notificar to notify tr. 24
novelar to write novels, tell lies/ fabulous stories intr. 10
novelizar to put into a novel, fictionalize tr. 31
nublar to cloud, become cloudy tr. (r.) 10
numerar to number tr. 10
nutrir to nourish tr. (r.) 133

obedecer to obey tr. 47
objetar to object tr./intr. 10
oblicuar to slant tr./intr. 10
obligar to compel, force, oblige tr. (r.) 30
obliterar to obliterate, erase tr. 10
obrar to work, act, be tr./intr. 10
obscurecer to darken, get dark, cloud tr./intr. (r.) 47
obsequiar to make a fuss of, lavish tr. 10
observar to observe, obey tr. 10
obstaculizar to hinder, obstruct tr. 31
obstar to impede, stand in the way intr. 10
obstinarse to persist, be obstinate r. 116
obstruir to obstruct tr. (r.) 110
obtener to obtain, get tr. 179

ocasionar to cause, occasion, provoke tr. 10

ocluir to occlude tr. (r.) 110

ocultar to hide, conceal tr. (r.) 10

ocupar to occupy tr. 10

ocuparse to be in charge of/busy with r. 116

ocurrir to occur, happen intr. (r.) (imp.) 133

ocurrirse to have an idea r. 133

odiar to hate, loath tr. 118

ofender to offend, be unpleasant, take offence tr./intr. (r.) 23

ofenderse to get upset r. 23

ofrecer to offer tr. (r.) 47

ofuscar to dazzle, blind tr. 24

oír to hear, listen tr./intr. (r.) **131**

ojear to glance, stare at tr. 10

oler to smell tr./intr. (r.) **132**

olfatear to sniff, scent, smell tr. 10

oliscar sniff, smell strong/high tr./intr. 24

olvidar to forget tr. (r.) 10

omitir to omit, leave out tr. (r.) 133

ondear to wave, sway, swing intr. (r.) 10

ondular to wind, wave tr./intr. 10

operar to operate tr./intr. (r.) 10

opinar to have an opinion, think intr. 10

oponer to oppose tr. (r.) 139

opositar to take part, be a candidate intr. 10

oprimir to oppress, press tr. 133

optar to choose, opt tr./intr. 10

orar to pray, make a speech intr. 10

ordenar to order, command, arrange tr. (r.) 10

ordenarse to tidy up, put in order r. 116

organizar to organize, arrange tr. (r.) 31

orientar to orientate, guide tr. (r.) 10

originar to originate, arise tr. (r.) 10

orillar to settle, approach the shore tr./intr. 10

orinar to urinate tr./intr. (r.) 10

ornar to adorn tr. (r.) 10

osar to dare, venture intr. 10

oscilar to oscillate, swing intr. 10

oscurecer to darken, obscure tr. (r.) 47

ostentar to make a show of, brag about tr. 10

otorgar to grant tr. 30

oxidar to rust, become oxidized tr. (r.) 10

oxigenar to oxygenate tr. (r.) 10

pacer to grace, pasture tr./intr. 47

pacificar to pacify, negotiate peace tr./intr. (r.) 24

pactar to agree, come to an agreement tr./intr. 10

padecer to suffer, endure, suffer from tr./intr. 47

pagar to pay tr./intr. (r.) 30

paladear to savour, taste, relish tr./intr. (r.) 10

paliar to palliate, alleviate tr. 10

palidecer to pale, grow pale tr. 47

palmear to clap; level off tr./intr. 10

palpar to feel, touch, grope tr./intr. 10

parar to stop tr./intr. (r.) 10

parecer to appear, seem intr. (r.) 54

parecerse to look like each other, resemble r. 54

parir to give birth tr./intr. 133

parlar to speak, talk tr./intr. 10

parlotear to chatter, prattle intr. 10

parpadear to blink, wink intr. *10*

participar to participate, notify of tr./intr. *10*

partir to divide; leave, set off tr./intr. (r.) **133**

pasar to spend time, pass, happen tr./intr. (r.) *10*

pasear to walk, promenade tr./intr. (r.) *10*

pasmar to stun, astound, chill, get blight tr. (r.) *10*

patear (= patalear) to kick, stamp one's feet tr./intr. *10*

patinar to skate, slide, skid intr. *10*

patrocinar to sponsor tr. *10*

pausar to pause, make pauses tr./intr. *10*

pecar to sin intr. *24*

pedir to ask, request tr. **134**

pegar to hit, stick, glue tr./intr. (r.) *30*

peinarse to comb r. *116*

pelar to peal tr. (r.) *10*

pelear to fight intr. (r.) *10*

penar to grieve, punish tr./intr. (r.) *10*

pender to dangle, hang, be pending intr. *23*

penetrar to penetrate tr./intr. (r.) *10*

pensar to think tr./intr. (r.) **135**

percibir to perceive tr. *133*

perder to lose tr./intr. (r.) **136**

perdonar to excuse, pardon, forgive tr. *10*

perdurar to last intr. *10*

perecer to perish, long for intr. (r.) *47*

peregrinar to go on a pilgrimage intr. *10*

perfeccionar to improve, perfect tr. (r.) *10*

perfumar to perfume tr. (r.) *10*

perjudicar to damage, harm tr. (r.) *24*

permanecer to remain, stay intr. *54*

permitir to admit, allow, permit tr. (r.) *133*

permutar to swap, exchange tr. *10*

perniquebrar to break one's leg tr. (r.) *143*

perseguir to persecute tr. *134*

persuadir to persuade tr. (r.) *133*

pertenecer to appertain, belong intr. (r.) *47*

perturbar to disturb, become upset tr. (r.) *10*

pervertir to pervent tr. (r.) *108*

pesar to weigh, grieve tr./intr. (r.) *10*

pescar to fish tr./intr. *24*

pestañear to blink intr. *10*

piar to chirp, cheep, peep intr. *10*

picar to pierce, sting, prick tr./intr. (r.) *24*

pillar to catch, plunder tr. *10*

pinchar to prick, jab tr. *10*

pintar to paint tr./intr. (r.) *10*

pisar to tread, step on, trample tr. *10*

placer to gratify, humour, please tr. *54*

plagar to infest, plague tr. (r.) *30*

planchar to iron tr. *10*

planear to plan, design, glide tr./intr. *10*

plantar to plant tr. (r.) *10*

plasmar to form, shape, mould tr. *10*

platicar to talk over, chat, talk tr./intr. *24*

plegar to fold tr. (r.) *30, 33*

pleitar to litigate, go to court intr. *10*

poblar to populate, stock tr./intr. (r.) **137**

podar *to prune, trim* tr. *10*

poder *to able, can* tr./intr. (r.) **138**

podrir (= pudrir) *to rot* tr. (r.) *142*

polemizar *to engage in controversy* tr. *31*

polvorear *to sprinkle, dust, powder* tr. *10*

ponderer *to ponder, consider* tr. *10*

poner *to put* tr. (r.) **139**

ponerse *to put on clothing, become* r. *139*

porfiar *to insist, persist* intr. *10*

portar *to carry, bear* tr./intr. (r.) *10*

posar *to pose, put, lay down* tr./intr. (r.) *10*

poseer *to process, own* tr. (r.) *117*

posponer *to postpone* tr. *139*

postergar *to postpone* tr. *30*

postrar *to prostrate, humble* tr. (r.) *10*

postular *to apply for, take part, apply* tr./intr. *10*

practicar *to practise* tr. *24*

precaver *to prevent, provide against* tr. (r.) *195*

preceptuar *to command* tr. *10*

preciar *to appraise, value* tr. (r.) *10*

precintar *to reinforce* tr. *10*

precipitar *to precipitate* tr. (r.) *10*

precisar *to specify, need, be necessary* tr./intr. (r.) *10*

preconcebir *to preconceive* tr. *134*

preconocer *to foresee, know beforehand* tr. *47*

predecir *to predict, foretell, forecast* tr. *57*

predestinar *to predestine, preordain* tr. *10*

predicar *to preach* tr./intr. (r.) *24*

predisponer *to predispose* tr. *139*

predominar *to predominate, prevail, command* tr./intr. *10*

preferir *to prefer* tr. **140**

prefijar *to prefix, prearrange* tr. *10*

pregonar *to proclaim, hawk, make public* tr. *10*

preguntar *to inquire, ask, question* tr./intr. (r.) *10*

prejuzgar *to prejudge* tr. (r.) *30*

preludiar *to prelude, clear the ground for* tr./intr. *10*

premeditar *to premeditate* tr. *10*

premiar *to reward* tr. *10*

prendar *to pawn, pledge, become fond of* tr. (r.) *10*

prender *to grasp, seize, catch* tr./intr. *23*

prensar *to press* tr. *10*

preñar *to get pregnant* tr. *10*

preocupar *to worry, be concerned* tr. (r.) *10*

preparar *to prepare, get ready* tr. (r.) *10*

preponderar *to preponderate, prevail* intr. *10*

preponer *to put before, prefer* tr. *139*

prescribir *to precribe, lay down, finish* tr./intr. *98*

presenciar *to witness, see, be present* tr. *10*

presentar *to present, display* tr. (r.) *10*

presentir *to have a premonition, predict* tr. *165*

preservar *to preserve* tr. *10*

presidir *to preside* tr./intr. *133*

presionar *to press, urge* tr. *10*

prestar *to lend, loan, be good for* tr./intr. (r.) *10*

prestigiar *to give credit* tr. *10*

presumir *to presume, suppose, show off* tr./intr. *133*

presuponer *to presuppose, budget* tr. *139*

pretender *to pretend, be after* tr. *23*

prevalecer *to prevail* intr. *47*

prevaricar *to prevaricate, act dishonestly* intr. *24*

prevenir *to prevent, prepare, warn* tr. (r.) *194*

prever *to foresee, anticipate* tr. *195*

principiar *to begin* tr. *10*

pringar *to dip, baste, take part, stain* tr./intr. (r.) *30*

privar *to deprive, be in favour* tr./intr. (r.) *10*

privatizar *to privatize* tr. *31*

probar *to prove, try (on), test* tr./intr. (r.) **141**

proceder *to proceed, continue* intr. *23*

procesar *to try, prosecute* tr. *10*

proclamar *to proclaim, declare* tr. (r.) *10*

procurar *to try, act as an attorney (for)* tr./intr. *10*

producir *to produce, cause* tr. (r.) *45*

proferir *to utter* tr. *108*

profesar *to profess* tr./intr. *10*

programar *to programme, plan* tr. *10*

progresar *to progress, advance* intr. *10*

prohibir *to prohibit, forbid* tr. **142**

prolongar *to prolong, extend* tr. (r.) *30*

prometer *to promise* tr. (r.) *23*

promover *to promote* tr. *128*

promulgar *to proclaim, announce* tr. *30*

pronosticar *to forecast* tr. *24*

pronunciar *to pronounce, articulate* tr. (r.) *10*

propagar *to propagate, spread* tr. (r.) *30*

propender *to lean towards, incline* intr. *23*

proponer *to propose* tr. (r.) *139*

proporcionar *to provide, furnish* tr. (r.) *10*

propulsar *to reject, propel* tr. *10*

prorrogar *to delay, postpone* tr. *159*

proscribir *to prohibit, banish* tr. *98*

proseguir *to follow up, proceed* tr./intr. *134*

proteger *to protect* tr./intr. *35*

protestar *to protest, object* tr./intr. *10*

proveer *to provide, supply* (past participle: **provisto**) tr./intr. (r.) *23*

provenir *to originate, come from, proceed* intr. *194*

provocar *to provoke, dare, make* tr. *24*

publicar *to publish, issue* tr. *24*

pugnar *to fight* intr. *10*

pujar *to struggle, raise* tr./intr. *10*

pulir *to polish* tr. (r.) *133*

pulsar *to play, pulse, throb* tr./intr. (r.) *10*

puntuar *to score, punctuate* tr. *10*

punzar *to prick, puncture, throb* tr./intr. *31*

quebrar *to break; smash* tr./intr. (r.) **143**

quedar *to stay, remain* intr. (r.) *10*

quejarse *to complain, grumble* r. 116

quemar *to burn, fire, be very hot* tr./intr. (r.) 10

querer *to love, want* tr. **144**

quitar *to release, remove, rob, strip* tr. (r.) 10

quitarse *to take off, withdraw* r. 116

rabiar *to rage, get furious; have rabies* intr. 10

racionar *to ration* tr. 10

radiar *to radio, broadcast, radiate* tr./intr. 10

raer *to wipe out, rub off, scrape, erase* tr. (r.) 26

rajar *to split, crack* tr./intr. (r.) 10

rallar *to grate, vex* tr. 10

rapar *to shave, crop, snatch* tr. (r.) 10

rapiñar *to plunder, pillage* tr. 10

raptar *to abduct, kidnap* tr. 10

rarefacer *to rarefy, become rarefied* tr./intr. 106

rasar *to skim, level* tr. 10

rascar *to scratch, itch* tr./intr. (r.) 24

rasgar *to tear, rip* tr. (r.) 30

raspar *to scrape* tr. 10

rastrear *to track, trace, rake* tr./intr. 10

ratear *to steal, pinch, creep, crawl* tr./intr. (r.) 10

rayar *to line, stripe, cross out, dawn* tr./intr. (r.) 10

razonar *to reason, explain* tr./intr. 10

reaccionar *to react* intr. 10

reactivar *to reactivate* tr. 10

realizar *to realize, fulfil, carry out* tr. 31

realizarse *to become fulfilled, happen* r. 31, 116

reanimar *to reanimate, revive* tr. (r.) 10

reapretar *to press (tight) again* tr. 33

rebajar *to reduce, lower* tr. (r.) 10

rebañar *to finish up, gather up completely* tr. 10

reblandecer *to soften, become soft* tr. (r.) 47

rebosar *to overflow, run over* intr. (r.) 10

rebuznar *to bray* intr. 10

recaer *to fall again* intr. 26

recalcar *to emphasize, list* tr./intr. 24

recalentar *to re-heat, warm up* tr. (r.) 27

recapacitar *to think over* tr. 10

recelar *to suspect, fear* tr./intr. (r.) 10

recentar *to leaven* tr. (r.) 33

rechazar *to reject, repel* tr. 31

recibir *to receive, get, welcome* tr./intr. 133

recibirse *to be admitted, graduate* r. 133

reclamar *to reclaim, claim, protest* tr./intr. 10

recluir *to confine, seclude, imprison* tr. (r.) 110

reclutar *to round up, recruit* tr. 10

recocer *to over-boil* tr. 34

recoger *to pick, gather, collect* tr. (r.) 35

recomendar *to recommend* tr. (r.) **145**

recompensar *to reward, compensate, recompense* tr. 10

reconciliar *to reconcile* tr. (r.) 10

reconocer *to recognize, acknowledge* tr. (r.) 47

reconstruir to rebuild, reconstruct tr. (r.) 110

recontar to recount tr. 50

reconvenir to remonstrate, reprimand tr. 194

recordar to remind, remember tr./intr. (r.) **146**

recorrer to travel, cross tr. (r.) 23

recortar to trim, cut off tr. (r.) 10

recostar to lean against tr. (r.) 53

recrear to amuse, entertain tr. (r.) 10

recrecer to increase, grow tr./intr. (r.) 54

redactar to edit, write tr. 10

reducir to reduce, cut down tr. (r.) 45

reelegir to re-elect tr. 84

reembolsar to reimburse, refund tr. (r.) 10

reenviar to send back, forward tr. (r.) 94

referir to refer, relate tr. (r.) **147**

refinar to refine tr. 10

reflejar to reverberate, reflect tr./intr. (r.) 10

reflexionar to reflect tr./intr. (r.) 10

reflorecer to blossom intr. 47

reformar to reform, alter, change tr. 10

reforzar to reinforce, strengthen tr. (r.) **148**

refregar to fray tr. (r.) 101

regalar to give gifts, make a present tr. (r.) 10

regañar to scold, growl, tell off tr./intr. (r.) 10

regar to water, irrigate tr. (r.) **149**

regatear to barter, bargain, haggle tr./intr. (r.) 10

regimentar to maintain discipline, organize tr. 33

regir to rule tr./intr. 134

registrar to record, search, examine tr. (r.) 10

regoldar to belch intr. 2

regresar to return, regress, go back tr./intr. 10

rehacer to redo, remake, rally tr. (r.) 106

rehogar to cook in batter/oil, stirfry tr. 30

rehollar to trample on tr. 2

rehuir to avoid, shun, flee, shrink tr./intr. (r.) 110

rehusar to refuse, decline tr. 10

reinstalar to reinstate tr. 10

reír to laugh tr./intr. (r.) **150**

rejuvenecer to rejuvenate tr./intr. (r.) 47

relacionar to relate tr. 10

releer to read gain tr. (r.) 117

rellanar to fill, stuff, refill tr. (r.) 10

relucir to shine intr. 45

remanecer to reappear unexpectedly intr. 47

remansar to form a pool tr. 10

rematar to end, terminate tr./intr. (r.) 10

remecer to rock to and fro tr. (r.) 47

remediar to remedy tr. 10

remendar to mend tr. **151**

remesar to pluck, remit, send tr. 10

remitir to transmit, remit tr./intr. (r.) 133

remojar to soak tr. (r.) 10

remolcar to tow, drag tr. 24

remontar to remount, rise, frighten away tr. (r.) 10

remorder to bite again tr. (r.) 126

remover to remove tr. (r.) 128

renacer *to be born again, be reborn* intr. *47*

rendir *to yield* tr./intr. (r.) *134*

renegar *to deny, renounce, detest* tr./intr. (r.) **152**

renovar *to renew* tr. (r.) *2*

renunciar *to renounce* tr./intr. (r.) *10*

reñir *to quarrel, scold* tr./intr. **153**

reparar *to mend, repair, observe* tr./intr. (r.) *10*

repartir *to deal card, distribute* tr. (r.) *133*

repensar *to think again* tr. (r.) *135*

repetir *to repeat* tr./intr. (r.) **154**

repicar *to ring, chime, mince* tr./intr. (r.) *24*

repisar *to pack down* tr. *10*

replegar *to re-double* intr. *30, 33*

repletar *to fill* tr. (r.) *10*

replicar *to retort, reply* intr. *24*

repoblar *to repopulate* tr. (r.) *137*

reponer *to replace, put back* tr. (r.) *139*

representar *to represent* tr. *10*

reprobar *to reprimand* tr. *141*

reprochar *to reproach* tr. (r.) *10*

reproducir *to reproduce* tr. (r.) *45*

requebrar *to compliment, woo* tr. *143*

requemar *to scorch* tr. *10*

requerir *to require, need* tr. **155**

resaber *to know very well* tr. *160*

rescatar *to rescue* tr. *10*

resembrar *to sow again* tr. *163*

resentir *to resent* tr. (r.) *165*

reseñar *to outline* tr. *10*

reservar *to reserve, keep* tr. (r.) *10*

resfriar *to cool, chill* tr./intr. (r.) *94*

resfriarse *to catch a cold* r. *94, 116*

residir *to reside, live* intr. *133*

resistir *to resist* tr./intr. (r.) *133*

resollar *to breathe hard and heavy* intr. *2*

resolver *to solve, resolve* tr. (r.) *200*

resonar *to resound* intr. *171*

respaldar *to support* tr. (r.) *10*

respectar *to concern* intr. *10*

respetar *to respect* tr. *10*

resplandecer *to shine, glitter* intr. *47*

responder *to answer, respond, reply* tr./intr. (r.) *23*

resquebrar *to split* intr. *143*

restablecer *to re-establish* tr. *47*

restallar *to crack, crackle* intr. *10*

restar *to deduct, subtract, remain* tr./intr. *10*

restituir *to restore, give back* tr. (r.) *110*

restringir *to restrain, restrict* tr. *52*

restriñir *to contract* tr. *133*

resucitar *to resuscitate* tr. *10*

resultar *to result in* intr. *10*

retar *to challenge, dare* tr. *10*

retemblar *to shake, tremble* intr. **156**

retener *to retain* intr. *179*

retentar *to relapse* tr. *180*

reteñir *to re-dye* tr. *181*

retirar *to withdraw* tr. (r.) *10*

retocar *to re-touch, touch up* tr. *182*

retorcer *to twist, sprain* tr. (r.) *184*

retostar *to re-toast* tr. *185*

retraer *to bring down, bring back* tr. (r.) *188*

retrasar *to delay, retard* tr./intr. (r.) *10*

retratar *to portray, make a portrait* tr. *10*

retribuir *to repay, reward* tr. *110*

retronar *to thunder again* intr. *190*

retrotraer *to antedate, date back*
tr. *188*

reunir *to unite, join, meet, assemble*
tr. (r.) *133*

revender *to resell, retail* tr. *193*

reventar *to burst, explode* tr./intr.
(r.) **157**

rever *to revise, look over* tr. *195*

reverdecer *to make green, give new*
vigour tr. (r.) *47*

reverter *to overflow* intr. *196*

revertir *to revert* intr. *108*

revestir *to reclothe* tr. (r.) *134*

revisar *to revise* tr. *10*

revivir *to revive, relive* intr. *198*

revocar *to revoke, appeal* tr./intr. *24*

revolar *to fly again* intr. *36*

revolcar *to roll about, trample, floor*
tr. *199*

revolcarse *to wallow* r. *116, 199*

revolver *to revolve, turn, mix* tr. (r.)
200

rezar *to pray* tr./intr. *31*

ridiculizar *to ridicule* tr. *31*

robar *to rob, steal* tr./intr. (r.) *10*

robustecer *to strengthen, become*
strong tr. (r.) *47*

rociar *to spray, sprinkle* tr./intr. *10*

rodar *to roll* tr./intr. **158**

rodear *to detour, surround* tr./intr.
10

roer *to gnaw, worry* tr. *26*

rogar *to beg, ask for* tr. **159**

romper *to break, shatter, tear* (past
participle: **roto**) tr./intr. (r.) *23*

roncar *to snore* intr. *24*

ronchar *to crunch, chew* tr./intr. *10*

rondar *to patrol, guard* tr./intr. *10*

rotar *to rotate* intr. *10*

rotular *to label, make a sign/*
inscription tr. *10*

rozar *to touch, rub* tr./intr. (r.) *31*

rubricar *to sign* tr. *24*

rumiar *to ruminate, reflect on,*
meditate tr. *10*

rumorear *to rumour* tr. (r.) *10*

saber *to know, how to; taste of*
tr./intr. (r.) **160**

saborear *to relish, taste and enjoy*
tr. (r.) *10*

sacar *to take out, get* tr./intr. (r.) *24*

sacrificar *to sacrifice* tr. (r.) *24*

sacudir *to shake, jerk, jolt* tr. (r.) *133*

salar *to salt, cure* tr. *10*

saldar *to settle, liquidate* tr. *10*

salir *to go out, leave* intr. (r.) **161**

salpicar *to splash, sprinkle, spatter*
tr. *24*

salpimentar *to season with salt and*
pepper tr. *10*

salpresar *to pickle, preserve with salt*
tr. *10*

saltar *to jump, leap, hop, skip* tr./intr.
(r.) *10*

saludar *to greet, salute* tr. (r.) *10*

salvar *to save* tr./intr. (r.) *10*

sanar *to cure, heal* tr./intr. *10*

sancionar *to sanction* tr. *10*

sangrar *to bleed* tr./intr. *10*

saquear *to pillage, sack, loot* tr. *10*

satisfacer *to satisfy* tr. (r.) *106*

secar *to dry* tr. (r.) *24*

sedar *to soothe, quiet, allay* tr. *10*

seducir *to seduce, entice* tr. *45*

segar *to mow, cut* tr./intr. **162**

seguir *to follow, continue* tr./intr.
(r.) *48*

sellar *to seal* tr. (r.) *10*
sembrar *to sow* tr. **163**
semejar *to resemble, look like* intr. (r.) *10*
sementar *to scatter (seed)* tr. *33*
sentar *to suit, fit* tr. (r.) *164*
sentarse *to sit down* r. **164**
sentir *to feel, regret* tr./intr. (r.) **165**
señalar *to point, signal, indicate* tr. (r.) *10*
separar *to separate, detach* tr. (r.) *10*
sepultar *to bury* tr. (r.) *10*
ser *to be* intr. (aux.) **166**
serrar *to saw* tr. *33*
servir *to serve, be of use* tr./intr. (r.) **167**
silbar *to whistle, hiss* tr. *10*
simular *to feign, simulate* tr. *10*
sintonizar *to synchronize, tune in* tr./intr. *31*
sisar *to thieve, filch, take in* tr. *10*
situar *to put, situate, locate* tr. (r.) **168**
sobar *to rub, slap, knead* tr. *10*
sobrar *to be in excess, be left over* tr./intr. *10*
sobregirar *to overdraw* tr. *10*
sobreponer *to superimpose, overcome* tr. *139*
sobresalir *to project, excel, stand out* tr. *161*
sobresolar *to resole* tr. *2*
sobrevenir *to supervene, follow, happen suddenly* intr. *194*
socorrer *to help, aid, assist* intr. *23*
sofocar *to smother, suffocate, choke* tr. (r.) *24*
solar *to sole, pave* tr. *2*
soldar *to weald* tr. (r.) *2*

soler *to be in the habit of* intr. **169**
solicitar *to solicit, request, apply* tr. *10*
sollozar *to sob, cry, whimper* intr. *31*
soltar *to loosen, undo, let go of* tr. (r.) **170**
solucionar *to solve* tr. *10*
solventar *to settle a debt* tr. *10*
someter *to subdue, submit, surrender* tr. (r.) *23*
sonar *to ring, sound* tr./intr. (r.) **171**
sonarse *to blow one's nose* r. *116, 171*
sonreír *to smile* intr. (r.) *150*
soñar *to dream* tr./intr. **172**
sopapear *to slap, box* tr. *10*
soplar *to blow, blow out* tr./intr. (r.) *10*
soportar *to support, endure* tr. *10*
sorber *to sip, suck* tr. *23*
sorprender *to surprise, astonish* tr. (r.) *23*
sorregar *to irrigate* tr. *33*
sortear *to sort, raffle, dodge* tr. *10*
sosegar *to tranquillize* tr./intr. (r.) *33*
sospechar *to suspect* tr./intr. *10*
sostener *to sustain, support, maintain, uphold* tr. (r.) *179*
soterrar *to bury, hide* tr. *33*
suavizar *to ease, soften, smooth* tr. (r.) *31*
subarrendar *to sublet, sublease* tr. *33*
subastar *to auction* tr. *10*
subir *to go up, rise, climb* tr./intr. (r.) **173**
subrayar *to underline, underscore* tr. *10*
subscribirse *to subscribe, agree to* r. *98*

substituir *to substitute, reduce* tr. 110

substraer *to take away, remove* tr. 188

subvencionar *to subsidize* tr. 10

subvertir *to subvert, disturb* tr. 108

suceder *to happen* intr. (r.) 23

sudar *to sweat, perspire* tr./intr. 10

sufrir *to suffer, endure, bear up, undergo* tr./intr. 133

sugerir *to suggest, hint* tr. **174**

sujetar *to subdue, subject, hold* tr. (r.) 10

sumar *to add, sum* tr. (r.) 10

sumergir *to submerge, plunge, immerse, sink* tr. (r.) 52

superar *to exceed, surpass, overcome* tr. (r.) 10

suponer *to suppose, assume, have authority* tr./intr. (r.) 139

suprimir *to suppress, omit, eliminate* tr. (r.) 133

surgir *to surge, appear, spout* intr. 52

surtir *to stock, supply, gush* tr./intr. 133

suspender *to suspend, hang* tr. (r.) 23

suspirar *to sigh* tr. 10

susurrar *to whisper, murmur* intr. 10

tachar *to cross out* tr. 10

tajar *to slice, chop, cut, trim* tr. 10

talar *to fell, cut down* tr. 10

tambalear *to stagger* intr. (r.) 10

tañer *to pluck, play strings* tr./intr. 23

tapar *to cover, hide* tr. (r.) **175**

tardar *to take a long time* intr. (r.) 10

tartamudear *to stammer, stutter* intr. 10

teclear *to type, run one's fingers over the keys* tr./intr. 10

tejer *to weave* tr. 23

telefonear *to telephone* tr./intr. 10

telegrafiar *to telegraph, cable* tr./intr. 10

teleguiar *to guide by remote control* tr. 10

temblar *to tremble, shake* intr. (r.) **176**

temer *to fear, dread* tr./intr. (r.) **177**

tender *to spread, layout; tend* tr./intr. (r.) **178**

tener *to have, possess* tr./intr. (r.) **179**

tentar *to feel, try; tempt* tr. (r.) **180**

teñir *to dye, stain* tr. (r.) **181**

terminar *to end, finish, terminate* tr./intr. (r.) 10

testar *to make a will or testament; erase* tr./intr. 10

tirar *to draw, pull, throw* tr./intr. (r.) 10

tocar *to touch, play* tr./intr. (r.) **182**

tolerar *to tolerate* tr. 10

tomar *to take, have* tr./intr. (r.) **183**

tontear *to be foolish, flirt* intr. 10

torcer *to twist, turn, bend* tr./intr. (r.) **184**

toser *to cough* intr. 23

tostar *to toast, roast, tan* tr. (r.) **185**

trabajar *to work* tr./intr. (r.) **186**

trabar *to join, lock, get entangled* tr./intr. (r.) 10

traducir *to translate* tr. **187**

traer *to bring* tr. (r.) **188**

tragar *to swallow* tr./intr. (r.) 30

traicionar *to betray* tr. 10

trajinar *to bustle about, rush around* tr./intr. (r.) 10

tramitar to negotiate, transact tr. 10

trancar to lock, stride tr./intr. 24

tranquilizar to tranquillize, calm down, quieten down tr. (r.) 31

transferir to transfer, postpone tr. 76

transformar to become, transform tr. (r.) 10

transfregar to rub together tr. 101

transigir to compromise, tolerate intr. 52

transitar to pass, travel intr. 10

translucir to be translucid, become clear, conjecture tr. 45

transmitir to transmit tr. 133

transponer to transfer tr. 139

transportar to transport tr. (r.) 10

trascender to transcend tr./intr. 136

trascolar to percolate tr. (r.) 36

trascordarse to remember incorrectly, forget r. 2, 116

trasegar to pour over, decant tr. 162

trasferir to transfer, defer tr. 108

trasladarse to move, transfer tr. (r.) 116

traslucir to be translucid, become obvious tr. (r.) 45

trasmontar to go over mountains tr./intr. 10

trasmudar to transmute tr. 129

trasoír to hear incorrectly tr. 131

trasoñar to make schemes, imagine wrongly tr. 172

traspasar to transfix, pierce tr. (r.) 10

trasquilar to shear, clip tr. 10

trastornar to turn upside down, disturb tr. 10

trasvolar to fly across tr. 36

tratar to treat, deal, try tr./intr. (r.) **189**

tratarse to be about 189

travesar to cross tr. (r.) 33

trazar to sketch, trace, draw tr. 31

trenzar to braid, plait tr. (r.) 31

trepar to climb, clamber tr./intr. (r.) 10

tributar to pay taxes, render tr. 10

tricotar to knit tr. 10

trillar to thresh, thrash, use frequently tr. 10

trinar to trill, warble, fume intr. 10

trinchar to carve, slice, arrange tr. 10

triplicar to treble tr. 24

triscar to mix up, set, consume tr./intr. (r.) 10

triturar to grind, crush tr. 10

triunfar to triumph intr. 10

trizar to tear to pieces tr. 31

trocar to barber, exchange tr. (r.) 24

trocear to cut into bits tr. 10

trompicar to trip, stumble tr./intr. 24

tronar to thunder, shoot tr./intr. (r.) **190**

tronchar to split, crack tr. (r.) 10

tronzar to slice, break into chunks tr. 31

tropezar to stumble, trip intr. (r.) 31, 33

trotar to trot intr. 10

tullir to cripple, disable, excrete tr./intr. (r.) 133

tumbar to fall down, lie down tr./intr. (r.) 10

tumultar to stir up, cause disorder tr. (r.) 10

tundir to thrash tr. 133

turbar to disturb, upset, perturb tr./intr. (r.) 10

tutearse to talk with familiarity using **tú** tr. (r.) 116

ubicar to locate, be located tr./intr. (r.) 24

ufanarse to boast r. 116

ultimar to finish tr. 10

ultrajar to offend, affront tr. 10

uncir to yoke tr. 45

ungir to anoint tr. 52

unir to connect, unite, join, bind, attach tr. (r.) 133

untar to aboint, grease, moisten, spread tr. (r.) 10

urgir to urge, press, be urgent tr./intr. (r.) 52

usar to use, employ, wear tr./intr. (r.) 10

usucapir to acquire legal right tr. 133

utilizar to utilize tr. (r.) 31

vaciar to empty tr./intr. (r.) 10

vacilar to vaciliate, stagger, waver, fluctuate intr. 10

vacunar to vaccinate tr. (r.) 10

vagabundear to roam, idle intr. 10

vagar to roam, wander intr. 30

vaguear to idle intr. 10

valer to cost, be worth tr./intr. (r.) **191**

vallar to fence tr. 10

valorar to appraise, increase value tr. (r.) 10

variar to vary tr./intr. (r.) 10

vedar to prohibit, forbid tr. 10

velar to stay awake, guard, watch over tr./intr. (r.) 10

vencer to defeat, overcome tr./intr. (r.) **192**

vendar to bandage tr. 10

vender to sell tr. (r.) **193**

vengar to avenge tr. (r.) 30

venir to come, arrive tr. (r.) **194**

ventar to sniff, blow tr./intr. 33

ventilar to ventilate tr. (r.) 10

ver to see tr./intr. (r.) **195**

veranear to spend the summer, holiday intr. 10

verificar to verify tr. (r.) 24

versar to turn around, turn intr. (r.) 10

verter to spill, pour tr./intr. (r.) **196**

vestir to dress, clothe intr. (r.) **134**

vestirse to get dressed r. **134**

viajar to travel intr. **197**

vibrar to vibrate tr./intr. (r.) 10

viciar to corrupt tr. (r.) 10

vigilar to watch over, look out for tr./intr. (r.) 10

vincular to relate tr. 10

violar to violate, rape tr. 10

virar to turn tr./intr. (r.) 10

visitar to visit tr. (r.) 10

vitorear to cheer, applaud tr. 10

vivir to live tr./intr. (r.) **198**

vocear to shout, cry out tr. 10

volar to fly tr./intr. (r.) 36

volcar to overturn tr./intr. (r.) **199**

voltear to overturn, revolve, turn around tr./intr. (r.) 10

volver to turn, return, do again tr./intr. (r.) **200**

volverse to turn round; become r. 200

vomitar to vomit tr./intr. 10

votar to vote, pass, approve tr./intr. 10

yacer to lie, lie at rest intr. 47

yuntar to pair, put oxen in harness tr. (r.) 10

zaherir *to blame* tr. *108*
zambullir *to dive* tr. (r.) *198*
zampar *to hide, stuff, gobble down* tr. (r.) *10*
zanjar *to dig, surmount* tr. (r.) *10*
zapatear *to tap/stamp one's feet* tr./intr. *10*
zarpar *to weigh, set sail, set out* tr./intr. *10*
zonificar *to divide into zones* tr. *24*

zozobrar *to be in danger, fail, sink* intr. *10*
zumbar *to buzz, hum, flutter around* tr./intr. *10*
zumbarse *to make fun of* r. *116*
zurcir *to darn, mend* tr. (r.) *187*
zurear *to coo* intr. *10*
zurrar *to thrash, beat, dirty* tr. (r.) *10*
zurriagar *to whip, lash* intr. *30*

English–Spanish glossary

The following glossary will help you to find some of the most common Spanish verbs, using English as your starting point. It is not intended to be a comprehensive list, so sometimes you will need to refer to a dictionary. If the Spanish verb you want is also listed in the main section of the book (indicated by a number in **bold type**), it is a good idea to check there on how it is used.

accept **aceptar 10**
achieve **lograr** *10*, **conseguir 48**
add **añadir** *133*
advise **aconsejar** *(counsel) 186;* **avisar** *(inform)* (**de** *= about) 10*
agree **estar de acuerdo** (**con** *= with,* **que** *= that) 99*
allow **permitir** *133*
annoy **molestar** *10*, **fastidiar** *118*
answer **contestar a** *10*, **responder a** *23*
apologize **disculparse** (**de** *= for,* **con** *= to) 116*
appear **aparecer; parecer** *(seem) 54*
arrive **llegar 119**
ask **pedir** *(request)* **134;** **preguntar** *(inquire, question) 10*
avoid **evitar** *10*

bath **tomar un baño 183; bañarse** *(bathe) 116*
be **ser 166, estar 99**
become **hacerse 26, llegar a ser 119; ponerse** *(turn get)* **139**
begin **comenzar** (**a** + *infin.*) **38, empezar** (**a** + *infin.*) **85, echarse** (**a** + *infin.*) **83**

believe **creer** *117*
borrow **pedir prestado** (**a** *= from)* **134**
break **romper** *23*, **quebrar 143**
bring **traer 188**
build **construir** *110*
buy **comprar 41**

call **llamar** *10; be called* **llamarse** *116*
can **poder 138**
carry **llevar** *119*
catch **coger** *(train, ball, disease) 35*
celebrate **celebrar** *10*
change **cambiar** *118*
check **controlar** *10*
choose **escoger** *35*
clean **limpiar 118**
climb **subir a** *173*
close **cerrar** *33*
come **venir 194**
complain **quejarse** (**de** *= about) 116*
cook **cocinar** *(prepare food) 10;* **cocer** *(what food does)* **34**
cost **costar 53**
count **contar 50**
create **crear** *10*

cry **llorar** *120*
cut **cortar** *10*

dance **bailar** *10*
decide **decidir(se)** *(de/en = about);* *(a + infin.) 133*
descend **descender** *66,* **bajar** *(de = from) 186*
destroy **destruir** *74*
die **morir** *127*
direct **dirigir** *52*
disagree **no estar de acuerdo** *99*
discover **descubrir** *133*
discuss **discutir** *133*
do **hacer** *106*
draw **tirar** *(pull) 10;* **dibujar** *(a picture) 186*
dream **soñar** *172*
dress **vestir, vestirse** *134*
drink **beber** *23*
drive **conducir** *45*
drop **dejar caer** *186*

earn **ganar** *10*
eat **comer** *39*
enjoy **gozar de** *31,* **disfrutar de** *10;* **divertirse** *(have a good time) 80*
enter **entrar** *10*
excuse **disculpar** *10*
expect **esperar** *10*

fall **caer, caerse** *26*
fear **tener miedo** *179;* **temer** *177*
feel **sentir** *165*
find **encontrar** *89*
finish **terminar** *10;* **acabar** *(de = to have just…) 10*
fly **volar** *36,* **ir en avión** *114*
follow **seguir** *48*
forbid **prohibir** *142*

forget **olvidar** *10*
forgive **disculpar** *10,* **perdonar** *10*

get **obtener** *179,* **conseguir** *(obtain) 48;* **buscar** *24,* **traer** *(fetch) 188;* **recibir** *(receive) 133;* **sacar** *(benefit) 24*
get down (from vehicle) **bajar(se) de** *186*
get on (into vehicle) **subir(se) a** *173*
get up **levantarse** *10,* **ponerse de pie** *139*
give **dar** *55*
go **ir** *114*
go away **irse** *114,* **marcharse** *116*
greet **saludar** *10,* **dar la bienvenida** *(welcome) 55*
grow **crecer** *54,* **aumentar** *(increase) 10;* **cultivar** *(plants) 10*
guess **adivinar** *10;* **acertar** *(be right) 1*

happen **pasar** *10*
hate **aborrecer** *54,* **odiar** *118*
have **tener** *179,* **poseer** *117;* **tomar** *(food) 183*
have to **tener que** *179*
have breakfast **desayunar** *10*
have lunch **almorzar** *9*
have supper **cenar** *10*
hear **oír** *131*
help **ayudar** *10*
hire **alquilar** *10*
hit **golpear** *(a person) 10;* **alcanzar** *(a target) 31*
hold **tener** *179*
hope **esperar** *10*
hurry **darse prisa** *55*
hurt **herir** *(injure) 108;* **doler** *(feel pain) 81*

imagine **imaginar** *10*, **fijarse** *116*
improve **mejorar** *10*, **perfeccionar**
   10
insult **insultar** *10*, **ofender** *23*
interest **interesar** *10*
invent **inventar** *10*

join **unirse a** *(person) 133;*
   participar *(en = in, con = with)*
   (activity) 10
joke **bromear** *10*
jump **saltar** *10*

keep **guardar** *(retain) 10;* **conservar**
   (preserve) 10; **quedarse con** *(not*
   give back) 116
kill **matar** *10*
kiss **besar** *10*
know **saber** *(fact) 16;* **conocer**
   (person/place) 47

lack **carecer de** *54*, **faltar** *10*
laugh **reírse** *(de = at) 150*
lead **conducir** *(take, convey) 45;*
   dirigir *(direct) 52*
learn **aprender** *23*
leave **dejar** *(leave behind) 186;*
   quedar *(remain) 10;* **salir** *(depart)*
   (de = from) 161
lend **prestar** *10*
let **arrendar** *(lease) 17;* **permitir** *5*
   (allow) 133
lie **mentir** *123*
lie down **acostarse** *3*
lift **alzar** *31*, **levantar** *10*
like **querer** *144;* gustar *(see 'The*
   verb **gustar***')*
listen **escuchar** *10*
live **vivir** *198*
look **mirar** *(look at, watch) 10;*
   parecer *(seem) 54*

look after **ocuparse de** *116;* **cuidar**
   de *(care for) 10*
look for **buscar** *24*
lose **perder** *136*
love **querer** *144*, **amar** *10;* **gustar**
   mucho, encantar *(see 'The verb*
   gustar*')*

make **hacer** *106*
mean **querer decir** *(signify)* **144;**
   pensar *(intend)* **135**
meet **encontrar; encontrarse** *89;*
   reunirse con *(get together)*
   133
mend **reparar** *10*
mind **molestar** *(bother) 10;* **cuidar**
   de *(look after) 10;* **preocuparse**
   (worry) **(de/por** *= about)* *116*
miss **perder** *(a train) 136;* **echar de**
   menos *(a person) 83*
mix **mezclar** *10*
must **deber** *56*

need **necesitar** *10;* **faltar** *10;* **exigir**
   (require) 84
need to **deber** *56;* **tener que** *179;*
   hay que *(from* **haber***) 104*

offer **ofrecer** *47*
open **abrir** *133*
order **mandar** *(command) 10;*
   arreglar *(tidy) 10*
organize **organizar** *10*
ought to **deber** *56*
owe **deber** *56*
own **poseer** *117*, **tener** *179;*
   confesar *(confess) 46*

pay **pagar** *30*
phone **llamar (por teléfono)** *10,*
   telefonear *10*

pick up **recoger** 35, **levantar** 10; **descolgar** (*a phone*) **67**

plan **planear** 10; **pensar** (*intend*) **135**

play **jugar a** (*a game*) **115**; **tocar** (*a musical instrument*) **182**

please **dar gusto a** 55, **agradar** 10

practise **practicar** 24

prefer **preferir** 140

pretend **fingir** 52, **pretender** (*claim*) 23

prevent **impedir** 111

promise **prometer** 23

pull **tirar** 10

push **empujar** 186

put **poner**; **ponerse** (*put on*) **139**

read **leer** 117

realize **darse cuenta de** 55

receive **recibir** 133

recognize **reconocer** 47

recommend **recomendar** 145

record **grabar** (*music*) 10; **registrar** 10

remember **recordar** 146, **acordarse de** 2

remind **recordar** 146

remove **quitar** (*take away*) 10; **sacar** (*extract*) 24

rent **alquilar** 10

require **necesitar** 10, **exigir** 84

reserve **reservar** 10

respect **respetar** 10

rest **descansar** 10

return **volver** (*go back*) **200**; **devolver** (*give/send back*) 75

ride **montar a caballo** (*a horse*) 10; **ir en bicicleta** (*a bike*) **114**

rise **levantarse** 116, **ponerse en pie** (*stand up*) **139**; **subir** (*go up, increase*) **173**

run **correr** 23

save **conservar** (*keep*) 10; **ahorrar** (*money*) 10; **salvar** (*rescue*) 10

say **decir** 57

say goodbye **despedir** (*see off*); **despedirse de 57**

see **ver** 195; **comprender** (*understand*) 23

seem **parecer** 54

sell **vender** 193

send **enviar** 94, **mandar** 10

serve **servir** 167; **atender** (*in a shop*) 21

share **partir** (*divide*) **133**; **compartir** (*have in common*) 133

shout **gritar** 10

show **mostrar** 62; **demostrar** (*prove*) 62

shower **ducharse** 116

sing **cantar** 29

sit down **sentarse** 164

sleep **dormir**; **dormirse** (*fall alseep*) 82

smell **oler** 132

smoke **fumar** 10

speak **hablar** (+ **de** = *of*) 105

spend **gastar** (*money*) 10; **pasar** (*time*) 10

start **empezar** (**a** + *infin.*) **85**, **comenzar** (**a** + *infin.*) **38**; **ponerse en camino** (*a journey*) **139**

stay **quedarse** 116; **permanecer** 54

steal **robar** 10

stop **parar(se)** 10, **detener(se)** 179; **cortar** (*supply*) 10; **dejar de** (*doing something*) 186

study **estudiar** 118

suggest **sugerir** 174

suspect **sospechar** 10

swim **nadar** 10

take **tomar** 183; **coger** (train) 35; **llevar** (lead, carry) 10

talk **hablar** 105

teach **enseñar** 10

tell **decir** 57; **contar** (a story) 50

thank **dar las gracias** 55, **agradecer** 54

think **pensar** 135; **creer** (believe) 117

throw **echar** 83; **lanzar** (a ball) 31

touch **tocar** 182

travel **viajar** 197

try **intentar** (to do) 10; **probar** (taste, try on) 141

turn **volver** 200, **dar vueltas a** 55, **girar** (change direction) 10; **cambiar en** (transform into) 10; **volverse** (to turn round, to become) 200

turn off **apagar** (light) 30; **cerrar** (tap) 33; **cortar** (gas) 10

turn on **encender** (light) 86; **abrir** (tap, gas) 133

understand **entender** 91, **comprender** 23

use **utilizar** 31, **usar** 10, **emplear** (employ) 10; **servirse** (be of use) 167

wait **esperar** 10

wake **despertar** 71; **despertarse** 116

walk **andar** 11, **pasear** 10, **caminar** 28

want **querer** 144

wash **lavar** 10; **lavarse** 116

watch **mirar** 10; **ver** (TV) 195

wear **llevar** 10, **poner** 139

work **trabajar** 186

worry **preocupar** 10, **preocuparse** 116

write **escribir** 98